D1411194

***The Southern Empire with Mountains and Rivers is where the
Southern Emperor dwells***

Her Sovereignty is registered in the Book of Heaven

Should You Dare to Invade This Nation

You Shall Be Beaten up into Pieces

General Lý Thường Kiệt

(1019-1105)

*(An 11th Century poem during Ly Dynasty,
in battles against the Chinese Song Dynasty)*

6/15/2020

DOSSIERS ON PARACELS AND SPRATLYS & NATIONAL SOVEREIGNTY

Nguyễn Văn Canh

Committee on Protection of Territorial Integrity of Vietnnam

COPYRIGHT

To my parents,

My wife, my children, and grand children

FOREWORD

Prof. Nguyen Van Canh has written a remarkably important book. He has prevented the world from forgetting important history by bringing forward documentation on sovereign rights in the South China Sea. Our global community is in debt to Professor Canh for his research.

The South China Sea is one of the most important international sea lanes in the world. It is the existential life support system for South Korea, Japan, and Republic of China, Taiwan. Its neutrality protects not only the over 300 million people of Southeast Asia but world peace.

Now for the first time in history a Chinese government seeks to "own" the South China Sea and through its military and political control of those waters and their surface features impose a self-seeking hegemony on East Asia and Southeast Asia.

Not since the Qing Dynasty's failed invasion of Vietnam in 1788 has a government in Beijing sent its forces into Southeast Asia.

There is no basis in history for China's claim of ownership or any other form of authority over the South China Sea and its surface features, in particular over the islands and shoals of the Paracel and Spratly chains.

The evidence presented by Prof. Nguyen Van Canh is of vital significance. It should be studied carefully by every government.

I recommend as most relevant to international law respecting sovereignty in the South China Sea the 1933 decisions of the French state of Cochin China and the royal government of Annam and Tonkin establishing civil administration over the Paracels and the Spratlys.

The global community must now address what can only be called an illegal trespass, even military aggression, against Vietnam on the part of China. The documents assembled by Prof. Nguyen Van Canh provide objective and conclusive evidence of the rights of the Vietnamese people to sovereignty over the Paracel and Spratly islands and surrounding waters.

Stephen B. Young,
Former Dean, Hamline University Law School
Saint Paul, Minnesota
Author with Prof. Nguyen ngoc Huy of "Human Rights in Traditional China and Vietnam" and
Author of "The Theory and Practice of Associate Power: CORDS in the Villages of Vietnam 1967-1972"

INTRODUCTION

This "Dossiers on Paracels & Spratlys and National Sovereignty" is published in order to present facts proving that the Archipelagos of Paracel (Hoàng Sa) and Spratly (Trường Sa) on the Eastern Sea (South China Sea) belong to the people of Vietnam. Documents include maps, photos and written papers or materials, for anyone needed in dealing with national sovereignty, an undisputable true sovereignty of the Vietnamese people.

In addition, the issue of real sovereignty is raised, because communist China is more determined than ever to occupy the entirety of Vietnam, not just the Paracels and Spratlys. The dossiers put on record the ill-intentioned efforts of Ho Chi Minh and his Communist Party, who gradually surrender our inherited fatherland to the invaders.

Finally, the Dossiers are dedicated for Peace and Security in Southeast Asia and the world.

Within the last 4 years, the situation on the Eastern Sea has changed rapidly with many incidents, raising serious concerns. That is, communist China has been aggressively constructing eight reefs and turning them into artificial islands, among the 17 reefs that they seized by forces, from the Spratly Archipelago belonging to Vietnam. They continue to build strong bases for military purposes.

What does Red China Empire want? - Expansion. These expansions are the occupation of Vietnam's Eastern Sea for China's military bases (already accomplished); as a staging base from there to move forward, to occupy the entire region of the Pacific Ocean, and the entire Asia (except Japan) in order to form the Great China Empire; and with a "String of Pearls" starting from Sihanouk Ville going through many seaports along the Southeast Asian coasts through the Indian Ocean to Djibouti, Red China paves the way to Africa. Currently Xi Jinxing has established a worldwide structure called One Belt One Road (OBOR or BRI), aiming at controlling Africa and Europe, and set up military bases filled with Chinese people everywhere, waiting for opportunities. The United States is the main target. Their plan is to defeat this enemy by the biochemical strategy, and then the entire world would lie in the hands of Red China. Therefore, eventually, communist China expected to achieve her dream by year 2049, as stated by this slogan: ONE WORLD, ONE DREAM and ONE CHINA.

That is called the "**Century of China**".

On this basis, this documentary book includes The Declarations by the Committee on Protection of Territorial Integrity of Vietnam, to alert the world leaders to the world security at risk, due to the Vietnamese communists' collusions. This issue is also presented directly to the President of the United States, the only nation capable of challenging Beijing's power.

October 1, 2018

Committee on Protection of Territorial Integrity of Vietnam

Table of Contents

PREFACE

DECLARATION (I)

OF VIETNAMESE INTELLECTUALS IN THE UNITED STATES ON VIETNAM'S SOVEREIGNTY OVER THE PARACEL AND SPRATLY ARCHIPELAGOS

According to the media, ten Mainland Chinese scholars came to Taiwan to attend a seminar on South China Sea, together with 100 local scholars on June 28 and 29 (1994). After two days of meetings, they declared that China has historical sovereignty over this disputed region. If this report is true, then it is an unlawful conspiracy of those Chinese named intellectuals of China and Taiwan. It can also cause misconceptions for the present and future about the true sovereignty over the two archipelagos of Paracel and Spratly.

The reported statement was just a continuation of what Mainland China and Taiwan have done in recent years, after the United States withdrawal from the Pacific Region.

On February 25, 1992, China passed a law, claiming those two archipelagos have been her own territorial waters, declaring that any research ship and military vessel navigating through the Dong Hai area (Vietnam Eastern Sea or South China Sea) must be authorized by Chinese authorities. On May 8, 1992, China signed a contract with U.S. Crestone Company for exploring and exploitation of oil and natural gas, in an area of 25,000 square kilometers west of the Crescent Group, within the Paracel Islands. This area is 400 kilometers off Vietnam coast, on the east. Immediately after the enactment of the law on sovereignty over the South China Sea, China sent troops to occupy Whitsun reef, the eighth reef of the Spratly Archipelago. The Reef is located at latitude 9o55' North and longitude 114o45' east.

In April 1988, China took six islands in this region. This well-known battle was conducted suddenly, using four destroyers encircling the Johnson South Reef and firing artilleries onto 74 unarmed Vietnamese soldiers in the water while they were moving construction materials into the reef. 64 people were killed. On May 4, 1992, China dispatched a tugboat and two military ships transporting troops landing into the Ladd Reef, and erected a landmark pole claiming sovereignty. On two days, August 19 and 30, 1992, China sent out two ships for oil exploration. The Nam Hai VI vessel was operating at 112 km southeast of the Ladd Reef seaport belonging to Vietnam, along the international corridor. Phan Dau V, the second Chinese ship, performed a geological research in the Hai Phong estuary area, 70 miles off the coast of Thái Bình.

Earlier this year (1994), Taiwan Petroleum Company and the National Offshore Oil Agency of China established a joint venture with Chevron from USA, for oil exploration in East Sea and South China Sea. This venture was carried out smoothly and easily, even though both sides have yet unified the country. However, this testifies to the fact that Taiwan and China reached collusion on business.

The above events were only part of a chain of China's continuous actions, reflecting a plot to occupy Vietnam territorial waters. In 1956, when the French army began to withdraw from Vietnam, China swiftly ordered her navy to occupy the Amphitrite Group, east of the Paracels. In 1974, when the United States already withdrew from Vietnam, China occupied the Crescent

Group in the west region. Until today, Red China has established a naval base and an airport, with hundreds of troops settled there.

In 1983, Mainland China redrew a U-shape map, to claim the entire southern sea as her territorial waters. This area includes the entirety of Vietnam's Eastern Sea, meaning the Philippines's coastal waters (West), Vietnam's coastal waters (East), and Malaysia's coastal waters (North).

Vietnamese intellectuals in the United States met today at the **Hoover Institution on War, Revolution and Peace**, Stanford University, to solemnly reject the statement from the Mainland China and Taiwan Conference, and confirm Vietnam's sovereignty over the two archipelagos of Paracel and Spratly. All of these islands have belonged to Vietnam geographically, historically and legally, under Vietnam's sovereign rights and jurisdiction.

Made at the Stanford University on July 22, 1994

Represented by: Professor Nguyễn Văn Canh

DECLARATION (II)

ON SOVEREIGNTY
OVER VIETNAM'S EASTERN SEA

Currently Red China, Taiwan, Philippines and Malaysia have deployed their troops on some of Vietnam's islands, in the Paracel and Spratly Archipelagos, on Vietnam's Eastern Sea (Dong Hai). At the Paracels, after having occupied the entire Paracel Archipelago, Red China established a naval base and an airfield for military aircrafts, freshwater reservoirs, and barracks for hundreds of military soldiers to occupy. In the Spratlys, China used forces to occupy eight islands, and put a landmark pole to assert her sovereignty over the Ladd Reef. The Philippines have occupied eight islands, Malaysia three islands, and Taiwan one island. Brunei only claims sovereignty, and with no military occupation on any island. The occupation of these islands by those countries is a violation of the territorial sovereignty of the Vietnamese people.

Facing the fact that several nations have divided and seized Vietnam territories, as what we have seen today on Vietnam's Eastern Sea, we the Overseas Vietnamese solemnly declare:

1. 10 days after Zhou Enlai's Declaration of Sovereignty over the Paracels and Spratlys, on September 14, 1958, Prime Minister Pham Van Dong under Ho Chi Minh's leadership, sent a diplomatic note to his counterpart to acknowledge Red China's sovereignty over the two archipelagos.

This is just an illegitimate transfer of a property of the people of Vietnam by the Communist Party of Vietnam (CPV) to the Communist Party of China (CPC). The two archipelagos belong to the people of Vietnam, not the CPV.

Any transfer of the national territory must be decided by the people of Vietnam. The CPV does not have a right to do so. In addition, the Paracel and Spratly Archipelagos at that time belonged to the Republic of (South) Vietnam. Therefore, the Vietnamese communists cannot transfer what they do not have.

2. The CPV has allowed parts of the nation's territories to be gradually possessed by foreign countries, and even acted as a passive partner in crime with the CPC, helping it seize Vietnamese territories. In January 1974, when Red China navy invaded the Crescent Group in the Paracel archipelago, the Republic of South Vietnam sent its Naval forces to protect it by exchanging fires in defense, while the CPV was completely silent. This is collusion with the enemy to commit such crimes. In the past few years, when Red China advanced further south, invading some other reefs in the Spratlys, Vietnam communist leaders voiced against it with weak objections, just asking Beijing not to repeat similar actions, implying Vietnam's approval of that occupation, or asking Beijing not to make any move further. The international media concluded that the languages used in the letter do not reflect any protests. At present times, Red China encroaches on territories by erecting structures on Mischief reef, planting flags around it. The reef is claimed by the Philippines. This nation on one hand protested strongly ageist China, and on the other, sent naval ships out and used explosives to remove them. The CPV leaders did not take any positive action to protect the territories.

3. Historically, the entire Dong Hai (Eastern Sea) has always belonged to Vietnam. From the Le Dynasty, the sovereignty over the Paracel archipelago was recorded as "the Golden Sand Island" (đảo Cát Vàng). The book of "Hồng Đức Địa Dư Chí" on the geography under King Le Thanh Tong (1460-1497) made this clear claim. Later, in the documents prepared by scholar Lê Quý Đôn (1726-1784) and Phan Huy Chu's geography book "Hoàng Việt Địa Dư Chí" printed in 1834, sovereignty was also mentioned several times.

4. In terms of asserting sovereign rights, under the Gia Long regime, the Vietnamese government officially occupied the Paracels, and Vietnam flags were planted in a solemn ceremony in 1916. Under many dynasties and successive governments of Vietnam, including the ones under the French colonial rule, several activities were continuously carried out on these offshore islands. The Paracel and Spratly archipelagos also have been directly placed under the territorial jurisdiction of South Vietnam's provinces. Governments had sent troops to occupy and exploit natural resources on these archipelagos.

5. There are geographical factors proving that these two archipelagos have been Vietnam's extended continental shelf. The position of these islands is closer to Vietnam than to other countries.

Made on April 29, 1995

COMMITTEE ON PROTECTION OF TERRITORIAL INTEGRITY OF VIETNAM

Represented by: Professor Nguyen Van Canh

The Committee was established on February 1, 1995. The Steering Board is the Council of Governors, including Prof. Vũ Quốc Thúc, Professor Nguyễn Cao Hách, Professor Nguyễn văn Canh, Attorney Vũ Ngọc Tuyền, and Attorney Võ Văn Quan.

***

A government that suppresses its College students who protest against aggressors, what kind of government is it?

They are representatives of the people of Vietnam, or they are representatives of the aggressors?

- Some people such as journalist/blogger Măng and blogger HT called the CPV leaders "Thái Thú" (China puppets, lackeys) who rule Vietnam on behalf of China, while college student Kim Duy mentioned about the assimilation, a process by which the CPV endeavors to make Vietnamese people become Chinese people. These thoughts are presented everywhere in this documentary book, for all Vietnamese people to ponder.

For years, the author of this "*Dossiers on The Paracel & Spratly Archipelagos and National Sovereignty*" has changed the title of Ho Chi Minh and the CPV, from Red China lackeys to Local Sino Henchmen (太守), they are now called Chinese puppets.

Their role is to suppress and exploit Vietnamese people, on behalf of Chinese communists. They have gave away portions of Vietnam's territorial land and waters to Han Chinese descendants, something that Beijing expansionists could never achieve throughout a 1000 year of domination of Vietnam. Within the past few decades, Ho Chi Minh and his accomplices have done such a "clever" work in this way: a portion of waters transferred to Red China. With Ho and accomplices as their puppets, placed in position of ruling Vietnam to do the job, the Chinese invaders will not be blamed for taking territories from Vietnam.

Currently, what is the role of Sino Puppets?

a) They assist the invaders to control the South China Sea,

b) They increase their activities to suppress any opposition from the people, using the entire regime's ruling engine with Leninist techniques to eliminate any popular uprisings against the Chinese invaders, the enemies of Vietnam people, and

c) They create conditions favorable for Chinese to come and settle in different areas throughout the country; they grant territorial concessions in strategic regions, either deep in the jungle or in the plateau or at sea coast; they grant major economic projects- energy, chemical, mines, road construction, metallurgy… they are turning Vietnam economy to the one that depends on China's.. They allow Chinese to be involved in directing and controlling the government's activities….

Still, that is not yet the final goal of Ho and the entire CPV. The Chinese communists also have a further dream: It is to **assimilate** 同化 the entire Vietnam population. With no hesitation, Truong Chinh, a Vietnam Communist Party leader, publicly declared that intent in 1951 and Vietnam becomes part of China.

At that moment, Ho and the Communist Party of Vietnam's mission will be completed.

RED CHINA DREAM

Slogans and Emblems of Beijing Olympic 2008

(Displayed in front of the former Republic of Vietnam's National Assembly House by Chinese Communist Youth sent from China to Saigon during the Beijing Olympics 2008)

"One World One Dream One China"

One World One Dream

One Dream: One world under the Communist Party of China.
THE CENTURY OF CHINA

The slogan on the poster: **"One World, One Dream - One China"** means that Vietnam and the entire world are within one nation: **China**, while the yellow China map includes three dashes drawn outside of mainland China. They are Paracels, Spratlys and the Middle Islands.

Those young Chinese blatantly displayed two banners above, along with many Chinese flags flying in front of the National Assembly Building once belonging to the Republic of Vietnam, in downtown "Ho Chi Minh" city (Saigon). They are free to publicly express those **desires** that really hurt the Vietnamese people's feelings, with no interference from police of the Socialist Republic of Vietnam (SRV), while Viet college students are hunted, harassed, and blocked, because the Vietnamese socialist regime fears that students could protest and speaking out, to demand the protection of the Paracel and Spratly Archipelagos. Police on Vietnam lands protects Chinese Youth. Vietnamese college students on their own motherland are not considered Vietnam citizens.

Both communist parties- China and Vietnam support and have carried out a policy of **comprehensive cooperation** in all fields of activities to achieve socialism. Such cooperation is "working together" in the name of *"***looking forward to a good future***"*. Practically, this is a warning sign: **the "One China" dream** that includes the nation of Vietnam and the world.

ONE CHINA

What is Beijing's dream? In a 2005 meeting, communist leader Chi Haotian 遲浩田 (Trì Hạo Điền), China's Defense Minister in a talk to senior officers mapped out China's strategy:

"…By just utilizing non-destructive weapons that could best kill as many people as possible, we could preserve the United States for us to use. There have been rapid developments in modern biological weapon technology, and new types of biological weapons invented, one after another.

…When comrade Deng Xiaoping was still alive with us, the Party Central Committee was wise to quickly make the right decision not to develop aircraft carriers, instead, they focused on developing the murdering weapons, capable of destroying a large population of a hostile nation

"OUR HISTORY PROOVED THAT ONCE WE ESTABLISHED SOMETHING, THEN NO ONE IN THIS WORLD COULD DO ANYTHING TO US. *In addition, if the United States as a world leader would be defeated, then other enemies shall surrender to us.*

…In China's history, while kingdoms changed, the wicked ones always won and the merciful always failed.

…We already have advanced technology and science, including "clean" technology on nuclear, genetic engineering, as well as biological weapons, and we could use powerful methods to exterminate the American people on a large scale.

If biological weapons would succeed in unexpected attacks on the United States, the Chinese would be able to minimize losses against the United States. However, if the attacks would fail, leading to a nuclear retaliation from USA, probably China would suffer a terrible disaster, in which over half of China's population would be destroyed. Thus we must use decisive methods to "wipe out" the United States and preserve America for our immediate use.

...While the enemies of the United States aimed at the inland area before U.S. Congress could finish the debate and authorize the President to declare war, the U.S enemies already would reach Washington, the capital.

... It is truly cruel to kill one or two hundred million Americans. But that is the only way to guarantee that we will make the Century of China 中國世紀, a century in which the Chinese Communist Party would lead the world".

*(Excerpts from Chi Haotian speech: **"War is not Far from us and is the Midwife of** the Chinese Century", August 08, 2005 (*www.peacehall.com and www.boxun.com).

Thus, an obstacle to prevent China from achieving her dream is America. So, America needs to be wiped out. When America collapses, all Western countries will surrender.

Conspiracy of China for Supremacy

-In October 1953, at the Conference of the Central Military Commission, Mao said: *"**We must conquer the earth. It is our goal.**"*...

-At the Politburo meeting of The Chinese Communist Party's Central Executive Committee, August 1965: Mao stated **"We must take control of Southeast Asia, including Cambodia, South Vietnam, Thailand, Burma, Malaysia and Singapore."**   .   (Excerpt: Vietnam's White Book, titled **"The Truth on Vietnam-China Relations in 30 Years"**, published by Ministry of Foreign Affairs, Socialist Republic of Vietnam (SRV), Hanoi, October 4, 1979, Sự Thật Publisher, Hanoi, October 1979).

-In the book **"A Brief History of Modern China**" published in Beijing in 1954, there were Maps of China territory including several neighboring nations, Southeast Asia and the South China Sea.

*"**Vietnam is a staging base to move south; we must seize this region at any cost.**"* (Quoted from communist Vietnam's White Paper 1979 on China's scheme of expansionism)

***

Some noticeable events

-On June 15, 1956: Ung van Khiem, Deputy Minister of Foreign Affairs of the Democratic Republic of Vietnam (North Vietnam), told Li Zhimin a foreign affair official of the People's Republic of China at his office: *"In history, the Paracels and Spratlys were parts of China."*

-On September 14, 1958, replying to China Premier Zhou Enlai's Declaration, Pham Van Dong, North Vietnam Prime Minister, sent a diplomatic note recognizing that the Paracels and Spratlys are China territories.

-On December 25, 1999, Le Kha Phieu, General Secretary of Vietnam Communist Party, together with SRV President Tran Duc Luong, went to China to sign a Treaty on Boundary Delimitation. With that Treaty, Vietnam communist leaders officially ceded many Vietnam borderlands to Red China: part of Ai Nam Quan 隘 南 關 (Friendship Pass), half of Ban Gioc Waterfall (Detian Falls), several mountain ranges of Ha Giang, Lang Son, etc.

- On December 30, 2000, the Communist Party of Vietnam signed two Treaties with China: a) Delimitation of the Maritime Boundary in the Gulf of Tonkin (Vịnh Bắc Việt /Gulf of North Vietnam) and b) Fishery Cooperation. With these two Treaties, Vietnam communist leaders have allocated to Red China over 11,000 square kilometers of the Tonkin Gulf, and allowing China to exploit resources in the Gulf.

- On December 12, 2007, Nong Duc Manh, General Secretary of CPV pledged to the clerk of Hu Jintao, general secretary of China communist party, to prevent college students in Hanoi and Saigon from protesting against Chinese occupation on the Paracels and Spratlys:

"For everlasting friendship with China, Vietnam leaders are willing to surrender everything."(1)

---

(1) Professor Carl Thayer: To my knowledge, China is also surprised about numerous protests in Vietnam. Party General Secretary Hu Jintao was quite upset, so he asked his secretary to telephone and rebuke Party General Secretary Nong Duc Manh. Beside his explanation and justification, Party General Secretary Nong Duc Manh promised that Vietnam will try harder to restrict protesters, and made that above statement. (Excerpt from an interview by TK, freelance reporter, about "Vietnam protests against China invading the Paracel & Spratly Islands of Vietnam, with massive college students taking to the streets on December 9, 2007 in Ha Noi and Saigon")

This book is composed of 3 Parts:

Part I

Contains maps and documents proving Vietnam's sovereignty over the two Paracel and Spratly Archipelagos, as well as photos of China military structures built on islands occupied by China, revealing their scheme to use South China Sea as a staging base for expansion.

Part II

Discusses the national sovereignty (currently) being surrendered to Red China, by Ho Chi Minh and his CPV. Under this situation, the invaders are gradually moving forward to own and dominate Vietnam.

Part III

Contains Appendices

Vietnam, a starting point for China to conquer the 'earth' to realize "One World One Dream One China". That is the Century of China.

PART I

MAPS AND DOCUMENTS

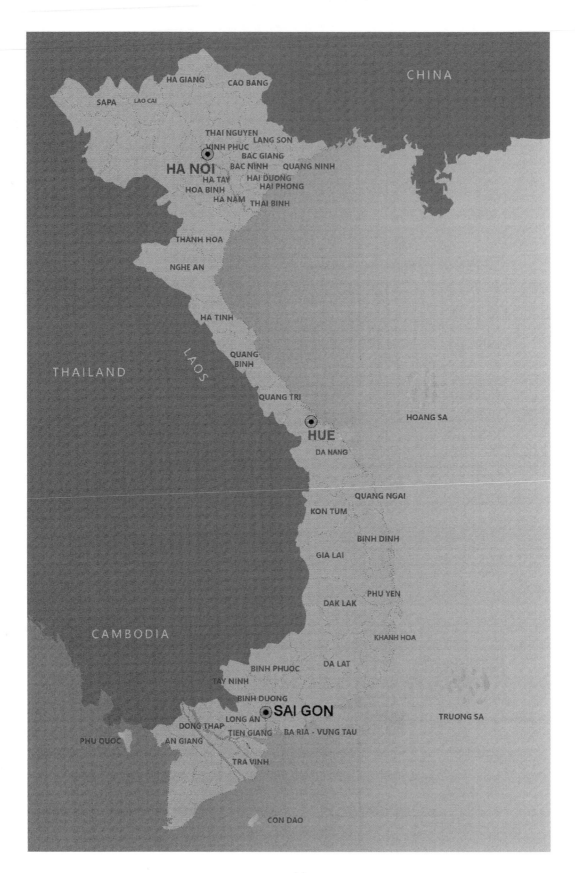

With support from communist China, Ho chi Minh and the CPV seized half of Vietnam in 1954 and later invaded South Vietnam. Since 1956, the communists have never hesitated to reveal their intention, either implicitly or publicly, to surrender Vietnam lands and sea to their 'master' China, including the Paracel and Spratly Archipelagos, **in exchange for aids to invade South Vietnam**. The recent surrendering of a partial land border, and part of the Tonkin Gulf in 1999 and 2000 is just a continuation of Ho policies.

Nowadays, in the process of annexing the South China Sea, Red China invoked this giveaway act by Vietnamese communists as reasons or evidence to justify her secret plan to occupy the entire Bien Dong as Vietnamese called, Vietnam Eastern Sea (South China Sea) by force.

Since ancient times, China has never claimed anything related to Vietnam's sovereignty on South China Sea. China's own writings on geography, history, or culture never had any trace on this subject matter.

In June 1994, about 10 Chinese scholars from mainland gathered in a Conference with about 100 "colleagues" in Taiwan. They issued a proclamation calling on overseas Chinese worldwide to assist them collecting evidence, to prove that the South China Sea belongs to China. Shortly after, Chinese media announced that an 'archeologist' found a few pottery pieces on some island, or another 'scientist' found some broken pottery on another island, to represent traces of Chinese people living there, meaning China has had sovereign rights over it. Beijing expansionists said China has had sovereignty over South China Sea since the Han dynasty, since the Three Kingdoms conflict, etc.... However, there were absolutely neither maps, nor any information on culture or history, illustrated or written by Chinese people in mainland or overseas, to prove that the South China Sea belonged to China, although scholars of ancient China were very knowledgeable on history.

Not until after the communists seized China in 1949, have people seen a map annexing the Paracels and Spratlys into China. With the most recent maps issued in June 1994, Beijing expansionists went further to again redraw the map "*Nam Hải*" (South Sea). The boundary of this map is close by Cam Ranh Bay and the coast of Tu Nghia district, Quang Ngai. Then, at the end of November 2007, they established Sansha district *Tam Sa* 三沙 (an area within Hainan Island) to manage the two archipelagos of Paracel and Spratly of Vietnam, with the purpose of completing the annexation of Vietnam's Bien Dong into China. That is the last stage, in the plot to seize Bien Dong. At this point, Beijing hegemonists could **think** they have legitimized China's sovereignty over this sea, in terms of international law.

We must also mention the military bases established on Woody Island (Phú Lâm) and other islands of the Paracel archipelago, since the early 1970s. Fortified structures have been built on the Fiery Cross Reef (*đá Chữ Thập*); a secure multi-story building was constructed on the Mischief Reef (*đá Vành Khăn*) of the Spratly Islands -- all related to the Beijing scheme. The construction of Sanya Base (*Tam Á*) in Hainan was recently revealed in April 2008 for nuclear submarines and jetties as docking stations for aircraft carriers, to protect the "property" seized from Vietnam and to control this ocean by force. This scheme does not stop there. They want to control the entire nation of Vietnam, to render Vietnam to China for use as a stepping-stone to advance into Southeast Asia, etc.

For the above reason, the **collection** of ancient maps of the Paracels and Spratlys, together with related photos, and documents is necessary to prove the following: a) The Vietnamese people have had absolute sovereignty over those archipelagos throughout many generations - an indisputable sovereignty, and b) China has had no relationship with those two Archipelagos.

The presence of communist Chinese government today on Vietnam's Eastern Sea, through acts of violence, is unjust. It violates the United Nations' Convention on The Law of The Sea, accepted internationally since 1982.

Therefore, it will help to reject all justifications of sovereignty claimed by Beijing expansionists. Further, it is important to condemn Red China's Puppets Ho Chi Minh and his accomplices, assisting their foreign masters to take a part of territory from the people of Vietnam. They have been local Sino Henchmen (太守) directed by a foreign nation in a scheme to occupy Vietnam lands and to assimilate the Vietnamese into Chinese people.

****

THE REPUBLIC OF VIETNAM
Reconfirmed Her Sovereignty After The 1974 Incident

In January 1974, Red China's navy engaged in battles to occupy the rest of the western Paracel archipelago, the Crescent Group (Nguyệt Thiềm).

The Republic of Vietnam Navy fought heroically and courageously China's powerful fleet of warships, but could not protect the islands.

During those fierce battles, the CPV leaders kept completely silent. That silence reflected the spirit of North Vietnam as an accessory to Chinese aggression. Since then, the entire Paracel archipelago has fallen into the hands of Red China.

The historic battle of the Republic of Vietnam navy against the aggressor to defend the Paracels is repeated here in a sense that a formal protest is made against Chinese aggressors:

On January 19, 1974, the South Vietnam navy was composed of one destroyer, two cruisers and one frigate equipped with light weapons, not for offshore battles. They had to be faced with at first 11 Chinese warships, then 30 others reinforced and two marine battalions, not to motion militias.

In the first 5 minutes of the battle, the ARVN Navy sank an enemy ship (corvette #271), and later, severely damaged three other Chinese vessels (#396, 389 and 274), one of the three malfunctioned in that first moment. The two rescue vessels 281 and 282 and other Chinese vessels were safe. Later, sources revealed that: Chinese Admiral Phuong Quang Kinh, the deputy commander of China South Sea Fleet, currently Front Commander, along with the Operation Staff were eliminated from battle. Four Chinese ship Commanders were, Colonel Quan Duc of the operation's Flagship (Commander of the Aviso Kronstadt #274); Colonel Vuong Ky Uy, Commander of the Aviso Kronstadt #271; Colonel Diep Manh Hai, Commander of the Torpeller #396; Lieutenant-colonel Trieu Quat, Commander of the Torpedo #389 were on the dead Chinese list. In summary, in this brief battle, on the Chinese side, one Admiral, four Colonels, six Lieutenant Colonels, etc.were killed on Vietnam's Paracel Islands.

For the Republic of (South) Vietnam (RVN), Lieutenant Commander Ngụy văn Thà, Commanding Officer of the Nhật Tảo minesweeper frigate, Navy Lieutenant Nguyễn Thành Trí, Executive Officer and 72 soldiers were heroically sacrificed, and 42 people were captured in the mission to protect our Fatherland. Among 42 people captured, there were members of the regional forces and civil employees on the islands.

Right after Red China's invasion of the entire Paracel archipelago, The Republic of Vietnam (South Vietnam) government issued the following Declaration:

RVN Declaration 74

[Home] [Up] [EARVNMM 98] [RVN Declaration 74] [SRVN Statement79]

Proclamation by the Government of the Republic of Vietnam (1974)

The noblest and most imperative task of a Government is to defend the sovereignty, independence and territorial integrity of the Nation. The Government of the Republic of Vietnam is determined to carry out this task, regardless of difficulties it may encounter and regardless of unfounded objections wherever they may come from.

In the face of the illegal military occupation by Communist China of the Paracels Archipelago which is an integral part of the Republic of Vietnam, the Government of the Republic of Vietnam deems it necessary to solemnly declare before world opinion, to friends and foes alike, that :

The Hoang Sa (Paracel) and Truong Sa (Spratly) archipelagoes are an indivisible part of the territory of the Republic of Vietnam. The Government and People of the Republic of Vietnam shall not yield to force and renounce all or part of their sovereignty over those archipelagoes.

As long as one single island of that part of the territory of the Republic of Vietnam is forcibly occupied by another country, the Government and People of the Republic will continue their struggle to recover their legitimate rights.

The illegal occupant will have to bear all responsibility for any tension arising therefrom.

On this occasion, the Government of the Republic of Vietnam also solemnly reaffirms the sovereignty of the Republic of Vietnam over the islands off the shores of Central and South Vietnam, which have been consistently accepted as a part of the territory of the Republic of Vietnam on the basis of undeniable geographic, historical and legal evidence and on account of realities.

The Government of the Republic of Vietnam is determined to defend the sovereignty of the Nation over those islands by all and every means.

In keeping with its traditionally peaceful policy, the Government of the Republic of Vietnam is disposed to solve, through negotiations, international disputes which may arise over those islands, but this does not mean that it shall renounce its sovereignty over any part of its national territory.

(Proclamation by the Government of the Republic of Vietnam dated February 14, 1974)

CHAPTER I: MAPS & DOCUMENTS ON SOVEREIGNTY

1. ANCIENT MAPS DRAWN BY VIETNAM

**MAPS SHOWING VIETNAM'S SOVEREIGNTY
OVER THE PARACELS AND SPRATLYS
MAP DRAWN UNDER THE LE DYNASTY
(1630-1653)**

THIÊN NAM TỨ CHÍ LỘ ĐỒ
(vẽ vào 1630-1653)
trong HỒNG ĐỨC BẢN ĐỒ

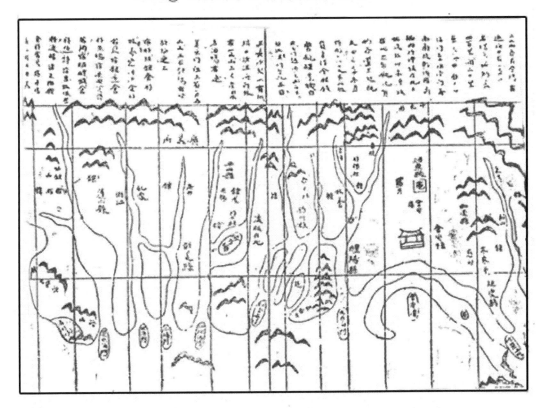

PHỤ ĐÍNH I

*Nguyên văn chữ Hán trích trong Toàn tập Thiên Nam Tứ Chí Lộ Đồ,
quyển I, nằm trong Hồng Đức Bản Đồ, hiện tàng trữ tại
To-yo Bunko, và được Viện Khảo Cổ Sàigòn dịch theo
vi ảnh số 100-891 năm 1962.*

Map by Đậu Bá Công Đạo, illustrated in XVII century with the terms "Bãi Cát vàng" ("Golden Sands", Hoàng Sa, Paracel), indicated the Paracel and Spratly Archipelagos, administered by Lord Nguyen.

According to history books and research materials by scholars, Dau Cong Luan was born and raised during the period of Trinh – Nguyen fierce conflict. Lords Trinh (Trinh Tac and Trinh Can) drove away the Yuan (Nguyen) army, which had to withdraw to the southern part of Vietnam. With a high ambition to conquer the South, Lord Trinh aimed at overthrowing the Nguyen administration in the South, and then retrieving the land, sea and islands back. The Lord then badly needed a geographical map of Đàng Trong 南河 (south of Gianh River). In 1682 (3rd year of Chính Hòa), Zen master Hương Hải escaped from South Vietnam to Thăng Long (north). He offered to Lord Trinh a map of Thuận Quảng area, illustrated from his memory. Therefore, in all aspects, this map was not good for Lord Trinh to use in order to move troops to Đàng Trong, to attack the Nguyen.

During 1680-1705 (Chính Hòa period), Dau Cong Luan disguised himself as an entrepreneur, and then sailed on merchant boats heading South. He intended to construct a more practical map of Dang Trong's landscapes. After many sea voyages along the coasts, from Central to South regions, he secretly surveyed and constructed a collective map of several locations, from Thuận Quảng going southbound. This map "Tứ Chí Lộ Đồ" provided roads drawn in four directions. After completing the map, Dau Cong Luan offered to Lord Trinh a proposal to conquer the South. VietBao.vn (according to Dân Trí.

PARACELS
(Under the Le dynasty, 17th century)

GOLDEN SAND
In the map "The Road to Quang Nam Area", Le dynasty

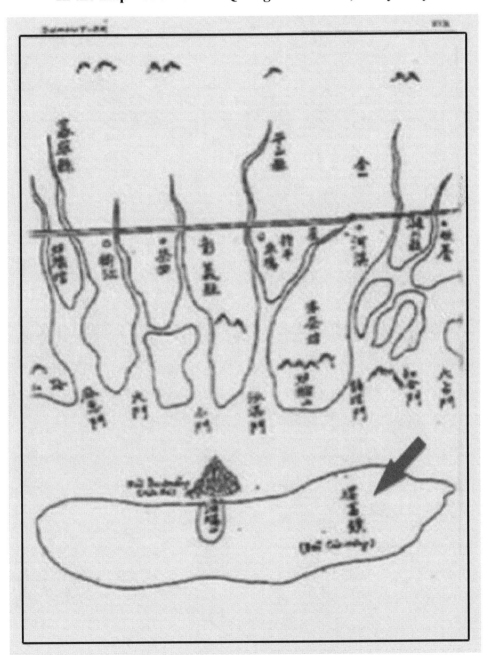

HOÀNG SA và TRƯỜNG SA
Đại Nam Thống Nhất : Toàn Đồ triều Nguyễn

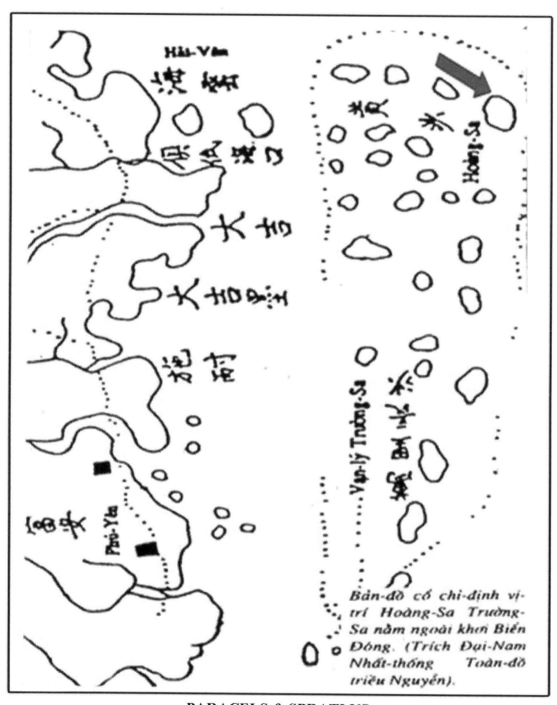

Bản-đồ có chỉ-định vị-trí Hoàng-Sa Trường-Sa nằm ngoài khơi Biển Đông. (Trích Đại-Nam Nhất-thống Toàn-đồ triều Nguyễn).

PARACELS & SPRATLYS

HOÀNG VIỆT ĐỊA DƯ (Geography of Golden Viet)
THE PARACEL AND SPRATLY ARCHIPELAGOS
1834

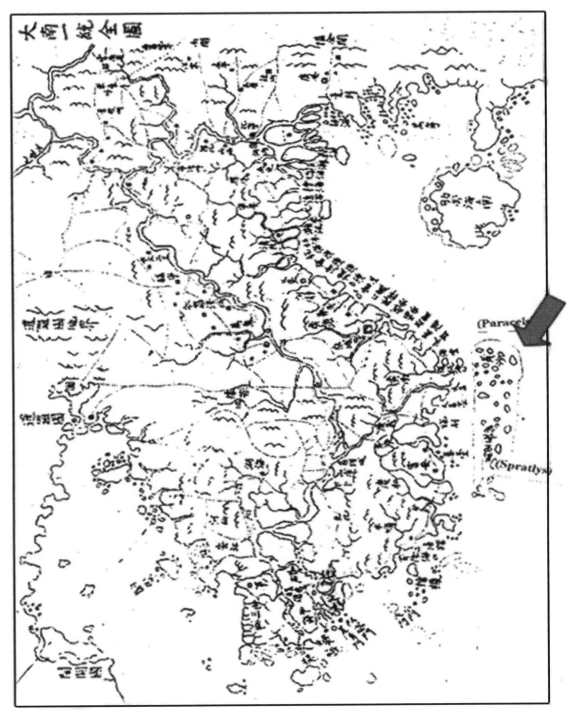

Carte de l'Indochine — Extrait de la Géographie de Hoàng-Việt-Đia-Du
1ᵉ année de Minh-Mạng 1834

2. MAPS DRAWN BY FOREIGNERS

2.1.   Map by RAMUSIO, 1554

2.2.   Map by GASTALDI, 1564

Annotation on two Oldest European Maps of the Paracel Archipelago:

An island group unveiled in 1554, from the hands of the cartographer Ramusio, is the Paracel Archipelago (Paracels) and is sketched as a sandbank with the notes "Canali donde Vengono gli liquij". [Paracel Archipelago Map by Ramusio, 1554]. Ramusio's notes on the Paracel Archipelago explained more clearly than Gastaldi's version in 1564, who confirmed that *"Canalli dove passapo i chini per andarea palohan, et a boru"* (the sea route through which the Chinese have crossed, to reach Palawan and Borneo). (*Paracel Archipelago Map by Gastaldi, 1564).*

2.3.   MAP by MATTEO RICCI, 1602

Ricci, an Italian missionary (1552-1610) constructed this map in 1602: THE PARACEL ISLANDS belong to Vietnam. The original copy is missing. Map redrawn by Tao Zhi, a Ming official. *(Documents by Đinh kim Phúc, Đất Việt newspaper Monday, January 18, 2010)*

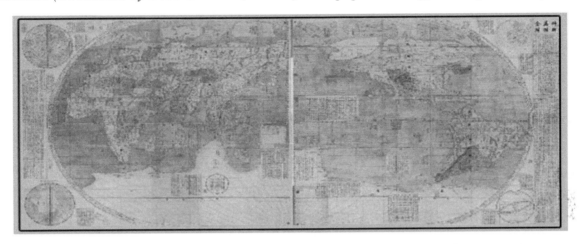

Tao Zhi (Ming dynasty) re-drew this map, named it *"Khôn Dư Vạn Quốc Toàn Đồ"* 坤輿萬國全圖". (World Atlas of All Nations).

A revision of this map, shown in Photo 1, now on display at the Miyagi Prefectural Library (Sendai City) and Kyoto University Library;

Photo 2: a part of Ricci's Far East map

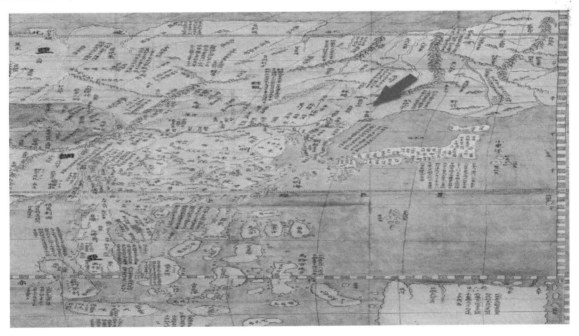

Photo 3

In these two maps (photo 2 and 3), the annotations are written in two languages: Chinese and Japanese. The territory of Vietnam today was noted by Ricci on Vietnam's history and geography and these annotations prove Vietnam's sovereignty over the Paracels and Spratlys

Photo 4

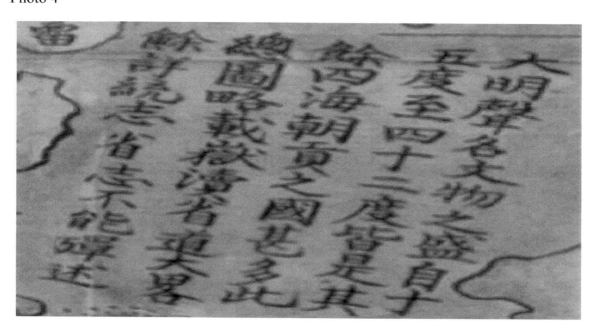

The Chinese passage in Photo 4 with annotations on the Eastern Sea, is read as: "Great Ming heard that the surrounding kingdoms worldwide around the four oceans, from 15° to 42°... are all rich and are all tributary nations. This general national map is simplified, without record of provinces, routes, mountains, rivers...", unable to record all clear details, as "*Đại Nam Nhất Thống Chí* 大南一統志 .

http://dantoc.net/?p=25537 1/20/2010
(the official geographical record of Grand Vietnam during Nguyễn dynasty, written in traditional Chinese, 1882).

<u>Photo 5:</u> The four Chinese characters are "*Vạn Lý Trường Sa* 萬里南沙"
(Great Length Spratlys) written on the map. Source: © Ba Sàm 2010.

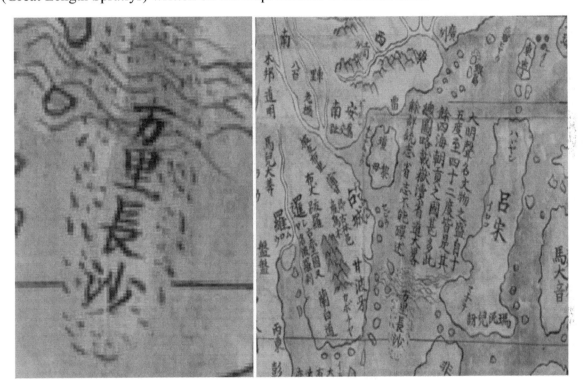

phụ bản in trong A.J. L. Taberd, Dictionarium Anamatico-Latinum
(Serampore,1838) trong đó có ghi đảo Cát Vàng

Map of "*An Nam Đại Quốc Họa Đồ*" is written in 3 languages: Han Chinese, Latin, and Quốc ngữ (modern Latinized national Vietnamese), constructed by Bishop Jean Louis Taberd in 1838, inscribed as Paracel or *Cát Vàng* (Golden Sand) has proven Vietnam sovereignty. In an article published in The Journal of the Asiatic Society of Bengal in 1837, Bishop Taberd also stated: "*The Paracels, or Paracel, Hoàng Sa - the Golden Sand Islands, have belonged to Vietnam*".

2.5. INDES, PETRUS, PLANCIUS PRACELS (Hoang Sa黄沙) BD8 1594

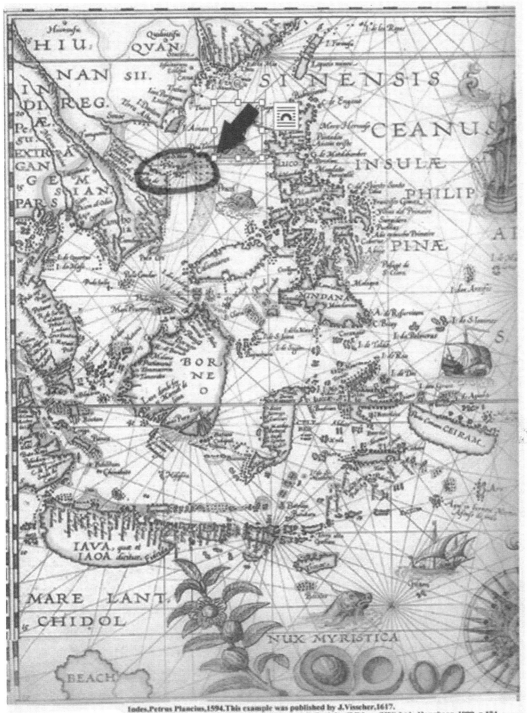

Indes,Petrus Plancius,1594.This example was published by J.Visscher,1617.
Thomas Suarez,"Early Mapping of Southeast Asia", Periplus Editions (HK) Ltd., Hongkong, 1999, p.174.
Cofta de Pracel has belonged to Cochinchina.

2.6.   VAN LANGREN

Carte de la péninsule indochinoise, 1595

2. Carte de la péninsule indochinoise, par les frères Van Langren, 1595.

Fig.111 Mainland Southeast Asia, Jodocus Hondius, 1606 (35.5 x 48.6 cm). Hondius shared the classic view of Southeast Asia' river systems, mapping five rivers from the Mekong westwards, as originating in a Himalayan lake associated, if not in Hondius' mind, with the kingdom of Lan Na in what is now northern Thailand. Note also the depiction of the Mergui Archipelago, off the Burmese portion of the Malay Peninsula, as an islet-studded sea, and the exaggerated representation of the island on which the Siamese court of Ayuthaya sat (the red island at the top in the Gulf of Siam).

As a youth, Hondius showed a talent for drawing and calligraphy, and later developed a fine reputation as an engraver. He also studied mathematics, Greek, and Latin, and the Lutheran faith. The Duke of Parma offered Jodocus the opportunity to continue his studies in Rome, but he declined the offer, probably to avoid religious conflict. Ironically, the Duke of Parma subsequently captured Ghent, where Hondius was living, and many Protestants were forced to flee, Jodocus among them. He resettled in England, where he carried on as an engraver and instrument-maker, as well as a maker of maps and portraits. He returned to the Continent in 1593 and set up shop in Amsterdam. Here he was successful as a maker of large wall maps and of globes, for which he had obtained, in 1597, the privilege from the States General. In 1604 he acquired the copperplates from the Mercator Atlas, which he began publishing two years later, supplemented by his own, more up-to-date, maps. Two of his new constitutions covered Southeast Asia; this map focusing on the mainland, and one devoted to the islands (fig. 112).

Jodocus Hondius,"Insular Southeast Asia",
Mainland Southeast Asia,India Orientalis,
1606, p.196.
Cofta de Pracel has belonged to Cochinchina

2.8.   JODOCUS HONDIUS

Jodocus Hondius
1616

The Paracel Islands were also displayed, or especially annotated, on the map drawn by Jodocus Hondius in 1613 showing Frael archipelago (*Hoàng Sa*/Paracel) including all islands of Vietnam from the southern Gulf of Tonkin to the entire southern sea of Vietnam, except Pulo Condor (*Côn Đảo*) and Pulo Cici (*đảo Phú Quốc*) which are drawn separately. Map 11

2.9.   INSVLAE MOLVCCAE, COSTA DE PRACEL, 1617

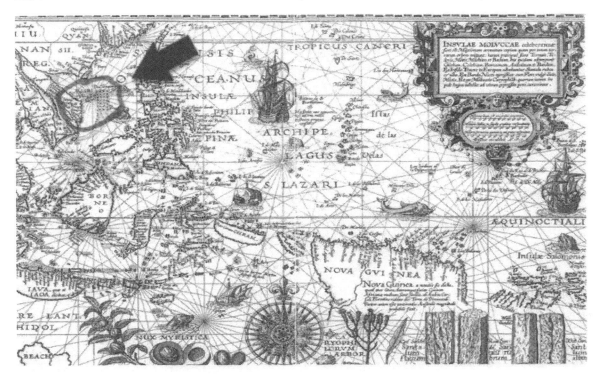

2.10. **MAP by ENGLAND, 1703**

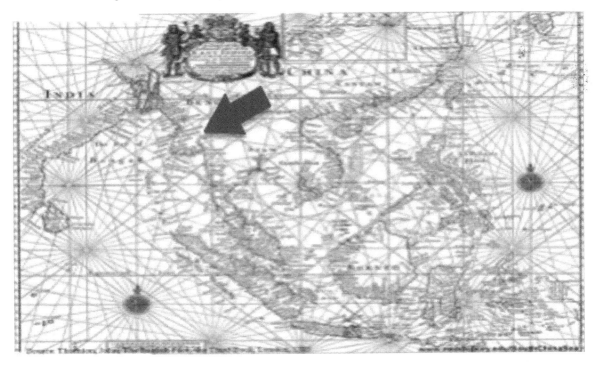

2.11. **MAP OF INDOCHINA PENINSULA by Priest DU VAL CAMBA (Champa), 1686**

CARTE DE LA PÉNINSULE INDOCHINOISE DU PÈRE DU VAL (1686)

2.12. EASTERN SEA MAP, COCHINCHINE, TONKIN

Paracels & Spratlys drawn in Holland, 1754

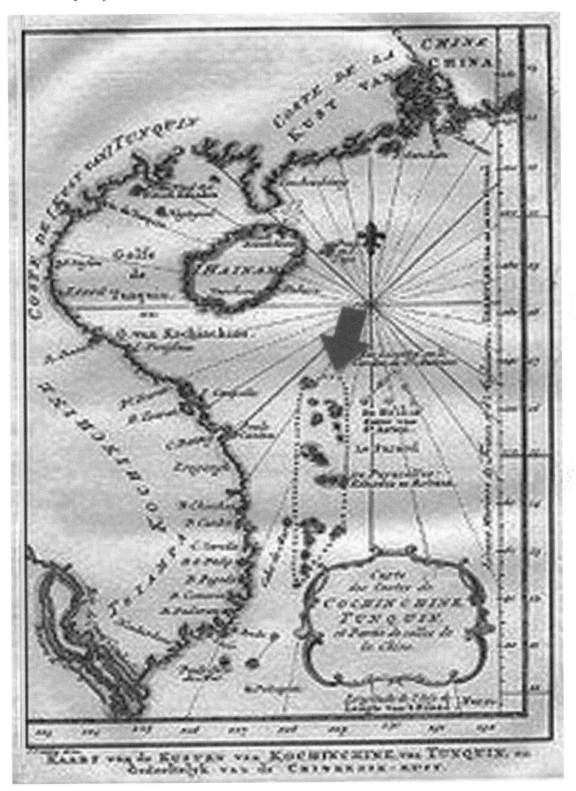

2.13. PARACELS

**GOLDEN SAND
IN THE MAP OF THE ENTIRE REGION
1780**

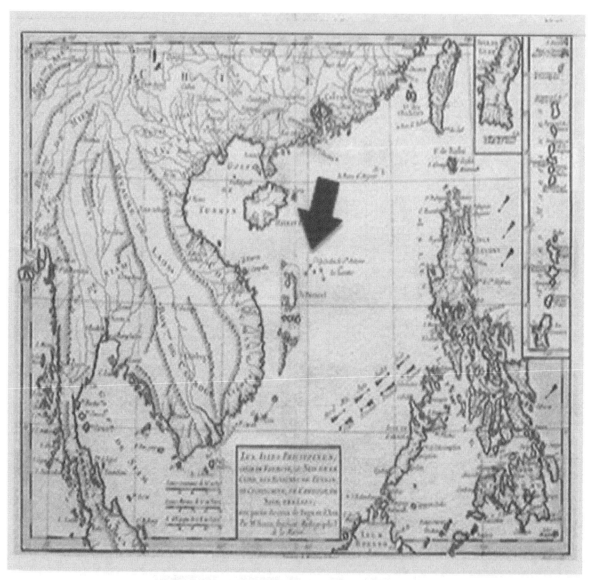

Bãi Cát Vàng, Bãi Cát Vàng... đau nhói lòng ta...
[Nguồn: BONNE (R), *Les Isles Philippines Celle De Formosa, Le Sud De La Chine Les Royaumes
De Tunkin, De Conchinchine, De Camboge, De Siam, Des Laos avec Partie de ceux de Pegu et
d'Ava. Paris 1780*]

2.14. EAST INDIES

PARACELS & SPRATLYS
belong to South Vietnam
1969

Phụ Bản III : Bản đồ "East Indies and Further India" trong Philips'
Pocket Atlas of the world, trong 48-49 xác định rõ ràng : "Paracel
Is, (South Việt Nam)", xuất bản tại London, 1969

2.15. NATIONAL GEOGRAPHIC SOCIETY

Distances between the nearest islands of Hoang Sa to points of Mainland, reprinted from Map of Southeast Asia, National Geographic Society, Washington DC, 1968 (See also, Vũ hữu San, "*Địa Lý Biển Đông với Hoàng Sa và Trường Sa*" (Geography of Biển Đông with the Paracels and Spratlys), *The Committee on Protection of Territorial Integrity of Vietnam*, 1995, p.109)

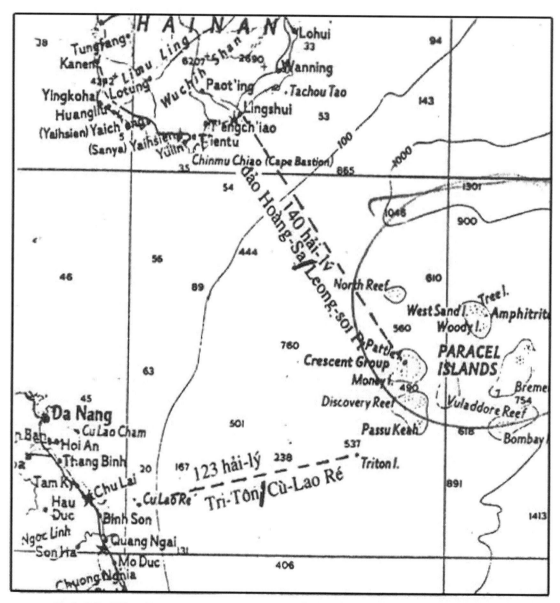

Hình 71- Bản-đồ ghi khoảng cách các đảo gần nhất của quần-đảo Hoàng-Sa đến các đảo gần đất liền (Trích từ Bản-đồ Southeast Asia- National Geographic Society- Washington DC, 1968).

2.16. VIETNAM SEA IN SOUTHEAST ASIA

The two archipelagos of Hoàng Sa and Trường Sa of the Republic of (South) Vietnam

BIỂN ĐÔNG TRÊN BẢN ĐỒ TOÀN VÙNG

3. DOCUMENTS ON SOVEREIGNTY

3.1. Scholar LÊ QUÝ ĐÔN

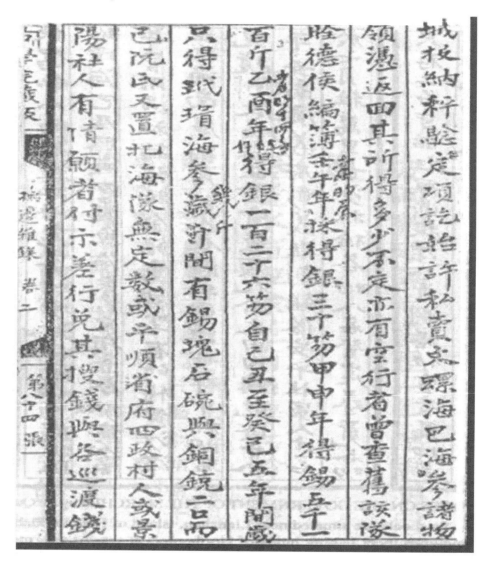

MISCELLANEOUS PIECES ON THE GOVERNMENT OF THE MAPS by Lê Quý Đôn. Vol.2: "I myself (i.e. Lê Quý Đôn) have examined the registers of team leader Thuyên Đức Hầu and found the following: The year Nhâm Ngọ (1702) the Company found 30 billions of silver".

The year of Giáp Thân (1704), 5100 units of tin. The year of Ất Dậu 1705), 126 billions of silver. From the year of Kỷ Sửu (1709) to the year of Quý Tỵ (1713), for a period of five years, the Company gathered several *cân (*units) of tortoise shells and holothurians. Sometimes, it only found some tin ingots, some ceramic bowls and two bronze guns". SOURCE: - Lưu văn Lợi "*The Sino-Vietnamese Difference on the Hoang Sa and Truong Sa Archipelagoes*", The Gioi Publishers, Hanoi, 1996, p.144.

3.2. ROYAL ORDINANCE of MINH MANG EMPEROR

On April 15, 1835, year of Ất Mùi (the 15th year of Minh Mạng) to dispatch a fleet of three boats and 24 marine soldiers from Quảng Ngãi province to the Paracel Islands for a mission.

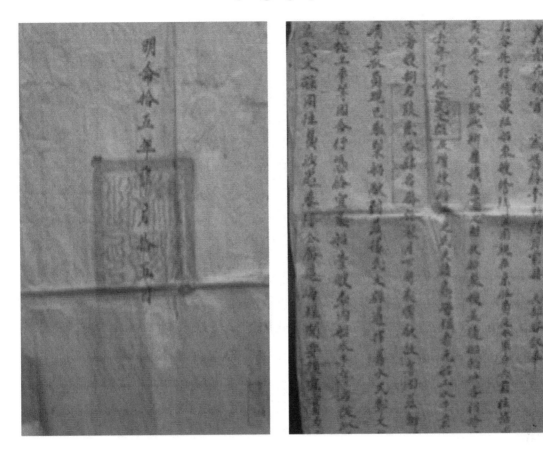

This ordinance was related to the Paracel archipelago

(Dân trí) – "In the morning of April 1, 2009, Dr. Nguyễn Đăng Vũ, Deputy Director of Vietnam's Department of Culture, Sports and Tourism of Quang Ngai proclaimed that*: The province just discovered a rare ordinance from the Nguyen Dynasty related to the Paracel archipelago. The ordinance has been preserved by the Đặng family at Dong Ho village, An Hai town, Ly Son district for more than 170 years.*

Mr Đặng Lên (clan of Đặng) - who has kept this royal ordinance, reported to Quang Ngai Department of Culture, Sports and Tourism, and confirmed that his family has kept the important documents related to the Paracel archipelago, which still remained intact. It was the Royal Ordinance of Minh Mang Emperor to dispatch a fleet of three boats along with 24 marine soldiers to the Paracel Islands, on April 15, 1835 (Ất Mùi, the year of Minh Mạng), in a mission to protect the Paracel Islands of Vietnam."

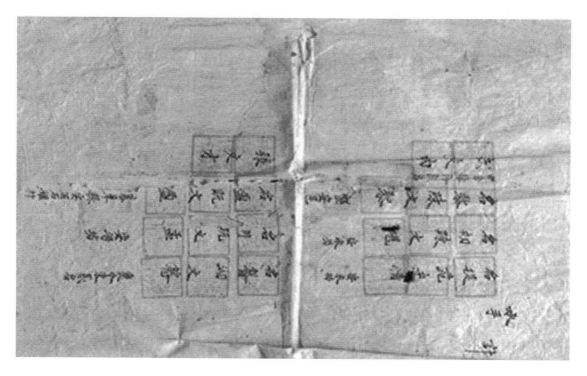

One of the 4 pages of the Nguyễn Dynasty's Ordinance has been kept in the home of Mr Đặng Lên. (Photo: Anh San)

"According to Dr Nguyễn Đăng Vũ, this ordinance clearly stated: to assign Mr Võ Văn Hùng at Lý Sơn to select young, strong and skillful people in swimming and diving, to join the fleet; to assign Mr Đặng Văn Siểm - an experienced seafarer to guide the fleet; to assign Mr Võ Văn Công going along, in charge of logistics... This is the only ordinance, since the time of discovery, kept by the clans living on Lý Sơn Island (Cù Lao Ré) in Quảng Ngãi Province (south central coast of Vietnam), related to the Paracel archipelago of Vietnam".

3.3. Other evidences: OFFICIAL ROYAL DOCUMENTS (Châu Bản)

To confirm Vietnam sovereignty over the Paracel Islands

Below are official documents written in Vietnamese and French, with Emperor Bao Dai's signature.

The official royal documents were written on February 3, 1939. There were two different documents (one in Vietnamese, one in French), but closely related to each other. In formatting, each document was typed on one side of a sheet of paper about 21.5 x 31cm. It is a good type of paper, exclusively used in the Majesty's Civil Cabinet under Emperor Bảo Đại. Therefore, in the upper left corner of each sheet, in addition to two French lines, "Palais Impérial" (Imperial Palace), on February 3, 1939, and *the Majesty's Civil Cabinet*" (Ngự tiền Văn phòng), every sheet also included the phrase printed in Han-Viet, the ancient Vietnamese: "*Ngự tiền Văn Phòng Dụng Tiên*" (Majesty's Civil Cabinet Treasury)

First document has the following content:

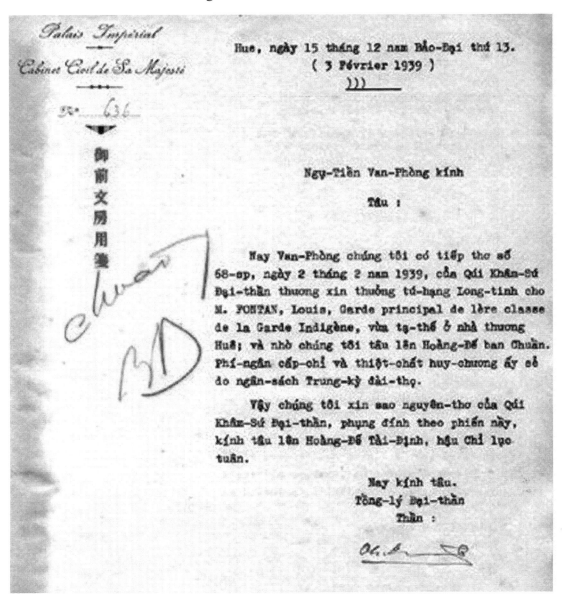

Hue, December 15, 1939, in the 13th year of Bao Dai
The Majesty's Civil Cabinet respectfully reporting to Your Majesty:

Our Office received a No.68-sp letter on February 2, 1939 from the Resident Superior respectfully requesting the "tứ hạng Long tinh" Medal to M. Fontan, Louis, Senior Guard of the 1st class of the Indigenous Guard, who recently passed away at Hue hospital; and asked us to bring this matter to the Emperor for blessing. The expenses and the actual cost of that medal will be covered by the Annam (Trung Kỳ) budget. Therefore, we would like to send a copy of the entire letter from the Excellency Ambassador, attached to this paper, respectfully sent to your Majesty for decision, for compliance. Respectfully, Prime Minister of the Imperial Cabinet (Tổng lý Đại Thần) [signed: Phạm Quỳnh].

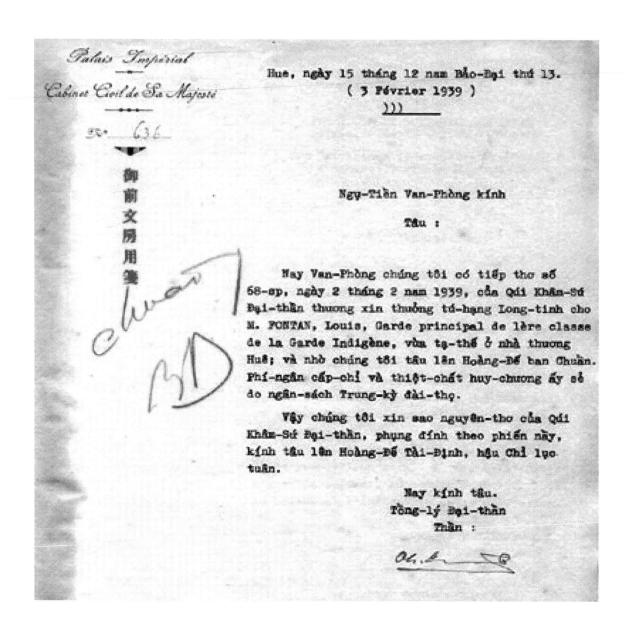

Palais Impérial

Cabinet Civil de Sa Majesté

N° 636

御前文房用箋

Hue, ngày 15 tháng 12 nam Bảo-Đại thứ 13.
(3 Février 1939)
)))

Ngự-Tiền Văn-Phòng kính

Tấu :

Nay Văn-Phòng chúng tôi có tiếp thơ số 68-sp, ngày 2 tháng 2 nam 1939, của Qúi Khâm-Sứ Đại-thần thương xin thưởng tứ-hạng Long-tinh cho M. FONTAN, Louis, Garde principal de lère classe de la Garde Indigène, vừa tạ-thế ở nhà thương Huế; và nhờ chúng tôi tấu lên Hoàng-Đế ban Chuẩn. Phí-ngân cấp-chỉ và thiệt-chất huy-chương ấy sẽ do ngân-sách Trung-kỳ đài-thọ.

Vậy chúng tôi xin sao nguyên-thơ của Qúi Khâm-Sứ Đại-thần, phụng đính theo phiến nầy, kính tấu lên Hoàng-Đế Tài-Định, hậu Chỉ lục tuần.

Nay kính tấu.
Tổng-lý Đại-thần
Thần :

Second document sent from the Resident Superior of Annam situated at the South bank of Huong River, written in French, briefly translated as following:

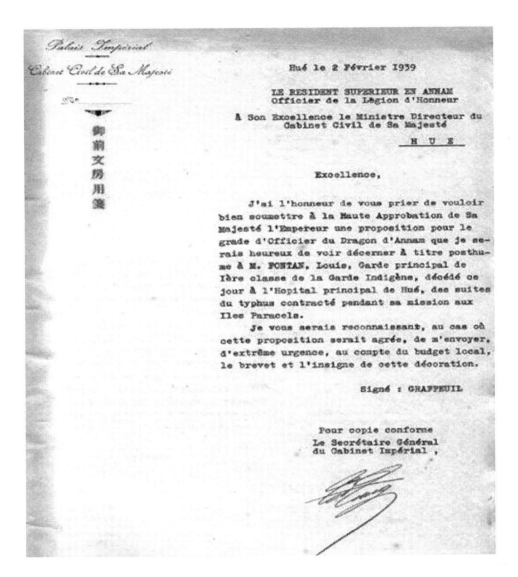

Hue, February 2, 1939 Resident Superior of Annam; National Order of the Legion of Honor.

To Minister of the Majesty's Civil Cabinet (Tổng Lý Ngự Tiền Văn Phòng), Huế.

Your Honor, I am respectfully asking you to please submit this proposal to the Majesty for approving the Long Tinh Medal Award of the Southern Dynasty (Le Dysnasty, 16th Century) awarded to Mr. Louis Fontan, a top-level tirailleur (lính khố xanh/french guardmen) who just died today at the Grand Hospital in Hue. He suffered from "typhus" fever, during the time he served at the Paracel Island.

In case this proposal is accepted, your honor, I would appreciate it if you could immediately send me that merit certificate and medal through the local budget account. Signed: Graffeuil. Copied from the original, The Majesty's Civil Cabinet Officer -[Signed: Trần Đình Tùng]

According to researcher Phan Thuận An, the contents of those two documents could be combined to be expressed simply as this:

"On February 2, 1939, Mr Graffeuil, the Resident Superior of Annam sent a letter to Mr Phạm Quỳnh, Minister of the Majesty's Civil Cabinet, proposing to Emperor Bao Dai to award the Southern Dynasty's *Long Tinh Medal*, to Mr Louis Fontan - who recently passed away.

Previously, he was the first-class squad team leader, of the Tirailleurs indochinois (lính khố xanh) stationed at the Paracel Islands. During his services here, he was sick with a dangerous type of malaria, and died at Hue grand Hospital. Immediately after his death, the letter was submitted.

After receiving this letter, Phạm Quỳnh, Minister of the Majesty's Civil Cabinet assigned Trần Đình Tùng, an officer under his direct authority, to make a copy of this letter, to submit to the emperor along with the proposal.

On February 3, 1939, the next day, the Majesty's Civil Cabinet submitted the proposal and copy of that letter to Emperor Bao Dai. In the proposal, although the Imperial Cabinet's Prime Minister did not recall the cause of Mr. Fontan's death (already mentioned in the letter attached) he suggested to award the "*tứ hạng Long tinh*" medal to that French official. This was a respectful attitude toward people under the colonial government. who well deserved the credit for defending the Paracel Islands of the Southern Dynasty.

After reading the proposal and the attached letter, Emperor Bao Dai immediately accepted the suggestion. The Emperor signed and "approved" with his initials "BĐ" (Bao Dai) in red pencil.

This meant, right after that, that everything proceeded as it should be. According to researcher Phan Thuan An: "We need to pay attention to the fact that although Louis Fontan was a Frenchman, and despite hardship, he defended Hoang Sa Island for Vietnam, so the Southern Dynasty highly valued his merits after death."

"Once again, this official royal document confirmed that before World War II and before the Japanese army invaded the Asia-Pacific region, the Paracel Islands had been under the sovereignty of Vietnam. And after the end of World War II, Hoàng Sa (Paracel) was returned to Vietnam sovereignty as before."

Ải Nam Quan (*Friendship Pass*)

3.4. Ordinance of Emperor Bao Dai, 1933

PROTECTORAT DE L'ANNAM

GOUVERNEMENT ANNAMITE

BULLETIN OFFICIEL EN Langue Annamite

—oOo—

南 朝 國 語 公 報

NAM-TRIỀU QUỐC-NGỮ CÔNG-BÁO

NĂM 1933 — Số 8

Cung lục DỤ số 10 ngày 29 tháng 2 năm Bảo-Đại thứ 18 (30 Mars 1933)

Chiếu chỉ các Cù-lao Hoàng-sa (Archipel des Iles Paracels) thuộc về chủ-quyền nước Nam đã lâu đời và dưới các tiền triều, các Cù lao ấy thuộc về địa hạt tỉnh Nam-Ngãi, đến đời Đức Thế-Tổ Cao-Hoàng-Đế vẫn để y như cũ là vì nguyện trước sự giao thông với các Cù-lao ấy đều do các cửa bể tỉnh Nam-Ngãi.

Chiếu chỉ nhờ sự tiến bộ trong việc hàng hải nên việc giao thông ngày nay có thay đổi, và lại viên Đại-diện Chánh-phủ Nam-triều ủy phải ra kinh-lý các cù-lao ấy cùng quan Đại-diện Chánh phủ Bảo-bộ có tàu rằng nên tháp các Cù-lao Hoàng-sa vào địa hạt tỉnh Thừa-thiên thời được thuận tiện hơn.

Dụ :

Độc khoản . — Trước chuẩn tháp nhập các Cù-lao Hoàng-sa (Archipel des Iles Paracels) vào địa hạt tỉnh Thừa-thiên ; về phương diện hành chánh, các Cù-lao ấy thuộc dưới quyền quan Tỉnh hiến tỉnh ấy.

Khâm thử.

VIỆT-NAM TẬP-CHÍ 25

47

3.5. Decree by the Governor of Cochin China to annex the Spratly Island and vicinities into Bà Rịa province (1933)

ANNEX 30

Decree by the Governor of Cochin China (J. Krautheimer), Saigon, 21 December 1933

THE GOVERNOR OF COCHIN CHINA,

Officier de la Legion d'Honneur

Having regard to the Decree of 20 October 1911;

Having regard to the Decree of 9 June 1922 for the reorganization of the Colonial Council of Cochin China and to the subsequent texts;

Having regard to the Opinion published in the Official Gazette of the French Republic of 26 July 1933 by the Ministry of Foreign Affairs relating to the occupation of certain islands by French naval units;

Having regard to letter No. 034, and letters No. 2243-AP of 24 August and 14 September 1933 from the Governor General concerning the annexation of the islands and islets in the Spratly or Storm group;

Having regard to the deliberations of the Colonial Council dated 23 October 1933;

Having heard the *Conseil prive,*

DECREES:

ARTICLE 1. - The island named Spratly and the islets named Amboyna Cay, Itu-Aba, Two Islands group, Loaito and Thi-tu which fall under it, situated in the China Sea, shall be attached to Baria Province.

ARTICLE 2. - The Administrator, Head of Baria Province and the Head of the Land Registry and Topography Department shall be responsible, each in so far as it concerns him, for implementing this Decree.

Saigon, 21 December 1933

(Signed) J. Krautheimer

Certified true copy of the original

Filed in the archives of the *Conseil prive*

3.6. The Governor General of Indochina established two administrative regions: the Crescent Group (Nguyệt Thiềm) and Tuyen Duc belong to Thua Thien Province (1939).

RESOLUTION

ANNEX 28

Decree by the Governor General of Indochina

The Governor General of Indochina

Grand Officier de la Legion d'Honneur No.

3282

Having regard to the Decrees of 20 October 1911 laying down the powers of the Governor General and the financial and administrative organization of Indochina;

Having regard to the Decree of 5 October 1936;

Having regard to the Decree of 28 December 1931 regulating the allowances and benefits in kind and in cash;

Having regard to Decree No. 156-SC of 15 June 1932 creating an administrative *delegation* in the Paracel Islands under the authority of Thua-thien Province (Annam) and named the *Delegation* of the Paracels;

On the proposal of the Chief Resident of Annam;

DECREES:

Article 1. - Decree No. 156-SC of 15 June 1932 shall be amended as follows:

Article 1. — Two administrative *delegations* shall be created in the Paracel Islands under Thua-thien Province (Annam) and named *Delegation* of the "Crescent and Dependencies" and "Amphitrite and Dependencies". The boundary between these two administrative districts shall be determined by the line of the 112th meridian, except where it intersects Vulladore Reef, which is wholly contained within the *Delegation* of the Crescent.

Article 2. — The officials in charge of these *Delegations* in their capacity as Delegates of the Resident of France at Thua-thien shall reside on Pattle Island and Woody Island respectively.

Article 3. — In this capacity, they shall each, to cover the costs of representation and tours of duty, be entitled to an annual allowance of 400 piastres (400$00) laid down in the Decree of 28 December 1934. This allowance shall be chargeable to the local budget of Annam, Section 12, Article 6, paragraph 3.

Article 2. — The Secretary General of the Government General of Indochina and the Chief Resident in Annam shall each, in so far as it concerns him, be responsible for the implementation of this Decree.

Hanoi, 5 May 1939

(Signed) J. Brevie

4. ANCIENT MAPS OF CHINA (show that Paracels and Spratlys are not parts of China)

ANCIENT MAPS OF CHINA DO NOT HAVE PARACELS AND SPRATLYS: SOUTHERNMOST POINT OF CHINA IS HAINAN ISLAND

4.1. THE NATIONAL MAPS

The ancient map (1)

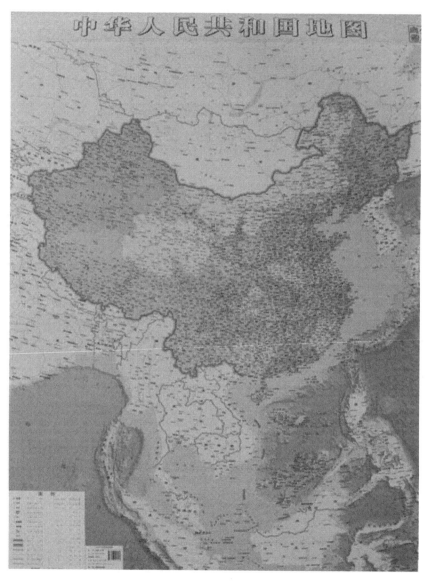

中华人民共和国地图

The People's Republic of China Map. Red China created this map, after taking over the government, having neither Paracels nor Spratlys.

The ancient map (2)

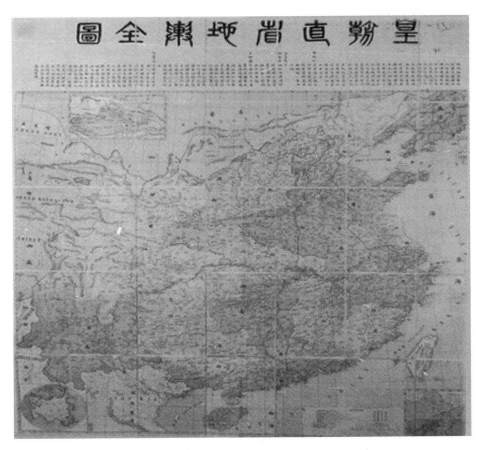

Hoàng Triều Trực Tỉnh Địa Dư Toàn đồ
(The royal dynasty provincial full geographical map)

This total geographical national map is a map collection under Qing Dynasty, published in Shanghai in 1904, reprinted in 1910. This map confirmed Hainan Island as the southernmost part of Chinese territory. That means, the Paracel and Spratly islands in the South China Sea are well outside of China's territory. This map collection was printed in color, created with more than 35 pieces glued on canvas. Each piece measured about 20x30cm.

According to Dr. Mai Ngoc Hong, one of the map's great values was its genuine content and skillfully crafted materials, for the purpose of constructing maps, during a long period of nearly 200 years, starting from the era of Kangxi Emperor 康熙帝 (1654 – 1722), only completed and published in 1904. According to him, this map was constructed with large documentary sources of information directly instructed by China's Emperor. It combined the intellect of the Western and Chinese scholars, reflecting its genuine, official and scientific value, for the first modern map of China. These map collections were printed according to Western designs and techniques, especially regarding the precise ratio scale.

"This map was not established by any private or local entity, but by China's Emperor together with the survey research scientists over a long period of time. Therefore, this is an undeniable historical record".

Map of Ancient China (3): German Chancellor Merkel presented this Map when Xi Jinping visited Berlin on March 28, 2014

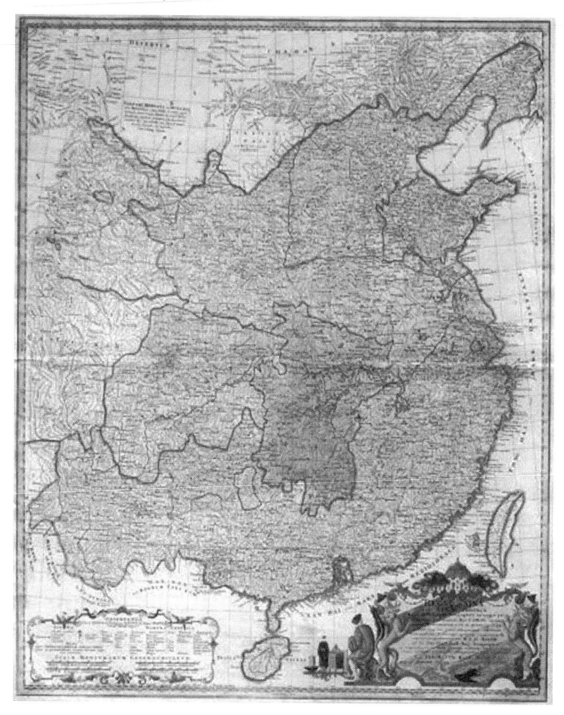

PHOTO: 1735 -Map of Ancient China: German Chancellor Angela Merkel presented to Chinese President Xi Jinping with a map of China from the 18th century, at the Chancellor's Office on March 28, 2014 in Berlin

Ancient Map (4)

Ancient Map (5): Under the QING DYNASTY

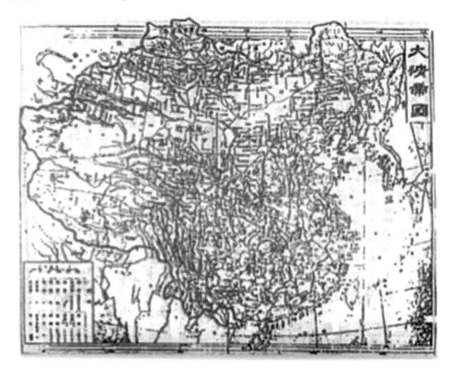

DA QING DI GUO QUAN TU大清帝國全圖 (National Map of the Qing Dynasty Empire). The map Da Qing Di Guo, *Đại Thanh Đế Quốc* 大清帝国, the official map of the Qing Dynasty Empire published in 1905, showing Hainan island at the extreme south of China; not mentioning the Xisha and Nansha (Nam Sa/Spratly/Truong Sa). Luu van Loi ' –id p. 154

4.2. GEOGRAPHY BOOKS THROUGH DYNASTIES "LỊCH PHƯƠNG CHÍ"

Xisha 西沙 (Tây Sa/Hoàng Sa/Paracel) and *Nansha* 南沙 (Nam Sa/Trường Sa/Spratly) were never included in mainland China. Phạm Hoàng Quân, Bvnpost Oct 31, 2010.

There are three types of ancient Chinese Geography Books: *Tổng Chí* (national), *Thông Chí* (provincial) and *Địa Phương Chí* (local). Those three types of geography books never listed Hoang Sa/Paracel and Spratly as Chinese islands.

4.2.1. National Map (Tổng Chí):

- The Tang Dynasty constructed many Maps. Later, the Qing Dynasty, based on those maps, especially the ancient maps of 813, composed the Atlas *"Nguyên Hòa quận huyện bổ chí"*. It said Hainan island province, under the Tang dynasty, consisted of four administrative divisions (châu): Nhai, Đam, Vạn An and Chấn of Lĩnh Nam province. At the southernmost are the two districts of Ninh Viễn and Lâm Xuyên, belonging to Chấn province (now known as Nhai and Hai Nam Districts).

- The Song Dynasty finished the document series *"Nguyên Phong Cửu Vực Chí"* (1080): the southernmost administrative unit, only reaching Nhai and Hai Nam districts, today.

- "On Ming Dynasty, there was a *"Đại Minh Nhất Thống Chí"* 大明一統志 (1461) including a national map called *"Thiên Hạ Nhất Thống Chi Đồ"* (People Unified Map) ... showing that the southernmost point of China only reached Quỳnh Châu district. The southernmost province of mainland China is Hainan 海南 (Hải Nam/South Sea). It is not related to Xisha (Paracel/Hoàng Sa/Tây Sa/Western Sands), or Nansha (Nam Sa/Trường Sa/Southern Sands).

-The Qing Dynasty has 3 sets of maps. The Atlas was prepared the 3rd time: *"Gia Khánh Trùng Tu Đại Thanh Nhất Thống Chí"* completed in 1842, also refers to Nhai province (châu) in city of Quynh Chau district (phủ).

4.2.2. Quảng Đông Province Map

The documents of the Ming Dynasty in 1535, 1602, and the Qing Dynasty in 1675, 1731, and 1882, such as "*Quảng Đông Toàn Tỉnh Tổng Đồ*" (complete map of Guangdong) show that the Guangdong boundary only reaches Quynh Chau district.

Map "*Quỳnh Châu phủ toàn đồ*" noted that "Quynh Chau is four-side surrounded by the ocean, and could not be surveyed at the eight adjacent places". In "*Quảng Đông Thông Chí*" by Nguyễn Nguyên, "*Quảng Đông Dư Địa Tổng Đồ*" (the Guangdong general geopolitical map) was constructed with Western techniques, with the theodolite system, and the limit to the south is only about 18.5 degrees north latitude, while Paracel lies within the latitudes 16-17.

4.2.3. Local Map

Quynh Chau district is located in the South. The map series "*Quỳnh Châu Phủ Chí*" was last compiled in the Qing Dynasty (1891). This map series cited words of the county chief Tieu Ung Thuc, written in this 1774 map series: "*Quynh Chau is in the middle of the sea; on the south is Chiem Thanh; west is Chân Lạp, Giao Chỉ; east is Thiên Lý Trường Sa (thousand miles Spratly), Vạn Lý Thạch Đường; the north adjoining Từ Văn, Loi Chau district*".

The Chinese know that Vạn Lý Trường Sa (Great Spratly) belongs to none of their provinces or districts.

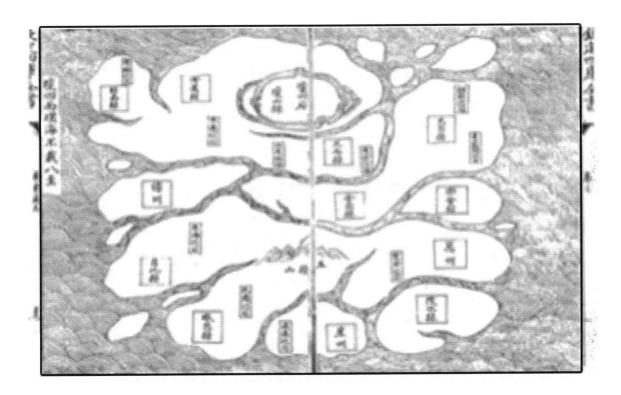

5. CHINA EXPANSIONISM:

INVASION OF THE EASTERN SEA (South China Sea)

5.1. SCHEME TO OCCUPY SOUTH CHINA SEA

THE 9-DASH LINE MAP OF CHINA - Map 15

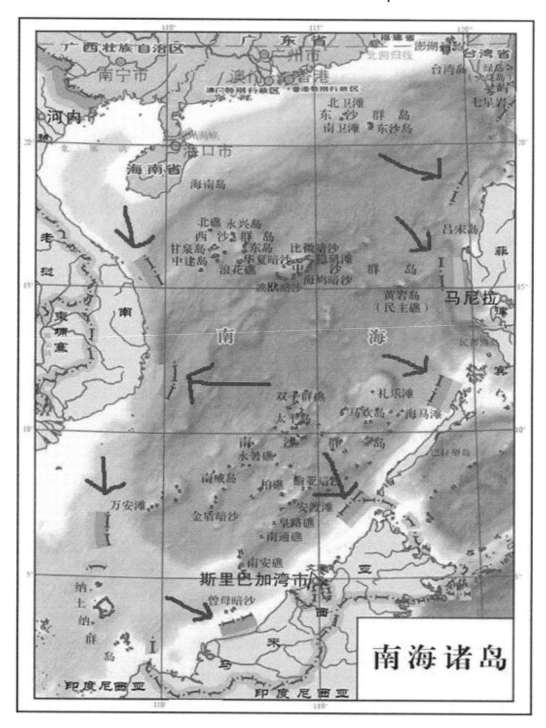

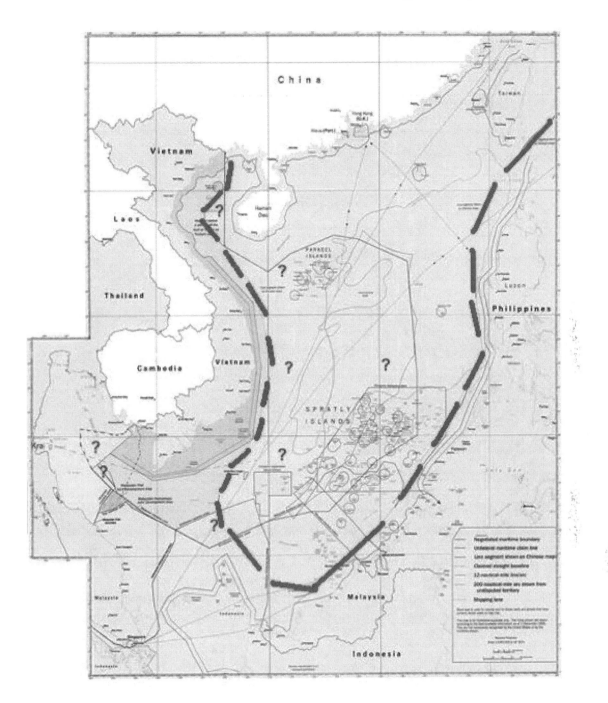

The borders on this map are connected. Because China did not publish the coordinates, we could use vision to compare: the distance between Hoàng Liễu (Hainan) and Cồn Cỏ, offshore of Vĩnh Linh, Đồng Hới, at the mouth of Tonkin Bay (according to the 2000 Agreement). That distance is 120 nautical miles. Half of that distance is 60 nautical miles. If we compare the distance from the "cow's tongue" line to the coastline of Tư Nghĩa district, Quảng Ngãi, the distance would be only about 40 or 50 nautical miles.

THE 10-DASH LINE MAP

The Inquirer Daily (Philippines) reported on June 25, 2014 that China lawlessly announced a new map, almost completely consuming the South China Sea by a "*10-dash line*" instead of "*9-dash line*" map as before.

China's official Xinhua News Agency has posted several photos of the new map released by Hunan Map Publishing Company with blunt annotations: "*The islands in the South China Sea have the same proportion as the mainland and are shown more clearly compared to the traditional maps*".

On November 1, 2013, the China National Survey, Map and Geological Information Agency (NASMG) announced the release of a new China map with vertical format, for the first time, with all 130 large and small islands in the South China Sea clearly marked. Until today, September 12, 2014, China has not released this map.

According to the Xinhua News Agency, until September 8, 2014, this new map has not yet been available, which was published by Sinomaps, and would be sold to the public in late January. A representative of this publishing company announced to the Xinhua News Agency that the new map, "*has important value in raising people's awareness of the national sovereignty, to protect the maritime rights and benefits, as well as expressing China perspective on the political diplomacy stance*".

Last year, China also published a new Passport with a map, to impose sovereignty over almost the entire **Vietnam's Eastern Sea** (South China Sea), called the "*cow's tongue line*" map.

DELIMITATION OF THE TONKIN BAY, 2000

DIVIDING THE TONKIN GULF AREA, 2000

- Red Line: The 1887 Convention (or 1884 Treaty, with the French)

- Black Line: The New Border Line

- Blue Line: The Common Fishing Ground and where eight fishermen in Thanh Hóa were killed by the communist Chinese on January 8, 2005.

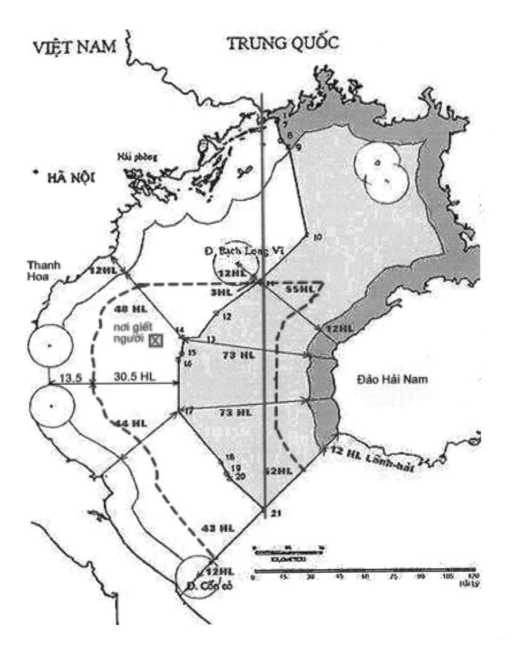

Map of the New Delimitation and the Common Fishing Ground

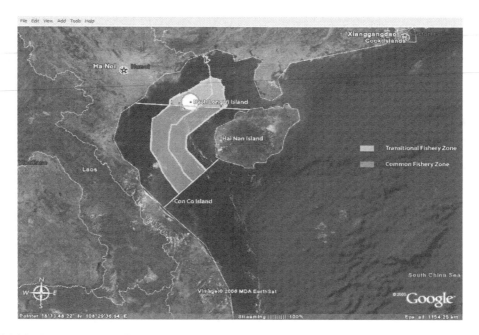

In this 2000 Agreement, Vietnam communist leaders surrendered to China 11,152 square kilometers in the Tonkin Gulf area, comparing to the 1887 Convention.

Map according to the Treaty of Tientsin (*Hiệp Ước Thiên Tân, 1885*),

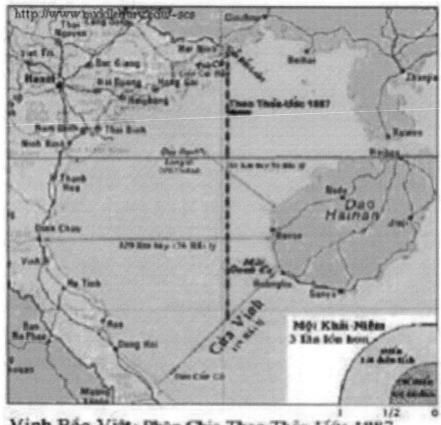

Vịnh Bắc-Việt: Phân Chia Theo Thỏa-Ước 1887

Already acquiring over 10.000 square kilometers sea waters, Red China is even allowed by Vietnam to "cooperate " in a joint fishing project in the Tonkin Bay. She advances deep into Vietnam's maritime territory to fish, plus four more years of coopreration in another area north of Bach Long Vĩ island in the Bay.

INTERVIEW

Professor Nguyen Van Canh on the Maritime Boundary Delimitation and Sino-Vietnamese Treaty in the Gulf of Tonkin (*Hiệp Định Phân Định Vịnh Bắc Bộ*) and the Fisheries Cooperation Agreement in the Gulf (*Hiệp Định Hợp Tác Nghề Cá ở Vịnh Bắc Bộ)* conducted by Professor Tran Cong Thien and Attorney Do Doan Que on March 16, 2002, excerpt from a book entitled "*Communism on Vietnam Soil*", Kiến Quốc, 2002, Book II, p. 325-333:

Professor Thien: Professor Canh, could you provide details on the Tonkin Gulf: surface area, and ratio of the territorial waters in the Gulf surrendered to China. What is the basis to determine that ratio? What about the Fisheries Cooperation Agreement?

Professor Canh: To enforce article 3 of the Tientsin Accord, the 1887 Convention specifies the Gulf boundary by the Paris meridian of 105o43' East. That line runs north-south, lying close to the eastern tip of Trà Cổ Island. On the map, a line was drawn according to the Convention called **The Red Line**.

According to this demarcation line, it has been calculated that Vietnam has 63% and China has 37% area of the Gulf.

Now, the communist leaders have a compromise: 54% for Vietnam and 46% for Red China. Therefore, Vietnam surrendered to China 9% of the Tonkin Gulf.

Attorney Quế: Therefore, professor Canh, can you tell how much area is lost?

Professor Canh: The total area of the Gulf is 123,700 square kilometers. According to the Treaty of Tientsin, Vietnam has 77,911 km², and China has 45,796 km².

Now with the new Agreement: Vietnam only has 66,798 km², and gave away 11,163 km².

Professor Thiện: What about the Agreement on fishery? Where is the common fishing ground, and what is the condition?

Professor Canh: The agreement on fisheries determined that about 27% of the Gulf area will be used for the fishing under the cooperation plan. It is equivalent to 33,500 km². This area is situated south of Bạch Long Vĩ island. In this area, both parties are to cooperate in fishery within 15 years. In addition, there is another zone called "transition", north of Bach Long Vi, for four years of fishery.

Using the new maritime boundary as the standard "*delimitation line*", each party contributes about 30.5 nautical miles in the Bay to the "common fishing area", with profits divided equally to each party.

Attorney Quế: Why the common fishing ground? Do the Vietnamese not have fishing capability, or can they not cooperate with any other third nation?

Professor Canh: There are plans to cooperate with a third nation in the Agreement. According to the published materials, the Agreement stated that in the exclusive economic zone in the Gulf (within the area of 30.5 nautical miles), each party has the right to sign agreement with a third party for fishery. Of course, there are questions on this matter: if there are such rights, then, there is no need to cooperate with China. People can only explain this matter in a general context of cutting and giving away territories. Vietnam is obligated to allow China fishing in our 30.5 nautical miles area, west of the boundary. It means to allow Chinese encroachment deeply on Vietnam's territorial waters, in addition to areas already being ceded.

Clearly, Vietnam is under Chinese pressure, so they have sovereign rights to control resources in the gulf area. Would Vietnam authorities dare to cooperate with a third country, to fish in this exclusive economic zone? The answer is: "wait and see". Not to mention whether Vietnam is able or dares to go fishing on the other side (east) of the boundary line, i.e. in China's exclusive economic zone. To cooperate in fishery is only a disguised tactic, to allow China to encroach deeply on Vietnam territories, to exploit natural resources. Everyone understands that Vietnam's state-owned fishing capability could not have a large-scale ship as that of China. And within a wide area like that, how could Vietnam be able to control the fishing harvest, for sharing profits? Furthermore, would Vietnam dare to control it? That is another subject.

What about the transition zone? Vietnam did not reveal the exact surface area, and its actual location. Le Cong Phung (negotiation team leader of communist Vietnam) vaguely said that this area is situated to the north of Bach Long Vi Island 白龍尾 (meaning White Dragon Tail). Phung enthusiastically announced, "we got the legal status of this island of Bach Long Vi". This means that China does not any more claim the island is hers.. When looking at the new maritime boundary, north of Bach Long Vi island, we see that section lies the middle of the bay, but within the area belonging to Vietnam. So, the transition zone is announced to be in the north of Bạch Long Vĩ island, so it would lie within Vietnam's territorial waters.

Professor Thiện: If there is such a joint cooperation, Professor, do you think there can be any harm?"

Professor Canh: China has fishing trawlers with a 60-mile fishing net. The trawlers could dredge across the sea floor, to catch numerous small fish at once. To do dredge fishing continuously within 15 years, the ocean would be devastated, out of fish. Many fish species have disappeared, as I was told, in Vietnam's coastal area. Vietnam communist leaders seem never to be concerned about the future of Vietnam, therefore they have no concern about protecting the young fish, sustainable for generations to come. Previously, after 1975, this type of ships came close to Vietnam's coast, using that destructive fishing method...

Attorney Que: The following question has a legal aspect. I think professor Canh has credentials to explain this matter. Was the Brévié boundary line of the Tientsin Treaty not helpful while negotiating, for the delimitation of the maritime boundary of the Tonkin Gulf?

Professor Canh: Before answering this question, I think we must talk about the boundary line called Brévié. I have reviewed all the treaties signed between France and the Qing Dynasty, especially the Tientsin Treaty and the two conventions attached to that treaty. There was no boundary line named Brévié. I think that the boundary line that Attorney Quế mentioned was called the Red Line. This line was drawn in the Map, designated in the 1887 Convention. That Convention agreement was signed by Constans, the French representative. It was signed in Beijing, with the Emperor's family member Cung (K'ing), of the Qing Dynasty. That Red Line should be called the Constans line. I did find the term "Brévié". It is the name of the Governor-General of French Indochina Joseph-Jules Brévié (1937-1939). He was involved in the Viet-Cambodia territorial delimitation in 1939. Thus, the time he was Governor-General was over a half of century away from that 1887 Convention. Perhaps, at that time, he wasn't born. Yet the current Vietnam-Cambodia boundary line is called the Brévié line.

Regarding your question, attorney, whether the Constans line was used as a legal basis for negotiation? Then the answer is No. The two negotiating parties did not consider the boundary line prescribed in that Convention in the Gulf. Vietnam agreed with China that this Constans line was only used to divide the Gulf for both sides. Like China, Vietnam also called it the "administrative line", therefore it has no legal effect, meaning, the administrative line is not the boundary line to delineate sovereignty of each country in the concerned region. So it is a borderless zone, people are free to navigate. For this reason, both parties have established the new boundary line in the Gulf area.

So the question is whether both parties used the Treaty of Tientsin (Hiệp Ước Thiên Tân), together with the 1887 Convention as the basis for the negotiations. And what position is the Constans line, or the Red Line, in that document, to delineate the new boundary?

At first, when Le Cong Phung replied to VASC Orient, he said those documents were "the basis" for Treaty negotiating on lands. But when it came to the Gulf Agreement, he did not mention those documents. He said the two parties depended on the "basis" as follows:

"First, the United Nations Convention on the Law of the Sea (UNCLOS) in 1982. Second, it is based on the natural conditions of Gulf of Tonkin, and most important, the geography on the Vietnamese side and the Chinese side and the resources in the Gulf, as a basis for the boundary delimitation". Later, VASC Orient suggested whether the "administrative line" in the Bay was governed by the convention, then he said it was not in compliance with the international law, i.e. the 1982 Convention on the Law of the Sea, and not suitable with the international reality.

If based on the 1982 Law of the Sea, and if we only look at the population factor, then the coastal Vietnamese population compared to Chinese living close to the disputed area would be an important factor in the Law of the Sea for boundary delimitation, since Vietnamese people occupy most of the entire Gulf. In addition, what is the international reality? Le Cong Phung did not present it. Isn't it true that in the decades since 1980, China has had regional activities, such as sending drilling platforms deep into the Gulf for oil exploration, such as the Hai Nam Ship or Phan Dau ship in 1982? Those ships entered deeply into the coastal area of Hai Phong and Thai Binh for oil exploration, and China declared them their territorial waters. This act of China was one way to exercise their sovereignty over the Bay.

Here, I'd like to raise the question: why did Vietnam Communist Party leaders avoid invoking the 1887 Convention to defend Vietnam's sovereignty over our territorial waters, even though the 1887 Convention explicitly stated that it was a Boundary?

According to Chinese documents, in 1973, China demanded Vietnam to negotiate for boundary delimitation of the Gulf. Vietnam authorities replied that Vietnam was at war, not ready to discuss this matter. The following year, in January 1974, Vietnam authorities replied to China's demand on this issue, that the boundary line was already established, signed by France and China in 1887. Chinese authorities denied it, arguing that the boundary line agreement signed by France and China in 1887 was only intended **to divide the ownership of the islands:** islands on the east of the boundary line belongs to China, and islands on the west belong to Vietnam. That is the line to manage the islands.

In order to justify this position, Han Niem Long, deputy foreign minister of China, who was in charge of negotiations, cited a provision of the 1887 Convention describing the delimitation of the Gulf's boundaries, said the following: "*as for the islands in the sea, those to the west of the southward red line drawn by the commissioners of the two countries, passing through the hill at the east tip of Trà Cổ (Wanzhu) which is to the south of Móng Cái and Jiutoushan island (Cu To island) and other islands, belong to Annam.*"

Meanwhile, this entire section is: "Au Kouang-Tong, il est entendu que les points contestés qui sont situés à l'est et au nord-est de Monkai, au-delà de **la frontière** telle qu'elle a été fixée par la commission de délimitation, sont atribuées à la Chine. Les iles qui sont à l'est du meridien de Paris 105 degree 43' de longitude est, c'est-à-dire de la ligne nord-sud passant par la pointe orientale de l'ile de Tch'a Kou ou Puanchan (Tra Co) et **formant la frontière** sont également attribuées à la Chine. Les Iles de Go-tho et les autres iles qui sont à l'ouest de ce meridien appartiennent à l'Annam".

According to the above document (Convention of 1887) when Ha Niem Long cited the above paragraph, he eliminated its first part, especially removing the words **FORMANT LA FRONTIERE**, that is, to remove the terms "forming the boundary" and telling Vietnam that this is the administrative line": only the line dividing the islands...The Convention stated clearly: the North-South line (Red) forming the border (formant la frontière). The boundary between two nations obviously divides the Gulf, meaning it determined the national sovereignty for each party…

I think that:

1) Han Niem Long intentionally removed the words "formant la frontière". It is a deceit, misinformation, an important decisive factor to render all Covenants null and void.

2) There is a legal principle applying undisputedly, that a treaty or a treaty's provision can only be voided when it is replaced by another equivalent document, or when both parties agree to abolish it.

3) Vietnam has accepted whatever China requested from 1974, until now, and in the current situation- as Le Cong Phung said - based on the international reality: to surrender 9% of the

Gulf to China, to establish a joint fishing area.... because of applying the Law of the Sea 1982 and of the international reality, it is an unequal, deceitful treaty: this treaty has become worthless.

5.2. EXPANSION INTO THE PACIFIC OCEAN

Extending the territorial sea: First and Second Chains of Defense

5.2.1. String of Islands line of defense: from Japan to the Philippines

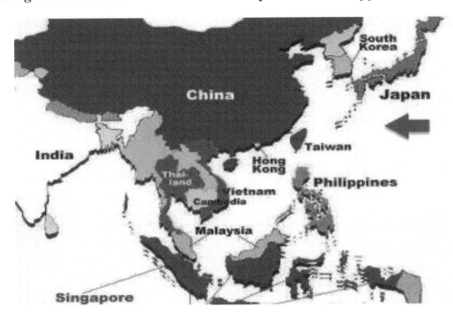

5.2.2. Distant or Far Sea Defense Line: From Indonesia to Guam then Australia.

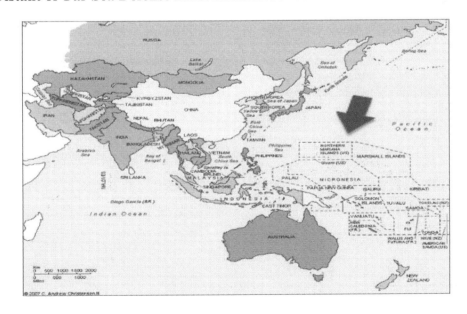

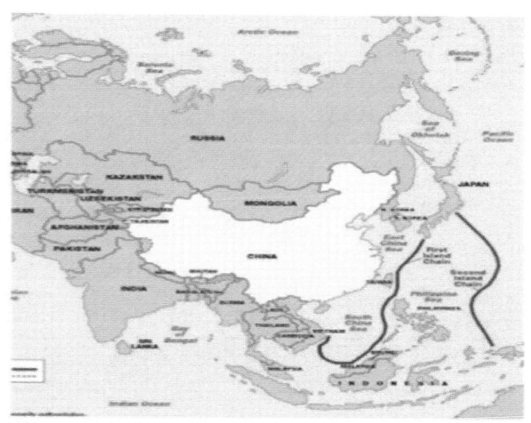

d Second Island Chains. *PRC military theorists conceive of two island "chains"*

Map 6.
Source: US Department of Defence, Annual Report to Congress: Military Power
of the People's Repub;lic of China 2007.

5.2.3. Scheme to Occupy The Entirety of Asia

A Great China Empire

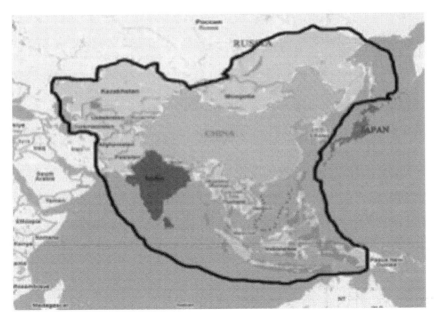

5.2.4. Expansion Westward: One Belt One Road / OBOR (TSBD-37) Occupying Europe and Africa and further

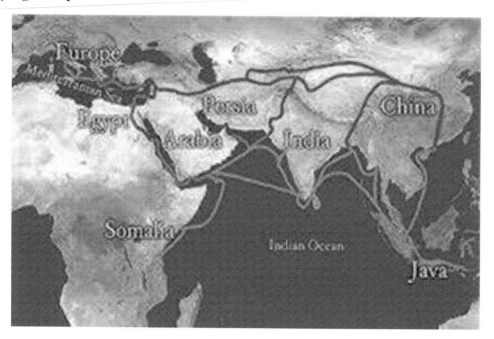

One Belt (red) One Road (blue)

The Belt (the new Silk Road)

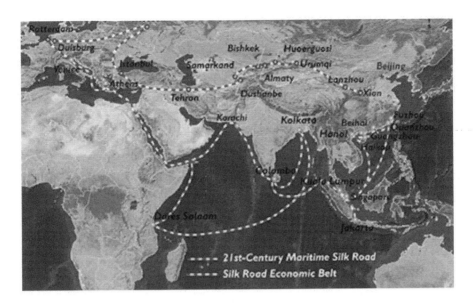

The Road

6. ANNOTATIONS OF MAPS

Map 1: Đông Hải (Eastern Sea). This map was named "Biển Việt Nam" (Vietnam Sea) with two archipelagos of Paracels and Spratlys. "The Republic of Vietnam" (RVN) is written on the bottom line. "Biển Việt Nam" was in Southeast Asia at large

Map 8: An ancient map issued in 1594 by Indes, Petrus Plaucius and published by J. Visscher in 1617. On this map are the words *"Costa de Pracel"* (Portuguese) or *"Coastal Paracels"* The Coastal Paracels was positioned on the lower part of the map, belonging to Cochin China (*Nam Kỳ* 南圻, in the South). On the top part, we saw the term *"Tunquin"* (rewritten as Tonkin, *Bắc kỳ* 北圻, in the North). Next, was the Royaume de Champa (Kingdom of Chàm)? On both sides were *Mecon Fluvius* (Mekong River) of Royaume de Camboja/Camboia (Cambodia/Cao Miên). Offshore, this "Costa de Pracel" Coastal Paracels encompassed a series of interconnected islands, stretching from a location equivalent to Quảng Nam – Đà Nẵng today, through Champa, going to Cambodia's offshore area which is Paracel (Paracel/Hoang Sa). This entire district has belonged to Vietnam. And those groups of interconnected islands later were called *Hoàng Sa* (Paracel) and *Trường Sa* (Spratly). Those groups of islands have never belonged to China.

Map 9 - Map 11: drawn by Jodocus Hondius, Portuguese, 1606 and 1617, including the entire Southeast Asia, including Tonkin, Cochin China, Champa (Chàm) and Cambodia (Miên). Champa and part of Cambodia now belong to Vietnam). Map 11 includes a series of islands in South China Sea now recognized as the Paracel and Spratly Islands. Map of Jodocus, similar to that of Indes shows the series of islands of Hoàng Sa (Paracels) and Trường Sa (Spratlys), stretching across the ocean, off the coasts of Vietnam, Champa and Cambodia

Map 15 and 16: Red China redrew the maps (the 9-dash line Map) is also known as "South China Sea". The boundary of this map is close to the Vietnam coastline. At Tư Nghĩa district,

Quảng Ngãi, the new boundary line lies on the meridian 110° west and on the 15° north latitude, and overlaps Vietnam's continental shelf as well as Vietnam's exclusive economic zone of 200 nautical miles, designated solely to nations bordering the ocean, according to the 1982 International Law of the Sea. With this new map, Communist China wants to seize the entire Vietnamese Eastern Sea (Đông Hải) of 3.5 million km². To occupy Bien Dong (South China Sea) is to block Vietnam from going offshore, connecting and integrating with the international communities. It is necessary and mandatory for the Vietnamese people along with other nations in the world, **to survive**, in the present as well as in the future. Hegemonistic Beijing's plot is to isolate Vietnam, to tightly control, to dominate the Vietnamese people. They suffocate the "living space of Vietnamese people". Clearly, there are other steps in their secret plan to annex 附件 Vietnam into Chinese territory, gradually *assimilate* 吸收 Vietnamese people to become "Chinese". Ho Chi Minh and his close assistants, Pham Van Dong and Truong Chinh, held key positions in the Vietnam Communist Party and other national positions to implement this mission.

The entire Vietnam Communist Party apparatus and its communist government machinery have taken ruthless bloody measures to carry out this conspiracy with Red China, a type of conspiracy advocated by Mao, as in Hanoi's White Paper of 1979, cited by Vietnamese authorities. China's scheme in this case is not different from what has been happening to the Tibetan people that the world has witnessed.

TSBD 37: One Belt - One Road is a Scheme to seize control of Africa and Europe. It was China's Aspiration to create a Century of China by the year 2049.

One Road (by Sea) today is a redraw of the Pearls Chain Scheme that went into effect and has been implemented for several decades now. It is a chain of ports from Southeast Asian sea route Straight of Malacca-Indian Ocean, beginning in Kampuchea / Cambodia to Myanmar, Bangladesh, to Sri Lanka, to Cocos Island and the Maldives, to Pakistan, then Tehran, and ending in Africa and also in Italy where One Belt ends. A continental Beltway from East to West: from China through nations of the old Soviet Union to Moscow, through the Baltic countries to Europe and meeting the end of the One Road in Italy.

These seaports are used as military bases, employing military power for expansion. As to Vietnam, in 2005, Tran Duc Luong, then president of Communist Vietnam, cooperated with China to establish to economic corridors: One, from Kunming, Yunnan, to Lai Chau, and ending at Hai Phong. Another one starting at Nanjing, Guangxi runs through Lang Son. And one beltway runs along the Bay of Tonkin southward. And three special economic zones: Vân Đồn, Quảng Ninh, Bắc Vân Phong, Khánh Hoà, and Phú Quốc to be established by Communist Vietnam lie within this beltway.

China has utilized "debt traps" to entice leadership of usually corrupted governments of developing countries with economic loans up to billions of U.S. dollars in order to finance the construction of infrastructures such as roads, power plants, high speed expressways, railways. Briberies accompany these development loans. When the due dates come, these debtor-nations usually unable to repay them are then forced to cede control of their strategic areas to China on long-term basis.

For example, Sri Lanka, owing 17 billion U.S. dollars, in 2017 had to lease Hambantota port and an industrial zone for 99 years.

Another example is Cambodia, which receives 5.3 billions U.S. dollars and China spent 3.8 billions U.S. dollars to construct a military base on a 4500 acre area at the seaport Koh Kong subject to a 99 year lease. This port overlooks the Bay of Thailand. This military base is under self-rule. Thailand itself was promised 20 billions to construct the Kra canal. The Maldives ceded control to China seaport Feydhoo Finolhu for a 99-year lease, beginning in 2017. Pakistan was indebted to China for 17 billions U.S. dollars so it has leased Gwadar seaport to China and permitted China to construct a military base nearby, both under China control for 40 years. Tehran is indebted to China for 9 billions U.S. dollars. Myanmar 7.3 billions U.S. dollars, so it ceded control of seaport Kyauk Pyu to China for 50 years, beginning in 2015. The Philippines, 20 billions U.S. dollars. Malaysia for 24 billions U.S. dollars, but the Malaysian new leadership withdrew from this loan because it saw that it could not repay the prospective debt. Djibouti ceded Obock seaport to China's use as a military base for 10 years. Kenya itself in 2017 ceded Mobata seaport to China, the gateway to East Africa.

In addition, in connection with the construction, Chinese engineers and workers are sent to the local areas, for example 20,000 Chinese "workers" live in the Aluminum mining project at Dac Nong, Vietnam. This is a plot to settle Chinese in the area so to form a Chinese community. The community is a sleeper force destabilizing the local government from the inside, if and when China starts a war for world domination. At the same time, this project plots the growth of these Chinese communities in attempts to populate the world with Chinese, as sketched out in 2005. (See pages 26-27, HS. Hoang Sa & Truong Sa & CQDT). A close examination of the detailed railway map of the beltway would reveal this plan, so does an examination of the seaports along the beltway.

Countries within China Beltway:

1. North Line A: North America (The United States and Canada) --north Pacific –Japan -- South Korea -- the Sea of Japan -- Zarubino port– Huichun --Yanji –Jilin-- Changchun -- Mongolia – Russia – Europe (northern Europe, central and eastern Europe, Western Europe,

Southern Europe)

2. North Line B: Beijing -- Russia -- Germany -- northern Europe.

3. Middle line: Beijing -- Xi 'an -- Urumqi -- Afghanistan --Kazakhstan -- Hungary -- Paris.

4. South Line: Quanzhou – Fuzhou – Guangzhou – Haikou—Beihai-- Hanoi - Kuala Lumpur – Jakarta – Colombo – Kolkata -- Nairobi –Athens – Venice.

5. Central Line: Lianyungang -- Zhengzhou -- Xi 'an -- Lanzhou --Xinjiang -- central Asia -- Europe.

Starting country: China.

Other countries: Mongolia, Russia.

8 countries in South Asia: Pakistan, Bangladesh, Sri Lanka, Afghan, Nepal, Maldives, Bhutan.

11 countries in Southeast Asia: Mongolia, Russia, Indonesia, Thailand, Malaysia, Vietnam, Singapore, Philippines, Myanmar, Cambodia, Laos, Brunei, east Timor

5 Central Asia countries: Kazakhsta, Uzbekistan, Turkmenistan, Kyrghyzstan, Tajikistan.

16 Countries of West Asia and North Africa: Saudi Arabia, UAE, Oman, Iran, Turkey, Israel, Egypt, Kuwait, Iraq, Qatar, Jordan, Lebanon, Bahrain, Yemen, Syria, Palestine.

17 Central and Eastern European countries: Poland, Rumania, Czech Republic, Slovakia, Bulgaria, Hungary, Latvia, Lithuania, Slovenia, Estonia, Croatia, Albania, Serbia, Macedonia, Bosnia and Herzegovina.

The other six states of the CIS: Ukraine, Azerbaijan, Armenia, Belarus, Georgia, Moldova.

As part of this project, China has thrown money into African countries and those of Oceania. The total planned investment is 1 trillion U.S. dollars over 90 countries.

At the second international conference on the One Belt One Road Initiative, held in Beijing last April, Li Keqiang disclosed that 129 nations and 50 international organizations participate in this project.

CHAPTER II: PHOTOS OF ISLANDS OCCUPIED BY COMMUNIST CHINA

POSITION OF THE PARACELS AND SPRATLYS

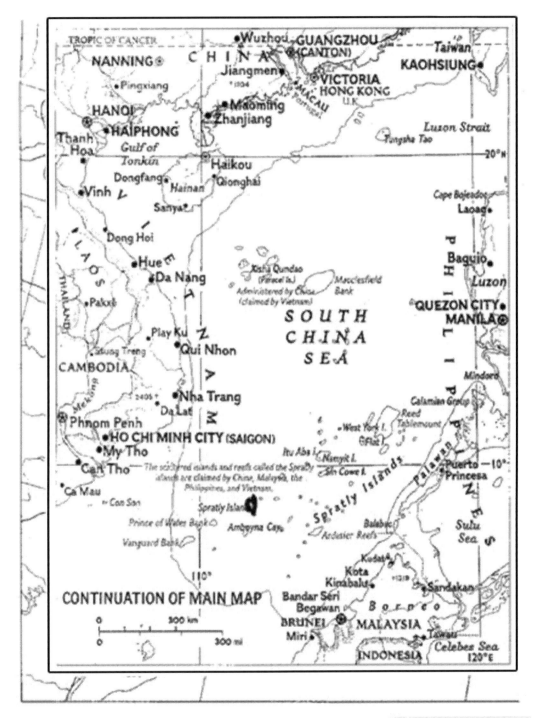

MAP OF OIL DRILLING SITES

MAPS OF OIL AND GAS EXPLOITATION

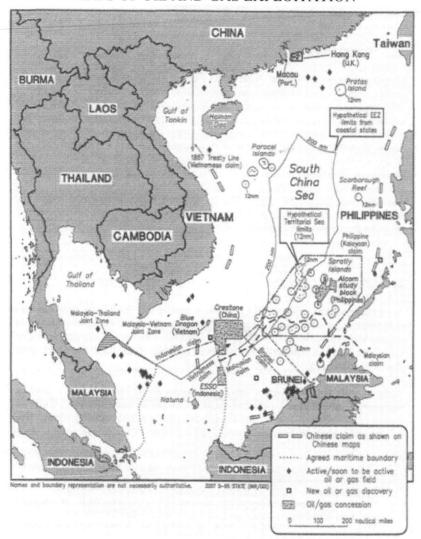

1. THE PARACEL ARCHIPELAGO

1.1. AN OVERVIEW: Remarks on the Paracel Islands

The term Paracels was used by Dutch brothers since 1595. Some people assumed this name came from the Portuguese, because "Paracels" means, "*reef*" (đá ngầm). Other people assumed Paracels was the name of a ship of Dutch East India Company. This ship sank at this archipelago in the XVIth century.

The Paracels (Hoàng Sa) is an archipelago situated on the north of the Eastern Sea (South China Sea). This archipelago consists of about 120 islands/islets. The islands are not large enough and cannot be self-sufficient for survival, so no people are living there permanently. In 1939, under the French colonial government, the archipelago was divided into two groups: The

Eastern group is called Tuyên Đức (Nhóm đảo An Vĩnh/Amphitrite), including islands such as đảo Cù Mộc (đảo Cây/Tree Island), Đảo Bắc (North Island), Đảo Phú Lâm (Woody Island), Đảo Linh Côn (Lincoln Island), Đảo Đá (Rocky Island), and the Western group is Nhóm Nguyệt Thiềm (also called Nhóm Trăng Khuyết/ Lưỡi Liềm/Crescent Group), including đảo Hoàng Sa (Paracel island), đảo Hữu Nhật (Robert island), đảo Bạch Quy (Passu Keah Reef), đảo Tri Tôn (Triton Island), đảo Quang Ánh (Money Island) đảo Quang Hòa (Duncan Island), đảo Duy Mộng (Drummond Island), etc....

- In 1630, the geography series Toàn *Tập Thiên Nam Tứ Chí Lộ Đồ* (Đỗ Bá) has an Ancient Map drawing area of Quảng Ngãi and Thăng Hoa Districts, with detailed annotations. The *"Golden Sand"* is Paracel.

-- In 1776, the documentary book *Phủ Biên Tạp Lục* (scholar Lê Quý Đôn) mentioned Đại Trường Sa (Great Spratlys), Đại Hoàng Sa (Great Paracels), Vạn Lý Trường Sa (Great Length Spratlys)

- In 1821, the *"Dynasty Charter"* (Phan Huy Chú) mentioned the "Hoang Sa Team" bringing six months of food supplies for staying in Hoang Sa (the Paracels). They took many valuable items from the stranded boats...

-In 1816, King Gia Long came to solemnly plant a flag and officially state Vietnam's sovereignty over this archipelago.

- In 1909, China landed on the Paracel Island, fired 21 cannons, planted China flags, and declared sovereignty over all occupied islands in this area. In 1921, the Viceroy 總督 (Tổng đốc) of Quangdong annexed the Paracels into the administration of Yaihien, Hainan island 海南 (Hải Nam). The French government did not respond.

- From 1920, the French Customs Service regularly sent a patrolling ship to the Paracel archipelago.

- In 1925, a delegation of scientists was sent by Nha Trang Institute of Oceanography to survey, and reported that this archipelago was on a plateau resting on the seabed, and attached to Vietnam's *continental shelf*.

- From 1926 to 1933, the French government sent battleships to spy on both Hoang Sa (Paracel) and Truong Sa (Spratly) archipelagos.

- From 1931 to 1939, France sent troops to be stationed at the Paracel islands.

- In 1946, France set up a radio station on Pattle Island (Đảo Hoàng Sa) to ensure navigation security for the South China Sea.

- In 1931, the Gouverneur-général de l'Indochine Française placed the Paracels as an administrative unit of Thua Thien province.

- The Ordinance No 10 of Bao Dai, the 13th signed on March 30, 1933 placed Hoang Sa in Thùa Thiên Province (photo attached).

During the colonial period, French people built military bases on the island of Hoang Sa (*Pattle*), and sent dozens of soldiers to guard and control the islands in the region. During the Japanese occupation, they built bunkers around this island for defense. After the Japanese surrendered, France returned to Indochina and sent troops to guard it.

After World War II, on October 29, 1947, Chiang Kai-Shek sent out 4 battleships to invade. After the confrontation, with the French, Chiang's troops had to retreat, but then occupied the Woody Island.

After the communists took over Mainland China in 1949, Red China also occupied several other islands in the archipelago, except one island called Pattle (Hoàng Sa). Of the 120 features in the Hoang Sa archipelago, there are 12 small islands with names, of which two relatively larger islands are Hoàng Sa (*Pattle Island*) in the Crescent Group (West group or *Nguyệt Thiềm*) and Woody Island (*Phú Lâm*) in the Amphitrite Group (*nhóm Đông/An Vĩnh, or Tuyên Đức*). No island is larger than 2.5 km². When Chiang's troops withdrew to Taiwan, Red China occupied some islands on the East in 1956. In 1974, China sent a fleet of battleships to occupy the entire Paracel archipelago. At that time, the Crescent Group belonged to the Republic of Vietnam. The Republic of Vietnam Navy (RVN) bravely confronted the powerful China Navy, fought to defend, but failed, and since then, China has controlled that entire archipelago. This counter-defense was to protect the Paracels, an act to protect Vietnam's sovereignty.

Paracel currently is the military base of communist China. China is also planning to turn the Paracel archipelago into a tourist center, and they announced this project in the mid-1990s. Currently, there are only the communist Chinese military troops on the Paracel Island.

Chinese Navy and soldiers are on the Paracel Islands.

BBC August 27, 2007: China began exploiting tourism in the Paracels.

China Daily, the Chinese Communist Party's English newspaper reported on August 10, 2008 about Hainan authorities planning to exploit tourism in the Paracels. This plan was recently approved by Beijing government. A Chinese reporter was quoted from this article, describing *"the Paracel Islands scenery is more beautiful than that of Hainan"."The water is so crystal clear that fish can be seen swimming, 10m below the ocean surface. Plants grow abundantly everywhere. There are many rare bird species, not seen anywhere else".*

CHINA ACTIVITIES TO ASSERT SOVEREIGNTY O VER THE PARACELS

China prohibited Vietnamese fishermen, from May 16 until August 1, 2009 for the sake of protecting marine resources from the latitude 12 up to the Guangdong offshore area.

On June 16 2009, China's navy captured two fishing boats at the Paracel area. On each fishing boat, there were 12 fishermen from Quang Ngai province; they were fishing near Lincoln Island. A Chinese naval ship, with a registered number 309, suddenly appeared near those fishing boats. Chinese navy soldiers jumped onto the fishing boats, lashed them to their ships, then pulled the boats to Woody Island. The next day, a third boat was captured, and also taken to Woody Island. On June 21, all of these fishing boat captains were forced to sign a report, written in Chinese characters, accusing them of violating Chinese territory. They were charged $US 31,000.00 penalty fines. 25 fishermen were released on June 25, with messages that they must pay penalties, so the remaining fishermen could be released.

Penalty Report - "Three fishing boats of Vietnamese fishermen from Ly Son island district were arrested by Chinese vessels, while fishing in the Paracel Islands area, on December 7 and 8. China confiscated two Vietnamese boats, allowing one to take the Vietnamese fishermen home, after taking away all boat fishing equipment. All 43 Vietnamese fishermen were released on the 10th, arriving at Ly Son Island at 19:00 pm on December 11".

Vietnam Newspapers reported that the three Vietnamese boats were boat QNg 96004 of Mr Lê Tân; boat QNg 96199 of Mr. Lê Văn Lộc, boat QNg 66398 of Mr. Dương Lúa. All crew lived on Ly Son Island. They were arrested by Chinese cruisers patrolling on December 7 to August 8 while they were operating in Vietnam's territorial waters.

The fishermen were forced to sign and were fingerprinted into paper reports written in Chinese characters". (Việt Hà, RFA correspondent 2009-12-13).

1.2. PHOTOS OF COMMUNIST CHINA'S MILITARY STRUCTURES

MAP OF THE PARACEL ARCHIPELAGO:
THE CRESCENT GROUP (NGUYET THIEM AREA) and
AMPHITRITE GROUP (TUYEN DUC AREA)

QUẦN ĐẢO HOÀNG SA

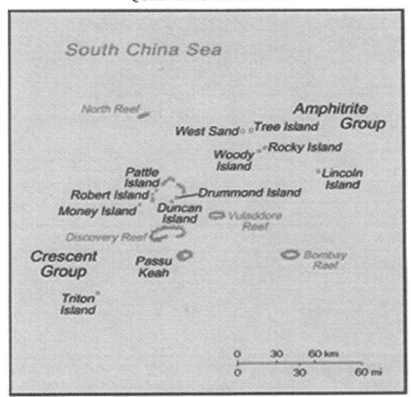

MILITARY INSTALLATIONS
Crescent & Amphitrite Groups

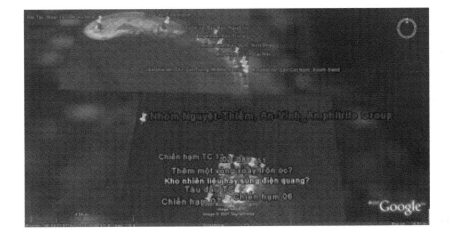

PATTLE (Crescent Group)

The Paracel Island

In this Paracel Island area of the Paracel archipelago on the afternoon of January 18, 1974 (December 26 of the lunar calendar), and in the battle of January 19, 1974, four battleships of the Republic of South Vietnam (HQ 4, 5,10 and 16) were gathered here, under the command of Colonel Hà văn Ngạc. The next day, they advanced to Quang Hòa (Duncan Island) and Duy Mộng island (Drummond island), fighting against the communist Chinese invaders. They had occupied these two islands previously.

WOODY

Woody Island-HSBD20

"Today, at the western end of Yongxing (Woody) Island, there are four silver water containers. Each can stores 5,000 cubic meters of rainwater. The rainwater, after going through technical treatment, such as filtering, sediment, sterilization and electro-coagulation, reaches the State standard for drinking water sanitation. This rain water project is called the "project of life" by Xisha people. They collect freshwater for the army and civilians. Xisha Island, far from the mainland, is more than 180 nautical miles away from Sanya City. On January 1, 1999, the program-controlled switchboard of Yongxing Island was successfully connected with the program-controlled switchboard of Sanya City post office. This marked the entry of Xisha's communication into the age of program control, and one can direct dial a phone call to everywhere in the country" (from China media).

Phú Lâm (Woody Island) is the most important Chinese communist military base in the Paracel archipelago, including many seaports, docks for warships, underground weapons depots, power substations, barracks for thousands of marines, seawater refineries and freshwater reservoirs, meteorological station, radar stations, telecommunication systems, and a large airport with many jet fighters. This is a military base used by China as a station for supplies, to support dozens of military bases built on remote areas in the South of Spratly Islands, to advance further East and South, and also to block Vietnam's offshore and coastal areas, meaning to encircle Vietnam.

Phu Lam supported the strategic axis of South China Sea. It is a place to detain, interrogate, confiscate, and punish Vietnamese fishermen from Ly Son Island to fish at the islands.

The Paracels belong to Vietnam.

(1)

(2)

(2a- 2017)

(3)

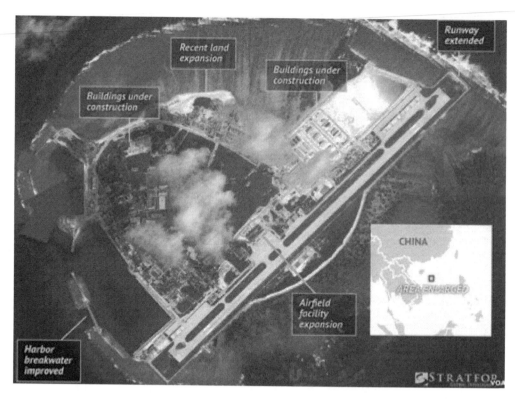

The cost for seaport expansion in 2015 was $13 million.

(3b)

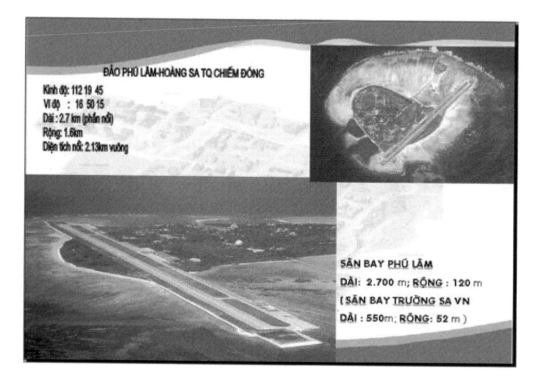

(4)

HCBD 20a: Seven battleships are stationed in Woody Island. There are two outpost stations in two seaports and helipads. Part of the runway was extended to 2,600 m long for artillery launchers. There are roads, trees, houses for the troops stationed there.

(5)

Two seaports with seven warships are seen along the island. Two outposts were built at the mouth of the base with a platform for helicopters. There is an oil ship off the coast.

(6)

A warship berthed along the dock, barracks for troops, roads and trees occupying a small part of the island

(7)

Woody Island (Đảo Phú Lâm) hsbd-20B

MISSILE DEPOTS

(8)

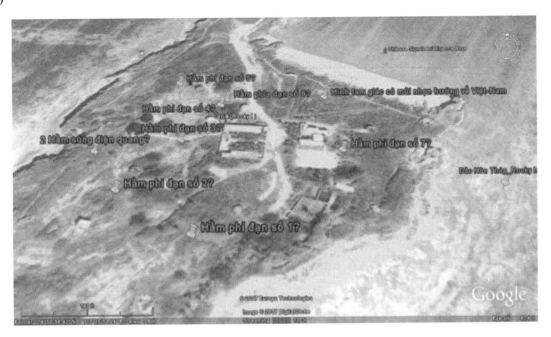

Woody Island: seven Missile Depots, two laser weapons depots, seven missiles (rockets), and two vaults for electro-optic guns.

MILITARY OFFICE

(9)

Military Headquarters

Apartment complexes

The battleships

(14)

Part of an airport

TRITON ISLAND/ ĐẢO TRI TÔN (THE CRESCENT GROUP)

HSBD-20H

TREE ISLAND HSBD-20E (1)

ĐẢO CÙ MỘC or ĐẢO CÂY

TREE ISLAND: COMO TOWER (2)

ĐẢO QUANG HÒA (DUNCAN ISLAND) HSBD-20H
MILITARY HEADQUARTERS (1)

Duncan Island (*Dao Quang Hòa*)
Naval battle occurred in the area of Duncan Island
(January 19, 1974, on the 27th of New Year (lunar year of the Tiger),

Please see Annotations below

COMMO TOWER (2)

Duncan, Communication Tower

ZHONY HSBD-20G

Zhony Dao, Paracel

ZHONGYE
HSBD-20H

Zhongye Dao, Airfield

ROBERT ISLAND (ĐẢO HỮU NHẬT) THSBD-20 I

YAGONG HSBD-2J

Yagong Island (*Đảo Ba Ba*), Paracel

MONEY ISLAND HSBD-20K

Money Island (*Đảo Quang Ảnh*) in the Crescent Group

ANTELOPE HSBD-20L

Antelope Reef (*bãi ngầm Sơn Dương*) Amphitrite Group (*nhóm đảo An Vĩnh*), Paracel

China military forces stationed on the Paracels

Vietnam's Paracel archipelago on South China Sea has become
China's strong military base

Various types of armored vehicles and heavy weapons were also moved to the Paracel Islands. The purpose of having these combat vehicles is not only for defense but also for the deployment, invasion, and expansion.

Radar Control Center in Hoang Sa is a place to gather intelligence information and monitoring the navigation of ships on Vietnam's Eastern Sea.

Communist China always shows her readiness for combat.

China has hundreds of troops on the Paracel Islands.

radar system installed on the island

The Paracel military seaport is the anchorage of various types of battleships, destroyers, and other civil or military ships.

Outside the Paracel Islands, there are many Chinese battleships patrolling

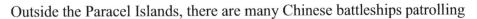

Submarines also participate in ocean patrolling in the Paracels.

Surveilllance ship patrolling

Fishery vessels are also utilized to patrol in the Paracel archipelago and its surrounding waters; nothing could stop the Chinese expansion and increasing of military strength, although China signed the DOC (Declaration on Conduct of the ASEAN in the South China Sea, 2002).

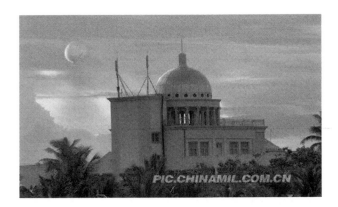

Meteorological station on the Paracels

1.3. Annotations on Photos of Islands in the Paracel Archipelago

HSBD.20: The Woody Island (đảo Phú Lâm), and Tuyên Đức region in the Paracel archipelago

When seizing this island in 1946, Chiang Kai-Shek's troops turned this island into a large military base: constructing roads for vehicles, building barracks consisting of five building complexes of six apartments, four building complexes of duplexes and two antenna towers 12m high. They built 50 extra facilities and a 100m-long coastal dock. When the French-Vietnamese war broke out in Hanoi, France opposed Chiang's occupation. French Admiral D'Argenlieu (the high commissioner for Indochina) deployed the Tonkinois battleship, with intention to recapture this island. Three officers and 60 soldiers were seen on the island. This group called for help. The Chiang Government in Nanjing opposed the French. French did not recapture it.

After the communists took over mainland China in 1949, Red China also occupied several other islands in this archipelago, including Phú Lâm (*Woody island*), excepting an island called "*Pattle*" (Paracel) under French rule. Later, this island was handed over to the State of Vietnam.

According to Jane's Defense Magazine, April 24, 2008: China increased its construction in the Paracels (Hoang Sa). In the late 1990s, according to this report, China already had an airport runway extending to 2600 meters on Woody Island, for jet bombers to use. Recent satellite images have shown China already added a 350-meter coastal dock on this island to accommodate warships, and towers used for satellite information and radar. Unverified information also stated that China has maintained an intelligence gathering base on Rocky Island, also known as North Island (*đảo Bắc*), on northern Woody Island (*đảo Phú Lâm*). Phu Lam has an area of 1.32 km^2

Photo 2: There were two outpost stations, five battleships and a large ship, an oil tanker, roads and trees, and houses for the stationed troops.

Photo 3: a battleship and a naval seaport dock.

HSBD 20 About Woody island, according to Shigeo Hiramatsu, author of "*China's Advances in the South China Sea*": "*Strategies and Objectives* ", Asia-Pacific Review, Vol. 8, No. 1, 2001:

- We later received information on the ten F7 Fighters permanently stationed at that airfield. Recently, I had the opportunity to view aerial photographs of this runway taken from an airplane. Four hangars could be clearly identified in the photographs, which would provide more than enough room for an entire squadron (at least 20 aircraft) to be stationed there. All kinds of aircraft could take off and land on the runway, including SU27 fighters, which China used to procure from Russia and now produces at home under license. A variety of facilities have appeared on the island over the last few years, including new buildings that resemble military barracks, purification systems for converting seawater into fresh water, orchards, and pig and poultry farms. In 1999, it was reported that they had also built equipment for collecting storm water in gutters on both sides of a runaway, and for purifying and storing it in underground tanks. It is no easy task even to replenish supplies on such a small island, one that is 300 kilometers from Hainan Island and twice that distance from the Chinese mainland. This makes the island completely impractical as a base for large-scale military operations, but it is invaluable for conflicts of a smaller scale, or for patrols, exercises, and civilian activities such as fishing. China's desire to exert influence over the Spratly Islands, which are so far from the mainland, must also be taken into account. While China's marine transport capabilities and engineering skills may be inferior to those of Japan, they have still reached a considerably high level, given that China was building a military base on six reefs in the Spratly Islands at almost the same time that it was building the runway on Yongxing Island.

HSBD.20A: Photo of Rocky Island (*Đảo Đá*), Pyramid Rock (*Đảo Hòn Tháp*) belong to Tuyen Duc area: having seven tunnels for missiles, and two tunnels for electro-optic guns.

In addition, Red China built an additional new seaport on Triton Island (Đảo Tri Tôn), located south of the archipelago, within the Crescent Group (*nhóm Nguyệt Thiềm*) (HSBD 23a).

HSBD-20F: The Duncan Island Naval warfare in Paracels

The naval battle at the Paracel archipelago occurred in the Duncan Island area on January 19, 1974 (on the 27th of New Year , *Tết Giáp Dần*)

On January 19, four battleships of the Republic of the South Vietnam Navy were separated into two divisions a) Division I consisted of the HQ-4 and HQ-5 battleships, entering the southwest area of Duncan Island (*đảo Quang Hòa*), directed by Lieutenant Colonel Vũ hữu San, the HQ-4 Battleship Commander; b) Division II consisted of HQ-10 and HG-16 heading toward the northeast of this island, directed by Lieutenant Colonel Lê văn Thự, the HQ-16 Battleship Commander. Colonel Hà văn Ngạc was commander of this operation, stationed on HQ-5 battleship. The HQ-5 was used as the Flagship (*Soái hạm*). HQ-5 was led by Commander Lieutenant Colonel Phạm Mạnh Quỳnh, Battleship Commander.

- At 7:30 am on January 19, 1974, a team of 30 members of the Republic of Vietnam Navy Amphibious Assault Special Forces (*Hải Kích*), commanded by Navy Lieutenant Lê văn Đơn, from battleship HQ-5 landed on Duncan Island (*đảo Quang Hòa*). The Amphibious Assault Special Forces, fully armed, moved into the island about a few dozen yards, intercepted by Chinese invaders. Both sides disputed about the sovereignty over the island. After awhile, the Chinese soldiers menacingly used guns to push the Republic of Vietnam Amphibious Assault soldiers back to the sea at their landing point.

- About 8:40 am, Col. Ngạc ordered Lt. Đơn to move East, occupying a small hill. When the commandos team began moving, the Chinese soldiers opened fire. Lieutenant Đơn and Navy SEAL's Corporal First Class (Hạ Sĩ Nhất) Đỗ văn Long died. Three other sea commandos were wounded. Observing the unfavorable situation, Colonel Ngạc ordered the sea commandos to withdraw, moving toward the battleship HQ-5. Soldiers who were killed and injured were transported back to battleship HQ-5, except Corporal Đỗ văn Long, who was sacrificed on the Duncan Island. (According to Vũ hữu San & Trần Đỗ Cẩm, *"Hải Chiến Hoàng Sa"* (Naval Battle at The Paracels), the Sea Commando Team, led by Captain Nguyễn Minh Cảnh, consisted of the "Navy SEALs" of the Coast Guards. The Sea Commandos team specialized in ambushing and fighting on lands, commanded by Navy Captain Trần Cao Sạ.

(vanttuyen.ne/index.php?view=story&subjectid=9234&chapter=7)

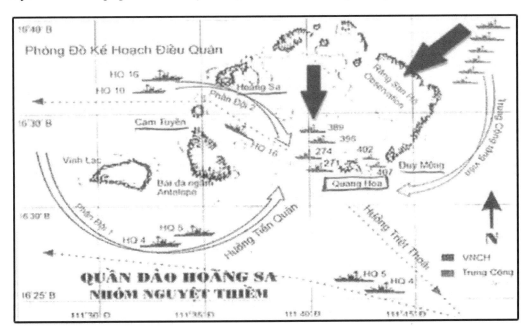

To possibly occupy the island, first, it was necessary to destroy the enemy ships and, with the order from Da Nang, Colonel Ngạc moved two battleships of Division II from the northeast to the northwest of Duncan Island. With such a move, they could deploy and re-occupy this island. These two divisions formed an arc from Northwest to Southwest of the island. The enemy force consisted of four battleships: 389, 396, 271, 274. They closely followed the four Navy battleships of the Republic of Vietnam Navy. In addition, the enemy forces also included four other battleships, not close to the area came for support. They were 402, 407, 281, 282.

-At 10:24, Colonel Ngạc ordered the battleship HQ-10 to open fire. Then other battleships simultaneously fired at the targeted Chinese warships. The battle began.

In the very first few minutes, the RVN Navy forces sank the Chinese flagship 274. The entire operation staff, under the command of Admiral Phuong quang Kinh, Deputy Commander of China's South Sea Fleet and also Front Commander was hit. Many died. They were the commander, four colonels, six lieutenant colonels. And also, among those who lost their lives were four battleship captains, two majors, seven lieutenant officers and some crew members;

The Aviso 271, the two minesweepers 389 and 396 were severely damaged, later scuttled, and four fishing boats carrying troops were sunk.Years later, there were reports that China mobilized 11 battleships for this naval battle at the Paracel region. Later, people learned that China actually mobilized a total of 42 ships and boats, including other forces for this maritime battlefield.

On the side of the Republic of Vietnam Navy (RVN), the HQ-10 battleship arsenal was hit, then broke up and sank. Major Ngụy văn Thà, the Navy battleship captain, was wounded but refused to escape by rescue boat. The captain went down with the ship. South Vietnam Navy Captain Nguyễn thành Trí, vice commander of the battleship, was severely injured then died on the rescue boat, after withdrawing.

The HQ-4 battleship had technical difficulty in firing, so it pulled out to be repaired. The strongest firepower of this combat squadron was the 76.2 mm cannon with automatic firing, 60 rounds per minute. Otherwise, the loss for the Chinese Navy would have been immeasurable. After 15 minutes of cross-fire, the battleship HQ-16 reported that it was hit accidentally by friendly fire. This ship lost power, tilted and had to retreat.

After 30 minutes of combat, all forces from the Republic of Vietnam Navy (RVN) had to withdraw from the battle zone. The loss of human lives: 74 soldiers were sacrificed, 42 people captured as war prisoners after landing on the island..

References:

- Bùi ngọc Nở, “*Trận Hải Chiến Hoàng Sa*” (The Naval Battle of Hoàng Sa), Thoi Luan, July 1, 2004. Bùi ngọc Nở was formerly Lieutenant of South Vietnam Navy, interim Head of Operations, Cruiser Trần Bình Trọng HQ-5, participating in the Naval Battle of Hoang Sa in 1974.

- Vương thế Tuấn, “*Hải chiến Hoàng Sa*” (The Naval Battle of Hoàng Sa)

http://www.youtube.com/watch?v=Os_39fe09RQ www.gatasi.com/tag/haichienhoangsa.

-Vũ Hữu San and Trần Đỗ Cẩm, “*Hải Chiến Hoàng Sa*” (The Naval Battle of Hoàng Sa) vanttuyen.ne/index.php?view=story&subjectid=9234&chapter=7)

HSBD-20I Robert Island (Đảo Hữu Nhật): Chinese soldiers shot Vietnamese fishermen while sheltering from storms. They were robbed and beaten. At the Paracel archipelago area, during May to July of 2009, Chinese soldiers sank the Vietnamese boats, prohibited Vietnamese fishermen to fish.

- On May 19, 2009, a “strange ship”, the term used by all Vietnam cmmunist media to pinpoint “Chinese ship” (by order of the Central Committee Directorate of Education and Propaganda) sank a Vietnamese fishing boat, registered number Qng-95348, in the Paracel area. All 26 fishermen were thrown into the sea, and after its mission, the “strange ship” quietly left the incident scene, without rescuing the victims. The Vietnamese victims had to hold on to anything floating, for survival. Fortunately, other fishing boats working nearby rescued them.

- On July 16, 2009, also in the Paracel area, another "strange ship" hit a Vietnamese fishing boat, registered number Qng2203. These fishermen came from Quang Ngai province. All nine fishermen were rescued by colleagues, but seven were injured.

Of course, the purpose was to warn the Vietnamese fishermen who work "illegally" in China's "territorial waters". This act was to help prohibit any non-Chinese people to set foot on territories occupied by China and turn this "territorial waters of China" into the seas under China's control When Vietnam was annexed into China, Vietnamese people could freely go offshore with Chna flgs and be protected by China.

Beating, confiscating, drowning, killing Vietnamese Fishermen to prevent them from sheltering in storms in Robert Island (đảo Hữu Nhật):

- On September 26, 2009, 17 Vietnamese fishing boats from Quang Ngai province went offshore, along with 200 fishermen to go fishing in the Paracel archipelago area. A strong storm suddenly came to this area, in the afternoon. They rushed to shore.

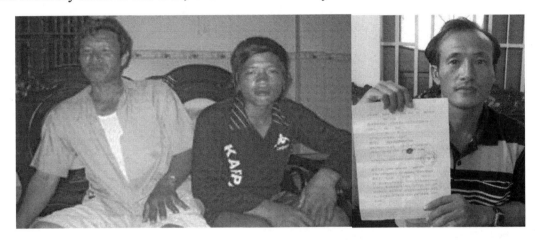

Mr Lê Du and his son were assaulted, and beaten on their faces, when taking refuge on Robert island. When arriving in the nearshore area, the first two Vietnamese fishing boats were fired on by the Chinese soldiers stationed on the island. Vietnamese fishermen had to escape. Other boats dared not go near the shore, and everyone had to anchor offshore. However, ships from Japan, Hong Kong and China were allowed to enter the island safely.

The next day, the wind was strong and waves were high. Frightened to be capsized, all fishing boats from Vietnam raised the white flag, and rushed to shore, with hope for survival, even though someone could be shot to death by the Chinese communist soldiers. Finally, everyone was safely sheltered in the "Chinese seaport" for three nights. However, in the morning of September 30, when the sky was calm, the ocean was quiet, while the Vietnamese fishermen were preparing to go offshore, suddenly, dozens of Chinese soldiers arrived and assaulted. Some held guns, others had hammers. They jumped onto each Vietnamese fishing boat. On Mr. Dương văn Thọ's fishing boat, the Chinese communist soldiers pointed guns at him and each crew member. A few people knelt down, arms raised in surrender. Others pleaded for mercy. On this boat, no one was beaten. Perhaps because, according to a fisherman's explanation, there was a military officer on that vessel. However, all fishing tackle, tools, personal belongings, including communication devices, and a total of one ton of fish were quickly robbed of.

Mr. Tho asked for the offshore GPS device to be returned, for ocean navigation. However, the Chinese did not return it.

On another boat belonged to Mr. Lê Du, both he and his son were brutally beaten. Both of them were interrogated, to search for hidden mobile telephones and other devices. Under severe torture, the son showed the hidden items in a rice bucket. Then this man was beaten for lying and hiding his mobile phone. Meanwhile, other Chinese soldiers searched and rifled through the Vietnamese personal belongings. The faces of Mr Lê Du and his son were swollen and bloody. Blood ran down from the son's eyes. All assets and belongings were seized.

Victims are treated after having reached shores

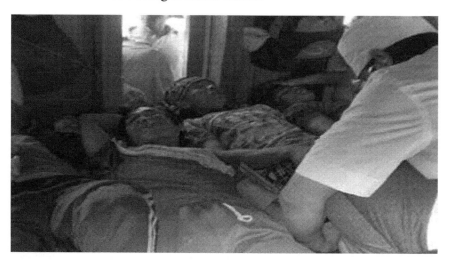

Photo: Vietnamese fisherman were robbed and massacred by the Chinese Communist naval forces in the Gulf of Tonkin. His corpse was stuffed in a fishing basket with ice, to be returned home to family.

2. THE SPRATLY ARCHIPELAGO

2.1.   AN OVERVIEW: Remarks on The Spratly Islands

The name "Spratly" was found in the Atlas "*Hồng Đức Bản Đồ*" of Vietnam. This Atlas was created in 1490, under the reign of King Lê Thánh Tôn. In the 19th and early 20th century, a number of sailors from some large European countries, such as Richard Spratly or William Spratly, arrived to the Spratly Archipelago. Since then, this archipelago has an English name "Spratly", and this name is generally recognized.

Global Security.org remarks on Spratly:

In 1939 the Japanese military government announced its decision to take possession of the Spratlys. France protested on 4/4/1939 when Japan announced it had placed the Spratlys "under its jurisdiction." In 1941 Japan forcibly took over the islands as part of its World War II strategy.

Military Base On Mischief Island

During the War, France defended the Spratlys from Japanese military forces. In 1949 Vietnam "inherited" from France all the rights over the Paracel Islands and the Spratlys Islands. Vietnam emphasized "*actual exercise of sovereignty over mere geographic contiguity*" as a basic ground for its claim. In the 1951, with the "*San Francisco Peace Treaty*", Japan relinquished all titles and claims to the Paracel Islands and the Spratlys Islands which belong to Vietnam. From 1956 to 1963, Vietnamese naval troops built "sovereignty steles" in the Spratlys.

The most proactive claimant in the region is China. In 1909 it seized some islands in Xisha (the Paracels). In 1946 it seized Itu Aba (in the Spratlys) and Phú Lâm Island (Woody Island) in the Paracels). In 1950's China seized additional Hoang Sa 黃沙 (Paracel) islands, which it forcibly repeated in 1974. Vietnam claims that these acts were unlawful and that the United States in 1974 conspired with China for the take-over of the Paracels.

In January 1974, Chinese military units seized islands in the Paracels occupied by South Vietnamese armed forces, and Beijing claimed sovereignty over the Spratlys. Following their conquest of South Vietnam in the spring of 1975, units of the People's Army of Vietnam (PAVN) moved offshore to occupy the Spratly Islands previously held by the Saigon regime. In 1978, Vietnam and the Philippines agreed to negotiate, but failed to settle their conflicting claims to the Spratly Islands. Foreign Minister Nguyễn Cơ Thạch, during a late-1982 visit to Indonesia, took a conciliatory position in discussing Vietnam's and Indonesia's competing claims to the Natuna Islands. In 1984 Hanoi made a similar gesture to Malaysia in order to help resolve their conflicting claims over Amboyna Cay.

China's massacre nn Spratly islands on March 14, 1988 possibly is related to Cambodia conflict. It potentially strengthened China's position at a future bargaining table. There was the ongoing dispute between China and Vietnam over sovereignty to the Spratly Islands. It erupted into an unprecedented exchange of hostilities. The situation was reduced to an exchange of accusations following the armed encounter. Vietnam repeatedly called on China to settle the dispute. Diplomatically, it won rare support from the international community and elicited little response from Beijing. A conciliatory mood was developed on both sides of the China-Vietnam border in 1989, partly because Vietnam's proposal to withdraw from Cambodia, which was a basic condition for improved relations between China and Vietnam.

http://www.globalsecurity.org/military/world/war/images/mischiefreef150.jpg

Mischief Reef is part of the Spratly Islands. Mischief Reef was discovered by Henry Spratly in 1791 and named by the German Sailor Heribert Mischief, one of his crew. China has sent naval vessels into the area and has constructed crude buildings on some of the islands. Beijing claims that the shacks are there solely to serve Chinese fishing boats. Manila describes the buildings as "military-type" structures. According to reconnaissance photos by the Philippine Air Force, these structures of course do not look like fishermen's sanctuaries. They were far more advanced, and seemed to have radar systems which were not normally associated with the protection of fishermen.

Itu Aba Island is used by Taiwan fishermen as a rest stop. Itu Aba Island is located at the northwest end of the northern part of the Spratly Archipelago near the Cheng Ho Reefs (Tizard Bank). In 1938, the Indochina Meteorological Service set up a weather station on Itu-Aba Island, which remained under French control from 1938 to 1941. When the World War II erupted in 1941, Japan took control of that weather station.

On 08 June 1956 Taiwan sent troops to occupy Thai Binh Island (Itu Aba - Peace Island), the largest island in the Spratlys. Vietnam claims that "as late as December 1973, the Far Eastern Economic Review of Hong Kong reported that a marker still stood there with the inscription: *France - Ile Itu Aba et Dependences - 10 Aout 1933 "* The northwestern part of the Tizard Bank consists of Itu Aba in the west, Center Cay in the center, and on the east side Sand Cay, all revised by Taiwan since 1955.

Since the end of World War Two, the ROC navy has guarded the island for over fifty years; they have a major responsibility to ensure the security of the South China Sea. A Taiwan, ROC garrison is stationed on Itu Aba on a permanent basis, building of roads and military installations an important task. As a result, the island now has well-built roads, and the soldiers keep it as clean as a well-kept park.

- On 3/30/1939, Japan decided to place the Spratly Archipelago under Japanese control, because there was a *"lack of local administrative government, causing disadvantages to Japan's interests"*. On 4/21/1939, the French Ambassador in Tokyo expressed disapproval. During World War II, Japan stationed her troops on these two archipelagos until she surrendered.

The Cairo Annoucement of 11/26/1943, which was confirmed at the Potsdam Summit in 1945 demanded the removal of Japanese claims over the Pacific islands that Japan had seized or occupied. At the San Francisco Peace Conference in 1951, Japan officially relinquished its sovereignty over the two archipelagos of Paracel and Spratlys After Japan surrendered, the disarmament of the Japanese army was carried out, by China in the North of the 16th parallel, and by G.B. in the south of the 16th parallel. Starting September 9, 1945, Chinese troops with

Lu Han entered Hanoi to handle the disarmament, and ended their duties in late August 1946 when the Chinese army withdrew, under an agreement to transfer China's responsibility to the French.

The Spratly Archipelago region has more than 300 islands, including the reefs. Most are small islands. Thai Binh Island (*đảo Itu Aba*) is now occupied by Taiwan. The French Government gained ownership of this island from April 10, 1933. At the same time, France owned several other islands in the Spratly region.

However, from October 29, 1946 to January of the following year (1947) Chiang Kai-shek's army sent four warships to occupy many of the Spratly Islands. They completely occupied Itu Aba Island (*đảo Thai Bình*) in December 1946.

After being pushed out to Taiwan, the Chinese Nationalist Party *(Trung Hoa Quốc Dân Đảng)* withdrew from the islands of Paracel and Spratly previously occupied, and only kept Itu Aba Island.

Islands under Vietnam's Control

1. Ladd Reef; 2. West Reef; 3. East Reef; 4. The Sprstla or the Big Spratly Island; 5. Eastern Spratly; 6. Amboyna Cay; 7. Alison Reef; 8. Tennent Reef; 9. Barque Canada Reef; 10. Pearson Reef; 11. Cornwallis South Reef;12. Discovery Great Reef; 13. Lansdowne Reef;14. Namyit Island; 15. Sand Cay; 16. Sin Cowe Island; 17. Sin Cowe East Island. 18.South Reef; 19. Southwest Cay (also called đảo Nam Tử); 20. Petley Reef.

Islands occupied by China

1. Đá Châu Viên - Cuarteron Reef - Huayang Jiao 华阳礁
2. Đá Chữ Thập - Fiery Cross Reef - Yonshu Jiao 永暑礁

3. Bãi Suối Ngà - First Thomas Shoal - 信义礁

4. Đá Gaven - Gaven Reef - Nanxun Jiao 南薰礁

5. Đá Gạc Ma - Johnson Reef South 赤瓜礁(occupied on March 1988)
6. Đá Ken Nan - McKennan Reef /Ximen jiao or Chigua 西门礁

7. Đá Lát - Ladd Reef - Riji Jiao 日积礁

8. Đá Len Đao - Lansdowne Reef - Qiong jiao 琼礁 (occupied on March 1988)
9. Đá Vành Khăn - Mischief Reef - Meiji Jiao 美济礁,

10. Đá Subi - Zhubi Reef - Zhubi Jiao 渚碧礁

(Source: Hung Nguyên "*Môi Hở Răng Lạnh*" vietnamexodus, April 26, 2008)

And Other Islands:

11. Gaven South Reef (Gaven Nam)

12. Half Moon Shoal (Bãi Trăng Khuyết);

13. Eldad Reef

14. Whitson/Whitsun Reef (đá Ba Đầu)

15. Whitsun Reef

16. Hughes Reef

2.2. MAP OF SPRATLYS & ISLANDS, ISLETS

MAPS OF THE SPRATLY ISLANDS

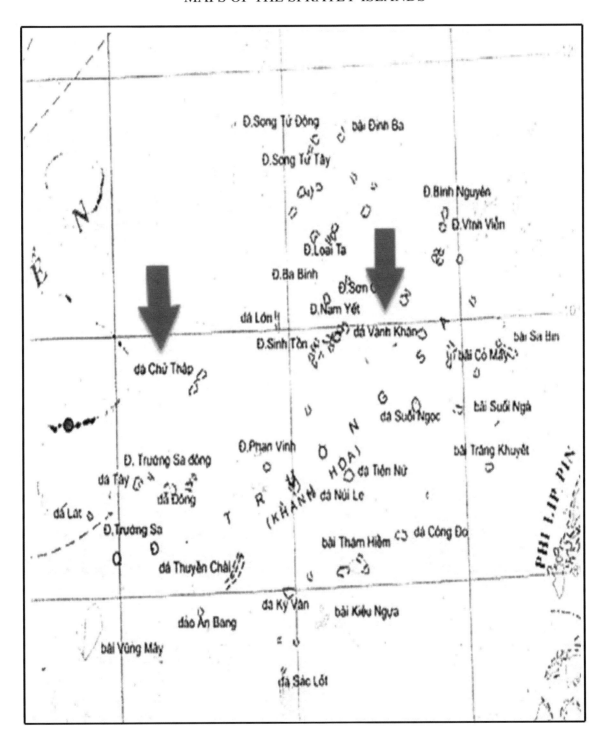

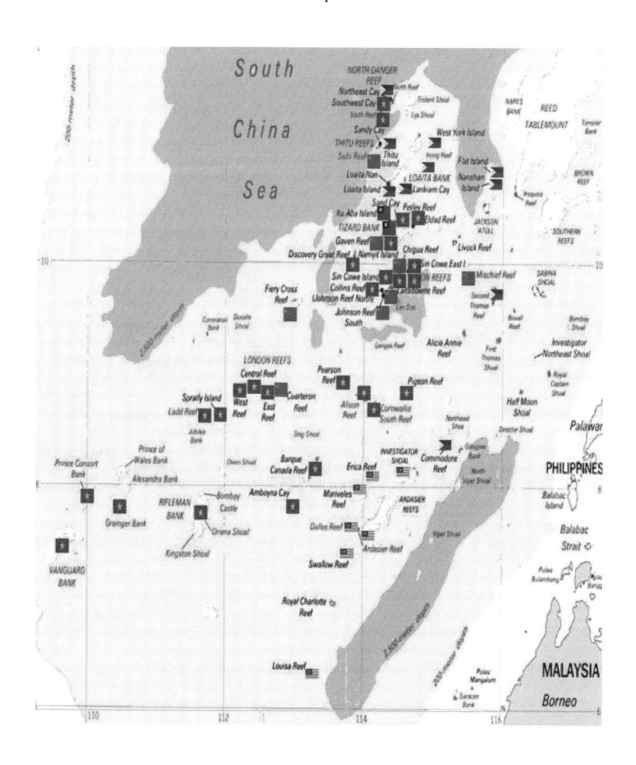

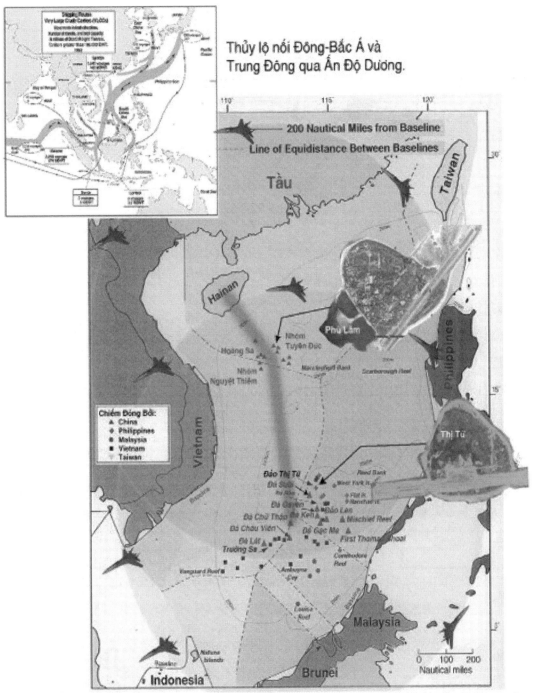

Thủy lộ nối Đông-Bắc Á và
Trung Đông qua Ấn Độ Dương.

Trục chiến lược Nam Hải - Hoàng Sa - Trường Sa. Hai vòng tròn màu xanh nhạt biểu thị tầm hoạt động
an toàn cho loại phản lực SU-27 của Không quân Hán tặc. *Ng:* middlebury.com, globalsecurity.org, googleearth.com.

PHOTOS OF SOME CHINESE MILITARY STRUCTURES & WEAPONS

SANYA: SECRET NAVAL BASE-TAM Á: SECRET NAVAL BASE, Hainan (TSBD-30):

Piers for Aircraft Carriers:

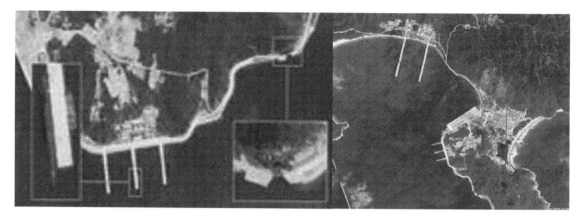

According to Richard Fisher, Jane Intelligence Review on April 24, 2008, China has completed an 800-meter-long pier, wide enough to transport and load-up to aircraft carriers and the ballistic missiles launched from submarines. It is capable of repairing large ships, and moving heavy equipment with troops onto the aircraft carriers and ships. In addition, according to The Australian (April 20, 2008), the Chinese Song S20 submarines are equipped with Yingji-8 anti-ship missiles. The ballistic missiles can be launched from submarines while submerged. The Song S20 was built in Wuhan, equipped with a quiet German diesel engine. One day, this Chinese submarine suddenly emerged among a United States Fleet, not far from the Japanese Okinawa island, to show-off the Chinese submarines' capabilities. This Song S20 is called 093. At times, the satellite noted the two 093 appearing in front of Sanya 三亚 base.

SANYA BASE - NUCLEAR SUBMARINE BASE:

China's Secret Nuclear Naval Base can house 20 nuclear submarines 094. According to Jane's Defence: "Perhaps the Chinese Communists are preparing to turn this area into depots, to hold a large part of their nuclear arsenal".

OVERVIEW OF SANYA'S NAVAL BASE, HAINAN

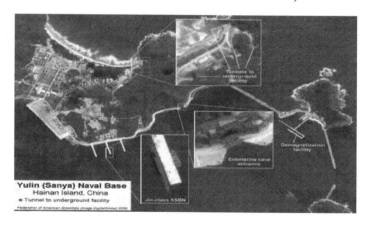

Chinese Aircraft carrier Liaoníng 遼寧

China built the Liaoning aircraft carrier. China bought an old and discarded Varyac ship from Ukraine, said to be used as a casino for gambling in Macao, but to build an aircraft carrier.

Since the late 1990's, China has purchased four ships of this type from Ukraine, Russia and Australia.

Nuclear submarines 094 (Jin Class) with six inter-continental missiles on each side, carrying nuclear warheads.

The Song-20 Submarines (?) are equipped with the Yingji-8 missiles, and operated quietly with the German diesel engine.

SHOW-OFF

Parade of South Sea Fleet

CHINA NAVAL FORCES DEPLOYMENT

to control the region

TSBD31

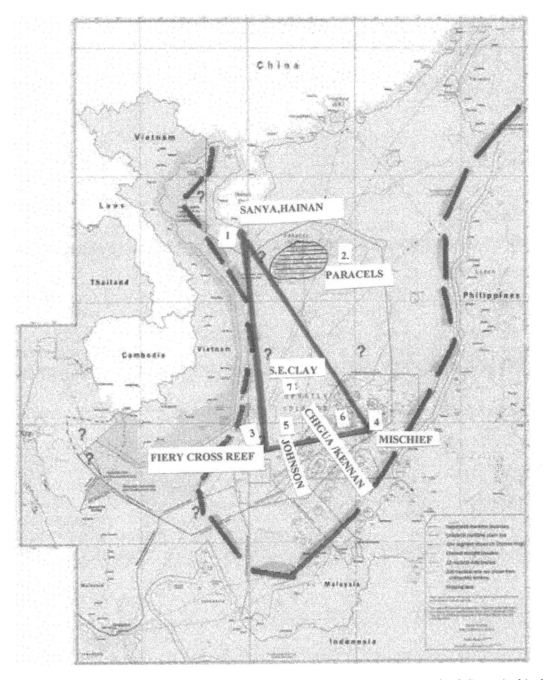

China's military purpose is a) to suffocate Vietnam (eliminate her Survival Space); b) then annex Vietnam to China; c) later on, to use Vietnam as a stepping stone to take over South East Asia.

THE TRIANGLE OF SANYA, FIERY CROSS REEF AND MISCHIEFS

FIERY CROSS REEF và MISCHIEFS

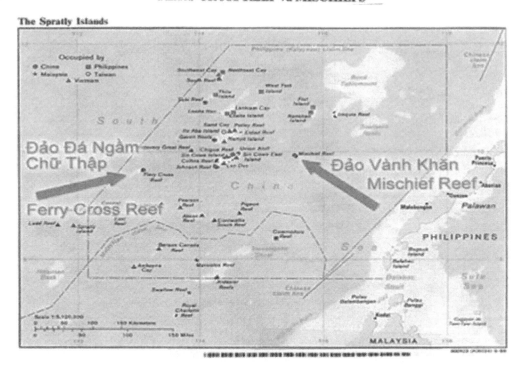

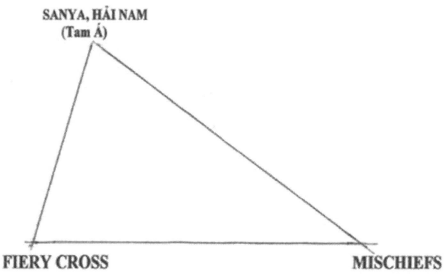

5 căn cứ xây trên Bãi Đá Ngầm **CHỮ THẬP, FIERY CROSS** và 1 cơ sở trên Bãi Đá **VÀNH KHĂN , MISCHIEFS** hợp với căn cứ **Hải Quân Tám Á** thành một Tam Giác chế ngự lãnh thổ Việt nam từ mặt Biển. Hai căn cứ quân sự này của TC nằm trên vĩ tuyến 9, ngang với cửa biển Hậu Giang (Sóc trang) đi ra. Tám Á cách Đà Nẵng 200 hải lý

SUBI REEF

Barracks, helipads, satellite communication antennas

(Russert, p.1962)

FIERY CROSS REEF
(Bãi Đá Chữ Thập)
(TSBD-32)

HEADQUARTERS (1)

SUPPLIES FACILITY (2)

The antenna has a frequency of 70-73 MHZ, operating range within the radius of 180 km. The two antenna towers broadcasted from the building are similar to the RW 2-1 equipment in the US Destroyers. James Bussert "China expands influence through electronics', Signal, Oct, 2003, p.6

MISSILE LAUNCHING PAD AND PLATFORM OF HELICOPTERS (116 m x 96 m) (3)

A report said that China plans to use thie platform to shoot down American satellites that provide guidances to American aircarft carriers. So they become ineffective.

MILITARY OFFICE (4)

UNDER CONSTRUCTION (5)

Red China's Activities to Assert Sovereignty on the Fiery Cross Reef

On September 4, 2009, the Chinese Navy conducted a military exercise landing on the Fiery Cross Reef, in the name of training for Border security. Their activities including: logistic supplies, visiting the working facilities and soldiers' activities on the island, parachuting, etc. More than 100 officers and soldiers participated.

MISCHIEF REEF
(Đá Vành Khăn)

(TSBD-34)

HEADQUARTERS AND LOGISTIC FACILITY (1)

-Oct. 1988, satellite communication antennas 215 m (Ian Storey, pp.46-50; pp 46-47

PLATFORM AND STORAGE (2)

In 2000, there were gun platforms and electronic devices placed at a small building in the North, with piers, landing helicopter docks, anti-aircraft guns and a missile system. Some reports said it was an anti-ship missile/silkworm (Sujit Dutta, *"Securing the sea frontier: China's pursuit of sovereignty claims in the South China Sea"* Strategic Analysis 29, 2 (April-June 2005), p.288.

Figure 3: Chinese Installation on Kennan Reef

PRC installation on Dongmen Jiao (probably Kennan Reef, see text), similar in design to that shown in Figure 4. Reprinted, by permission, New China Pictures Company (Beijing).

JOHNSON SOUTH REEF

(Bãi Đá Gạc Ma)

Nguoi-Viet Online, 25 January, 2008

Two satellite communication antennas, 2.5 meters in diameter and 2.4 meters high, are located on the roof of two-story concrete buildings (Ian Storey. "*Manila looks to USA for help over Spratlys*", Jane Intelligence Review 11,8 (Aug 1999) pp. 46-50 & 46-47). This island and five other islands were occupied by China in March 1988

SPRATLY ISLAND (within the Spratly Archipelago)

Spratly Island is the largest island still occupied by the Socialist Republic of Vietnam

In July, 2007, the Chinese Navy killed a Vietnamese fisherman and sank some Vietnamese fishing boats in this area, because of "*violating their territorial sea*", witnessed by a navy ship of the Socialist Republic of Vietnam.

ITU ABA (Taiping Island/Đảo Thái Bình)

1. Itu Aba, occupied by Taiwan- TSBD 16

2. A long 1,150m Runway on Taiping Island, was expanded in two years, 2009

3. Border Marker, BBC video

EAST-WEST SEA LANE: MALACCA STRAIT

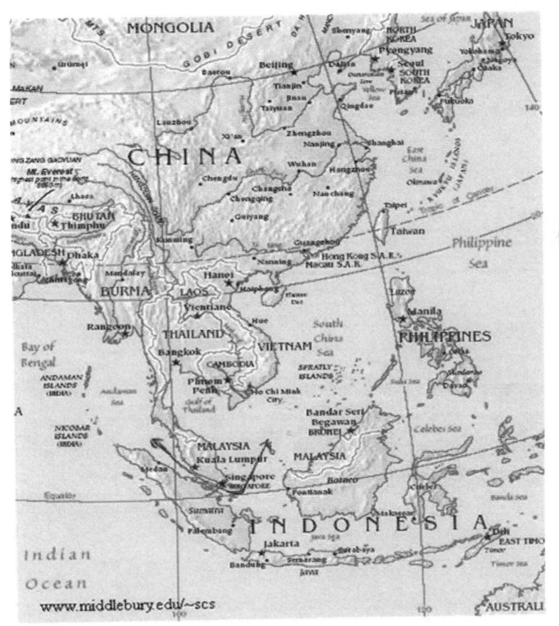

Hành lang lưu thông giữa Đông và Tây qua eo biển Malacca

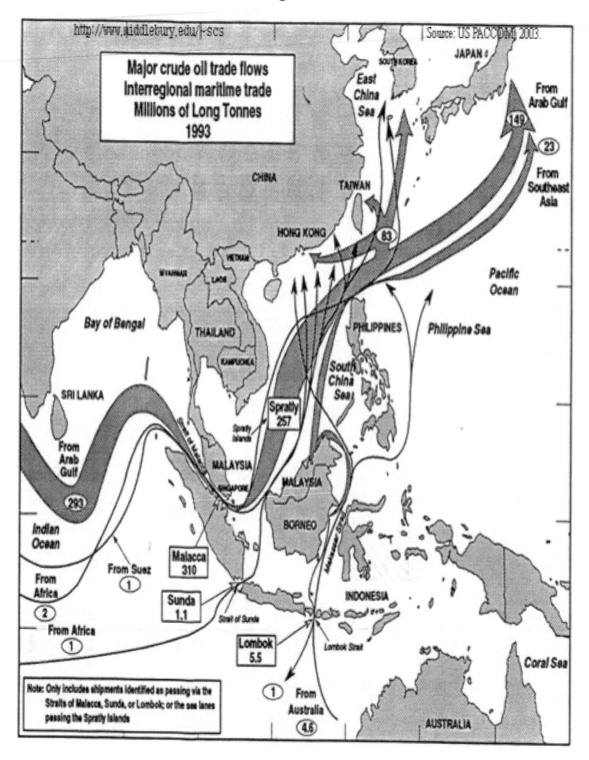

The total value of international trade in 2012 via Malacca was US $5,000 billion. The US trade alone is 1,300 billion.

NEW BILL, OLYMPICS 2008

Bank notes issued on the occasion of the Beijing 2008 Olympic Torch Relay -TSBD 37

Falsifying the evidences on sovereignty: The Spratly island has no Chinese inhabitants. China only occupies a number of reefs. 100 years later, the Beijing expansionists would bring up these pictures to prove their Chinese currency had circulated there.

The "*Thổ Địa Giới Tiêu*" 土 地 界 標" (Land boundary marker) inscribed on a plastic pole was also found on June 2009 at the bottom of sea near the Poulo Condor island of Vietnam found by Diệp đình Huyen, Dalat.

2.3. ANNOTATIONS:

TSBD 30 **Sanya Base** (Tam Á). There are 2 sections:

The **section for nuclear submarines** with entrance leading to the base, which is a tunnel deep inside the mountain. Jane's Defense, April 24, 2008: Sanya Naval Base (Tam Á) is called a secret base, because in nearly five years, China has built this military base secretly.

Last April, Jane's Intelligence Review reported on this base. According to the intel agents, that base could house 20 nuclear submarines of second generation type 094. They also reported that the satellite images show a number of tunnels and entrances for submarines. This type of submarine is equipped with long-range missiles. Each missile is equipped with several atomic warheads. The satellite images earlier this year showed a 094 submarine appearing at this base. Red China currently has five 094 submarines. The US Department of Defense predicts that in the next five years, China will have five more.

In addition, according to The Australian Magazine, April 20, 2008, many Chinese submarines are equipped with Yingji-8 anti-ship missiles that can be launched while submerged, and can fire at aircraft carriers on the surface. The incident of the Song S20, built in Wuhan, which has a quiet German diesel engine, and is difficult to be discovered, suddenly appeared among a United States Fleet, not far from the Japanese Okinawa island in April 2007, to show-off the Chinese submarines' capabilities.

Jin class submarine, 094

The 5,000m-deep area of the ocesn located at the entrance of the base is an ideal place for this type of submarines.

"Perhaps communist China is preparing to turn this place into depots for a majority of her nuclear arsenals, and may even use this place from which to launch nuclear weapons".

Section for aircraft carriers. This section consists of three piers for the aircraft carriers.

Richard Fisher, Jane Intelligence Review, April 24, 2008: China has completed an 800-meter-long pier, wide enough to transport and load-up the submarine-launched ballistic missiles on the aircraft carriers, as well as capable of repairing large ships, and moving heavy equipment with troops onto the aircraft carriers and ships, for sophisticated marine operations. The Chinese communists intended to construct three piers, assisting six aircraft carriers to anchor at the same time, after establishing the two South Sea Fleets.

Richard Fisher.Jr., Chinese Naval Secrets. Asian Wall Street Journal, May 5th, 2008. Both to protect its SSBNs and to defend China's growing interest in securing sea lanes to critical resources in distant areas like Africa, the Persian Gulf and Australia, Sanya can be expected to host future Chinese aircraft carrier battle groups and naval amphibious projection groups. Some Chinese sources suggest that the PLA could eventually build four to six aircraft carriers.

This military base could accommodate six aircraft carriers. Currently, China is repairing a Russian aircraft carrier (Kuznetsov), but in the next four or five years, they will have six aircraft carriers, meaning the 2 fleets of aircraft carriers are parts of the South Sea Fleet 南海舰队 (also called the Southern Theater Command Navy).

BBC, November 7, 2008: Chinese Major General Tien Loi Hoa, Director of the Office of Foreign Affairs, China Defense Department, said that if China owns aircraft carriers, she would not use them to go worldwide. In an interview with the British newspaper, The Financial Times (FT), General Tien said: *"Any Navy of a powerful nation would dream of having an aircraft carrier".* But he also said*: "the Navy of a powerful nation having over 10 fleets with aircraft carriers as Flagships, aims at other strategic goals. China has only one or two aircraft carriers for coastal defense. Even if someday we would have [more] aircraft carriers, we would not use them on global targets".*

China was considered to have plans to gradually order two or three aircraft carriers before 2015, as intended. Their ships could be smaller than the giant U.S. Nimitz aircraft carriers. China already bought four discarded aircraft carriers from Australia, Russia and Ukraine. China is repairing battleships to equip its Fleets, to be completed within a few years.

Jane's Defense Weekly, a journal on defense, reported last month that the People's Liberation Army were training 50 students to become navy pilots, capable of flying the folding wing aircrafts from the aircraft carriers. In March 2007, a communist China-backed newspaper in Hong Kong reported that China might have its first aircraft carrier in 2010.

The Varyag from Ukraine

In addition, there are landing crafts, destroyers, minelayers, and fast battleships, to deploy troops to China's desired areas. The submarines are capable of firing long-range missiles over ten thousand kilometers, capable of firing from Hainan to most areas of North America. The most powerful forces of the Chinese navy lie in the South Sea Fleet. Among 57 Chinese submarines, 32 of the most advanced subs belong to this fleet. According to this new information, in Sanya, China has made tunnels in the mountains, that could accommodate 20 nuclear submarines. Therefore, clearly, China's strategy is to advance to Vietnam's Eastern Sea of Southeast Asia, moving toward Guam island and the Indian Ocean. Sanya military base is situated about 200 nautical miles northeast of Da Nang, and will control Vietnam, especially Central Vietnam.

Shangri-La Dialogue, Singapore - A meeting was held in Singapore for three days, from May 30, 2008 among several powerful countries, discussing the South China Sea Security, with the presence of the U.S. Secretary of Defense. The theme *"Challenges to stability in Asia Pacific; maritime dispute in the Asia Pacific region"*.

Some other details noted at the conference:

- In an annual report to Congress, the U.S. Department of Defense warned about Beijing developing various types of missiles, capable of attacking the U.S. battleships right on the sea, about different types of inter-continental missiles, as well as weapons to shoot down Amrican satellites, so that the U.S.A couldn't use high-tech to control the battle.

According to Admiral Sureesh Mehta, the naval commander of the Indian Navy, the fact that Sanya base could accommodate over ten nuclear submarines is a worrisome matter, because this type of submarine has a range from 7000 to 15,000 kilometers. India doesn't want to deal with the presence of a large number of nuclear submarines next door.

- The Commander of U.S. Forces in the Pacific, Admiral Keating, emphasized the United States's determination to maintain her leading role in the Pacific Ocean region. According to him, Beijing certainly will fail if it competes with Washington on the military front.

TSBD.31: The triangle's base line consisted of military bases built on the Fiery Cross Reef (including 5 photos) stretching toward the Mischief Reef. The two ends of this baseline move up toward Sanya base on Hainan Island. This triangle dominates the entire surface of Vietnam's Eastern Sea. With the new map published again in June 2006, China dominated Vietnam from the South China Sea, strangling the nation's survival space. Vietnamese people can only go offshore after Vietnam becomes China's territory, and Vietnamese people become Chinese. By this time, the Vietnamese assimilation into China is being strongly pushed forward, as Truong Chinh announced in 1951 in the name of the Labor Party, under Ho Chi Minh's leadership.

The Australian, April 24, 2008: The Chinese navy has rapidly acquired a blue-water capacity. China has 57 submarines. Five of them are nuclear-powered, with many equipped with Yingji-8 anti-ship cruise missiles that can be launched while submerged..

TSBD.32: Fiery Cross Reef (*Bãi đá ngầm Chữ Thập*). Photos taken by satellite in December 2007, shows it is the largest Chinese military complex in this archipelago. China has a fortified structure of 116 meters long, 96 meters wide, with a square section exposed, each side 34 meters long. This dimension is wide enough to serve as the landing zone for the Change Z-8 helicopter, largest of China's Navy. This large area could also be used to install the surface-to-air rocket launchers controlled by satellites, airplanes or battleships. According to photos taken in December 2007, these buildings could be used as air defense missile launchers or high-frequency communications stations. In addition, there is a Command Post on one area, an office on another area, a storage of supplies, and a base under construction. This is a very important base area adjacent to Vietnam's coastlines, blocking all activities from the Vietnam mainland, and preventing Vietnam from advancing southward from the central archipelago, and also to protect Vietnam's territorial waters.

TSBD34. The Mischief Reefs. In the photos, three military ships were found stationed there. This is evidence that this place could potentially provide temporary shelter and logistics for a small Chinese navy unit.

About the Three-Floor Structure: Previously, in 1994, China installed a building structure on the Mischief Reef (*Đá Vành Khăn*) area near the Philippines. When the Filipino Deputy Foreign Minister visited China to protest and inquire about that building structure, China replied that it was a temporary building structure, to assist the Chinese fishermen sheltering during storms and rains. The Philippines navy set up explosives to demolish those building structures. There are now more durable structures installed on this reef, and in recent years people have seen Chinese military ships here. It is considered to be a small logistics facility.

According to Shigeo Hiramatsu, author of "China's Advances in the South China Sea: Strategies and Objectives" Asia-Pacific Review, Vol. 8, No. 1, 2001:8. 1, 2001:

It has been reported that China built permanent buildings out of reinforced concrete on the Philippines' Mischief Reef during late 1998 and early1999. Three pictures released by the Ministry of National Defense of the Philippines showed three different buildings, which suggested that the buildings had been built in three different locations. There was also a report that a fourth building had been built in another location. It was predictable that China would also build permanent facilities on Mischief Reef, after the series of advances that had followed its first encroachment upon the Spratly Islands area off southern Vietnam in 1988. The reef is quite large and roughly circular (about 8 kilometers from East to West, and about 6.5 kilometers from North to South), and the permanent buildings would have been built on four locations on the inner reef. An aircraft carrier, such as the PLAN will no doubt eventually own, would be able to anchor quite easily on Mischief Reef.

In January 2000, photographs of Mischief Reef in the Spratly Islands were shown to the foreign ministers of the other eight ASEAN countries by the Philippine foreign minister, Domingo Siazon. The photographic evidence showed that China had expanded installations on the reef since 1995, when it first started building what it said were shelters for fishermen. There are now four sites on the reef with installations that could be connected to form a fortress, like Gibraltar, or a five-star hotel for fishermen.

TSBD.36. Itu Aba Island or Thái Bình (Taiping) is in the Trường Sa Islands.

During World War II, Thai Binh Island was occupied by the Japanese army. When Japan surrendered, Chiang Kai-shek was assigned by the Potsdam Conference to enter North Vietnam (north the 16th parallel) to disarm the Japanese army, while G.B. in charge the South. Taking this opportunity, the Chiang Kai-shek army seized Thai Binh Island from the Japanese army, although this island lies deep in the South, on the 10.24' parallel, in the Spratly Archipelagon. Chiang's mission was to disarm the Japanese only. He had no rights to occupy any island. In this case, he took the Itu Aba that lies in the far South, within the jurisdiction of GB..

When Chiang was defeated by Mao, he fled to Taiwan and continued to occupy the island. Therefore, the occupation and administration of Thai Binh island today is an illegitimate act.

Thai Binh is the largest island. It has a meteorological station, a radio, a lighthouse and an airport of 2 km-long.

November 20th, 2007: Taiwan's Ministry of Foreign Affairs issued a statement, including the following section: "Historically and geographically, Spratly, Trường Sa (Changsha), is the traditional territory of Taiwan. The sovereign rights over these islands are indisputable." The statement also said Taiwan has deployed troops to Taiping Island (Thai Binh/Itu Aba Island) for many years, and built a runway to transport the necessities to this location. The DPA news agency quoted the opposing lawmakers of Taiwan saying, the crossway was expanding over Thai Binh Island to prepare for Chen Shui-bian 陳水扁, President of the Republic of China (2000-2008) to visit this island, before his second term ended in May 2008. Manila Times: On June 28, Mr. Donald Lee, a Representative from Taiwan in Manila said: *"On Itu Aba Island (Thai Binh), there are more than 200 coast guard personnel and a new runway"*.

Military News leader visiting disputed Spratly islands. AFP Feb.7, 2008

Taiwan President Chen Shui-bian (2nd L) looked at a memorial during a visit to the Spratly islands on Saturday, visited the Spratly islands, oversaw the opening ceremony of a newly-built runway (1,150-metre-long or 3,800-feet). Speaking at the ceremony, Chen proposed A *"Spratly Initiative"* calling for a peaceful solution to the disputed claims of the group and promoting marine conservation in the region.

"Facing the complicated and sensitive territorial and sovereignty disputes in the South China Sea, Taiwan urges the countries involved to peacefully resolve the issues". Chen left Taipei early Saturday on his presidential jet to a base in Taiwan's south where he took an air force C-130 transport plane to the Spratlys in a clandestine test flight. The Philippines on Saturday expressed *"serious concern"* over Chen's trip.

Also according to that article, the Taiwan Navy sent a Kidd-Class destroyer to this sea area to protect President Chen Shui-bian. According to the latest news from the Inquirer,

Claro Cristobal, spokesperson of the Philippines Foreign Ministry reported that the airplane of Chen Shui-bian landed on the Island of Ligao (Filipino term), but was not sure whether it was Taiping Island (?) in the Spratly Archipelago, on Saturday afternoon. Philippines Foreign Minister, Alberto Romulo immediately voiced his opposition on this matter, saying: *"an irresponsible political move"*.

When DCVOnline published this article, the Ministry of Foreign Affairs of the Socialist Republic of Vietnam still kept silent until March 30, after the Philippines' objection, Le Dung finally protested.

BBC, March 30, 2008. The Foreign Ministry of the Socialist Republic of Vietnam issued a statement opposing Taiwan's activities on the Tizard Bank (*Bàn Than*), in the Spratly Archipelago. Vietnam's foreign ministry spokesman Le Dung, said: *"This is an act of widening encroachment, seriously violating Vietnam's territorial sovereignty"*.

According to national media, on March 23, Taiwan sent out a swift boat with eight people to Tizard Bank, starting the measured survey. The Taiwanese erected four concrete columns, about three meters apart, forming a square. Then the boat returned leaving people there.

TSBD37. Photos of the Chinese *Yuan*元 currency, special edition, issued for the Beijing 2008 Olympic Torch Relay.

When organizing the Beijing 2008 Olympic Torch Relay (in August), Red China issued special edition "Yuan": 1, 2, 5, 10 *yuán* clearly identified to be *"used only on the Spratly Archipelago"*.

Why did China issue this yuan currency? For long-term goals, such as for 100 years hence, the Han clan will use the yuan currency as evidence that Chinese ancestors "used Chinese currency on this archipelago" though the 8 reefs/shoals/rocks she has occupied from Vietnam are just features submerged in the waters without any habitants. That evidence is an important point, and necessary in International Law and Justice, to prove that Chinese ancestors had *"exercised sovereign rights"* for a long time there, even though this is clearly a deceptive act.

Red China's National Council of Minister established Tam Sa City to prove their actual occupation, a must-have element to justify sovereignty, even though it is only an acknowledged government on paper. But it helps to prove the sovereign rights, in the future, for example in the next 100 years. Who knows about this deceit? Perhaps that "incident" might become real in the future. Also, we need to add another example in this conspiracy: Three years ago, Red China celebrated a grand opening of Đức Thiên Waterfall, in a tourist area called "*Đệ Nhất Hùng Quan*" ("best mighty wonder"). The culture and press secretary of China's Embassy

138

invited Vietnam Communist Party leaders, from the press and tourism department, to attend this grand ceremony. The SRV leaders excitedly joined the event, indeed, to happily witness and acknowledge that Bản Giốc Waterfall, Vietnam's most majestic and beautiful area in the world, being transferred into the possession of Red China. If later, a younger Vietnam generation would demand the returning of that waterfall, then Red China would cite the evidence: the Socialist Republic of Vietnam officials were present at that ceremony, and agreed to transfer that waterfall to China.

Under similar arguments and methods of action, the Chinese cited the words of Deputy Minister of Foreign Affairs Ung văn Khiêm to Li Zhimin, Charge' d' affairs at China Embassy in Hanoi: "Historically, the Paracel and Spratly Archipelagos have belonged to China", even though it was just empty words, over a half-century ago, and true or not, that statement was only in private conversation. Everyone knows, legally, especially on territorial disputes, such a statement would not prove sovereignty. Being weak on reason, with no solid foundation, Red China cited the words of Ung Van Khiem as a means to prove sovriegnty.

In short, to establish a governance body is an important point, required by the International Law, for the "true possession", to "win" on a legal basis when this matter is brought before the court. It is also a method of proving the sovereign rights over that territory. Issuing Chinese currency is one of many tasks, in a grand scheme, to display the exercise of sovereignty. To construct and distribute China maps to visitors in Beijing, including the Paracels and Spratlys, during the 2008 Olympics, also was part of this scheme.

More on this matter:

1) The torch relay was planned to go across (actually to stop) an island (that China has previously occupied by force) in the Paracel or Spratly Islands area to prove that there are their activities on the islands, especially on the 2008 Beijing Olympics. This is a great event because a billion people on this planet look att it. It is used as an excellent symbol of exercising sovereignty. But most important, the silence of the Socialist Republic of Vietnam implies that China has sovereignty over the subject island when the torch stops on it **Due to the fierce opposition of college students in Hanoi and Saigon, China quietly cancelled the Olympic Torch going across the islands.** Part of the Red China conspiracy was defeated. Vietnam's "silence or complicity" was not revealed.

2) China's National Council of Ministers officially established Sansha District in late November 2007, with the purpose of completing the process of seizing both of these archipelagos.. **Because of the Vietnamese students' strong reactions against it**, the **Wenchan authorities (Hainan province) declared that they have no plan to establish Sansha district, since it is a disputed matter with a foreign government (Vietnam).** Shortly thereafter, on the occasion of the Chinese leaders' embarrassment, the CPV leaders allowed the People's Committee of Nha Trang to make statements opposing the Chinese project to cover up their cowardice and their "country selling" acts.

There are two remarks on this matter a) the Vietnamese people must recognize the wisdom and courage of young people and college students and journalists for their strong opposition to the establishment of Sansha District. Because of the protests, they were hunted, threatened, arrested, and persecuted by the Vietnamese Communist authorities, from when Sansha District was established in late November 2007, until the day Beijing Olympic torch went through Saigon on April 29, 2008. Even now, some people still remain in prison.

b) the fact that the Wenchan authorities denies the establishment of the Sansha District raises several issues: 1) The National Council of Ministers previously set it up and now the Wenchan authorities, a subordinate administtative unit can't deny its existance, abolish or replace it.. 2) It is the Natioanl Council of Ministers who must abolish it by an equivalent act. In the totalitarian system of communist China or Vietnam, the communist party makes all decisions and a governnental agency has a duty to execute. The Wenchan declaration is just a tactic to help reduce tensions among Vietnamese at that moment.

***

About Wenchan's cancellation of the Resolution by National Council of Ministers of the People's Republic of China establishing Sansah District, the Committee on Protection of Territorial Integrity of Vietnam, on December 21, 2007 demanded that China's Council of Ministers abolish the Resolution to establish the agency, not by a subordinate administrative unit. In that proclamation, the Committee declared that this is just a tactic to ease the tense situations caused by the Vietnamese college students' protests, and help distract from these very matters.

***

PART II

NATIONAL SOVEREIGNTY

**HOW HO CHI MINH AND THE VIETNAM
COMMUNIST PARTY
STEP BY STEP SURRENDER
SOVEREIGNTY TO COMMUNIST CHINA**

TWO GRAND SCHEMES OF RED CHINA WITH COMMUNIST VIETNAM AS CONSPIRATOR

ASSIMILATION OF THE PEOPLE OF VIETNAM (SINICIZATION) INTO CHINESE

Under the guise of popular resistance against the oppressing and exploiting French colonialists, to achieve independence, happiness and freedom for the people of Vietnam, Ho Chi Minh and the Vietnamese communist Party silently have served the Communist Party of China and its interests. To day, the guise of independence is still mentioned, even though no more colonial power exists in Vietnam. The Vietnamese communist leaders have always publicized the goals of freedom, happiness, social justice, civilized society (the types of propaganda that Hoang Minh Chinh promoted some times ago about a national plan of development for social welfare for the people of Vietnam) to deceive or mislead the populace. China is moving forward to execute their conspiracy to assimilate Vietnam into Chinese (Sinicization),

This scheme was revealed publicly through a flyer by Truong Chinh, General Secretary of the Labor Party (predecessor of the Vietnamese Communist Party) disseminated in 1951 in South Vietnam. In the flyer, Truong Chinh called for a) Vietnam becoming Chư Hầu (Subordinate/Client State or vassal state) of China; b). Abolishment of Chữ Quốc Ngữ (Vietnamese Latinized written language, based on alphabet,) and retuning to use of Chinese characters. This project is being carried out to day, and will be discussed later in this book; c) wiping out the so called "itellectuals" trained in schools of colonialist and imperialist countries......Intellectuals were brutally lidiquated in two programs: Land Reform Program and Attack to Bourgeoisie class after the CPV came to power in Vietnam…...

Becoming a Chư Hầu of China, abolishment of Chữ quốc Ngữ (and returning to the use of Chinese characters), and liquidation of intellectuals are important projets in the assimilation of Vietanese into Chinese.

Truong Chinh called upon Vietnam to become a " chư hầu" of China. He said " China is the first civilized counry all over the world. China is our MASTER", "no shame to acknowledge it" (see photo of the attached document below).

We need to mention the meaning of chư hầu, "subordinate or client state or vassal state". This term was used by the Manchu when negotiating to sign the 1885 Tianjin Treaty between Patenôtre, a French government representative, and Li Hong Zhang about the Vietnam-China boundary delimitation. Li Hong Zhang repeatedly said many times that "North Vietnam" had been a chư hầu of China for the past 600 years, thinking it was China's territory. Li Hong Zhang mentioned it with the purpose "to claim for more lands" for China, because Zhang thought that treaty was signed with great disadvantage for China. It is an unequal treaty. With that 1885 treaty, France and China set a new boundary with the 1887 Convention, requiring the Chinese troops to withdraw completely behind their own border. By withdrawing troops, China had no rights over its "chư hầu", e.i, China lost all. In that spirit, Truong Chinh mentioned the word "Chư hầu".

In order to carry out the plot of becoming a " chư hầu", the First Secretary of (communist) Labor Party Truong Chinh led the Land Reform campaign in North Vietnam to massacre the landlord class, in the countryside and bourgeoisie class, including intellectuals, and at the same time destroying Vietnamese culture (cultural genocide). To wipe out people's materials and spirits was a necessary condition for this campaign. Mentally, the campaign was to eliminate all traces attached to people of Vietnam (cultural genocide), to easily "assimilate" Vietnam into Chinese "civilization". Such a move would facilitate the "Sinicization" (Hán hóa) of Vietnam into China. This rampant brutal killing carried out from 1953 to 1956, by the Chinese communist methods, is a typical example of wiping out material resources. Today, it is known definitely that the Chinese advisers directly controlled the killings. Many documental resources mention the many powerful Chinese advisors. During that period, Ho Chi Minh only dared to complain about their cruelty in private places. This devastating destruction (including slaughtering dogs) dissipated the potential of resistance against the foreign assimilation. The traditional education was also thoroughly abolished and replaced by the socialist education, meaning to construct a "new man" (new Soviet man), with new customs, new styles, new way of thinking etc... as the foundation for "new society" within this direction of communism...

Therefore Vietnam could be "assimilated" into Chinese culture (Sino-tization/Sinicization) to become "Chinese citizens". This was Truong Chinh's goal and Mao's dream.

Also, during the process of "socialist construction", after the seizing North Vietnam by Ho, to wipe out other social classes, especially the "bourgeois nationalism" in cities, Do Muoi was entrusted with the mission to exterminate that social class in a campaign called "attack to the bourgeois" (capitalist reform in South Vietnam). Once the national potential (strength) no longer exists, hopefully Vietnam would be on the expanding road to sinicization (see photo of Truong Chinh's Call, in Part II, Chapter III).

Phạm Văn Đồng sent a diplomatic note to Zhou Enlai to recognize China's soverignty, over the two archipelagos, as a first step in the process of annexing Vietnam to China, in accord with Truong Chinh's dream for the Vietnamese people to be "sinicized" into Chinese (Hán hóa), together with other works of the Vietnamese communist Party over many decades up to now. Clearly, those are acts of the local puppets, scientifically calculated by the Beijing supremacists/expansionists, utilizing the techniques of the communist doctrine of Lenin's " organization weapons" (using an organization as a strugle weapon to seize power) to assist these northern enemies to obtain opportunities of advancing further in their conspiracy to erase Vietnam on the world map. In December 2007, General Secretary Nong Duc Manh also pledged to Hu Jintao's secretary that "**for the everlasting friendship with China, the Vietnam leaders will render all** (all what they have to China)" to show their submission to China.

The 16 "golden words" 十六字方针 given by the Beijing supremacists in early 1990s ("**long-term stability, looking forward to future, friendly neighbors, comprehensive cooperation**") were always repeated when the Vietnamese communist leaders visited China, to show respect and to pledge compliance with China's demands. The first four of those 16 words are "comprehensive cooperation", expressing the will of Vietnamese Communist Party to unite with Chinese communist Party to become one, and the two communist nations to be one. The last four words are "looking forward to the future". What future? That was Mao's stated goal, and the Chinese communist Party aimed at it: **Vietnam and China are one entity**. This goal has been revealed in Vietnam White Book of the year 1979, at a time when the CPV took the role of Moscow's puppet against China. And the goal was again written on a poster "Unify the Nation" and "One China, One Dream" that was displayed by Chinese youth in Hanoi and Saigon during the Olympic 2008.

This is a serious crime that Ho and his accomplices committed against the Vietnamese people. It was they who opened doors to guide the northern Beijing invaders into our home, assisting them to seize our people's country. Our people have shed blood and bones to protect Vietnam's national independence and territorial integrity, over many generations since King Hung Vuong founded Vietnam five thousand years ago.. Now this has become meaningless. What has been happening are warning signals that the Vietnamese people will face a horrible dark future. Over 1000 years of dominating Vietnam, still, China was unsuccessful in assimilating this nation. However, within a half of a century, Ho and his accomplices did more than what the Northern expansionists expected. The effort to "dedicate everything" that Nong Duc Manh pledged, has revealed the extraordinary result of Vietnam's Communist Party leaders contributing to that plot.

This part includes the following chapters:

Chapter I: Documentss relatting to Selling a Nation
Chapter II: Acts of Selling a Nation
Chapter III: Acts of Assisting the Foreign Invaders
Chapter IV: Process for China to Enslave the People of Vietnam

CHAPTER I: DOCUMENTS RE. SELLING A NATION

Asale is composed of two parts: the seller has a duty to transfer a 'objct' which is in this case "Vietnam territory" to Red China, and the buyer has a duty to hand 'money' which is "aids" to Communist Vietnam to fight the two wars: one against the French and the other agaisnt the American imperialists, actually to invade South Vetnam. This "aids" is revealed in a chapter below, especially with admissions by Pham van Dong and Nguyen manh Cam. It turned out that it is an advance by Red China to pay for the wars. This includes the costs of weapons, ammo., medecines and other military supplies, possibly the 'salaries of thousands of Chinese military personnel" fighitng on Vietnam soil. Deng xiaoping later disclosed that the amount for the first war was 20 billion dollars. The amount for the second war is unknown.

1. ON LAND

Le Kha Phieu, General Secretary of the Vietnamese Communist Party, together with SRV President Tran Duc Luong went to Beijing China to sign a **Border Treaty on December 25, 1999.** The following locations are already within China territories:

- At Hà Giang province, the mountain ranges 1250, 1545, 1509, 772, 223; The mountain range 1509 is Núi Đất (Earth Mountain) which belonged to Thanh Thủy village, Vị Xuyên district. China renamed it Lao Son. This mountain range is 1422m high, extending across the entire region. The importance is the 662 elevation and 20 other highlands lying toward the East. The range 1250 is Núi Bạc (Silver Mountain) belonging to Yên Minh district. China named it Giải Âm Sơn.These two mountain ranges control the access roadways from China to Vietnam.

- In Lạng Sơn, the mountain ranges 820 and 636 belonging to Quốc Khánh village, Tràng Định district, and Bình Độ area 400, behind the boundary marker 26 (Treaty of Tianjin), which belongs to Cao Lộc district.

-The land area north of the Bản Giốc waterfall in Cao Bằng province; a land area north of the Nam Quan Pass in Lạng Sơn province having the same fate. Other places, about 72 locations along the border of 1400 kilometers, are as yet unknown.

Let's listen to Vietnam Communist leaders' arguments on border negotiations as follows: (quoted from the interview by Ly Kien Truc, editor in chief, Văn Hóa Newspaper, conducted on September 23, 2008):

- Le Cong Phung (Vietnamese Ambassador in US): "...People accused, opposed me as head of the negotiating delegation. People said I sold to China about 5-7 hundred km² of lands on the border...In fact,"it is only a difference of 227 km² on the 64 points across the entire border. Therefore, we only discussed the delimitation of 227 square kilometers.... And the final result is that Vietnam gains an additional 113 km² and China controls 114 km². Thus the difference is just over 1 km, during the entire process of negotiation and delimitation.

- ....Regarding the highlands, I also want to tell you guys that in 1979, China attacked Vietnam. After that war, basically China went back to the old boundary line. China kept and occupied about 27 places on Vietnam's lands, most of which are the highlands.

... In the negotiation process, we asked China to return the highlands. Before signing the treaty, China returned 15 highlands. There are 12 highlands left. We fought forcefully, and finally we have six highlands. Finally, we moved the boundary line up between those high places".

Verifying with a few numbers and places quoted from the document *"Border Issues Between Vietnam and China"*, published by the Vietnam communist party 1979 (Su That Publisher, 1979), shows that Le Cong Phung completely lied. Vietnam actually has lost a lot of land.

1) What about the difference of over 1 km along the 1350-km border?

China has occupied the following Vietnamese lands:

a) Trình Tường area, Quang Ninh province. China has occupied this 6-km area, encroaching over 1 km into Vietnam. This area is now annexed into Đồng Tâm communes at Dongxing 东兴 district in China. The new boundary line is pushed back to the hill of Khâu Trúc in Vietnam.

b) And the villages of Thanh Loà, Cao Lộc district in Lạng Sơn province; Khắm Khâu of Cao Bằng province; Tà Lũng, Là Phù Phìn, Minh Tân of Hà Tuyên province; Năm Chảy village at Hoàng Liên Sơn mountain (this village stretched over 4 km long and over 1 km deep) now is situated in Chinese territory. Particularly in Năm Chảy village, Vietnam lost about 300 hectares of land. About 40 similar locations on the borderline were occupied by China, to have Chinese people move in as legal immigrants.

c) Nam Quan Pass. In 1955, Ho Chi Minh asked Mao Zedong to extend an additional 300 meters of railroads from China going into Vietnam, so both sides' railroads would be connected for convenient transportation. Mao approved. After awhile, Ho said that Vietnam's borderline was 300 m apart from the conjunction area, in the north, as it had been for a hundred years. Ho was told: the current border is where the railroads connected.

Lost 300 meters! Ho was silent. Not yet. Later on, Chinese soldiers carried the boundary marker No.18 (on border at Ải Nam Quan on Highway 1, 200m further into Vietnam territory. Therefore, that location lost about ½ kilometer.

d) Bản Giốc Waterfall (Detian Falls): At boundary marker No.53 in Đàm Thúy village, Trùng Khánh district, Cao Bang province, on Qui Thuận river is Bản Giốc waterfall of Vietnam. China sent 2000 soldiers to Vietnam, to pour reinforced concrete across the border river, redrew the maps, occupied a part of Bản Giốc Waterfall and even seized the Pò Thoong dune of Vietnam.

Detian waterfall. North side of China. 德天瀑 布 中国侧（北边较大的）

The main northern part of Bản Giốc Waterfall now belongs to China. China renamed it Detian (Đức Thiên) Waterfall 德天瀑布, the Great Marvel of South China.

The southern fall is left for Vietnam

Detian

Photograph by Mossikov

Source: article by blogger Măng
Photo by: blogger Điếu Cày

Overview of Bản Giốc/Detian Waterfall

Notes: On September 14, 2002 in an interview with Nhan Dan Online, Le Cong Phung announced a new boundary marker to divide Bản Giốc Waterfall in half. This new boundary marker is located on a "dune" in the middle of the stream. The Bản Giốc waterfall photo was published. In this photo, this waterfall consists of two parts: the North on the right, South on the left. China seized the Fall's largest part lying on the right side, renamed it DeTian (Đức Thiên) Waterfall, the Great Marvel.

Xinhua News Agency and the Cultural Attaché of the China Embassy in Hanoi (author called him Sino Puppet) on the National Day 2004, China invited the Socialist Republic of Vietnam's press team to attend the opening ceremony of the tourism fair and the inauguration ceremony of the DeTian Waterfall now belonging to China (in Sung Ta town). Vietnamese authorities from the press and tourism department were invited to attend the inauguration ceremony of this Duc Thien Waterfall, including "Director of the Press Department, the Director of the Tourism Department" and many in the media. The delegation attended a solemn reception to witness that waterfall now becoming the property of Red China. This was a celebration of the achievements of the Sino-Vietnamese friendship, between the two parties and the two states.

e) Removal of (destroying) the (old) boundary marker No.136 in Cao Bằng province, the markers No. 41, 42, 43 in Lạng Sơn province in the areas of Kùm Mu, Kim Ngân and Mẫu Sơn (9 km long) pushing 2.5 km further into Vietnam: lost an area of 1.000 hectares; the area of Nà Pàng - Kéo Trình (marker 29, 30, 31) in Cao Bằng province, stretched 6 km 450 long, 1 km 300 encroaching further on Vietnam lands. An area of 200 hectares. is lost. The Vietnamese communists remove all the old markers and no vestige of the old borderline is left.

Vietnam communist leaders destroyed old boundary markers set by the Tianjin Treaty (1885).

f) Using violent force to suppress Vietnamese people, deporting them, burning houses, pushing them away, seizing their homes and lands, Then Chinese migrants were encouraged to settle into many places, replacing Vietnamese citizens...

2. About the highlands

Finally "there are 6 highlands" and "we move the boundary line in between those highlands". This justification shows 27 places mentioned above which actually belong to Vietnam, and so they were previously within Vietnam. Red China has occupied those 27 highlands. Now because of "fierce disputes", China returned some, except for six highlands. As understood, those six "highlands" are the mountain ranges situated along Vietnam border. Now Phung has "succeeded" (sic) in moving the borderline in between the highlands, or between those mountain ranges, and therefore no land was lost.

So, if this statement is true, he allegedly agreed to surrender a land area from the half (½) summits of 6 mountain ranges in the North

In addition, how can Phung explain the following mountain ranges mentioned above:

- The mountain ranges 1250, 1545, 1509, 772 and 233 in Hà Giang province now belong to China. The mountain range 1509, Núi Đất (Earth Mountain) belongs to Thanh Thủy village,

Vị Xuyên district, which China renames Lao Son. Also the 1250 range Núi Bạc (Silver Mountain) in Yên Minh district now is named Giải Âm Sơn Range by China.

These high elevations were a strategic position to defend Vietnam against the Northern forces. These mountain ranges now belong to China.

- The mountain ranges 820 and 636 in Quốc Khánh village, Tràng Định district, Lạng Sơn province, lying near Nam Quan Pass on the west, next to highway 1, are also taken by China. The Bình Độ area 400, in Cao Lộc district of Lạng Sơn province, behind the boundary marker 26, East of highway 1, shares the same fate. These mountain ranges are important strategic areas for national defense against invaders from the North. The strategic rugged terrain here has assisted our ancestors in defeating the Chinese invaders. With those lost highlands, Vietnam would face enormous difficulties in protecting the nation. Therefore, the communist Vietnamese have assisted communist China to easily occupy Vietnam in the future.

So with the evidence mentioned above, how could the communist Party explain to the people of Vietnam about "only 1 kilometer difference"?

"GRAND CEREMONY" TO DEDICATE NAM QUAN PASS TO CHINA

on February 23, 2009

The dedication ceremony for Nam Quan Pass and some other locations on the borderline known as the "Celebration of a new boundary" was held on February 23, 2009 at Nam Quan Pass, at the boundary marker 'zero' km.

Overview of the Grand Ceremony at Nam Quan Pass, designed by China .

Now the boundary marker "0" changes again. President Nguyen Minh Triet, General Secretary Nong Duc Manh and Ho Cam Dao had drums and "thanh la" (a Viet traditional musical instrument) to make the ceremony more solemn.

Deputy Prime Minister Pham Gia Khiem and Chairman of Guangxi

Deputy Prime Minister Pham Gia Khiem held the hand of Chairman of Guangxi Province, on stage. This photo shows the Socialist Republic of Vietnam (SRV) being treated as a Chinese province. Once being annexed into China, Vietnam is unlikely to become a province, perhaps a district or an autonomous region, similar to the Zhuang Autonomous Region under Guangxi Province.

At the same time, on this day, the disputed border lands belong to China forever. And here is the result of the Sino-Vietnamese Boundary Demarcation Task Force that has been working "silently" for over a decade.

2. ANNEXASION OF VIETNAM INTO CHINA

In 1958, Pham Van Dong, as the Prime Minister of Ho Chi Minh, sent a diplomatic note to Zhou Enlai to recognize the Paracel and Spratly Islands as Chinese territories. This was an act publicly showing an annexation of part of Vietnamese territory into China.

Since then until now, successive leaders of the Communist Party of Vietnam have gradually implemented these schemes. The signing of the Treaties on Land Borders and the Gulf of Tonkin, at the same time, was a first step. Though the Land Border Treaty (partial lands already conceded) was signed for security reasons, borders are wide open. With the *"two economic corridors"* agreement that Tran Duc Luong, as a Chief of State, signed with China in 2005 (one from Kunming to Lao Cai extending to Hanoi, and the other from Nanning through Lạng Sơn to Hanoi), Vietnam communist leaders have not only helped Red China to achieve its goal of economic expansion, but also allowed the Chinese population to freely move into Vietnam. On one front, merchandise from Yunnan and Guangxi flows to Vietnam (as far as South Vietnam), and to Southeast Asia via Hai Phong port. These corridors serve the needs of economic development and improvement of the people's living standards for the two Chinese provinces, since they are located deep in the mainland. On the other front, more importantly, by 2019, about 90% of large ecconomic development projects throughout the country including heavy insdustries as metal production, mines, energy, chemical plants …. have been operated by Chinese corrporations where Chinese come to work and build Chinese colonies where local authorities are not allowed to get in The Vietnam economy now depends on that of China.

The agreement also includes an *"economic belt"* that runs along Vietnam's coast side to the South.

Chinese people have spread across the borders, to live and settle in Vietnam. A Chinese slogan is thus implemented in reality: "mountains connected to mountains, rivers connected to rivers" for China and Vietnam. With this "open border" policy, people are witnessing Chinese immigrants settling down along Vietnam's border, especially in Hà Giang, Lạng Sơn, Cao Bằng etc. Vietnamese secret police and military forces safeguard those "secret" moves. The Communist Vietnam government forbids any Vietnamese to "observe" this area. Since the treaty has been in effect, any curious people observing this area are arrested, and forbidden to approach. In the long term, these border boundaries will need to be reconsidered to be "consistent with reality", as Le Cong Phung proposed. And at that point, the border will be re-adjusted and changed so it will conform with new reality. Vietnam's territory will be narrowed further.

Moreover, the presence and actions of numerous Chinese youth groups marching on the streets of Saigon during the 2008 Beijing Olympic Torch relay is another example. A group of Chinese raised the signs *"Unify the Country"* with a Chinese Map and the three colored lines, symbolizing the Paracel 黄沙 and Spratly 南沙 Islands offshore, right in front of the Congress building which once belonged to the Republic of Vietnam in Saigon. About 30 young Chinese demonstrated with the slogan "Hoàng Sa and Trường Sa are the Chinese flesh and blood", in front of the China Embassy, located on Hoang Dieu Street in Hanoi, under the protection of the Socialist Republic of Vietnam police in uniform. All of those events reflected parts of the plan. Moreover, there were cases of Chinese gangsters carrying guns and publicly killing people in Hanoi, also with the protection of Vietnam police.

Even though there is a Treaty setting the new boundary in the Tonkin Gulf area, Vietnamese fishermen were killed by China's navy (January 2005) or were captured and imprisoned in China, then undergoing trial for violating the territorial sea of China, even though they fished within Vietnam's territorial waters, under the new boundary agreement (see map attached below). In many cases, Vietnamese fishermen were captured and imprisoned at Hainan Island. Conversely, each year, thousands of Chinese fishermen blatantly enter Vietnamese coastal territory to fish. Not to mention the Chinese fishermen who "strip" or confiscate the catch of Vietnamese fishermen, when Chinese fishermen approach and ask them to show their commercial fishing license. Now, with the *"economic belt"*, Chinese people including communist Chinese fishermen have more incentive to commit these acts.

Sometimes Red China also sends oil exploration vessels closer to Vietnamese territory for geological research. Recently, a search was carried out right off the coast of Danang, and the Vietnamese communists made no assertive response to protect Vietnam's territorial waters. In addition, the blatant Chinese takeover of the Paracel archipelago by forces in 1956 and 1974 in the South China Sea, together with silence from Ho Chi Minh and north Vietnam communist leaders, shows evidence of communist Vietnam's complicity.

The battle of January 1974 is a significant and important example of this. As we know, when China sent their warships to occupy some islands in the Crescent Group, the Republic of South Vietnam Navy (RSVN) bravely fought to regain control of this archipelago, to confirm and defend Vietnam's sovereignty, while Vietnamese communist leaders were completely silent: a blatant act of complicity. An important relevant point: the Soviet Union, a master, a patron, nurturer and active supporter of the Vietnamese communists, harshly condemned the Chinese aggression. The speaking up of Soviet Union was a very important action for Vietnamese communists in defending their sovereignty against Beijing's dominance. However, north Vietnam's silence in this situation meant refusing the Soviet Union's help that could protect Vietnam's own sovereignty and lands.

I should also note that the Soviet Union in this period was still the mainstay of VC support. This silence meant refusing Soviet support, taking side with China instead, and choosing China as their mentor. This behavior has a very important meaning in regards to the long-term goal of recognizing the South China Sea as China's territorial waters, just as did Pham Van Dong in his diplomatic note written to Zhou Enlai in 1958.

Such incidents currently help people to gradually see more clearly that the Vietnamese communists have surrendered the South China Sea to China.

And in the Spratly region? China has greatly increased its exercise of sovereign rights: to launch oil/gas exploration ships somewhere in the area, to have military drills with live ammunition (usually in November, as in 2007); to prohibit Vietnamese fishing in the South; not to have any reactions against China's Navy shooting and killing Vietnamese fishermen or sinking their commercial fishing boats near Spratly Island (July 2007); to forbid foreign oil companies exploring for oil, even in South Côn Sơn basin (north of the 8th parallel). That is the case of the BP company of UK. This company had to retreat from searching and exploiting for oil and gas, even though they and Mobil have contracts signed with Vietnam to explore oil and gas there

In May 1992, China allowed the US Crestone company, headquartered in Denver Colorado,, to explore for oil and gas in an area of 25.000 square kilometers at the Paracel archipelago. Thompson, president of this company, boastfully declared that the Chinese military would protect his company while performing work in this area.

On what basis would China do that? First, the Chinese National Assembly passed a law in February 1992 declaring that any military vessels or research ships passing South China Sea have to be authorized by China. If not complying, ships would be sunk. That is the legal basis established to "legalize" their sovereignty rights. They announced the boundary of the new 9-dash map of Chinese territorial waters over the entire Biển Đông, the Vietnamese Eastern Sea (in China, it is called Nam Hải 南海, South Sea). They annexed the Paracels and Spratlys into China by establishing an administrative organization called Sansha District, in Hainan Province to govern the maritime region. As such, they consider the Eastern Sea as their property.

The reason for this invasion, cited by China, is the diplomatic note from prime minister Pham Van Dong sent to Zhou Enlai in 1958. The Vietnamese Communist leaders did not transfer the territorial sea as agreed, therefore China used military tgmeans to enforce that promise.

How many islands has China occupied in the Spratly archipelago? So far, nobody knows for sure. At first in 1988, Chinese soldiers invaded six islands, including the Fiery Cross Reef, at the 9th parallel (across Hau Giang river mouth). By 1995, the international press mentioned the number 10. Nowadays, that number is much higher.

China has built extensive military bases at the Fiery Cross Reef. The satellite photos revealed that there are five different military facilities scattered on this reef: a military headquarters at one place; in other places, there is an office, a logistics warehouse, a platform for rocket launcher with a landing area for helicopters. The photos also show other Chinese military facilities under construction at other reefs. On that reef, there was a bulldozer and a ship dumping materials onto this location, and workers are doing construction work. All are durable structures, reinforced concrete, similar to all other bases on the two archipelagos of Paracels and Spratlys. They are built on the underwater foundations.

This is evidence reflecting China's determination to seize Vietnam's maritime territory, and control these islands for economic and military purposes etc, in their plan for future expansion, although at great expensess.

Across from the Fiery Cross Reef towards the East, another military base was built on the Mischief Reef. This is a huge 3-story building rising out of the water, painted yellow like a grand hotel, together with another structure nearby. According to the international media, this is a Chinese naval headquarters, with a small logistics base. In addition, there are two more building structures at two other places in the Mischief Reef area. One of these two structures is under construction. With the two bases on the Fiery Cross (near longitude 13) and Mischief (longitude 115) also situated north of the 9th parallel, we can draw a triangle connecting Fiery Cross and Mischief to Sanya base at Hainan Island (the base for nuclear submarines and aircraft carriers). We can see China navy forces ready to encircle all the islands where Vietnam troops are stationed. From there, Red China has encircled this entire sea surface, from Móng Cái (with the Tonkin Bay Area Treaty 2000) to the South, going through the entire Spratlys, all the way to Malaysia, to strangle Vietnam. There are also other bases constructed on the Spratly Archipelago such as on the Chigua reef, located on the 10th latitude and Johnson, may be later, they will build more military bases somewhere. At the Mischief Reef, it is known that there are three bases. There have been reports that a fourth base is being built.

To day, 2019. 8 reefs in Spratlys have been reclaimed and 3 of them becone large artificial islands with fortified multi-storey buildings, sea portts, large airfiileds to accommodate bombers like stealth J. 20, ammo depots inluding missiles, radomes, hangars for planes and depots for supplies like Subi, Mischiefs and Fiery Cross where one squadon of 24 fighters have been deployed on each.

To the north of Spratly, Chinese military bases are scattered in the Paracel archipelago, dominating Vietnam from the 16th parallel (Thừa Thiên/Quảng Nam/Đà nẵng) going south.

It won't be a surprise if later Vietnam announces the withdrawal from 21 occupied islands, especially from Spratly Island, the largest of the Spratly Archipelago, where there is a small unit of Vietnamese troops stationed.

With these examples, we see that China's navy is being used to prepare for the enforcement of territorial sovereignty, outlined by the New Map since 2006. If they succeed in this conspiracy, then the entire territory of Vietnam from (Ải) Nam Quan Pass to cape Cà Mau will become a province or a district/county of China. It won't be long. At that moment, the mission of Ho chi Minh and his accomplices will be accomplished. And a Chinese communist Party secretary will be officially appointed from Beijing to Vietnam to exert strict control, like the role of Hu Jintao as the former Tibetan secretary. Similar measures of mass killing and assimilation will be directly carried out by Chinese officials, brutally as in recent history. Anyone wanting to escape Vietnam by sea will be executed, because the entire Vietnam nation will have been tightly surrounded and tightly locked.

Vietnam communist leaders also will contribute to the further advance of China: not just by dominating Vietnam. As Mao Tse-Tung said: Vietnam will be a springboard for China to advance into Southeast Asia.

3. THE TONKIN GULF AREA

The CPV leaders signed **two Treaties** with the Chinese communists on December 30, 2000:

The Sino-Vietnamese Agreement on Maritime Boundary Delimitation in the Gulf of Tonkin. According to the delimitation at the Gulf of the Tientsin Treaty, 1885 (Hiệp Ước Thiên Tân), the map illustrators drew a **straight red line** from Móng Cái near the meridian of 108, passing Trà Cổ Island, going to the Sea mouth, in the direction of Thừa Thiên- Quảng Nam, known as the **Red Line** dividing the Gulf.

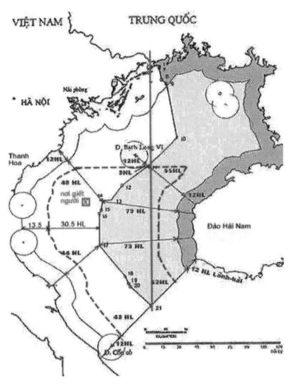

The total surface area of the Tonkin Gulf is 123,700 km². The Red Line divides the Bay into two parts: 63% belonging to Vietnam and 37% to China. Therefore, Vietnam has 77.931 km² and China has 45.769km². Under the 2000 treaty, a new maritime boundary line was drawn along the Gulf's curved shape, and lying in the middle of the two sides. The boundary line runs through all 21 points. Point 1 starts from the two borders joined at Móng Cái. The 21st point lies between the Gulf's mouth, between Hoang Liu, Hainan and Cồn Cỏ, Vĩnh Linh, south of Đồng Hới, Quảng Bình. Such a maritime boundary delimitation leads to this result: Vietnam lost 54% or 66,789 km², and China gained 46% or 45,510 km². Therefore, Vietnam surrendered to China 11,152 km². With this treaty, deputy foreign minister Le Cong Phung, who was in charge of negotiating, praised it as an achievement.

Treaty on Fishery Cooperation. Not over yet! Another one is called the Treaty on Fishery Cooperation. The goal is for both sides to cooperate on fishery. This treaty governs two regions.

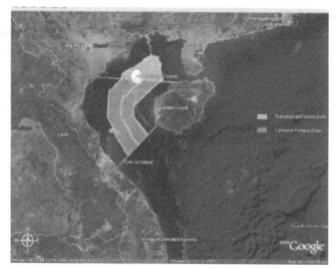

-The area South of the 20th parallel is situated in the south of Bach Long Vi island. The region covers an area of 35,000 km². The effective period is 12 years, with 3 years extended. To have 35,000 square kilometers, each side must contribute 30.5 nautical miles, counting from the middle boundary line of the bay.

Map of fishing cooperation

- Another area is situated in the North of Bach Long Vĩ Island 白龍尾 (White Dragon Tail). This region is smaller, valid for 4 years.

About the GULF OF TONKIN area, Phụng declared: "We delineate the Tonkin Gulf with China, based on the international law. ... When signing the agreement, if we compare the area between us and China, we have 8,000 km² more than China. We do not lose. Why did China consent to give us over 8 thousand square kilometers? Because we have a concave coastline, it contours inward this way. China's Hainan coastline contours outward this way. .... Saying that we lost 10 thousand square kilometers? No, unreasonable, not correct. We also don't want to specifically recall how we divided it, in what way.... There are times of negotiations that China voluntarily gave up three thousand square kilometers to us, at a different area, so they could take this area, only about 150 km². But we disagreed. We did not take the water. The water surface? For what? We calculated on the area below it, while guarding the sovereignty over the land, also guarding the national interests".

Phụng emphasized "the international law" and especially the Treaty of Tientsin in 1885 (Hiệp ước Thiên Tân) as basis of negotiation. He concluded: Vietnam did not lose 10,000 km² but gained 8000 square kilometers "given to Vietnam" by China. Moreover, communist China voluntarily gave to communist Vietnam 3000 square kilometers. In exchange, China only wanted 150 square kilometers and Vietnam disagreed....and "able to preserve the sovereignty over lands and national interests".

With that statement, Vietnam leaders had a "great success" in negotiating with the Chinese enemies, descendants of the greedy Han dynasty. From ancient times, the Chinese were accustomed to encroach on Vietnamese lands, meter by meter. There have been well-known cases of land loss, condemned by the CPV, but Phung concealed them. There are enclosed places banned to the public, in deep mountains and forests, or at remote places in the Gulf of Tonkin. Would anyone dare to seek the truth, by all means and opportunities?

Phụng seems to be "very pleased", if not proud, to say China "has given us" 8,000 square kilometers. China even volunteered to give another 3,000 kilometers that "we" didn't ask. Only to exchange for 150 kilometers.

This issue is related to the delimitation of the Tonkin Gulf, originated from the Tientsin Treaty, signed by the French and the Qing Dynasty in 1885. To enforce this Treaty, both parties signed a document called the 1887 Convention, setting the boundary in the Gulf of Tonkin. In this region, they drew a map dividing the Bay into two sections. On the map, they drew a North-South straight line, starting from Móng Cái, crossing Trà Cổ Island going down into the mouth of the Bay: on the East, at one point on Hainan Island is Hoang Lieu, and on the West is Cồn Cỏ Island of Vietnam. That boundary is named the Red Line, and the Convention called it "the delineation line" in the Gulf of Tonkin.

The Tianjin Treaty (Tientsin Accord) was signed by French minister Jules Patrenôtre and Chinese general Li Hongzhang of the Qing Dynasty, in June 1885. Is it "the international law". That treaty has been effective for over 100 years. The Red Line is the Delineation Line dividing the Gulf. China now demands to review the delimitation (boundary) of this Gulf, in her plot to occupy more of Vietnam's territorial waters. China unlawfully declares the Red Line has been only "the administrative line" for the purpose of "management" of the Gulf, referring to islands in this area. China demands elimination of that red line, to establish a new "official boundary line". Vietnam leaders concedes, to redraw a boundary going through 21 points in the middle of the Gulf, dividing it in half, as governed by that Treaty of 2000. As a result, 11,152 square kilometers of Vietnam's territorial sea were bestowed to Red China empire.

The Han descendants got 11,152 square kilometers! In addition, they even demanded to use both common fishing grounds, in both areas of the Tonkin Gulf. Not a word of praise from Phung, about the common fishing treaty. China could catch fish with a fleet of large fishing ships, with long nets covering 60 nautical miles (about 100 kilometers). Within 15 years "dredging" the Gulf, China could wipe out fish and deplete ocean resources. Numerous species of fish would be soon extinguished. Thanh Hóa fishermen only have wooden boats. They neither have steel vessels with hundreds of horsepower, nor high-tech equipment or fishing tackle, to compete with China's state-owned fishing industry. So how could Vietnamese fishermen cooperate with Chinese fishermen to share fishing resources? On January 8, 2005, Thanh Hoa fishermen were shot dead by Chinese naval ships, on the "new" Vietnam territorial waters.

In short, how could Vietnam's communist leaders explain to the people of Vietnam, such a statement by Lê công Phụng?

CHAPTER II: ACTS OF SELLING A NATION

aracel and Spratly Archipelagos have never belonged to China, although the Chinese communists have always cited their **historical** sovereignty over them. They said they have had ownership of those archipelagos since Han dynasty. The above ancient maps show China's maritime boundary only reaches Hainan Island.

1. COMMUNIST CHINA SEIZED VIETNAM LAND

The first time was in 1909, when Ly Chuan was patrolling the sea, he named 15 islands in the Paracel archipelago.

The second time in 1935, the Land and Sea Survey Committee (of China) published the Chinese-English glossary of islands in Nanhai 南海 (Nam Hải/South Sea), listing the names of 136 islands in Nanhai.

The third time in 1947, when the "resistance" was near victory, China's Ministry of Internal Affairs published a "Glossary of old and new names for the islands in Nanhai (China)", including the names of 172 islands.

Currently, the Chinese invaders have openly wanted to control the South China Sea and officially regarded this maritime region as their own property arguing that **they have historical soverignty over the islands**.. They enacted a law (1992) to define authority over the South China Sea; signed a contract with a foreign oil company to explore oil (Crestone, 1992), practiced military drills with live ammunition (11/2007), shot and killed Vietnamese fishermen fishing near the Paracel islands, for "violating the territorial sea" (July 7, 2007.....), forbade a foreign oil company to search for oil in southern Côn Sơn island, causing UK's BP company to leave, even though there was a signed agreement for oil exploration in Vietnam (5/2007); installed the sovereignty markers on Đa Lạc island (1992); they built up, set up military facilities on Fiery Cross reef, Mischief reef, etc. Sanya base has been used as a shelter and supply base, for many nuclear submarines and a aircraft carrier to defend this sea. They set up Sansha administrative authority (11/2007) to govern this sea. They mean to officially annex these two archipelagos into China, to be governed by that administrative body.

The Vietnamese communists raised their voices in false protest. They actually accepted the foreign occupation of our Vietnam territory. After 1988, Vietnam's leaders took absolutely no positive action to defend our national assets against the invaders. In such an implicit way, the transfer of South China Sea was completed when China established Sansha. Over time, China hope that these two archipelagos would become a 'done deal' for China.

To defend their sovereignty over South China Sea, Chinese authorities invoked some acts of Hồ Chí Minh surrendering Vietnam territorial waters, as reasons for their occupation. They used force to invade the Paracel archipelago in the years of 1956, 1974, (with complicity of Ho Chi Minh and the Communist Party of Vietnam), and six reefs in Spratly islands in 1988, and some more in 1992 and 1995. Then they constructed fortified military bases on some islands, bringing troops to occupy, to defend "sovereignty". In addition to protecting ownership of the South China Sea, the Chinese Communist Party's secret plan is to go further controlling the entire Vietnamese territory, to use Vietnam as a staging base for advancing into Southeast Asia and further.

2. ARGUMENTS BY CHINA TO CLAIM ITS SOVEREIGN RIGHTS

2.1. The Diplomatic Note of Pham Van Dong:

The most important evidence that China relies on to justify her sovereign rights is Phạm Văn Đồng 's official letter to recognize the Hoàng Sa 黄沙 (Paracel) and Trường Sa 南沙 (Spratly) Achipelagos as China's properties. As Prime Minister of the Ho Chi Minh Government, Phạm Văn Đồng sent a diplomatic note to Zhou Enlai in 1958, indirectly confirming China's sovereignty over these archipelagos.

The Diplomatic note stated:

Prime Minister of the Democratic Republic of Vietnam

Dear Comrade Minister,

We would like to clearly inform Comrade Prime Minister:

The Democratic Republic of Vietnam Government recognized and endorsed the declaration dated September 4, 1958, of the People's Republic of China Government, deciding on China's territorial waters.

The Democratic Republic of Vietnam Government respects that decision, and will instruct the responsible State agencies to thoroughly respect China's 12 nautical miles of territorial waters, in all relationships with the People's Republic of China on the sea.

Our respectful greetings to Comrade Prime Minister

September 14, 1958.

THỦ TƯỚNG PHỦ
NƯỚC VIỆT-NAM DÂN-CHỦ CỘNG-HÒA

Thưa Đồng chí Tổng lý,

Chúng tôi xin trân trọng báo tin để Đồng chí Tổng lý rõ :

Chính phủ nước Việt-nam Dân chủ Cộng hoà ghi nhận và tán thành bản tuyên bố, ngày 4 tháng 9 năm 1958, của Chính phủ nước Cộng hoà Nhân dân Trung-hoa, quyết định về hải phận của Trung-quốc.

Chính phủ nước Việt-nam Dân chủ Cộng hoà tôn trọng quyết định ấy và sẽ chỉ thị cho các cơ quan Nhà nước có trách nhiệm triệt để tôn trọng hải phận 12 hải lý của Trung-quốc, trong mọi quan hệ với nước Cộng hoà Nhân dân Trung hoa trên mặt bể.

Chúng tôi xin kính gửi Đồng chí Tổng lý lời chào rất trân trọng./.

Hà-nội, ngày 14 tháng 9 năm 1958

PHẠM VĂN ĐỒNG
Thủ tướng Chính phủ
Nước Việt-nam Dân chủ Cộng hoà

Kính gửi :
Đồng chí CHU ÂN LAI
Tổng lý Quốc vụ viện
Nước Cộng hoà Nhân dân Trung-hoa
tại
BẮC-KINH.

ANNEXE 4

La note adressée le 14 septembre 1958 par le premier ministre vietnamien Pham Van Dong au premier ministre Zhou Enlai.

Let's read the declaration of Communist China:

《中華人民共和國政府關於領海的聲明》

(1958年9月4日全國人民代表大會常務委員會第一百次會議批准)

中華人民共和國政府宣布：

(一)中華人民共和國的領海寬度爲十二海里(浬)。這項規定適用於中華人民共和國的一切領土，包括中國大陸及其沿海島嶼，和同大陸及其沿海島嶼隔有公海的台灣及其周圍各島、澎湖列島、東沙群島、西沙群島、中沙群島、南沙群島以及其他屬於中國的島嶼。

(二)中國大陸及其沿海島嶼的領海以連接大陸岸上和沿海岸外緣島嶼上各基點之間的各直? 爲基?，從基?向外延伸十二海里(浬)的水域是中國的領海。在基?以內的水域，包括渤海灣、瓊州海峽在內，都是中國的內海。在基?以內的島嶼，包括東引島、高登島、馬祖列島、白犬列島、烏島、大小金門島、大擔島、二擔島、東椗島在內，都是中國的內海島嶼。

(三)一切外國飛機和軍用船舶，未經中華人民共和國政府的許可，不得進入中國的領海和領海上空。

任何外國船舶在中國領海航行，必須遵守中華人民共和國政府的有關法令。

(四)以上(二)(三)兩項規定的原則同樣適用於台灣及其周圍各島、澎湖列島、東沙群島、西沙群島、中沙群島、南沙群島以及其他屬於中國的島嶼。

台灣和澎湖地區現在仍然被美國武力侵佔，這是侵犯中華人民共和國領土完整和主權的非法行爲。台灣和澎湖等地尚待收復，中華人民共和國政府有權採取一切適當的方法，在適當的時候，收復這些地區，這是中國的內政，不容外國干涉。

DECLARATION OF THE GOVERNMENT OF THE PEOPLE'S REPUBLIC OF CHINA ON THE TERRITORIAL SEA

(Approved by the 100th Session of the Standing Committee of the National People's Congress on 4th September, 1958)

The People's Republic of China hereby announces:

(1) This width of the territorial sea of the People's Republic of China is twelve nautical miles. This provision applies to all Territories of the People's Republic of China, including the mainland China and offshore islands, Taiwan (separated from the mainland and offshore islands by high seas) and its surrounding islands, the Penghu Archipelago, the Dongsha Islands, the Xisha islands, the Zhongsha Islands, the Nansha Islands and other islands belonging to China.

(2) The straight lines linking each basic point at the mainland's coasts and offshore outlying islands are regarded as base lines of the territorial sea of the mainland China and offshore islands. The waters extending twelve nautical miles away from the base lines are China's territorial sea. The waters inside the base lines, including Bohai Bay and Giongzhou Strait, are China's inland sea. The islands inside the base lines, including Dongyin Island, Gaodeng Island, Mazu Inland, Baiquan Island, Niaoqin Island, Big and Small Jinmen Islands, Dadam Island, Erdan Island and Dongding Island, are China's inland sea islands.

(3) Without the permit of the government of the People's Republic of China, all foreign aircraft and military vessels shall not be allowed to enter China's territorial sea and the sky above the territorial sea.Any foreign vessel sailing in China's territorial sea must comply with the relevant orders of the government of the People's Republic of China.

(4) Articles (2) and (3) mentioned above are also applied to Taiwan and the surrounding islands, the Penghu archipelago, Đông Sa archipelago, Xisha 西沙 (Tây Sa/Paracel/Hoàng Sa) archipelago, Trung Sa archipelago, Nansha 南沙 (Nam Sa/Spratly/Trường Sa) archipelago and other islands belonging to China.

Taiwan and Penghu are still occupied with force by the USA. This is an illegality violating the People's Republic of China's territorial integrity and sovereignty. Taiwan and Penghu are waiting for recapture. The People's Republic of China has rights to take all appropriate measures to recapture these places in due course. It is China's internal affair which should not be interfered with by any foreign country.

Remarks: By this declaration of the Chinese congress, the question is whether or not there was an undisclosed transfer of ownership of the islands to China. As a result, China then unilaterally made such statemant and Pham van Dong quickly sent the note recognizing the fact. If there was no scuh a transfer, Ho would have given away the islands to his mentor.

2.2. Statement of Ung Van Khiem:

The following information also provides a detail cited by China, to justify sovereignty over the South China Sea. Those were the words of Ung van Khiem, Deputy Foreign Minister of the Democratic Republic of Vietnam telling representative Li Zhimin of the People's Republic of China on June 15, 1956 that the Paracel and Spratly Islands historically belonged to China. This statement was made in the office of Ministry of Foreign Affairs of North Vietnam, witnessed by a Ministry official. This matter was made known by China. Whether or not it is true, no one knows.

If it was true, then those were just words exchanged in private between two people, when Li visited Khiem in his office. Normally, in the practice of diplomacy, if there is an important issue such as the Paracels and Spratlys, it must be conducted publicly, with a formal announcement immediately after the meeting. Especially in this case, the above officials were not high-ranking officials authorized to make such important decision. As in the case of Pham Van Dong's diplomatic note, this statement is illegitimate, not legally binding.

Since it is illegitimate, the invocation is just an excuse to justify aggression by force.

2.3. Hanoi's Textbook of Geography prior to 1974:

In the Geography textbooks (for 9th graders) appoved by Ministry of Education to teach at school, there was a lesson saying that Hoàng Sa 黃沙 (Paracel) and Trường Sa 南沙 (Spratly) Archipelagos formed a circle to protect China. Hoàng Sa and Trường Sa Archipelagos once belong to China and they are used to protect China.

The event has nothing to do with the transfer or claim of Red China's sovereignty over those two archipelagos.

2.4. Analysis on Act of Selling the Nation

What did the international press and scholars say about Phạm văn Đồng's diplomatic note to acknowledge the Paracels and Spratlys belonging to China?

The following is an excerpt of some original documents on this subject matter:

2.4.1. Todd Kelly "Vietnamese claims to the Truong Sa archipelago"

Source: A Journal of the Southeast Asian Studies Student Association, 'Explorations in Southeast Asian Studies' Vol 3 Fall 1999.

On June 15, 1956, two weeks after the Republic of Viet Nam reiterated the Vietnamese claims to the Truong Sa Islands, the DRV Second Foreign Minister told the PRC Charge d'Affaires that, "according to Vietnamese data, the Xisha and Nansha Islands are historically part of Chinese territory." Two years later, the PRC made a declaration defining its territorial waters. This declaration delineated the extent of Chinese territory and included Truong Sa. In response, the DRV Prime Minister, Pham Van Dong, sent a formal note to PRC Premier Zhou Enlai stating that "The Government of the Democratic Republic of Viet Nam respects this decision."

2.4.2. Far East Economic Review, March 16, 1979, p. 11.

In September, 1958, when China, in its declaration extending the breadth of Chinese territorial waters to 12 nautical miles, specified that the decision applied to all Chinese territories, including the Paracels and the Spratlys, Hanoi again went on record to recognize China's sovereignty over the two archipelagoes. Phạm Văn Đồng stated in a note to Chinese leader Zhou Enlai on September 14, 1958: "The Government of the Democratic Republic of VN recognizes and supports the declaration of the Government of the People's Republic of China on its decision concerning China territorial sea made on 9/4/1958 (see Beijing Review June 19, 1958, p.21 -- Beijing Review-- August 25, 1979, p.25 -- The existence of such a statement and its contents were acknowledged in VN in BBC/FE, no. 6189, August 9, 1979, p. 1)

NGUYEN MANH CAM's ADMISSION TO SELLING THE COUNTRY:

As Foreign Minister Nguyen Manh Cam has admitted….. (Vietnam News Agency, 3 December 1992):

"Our leaders' previous declaration on the Hoang Sa (Paracel) and Truong Sa (Spratly) archipelagoes was made in the following context: At that time, under the 1954 Geneva agreement on Indochina, the territories from the 17th parallel southward including the two archipelagoes were under the control of the South Vietnam administration. Moreover, Vietnam then had to concentrate all its force on the highest goal of **resisting the US aggressive war to defend national independenc**e. It had to gain support of friends all over the world. Meanwhile, Sino-Vietnamese relations were very close and the two countries trusted each other. **China was according to Vietnam a very great support and valuable assistance.** In that context and stemming from the above-said urgent requirement, our leaders' declaration [supporting China's claims to sovereignty over the Paracel and Spratly islands] was necessary because it directly served the fight for the defense of national independence and the freedom of the motherland.

More specifically, it aimed at meeting the then immediate need to prevent the US imperialists from using these islands to attack us. It has nothing to do with the historical and legal foundations of Vietnam's sovereignty over the Truong Sa and Hoang Sa archipelagoes" (remarks to a press conference in Hanoi on December 2, 1992 carried by Vietnam News Agency, December 3, 1992).

These statements show that all that the Chinese have alleged above are true. What happens today related to these two islands are merely consequences of the wicked settlement of these two communist brothers in the past. No one in the world community wants to step in to settle the dispute between Communist Vietnam and PRC. The reason is very clear: diplomatic note and recognition by Vietnamese Communists can't be erased by a small country like VN which has wanted to play a trick by cheating China. Moreover, Vietnamese Communists can't stay away from China while they have to follow Chinese "doi moi" (renovation) to go forward to socialism.

2.4.3. Eye on Asia– FEER, February 10, 1994

PHẠM VĂN ĐỒNG ADMITTED SELLING THE COUNTRY

"Saigon - Hanoi - Paracels Islands Dispute" – 1974, by Frank Ching, Far Eastern Economic Review Reference: Vol. 157, No. 6, February 10, 1994 "Vietnamese communists **sel**l the Paracel and Spratly islands, but now want to say no."

According to Chinese Ministry of Foreign Affairs's "China's Indisputable Sovereignty Over the Xisha and Nansha Islands" (Beijing Review, Feb. 18, 1980), Hanoi has "settled" this matter with the Chinese in the past. (In the past, Hanoi already "delivered" to China these archipelagos).

They basically claimed:

In June 1956, two years after Ho Chi Minh's government was re-established in Hanoi, North Vietnamese Vice Foreign Minister Ung Van Khiem said to Li Zhimin, Charge d'Affaires of the Chinese Embassy in North Vietnam, that "according to Vietnamese data, the Xisha (Tây Sa = Hoang Sa, Paracels) and Nansha (Nam Sa = Trường Sa, Spratlys) Islands are historically part of Chinese territory".

On September 4, 1958, the Chinese Government proclaimed the breadth of its territorial sea to be twelve nautical miles which applied to to all territories of the PRC, "including ... the Dongsha Islands, the Xisha Islands, the Zhongsha Islands, the Nansha Islands..." Ten days later, Pham Van Dong stated in his note to Zhou Enlai that "the Government of the Democratic Republic of Vietnam recognizes and supports the declaration of the Government of the People's Republic of China on China's territorial sea made on September 4, 1958. "One more thing to notice is that PRC threatened only the territories Vietnamese claimed and left open claims of other countries. It was very clear that Mr Ho Chi Minh, through Pham Van Dong, gave PRC "a big pie" because at that time Mr **Ho Chi Minh was preparing for invading South Vietnam. Mr Ho needed colossal aid and closed eyes to accept all conditions of Beijing.** It was easy for him to sell "only on paper" two archipelagoes which still belonged to South Vietnam by then.

For this, Vietnamese communists waited for a meeting of ASEAN countries in Manila, and used this opportunity as a safe buoy and immediately signed a paper requiring these countries to help Vietnam to solve this problem "fairly".

For its part, after taking islands of communist Vietnam, China showed amicability to Malaysia and Philippines and said that China was ready to negotiate resource areas with these two countries, brushing VC aside. China did say that it would not accept any foreign countries to get involved in this matter between it and communist Vietnam.

Later, Pham Van Dong denied his past wrongdoing in an issue of Far Eastern Economic Review, March 16, 1979. Basically, **he said that he acted because it was "wartime".**

Here's an excerpt from this article on p.11:

"According to Li (Chinese Vice-Premier Li Xiannian), China was ready to share the gulf's water "half and half" with the Vietnamese, but at the negotiating table, Hanoi drew the line of Vietnamese control close to Hainan island. Li also said that in 1956 (or 1958), Vietnamese Premier Pham Van Dong supported a Chinese statement about sovereignty over the Spratly and Paracel islands, but since late 1975, Vietnam has been in control of part of the Spratly group - the Paracels being under Chinese control. In 1977, Dong reportedly said of his 1956 stance :"**That was the war period and I had to say that**".

Because of his eagerness to create disastrous war for both areas North and South, and to contribute to international communism, Mr **Ho Chi Minh did promise, without dignity, a "future" land for Chinese to grab, not knowing for sure that whether or not the South Vietnam would be swallowed.**

As Dong said, "That was the war period and I had to say that". Who created the Vietnam War and was ready to do all it could, to get South Vietnam, even to sell land? **Selling land during the war time and when it was over Pham Van Dong denied it by just falsely laying the blame on the war...**

2.4.4. "A History of Three Warnings" by Dr. Jose Antonio Socrates,

Univ. of the Philippines, Geologist, actively monitoring Spratlys Island.

This document consists of 3 paragraphs as following:

1. FIRST PART: DIVIDING THE PARACELS

When in 1957 China protested Vietnam's move on Robert Island, Saigon was already in control of two other islands of the Crescent Group: Pattle and Money Islands. The three islands held by South Vietnam are on the western side of the Crescent Group. Then in August 1958, Saigon took over Duncan Island in the eastern sector of the Crescent, thus facing the Amphitrite Group. **Two weeks later the PRC government declared its sovereignty over the whole of the Paracels. They were supported by North-Vietnam.**

1) STATEMENT BY THE MINISTRY OF FOREIGN AFFAIRS OF THE SOCIALIST REPUBLIC OF VIET NAM ON THE HOANG SA AND TRUONG SA ARCHIPELAGOS (AUGUST 7, 1979)

On July 30, 1979, China made public in Peking some documents in an attempt to justify its claim of sovereignty over the Paracels and Spratly archipelagoes. As regards this issue, the Ministry of Foreign Affairs of the Socialist Republic of Vietnam declares:

……

a. The Chinese interpretation of the September 14, 1958 note by the Prime Minister of the Democratic Republic of Viet Nam as recognition of China's ownership over the archipelagoes is a gross distortion since the spirit and letter of the note only mean the recognition of a 12-mile limit for Chinese territorial waters.

....

2) DRV's RECOGNITION OF CHINA's SOVEREIGNTY OVER THE NANSHA ISLANDS

a. Vice Foreign Minister Dong Van Khiem of the Democratic Republic of Viet Nam received Mr. Li Zhimin, charge d'affaires ad interim of the Chinese Embassy in Viet Nam and told him that "*according to Vietnamese data, the Xisha and Nansha Islands are historically part of Chinese territory.*" Mr. Le Doc, Acting Director of the Asian Department of the Vietnamese Foreign Ministry, who was present then, added that "judging from history, these islands were already part of China at the time of the Song Dynasty."

b. Nhan Dan of Viet Nam reported in great detail on September 6, 1958 the Chinese Government's Declaration of September 4, 1958 that the breadth of the territorial sea of the People's Republic of China should be 12 nautical miles and that this provision should apply to all territories of the People's Republic of China, including all islands on the South China Sea. On September 14 of the same year, Premier Pham Van Dong of the Vietnamese Government solemnly stated in his note to Premier Zhou Enlai that Viet Nam *"recognizes and supports the Declaration of the Government of the People's Republic of China on China's territorial sea"*.

It is stated in the lesson *"The People's Republic of China"* of a standard Vietnamese school textbook on geography published in 1974 that the islands from the Nansha and Xisha Islands to Hainan Island and Taiwan constitute a great wall for the defense of the mainland of China.

2.4.5. RFA 12/12/2007

In 1977, former Prime Minister Pham Van Dong expressed his perspective in 1956 that *"it was wartime and I must say so"*. During wartime, Hanoi needed ample support from Beijing, such as military necessities, consulting, or mobilizing the international communities.

Thus, on Tuesday December 11, 2007, why did China Foreign Ministry's spokesperson say that "Vietnam in many historical periods had different perspectives on this sovereignty issue and China clearly knows that"?

Nguyên văn công-hàm của *"Chính-phủ nước Việt-Nam Dân-ch Cộng-hòa công-nhận quyết-định về hải-phận của Trung-quốc"* đăng trong *Nhân-Dân*, số 1653, ra ngày Thứ-hai, 22 tháng năm 1958.

VIỆT-NAM TẬP CHÍ 41

In a press conference in Hanoi on December 2, 1992, former Vietnam Foreign Minister Nguyen Manh Cam explained, and it was published by Vietnam News Agency on December 3, 1992. He said: *"Our leaders previously confirmed the Paracels and Spratlys like that, because of the 1954 Geneva Agreement on Indochina, Everywhere, on all territories from the 17th parallel going South, belonged to the South Vietnam government, including both of these islands.*

In addition, during that time Vietnam had to focus all forces on the war against the US, so it needed friends everywhere. China-Vietnam friendship was bonding and the two countries fully trusted each other. Vietnam views China as a big and valuable source of support. In that spirit, because of the urgent situation, our leaders' viewpoint (i.e. to support China's declaration of sovereignty over the Parcels and Spratlys) was necessary because it served the war defending our fatherland.

In particular, it also aimed for the urgent need at that time to prevent the imperialist USA from using those islands to attack us. The fact that our leaders temporarily recognized that China had nothing to do with Vietnamese sovereignty, historically and legally, over the archipelagos of Paracel and Spratly".

The expressions of Nguyen Manh Cam, former Foreign Minister of Vietnam, published on December 3, 1992 by the Vietnam News Agency, proved what was expressed by the spokesperson of China's Foreign Ministry: "In many historical periods, Vietnam had different perspectives on this sovereignty issue, and China clearly knows that".

Diplomatic messages exchanged between Prime Ministers, warm statements of leaders in good friendship, in need of each other, and publicly announced, being preserved in the official national archives, and noted by the international press, is this still legitimate? China insisted on clearly knowing that.

Then in the Saigon Liberation newspaper published in May 1976, an article was written: "China is great to us, not just a comrade, but also a trusted master who has been bearing us enthusiastically for the presence we have. Therefore, it doesn't matter whether Vietnam or China has sovereignty over Hoang Sa"! (quoted by Le Minh Nguyen's *"Làm Thân Cỏ Cú"*)

2.4.6. Pham Van Dong was Prime Minister for 32 years (BBC January 24, 2008).

In 1958, North Vietnam's Prime Minister Pham Van Dong signed a letter which later became very controversial. The letter on September 14, 1958 stated that the Democratic Republic of Vietnam government agreed with a Beijing statement on China's territorial waters. Many considered this letter as reflecting North Vietnam's acknowledgment of China's sovereignty over the Spratly and Paracel Islands. Recently, after the disputes between the two nations on sovereignty over the two islands, the letter of Pham Van Dong was again discussed, although unofficially in Vietnam and among overseas Vietnamese. So what opinion do overseas analysts have about the letter?

BBC Vietnamese asked Dr. Balazs Szalontai, a scholar on Asia who lives in Hungary. At first, he explained the two different views of North Vietnam in the 1950s and 1974 when the Paracel islands were occupied by China.

Dr. Balazs Szalontai: In the years 1955-1958, the North Vietnamese leaders had not yet reached the goal of national unity, while dealing with internal difficulties and the lack of international support. Their main ally at that time was China. In this situation, Hanoi could not hope to establish control over the Paracels and Spratlys in the near future. Therefore they could not have major disagreements with China over the islands. At this point, the North Vietnam government sought assistance from China, and they tried not to make public statements supporting China's specific claims on sovereignty, nor sign any binding document that would publicly surrender Vietnam's sovereignty over these islands.

In 1974, the situation was completely different. The unification of Vietnam was no longer a vague possibility. Assuming China did not intervene, Hanoi could easily take the islands along with the rest of the South. From 1968 to 1974, the North Vietnam-China relationship was cold, while the Soviet Union stepped up its support for the North. In that situation, of course, North Vietnam's views of China were more resistant, comparing to 1950s.

For similar reasons, China's attitude became more unfriendly. By 1974, Beijing no longer hoped Hanoi would follow them and resist Moscow. Indeed, in late 1973 and early 1974, the Soviet Union could feel that the US-China reconciliation had not brought the expected results. Washington had not given up diplomatic relations with Taiwan, nor dropped her intention to seek peace with the Soviet Union. In contrast, Soviet-US relations had progressed well. Thus by 1974, Chinese leaders once again felt besieged. Therefore, they sought to improve their strategic position in Southeast Asia, by taking the action of occupying the Paracels, and increasing support for the Khmer Rouge and the communist guerrillas in Burma.

BBC: In your opinion, in what context was the letter of Prime Minister Pham Van Dong written?

- The Socialist Republic of Vietnam Government acknowledged and approved the statement of the People's Republic of China on September 4, 1958, on the resolution of China's territorial waters. The RVN Government respected that resolution, and instructed responsible State agencies to thoroughly respect China's 12 nautical miles of territorial waters in relation to the People's Republic of China on the sea ...

Dr. Balazs Szalontai: First, let's talk about China's statement. It was born in the context of the United Nations Conference on the Law of the Sea in 1956 and the agreements signed afterwards in 1958. Understandably, China, though not yet a member of the United Nations, still wanted to have a voice on how to resolve those issues. Because of that, we had China's statement in September 1958. As I said above, during these years, North Vietnam could not upset China. The Soviet Union did not provide enough support for the reunification, while Ngo Dinh Diem in the South and the US government were unwilling to agree to hold elections as stated in the Geneva Agreement. Pham Van Dong therefore felt the need to lean towards China. Still, he seemed cautious enough to make a statement supporting the principle that China had sovereignty over 12 nautical miles of territorial waters along its territory, but refrained from defining this territory. Although China's previous statement was very specific, and mentioned all islands, including the Spratlys and Paracels that Beijing claimed as their sovereign rights, North Vietnam's statement mentioned no specific territorial sea boundaries.

In this bilateral territorial dispute between the interests of Vietnam and China, the North Vietnamese view, in the diplomatic sense rather than legal, was closer to the Chinese view, than that of South Vietnam.

BBC: In addition, people heard about Ung Van Khiem's statement agreeing with China in 1956, when he was North Vietnam's Deputy Foreign Minister. China publicly referred to this statement. Does it help us better understand Pham Van Dong's letter?

Dr. Balazs Szalontai: On the website of China's State Department, in the middle of 1956, Ung Van Khiem told a Chinese provisional representative that Hoàng Sa 黄沙 (Paracel) and Trường Sa 南沙 (Spratly) historically belonged to China. At first I doubted the truthfulness of this statement. In 2004, China's State Department even removed controversial chapters of Korean history from its website. That is, they were willing to change history to serve themselves.

I also accept the argument that if indeed Khiem said so, it meant that the North Vietnamese leaders actually intended to give up Vietnam's sovereignty over the Paracel and Spratly Islands. But now I think differently. One reason is that I have re-examined the border agreements between Mongolia and the Soviet Union and I realized that Ung Van Khiem's statement actually was nonbinding. In the communist system, an official's statement like that of Khiem is considered to represent the official viewpoint of the team leaders. But the team leaders could also ignore him and his statements, by removing him for unrelated reasons. That was the fate of Mongolian Foreign Minister Sodnomyn Averzed in 1958. While negotiating on the Soviet-Mongolian border, he had a hard-line viewpoint, and most likely because he followed the leadership's orders. But when Soviet Union refused to release Mongolia's claimed territory, and criticized Averzed's "nationalist attitude", Mongolia removed him.

China's Premier Zhou Enlai received the letter from Vietnam's Prime Minister Pham Van Dong in 1958. As in the case of Ung Văn Khiêm, at that time he was just a vice minister. It was only a verbal statement, in private talk with a Chinese provisional representative. In the communist system, a verbal statement does not have the same power as a well-prepared written statement that addressed territorial matters. It also has no weight as a verbal statement of the senior leaders like the prime minister, head of state, or general secretary. Clearly, North Vietnamese leaders did not sign or pronounce such an agreement. Otherwise, China would have announced it.

BBC: In your view, does Pham Van Dong's letter have any legal meaning?

Dr. Balazs Szalontai: It weakens Vietnam's perspective a little bit, but I consider it as having no legal binding. In my view, China's statements emphasizing the principle "silence implies consent", ignores the fact that it was not the legitimate South Vietnam Government which publicly protested China's claims and tried to defend the islands, but could not prevent China from seizing the Paracels. China simply ignored the opposition of Saigon. If Hanoi objected at that time, the results would be the same.

BBC: What can one do with Dong's letter today? For a long period, Vietnam has been silent. Do you think the Vietnamese people could openly debate it now, without fearing that it would only benefit China?

Dr. Balazs Szalontai: In my view, since Pham Van Dong's letter has only limited legitimacy, a public discussion on the issue would not be harmful to either Vietnam or China. But of course, the governments of the two nations could look at this issue differently.

Dr. Balazs Szalontai was professor at the Mongolian University of Science and Technology, and is currently an independent researcher in Hungary. He is author of a book on Kim Nhat Thanh during the Khrushchev period (Stanford University and Woodrow Wilson Center, 2006).

In short, Ho Chi Minh truly had a plot to transfer the Paracels and Spratlys to communist China, in exchange for Chinese aid in invading the Republic of (South) Vietnam.

***

In fact, legally, this was an administrative letter sent to a government partner. That letter was not legitimate in transferring lands or waters. Technically and legally, the transfer of territory must be made by a Treaty and this treaty must comply and meet strict conditions to be legitimate, and therefore effectively binding .For example, even though the 1999 and 2000 Treaties between Vietnam and China were officially signed and ratified by the National Assembly, they had numerous errors,/ defects and thus were illegitimate or void. China cited that letter on their Foreign Ministry's website, to prove that Ho Chi Minh's government officially acknowledged Biển Đông (*Eastern Sea*) as Chinese territory. Because there is no other legitimate and strong evidence, this letter is used. China even cited words of Ung Van Khiem and Li Zhimin, witnessed by Le Doc, a diplomat of the Democratic Republic of Vietnam, mentioned in the above documents. Politically, perhaps this letter or Ung Van Khiem's statement revealed something secret that Ho Chi Minh deliberately concealed, as this issue was explained by *Far Eastern Economic Review* magazine.

2.4.7. Four points to mention here about Pham Van Dong's Statement are:

1) No one can transfer to anyone anything he does not have.This is the case of the Democratic Republic of Vietnam, as with Pham Van Dong sending the diplomatic note mentioned above: They are not owners of the two Archipelagos of Paracel and Spratly. These two archipelagos are owned by the Republic of (South) Vietnam. It is possible that Dong's statement is only the one made by a third person, an outsider, to loudly protest or support, in order to please an ally, especially when that ally is his communist master. This is what Vietnam did when President Bush attacked Saddam Hussein. In the first two months of the war, Vietnam communist leaders mobilized people in 39 provinces and towns to protest against the imperialist USA invading Iraq, only because Saddam Hussein was Vietnam's friend. Perhaps Ho made such statements

to please China. Ho had nothing to lose, because those two archipelagos belonged to South Vietnam. So now there are disastrous consequences.

2) In the diplomatic note, Pham Van Dong endorsed Zhou An Lai's statement and respected it. In the statement, Zhou immediately claimed China to be owner of those two archipelagos. In reality, China has never legally acquired ownership of these two archipelagos. This is only a unilateral act of an aggressor to seize lands and property. When Red China was not the owner, the approval of Pham Van Dong had no value. This was an illegitimate act, before Pham Van Dong sent the letter to confirm it.

3) Declaring the 12 nautical miles of territorial sea, according to the Law of the Sea Let us suppose that if China truly possesses sovereignty over the Paracel and Spratly Islands, then outside of that territorial sea of 12 nautical miles, the law of the sea prescribes the continental shelf and the exclusive economic zone, 200 nautical miles wide. Of course, an island must have sufficient self-sustaining conditions to earn that status. When claiming the 12 nautical miles, it is understood that China accepts the international maritime law. Now with the map published in June 2006, China redrew the entire South China Sea as their territorial sea. So is this hegemonic behavior, regardless of the Law of The Sea recognized internationally?

4) An administrative letter, such as a diplomatic note, is not legitimate in the transferring of territorial lands or seas. The transfer of land at least must be approved by a national assembly.

In short, there is no transfer of sovereignty to China, even though the note shows voluntary support from Ho Chi Min to a unilateral Chinese statement. People in the civilized world would not believe that this is a document of transfer of soveriggnty..

***

Above, I said technically it is not legally binding. However, China has kept on emphasizing on it and raising it. Finally, China had publicly announced this archived diplomatic note. Hanoi leaders couldn't deny it. **Pham Van Dong, then Nguyen Manh Cam, Vietnam Foreign Ministers admitted that they did recognize China's sovereignty over those two archipelagos. However they vaguely cited reasons, and blamed "the war"... to avoid exposing the truth**, as revealed later by the Far Eastern Economic Review, March 16, 1979. The magazine wrote, "**This is a shady arrangement between two communist brothers... The diplomatic note and the admission from the Vietnamese communists could not be erased by a small nation like Vietnam 'playing tricks' to deceive China**".

About the reason for which Ho surrendered Vietnam's Eastern Sea to China, Frank Ching of FEER, on February 10, 1994 wrote: "Mr Ho needed colossal aid and closed his eyes to accept all conditions of Beijing. It was easy for him to sell "only on paper" two archipelagos, which still belonged to South Vietnam by then". That is why Vietnam's communist leaders were "mute as clams" on sovereignty over Vietnam's Eastern Sea. This is the inherent behavior of the Red China hegemonists: the strong bullying the weak, and communist Vietnam was trapped in this game. The consequences have been devastating for Vietnam. Because of Ho chi Minh's lies and ambiguity, the People of Vietnam pay the price.

2.4.8. Press Conference at the Chinese Embassy in Hanoi on September 15, 2008.

Beijing declared that this is the 50th anniversary of Zhou Enlai's declaration of territorial waters, and Phạm văn Đồng sending a diplomatic note to acknowledge that territorial sea limit. Why did they declare it on this occasion, and did it at Chinese Embassy in Hanoi, not in Beijing?

The deep and hidden intention of Beijing was to reaffirm Beijing's sovereignty rights over these two archipelagos that Ho Chi Minh transferred to them. The reaffirmation **right in front of Vietnam communist leaders at the Vietnam capital** is to remind them that they have duty to carry it out, also remind the Vietnamese people that Ho had transferred it, that China 's sovereignty over the two islands is indisputable. that all opposion to it be suppressed. Those who violate the China waters will be severely punished. This is the case of Vietnamese fishermen whio claimed doing fishing in their traditional waters of the Paracels area: being shot dead, imprisonment, ransson, sinking boats…

That declaration was also related to Vietnam Prime Minister Nguyen Tan Dung's visiting trip to Washington in June. He has tried to lure US capitalist ExxonMobil into oil exploration in the South China Sea. Since the United States would protect the interests of the oil company, this declaration was also to warn the US that South China Sea now belongs to China.

Finally, to publicly announce that diplomatic note right at Vietnam capital was to internationally confirm the People Republic of China's authority over these two archipelagos.

***

In short, what China cited to justify her sovereignty over the Paracel and Spratly Islands is not legitimate. An administrative letter on sovereignty is not legitimate, nor legally binding. Any desire to transfer the sovereignty rights, even if selling lands or selling sea, meaning to transfer lands or sea to a partner, is required to have the people's consent, through a legitimate referendum or a treaty ratified by Natioal Assembly.. A simple declaration of sovereignty, as in the case of Ung văn Khiêm is illegitimate. Red China knows that historically, it had nothing to prove sovereignty over these two archipelagos. In 1994, over 100 scholars from both sides, China and Taiwan, conferenced together. They mobilized the overseas Chinese worldwide, to assist in searching for evidence to prove their sovereignty. They also called the Chinese government to fight (politically), to help assert and defend their sovereignty over the two archipelagos of Vietnam. (see *"Communism on Vietnam Soil"*, Nguyễn Văn Canh, published by Kien Quoc, 2002 pages vii-ix).

Unable to justify their sovereign rights, China used violence to seize these archipelagos. Is is an act against the International Law: *The United Nations Charter and the Unites Nations Convention ot the Law of the sea, 1982*. China hope that such occupatin and continuous asserting sovereignty over those islands would be a "fait accompli" in the future, and that Vietnam's Eastern Sea would become legal China territory in the long-term future.

All people of Vietnam, especially the overseas free Vietnamese, must have a solemn duty to oppose this plot. We cannot allow the Chinese invaders to carry out such wicked conspiracy.

It is imperative that the genuine free people of Vietnam denounce to the world the abusive acts of Ho Chi Minh and the CPV, leading to the current unpleasant situation. They have suppressed Vietnamese people who stand up to defend the Fatherland, such as the Vietnamese college students who have demonstrated since early December 2007.

The following old records show objections to the North Vietnamese Communists supporting China's occupation of the Paracels: South Vietnam Newspapers Chính Luận, Hòa Bình, Sóng Thần published articles on the Paracels in 1974.

VIETNAMESE STUDENTS of THE REPUBLIC OF VIETNAM PROTESTS AGAINST CHINA'S INVASIONS, Saigon, January 1974

CHAPTER III: THE CPV ASSISTING FOREIGN INVADERS

The slogan used by Ho Chi Minh and his accomplices, during the period of anti-French colonialism, such as "fighting for the national independence", were detected later on by the people as a deceit. Their goals and activities were to serve two foreign nations: the Soviet Union and Red China.

In Chapters I and II, I have listed the **documents and acts** re. Ho and the CPV, playing the role of the native Sino Puppets tasked with "selling" our lands, surrendering our sea, even "selling " the Vietnamese people to China.

In this Chapter III, I have collected public materials which have been scattered everywhere, revealing Ho and CPV's **moves** to pursue the above goals. These public materials were researched, evaluated, and interpreted. They have been integrated so as to give readers an overview of what the CPV have done under this situation. From there, people can predict what is the future of Vietnam.

1. ANTI-FRENCH RESISTANCE FOR NATIONAL INDEPENDENCE OR SCHEME ASSISTING RED CHINA TO ASSIMILATE PEOPLE OF VIETNAM

During the resistance war "against the French for national independence", Vietnam communist leaders raised the slogans as: **independence, freedom, happiness** for the people. The slogans attracted Vietnamese people to fight the war agains French colonialists. Vietnamese enthusistically voluntered to go to front line. So much blood had been shed and sacifice made for those noble goals. Today, the results are empty.

The secret purpose of the Communist Party is revealed.

Independence? After the war against France, there was a brief moment of independence, because the French colonialists had gone. However, the party secretly brought in another foreigner. This foreigner or foreign nation is more clever, playing a role of guidnaces behind the scenes, to orchestrate a group of puppets to act. This foreign nation is China, embodied with ancient Han dynasty policies. They have experiences of 1,000 years of dominating Vietnam, with a goal to take lands and to Sinicize (Hán hóa) people of Vietnam, though as yet unsuccessful. Now they stand behind PCV leaders, giving commands for them to execute. The issues of land selling, surrendering the Paracels and Spratlys are examples.

Happiness and freedom? After seizing power in North Vietnam, horrific mass killings occurred during the Land Reforms Program. Other communist campaigns such as Agricultural cooperations, Attacks to bourgeoisie class, Coomerce anh Industry Reform including confiscation of people's assets, and restructuring of the entire society by brutal means bring much sufferings to the people under totalitarian rules. The people are deprived of all basic human freedoms; all privileges are reserved for members the ruling class....

5% of the total 17 million people in the North was eliminated,

So, *"independence, freedom, happiness"* were just a guise to mislead, to assist the communist Party in gaining power. After seizing the government power, the Communist Party then gradually utilized necessary measures to carry out its objectives so that in the long-term, it could advance to the assimilation of the Vietnamese people, as Truong Chinh advocated in the following statement. Let us read Truong Chinh's Announcement to have a better knowledge of that ultimate goal of Ho and his accomplices.

THE DEMOCRATIC REPUBLIC OF VIETNAM,
THE ADMINISTRATIVE COMMITTEE OF THE RESISTANCE, YEAR VII (1)
VIETNAM LABOR PARTY'S GENERAL SECRETARY, No 284/ LĐ 284/LĐ
INDEPENDENCE - FREEDOM - HAPPINESS

Dear fellow countrymen!

Why accept a weird language from the capitalist white, penetrating our beloved Vietnam, a long-term **vassal state (chư hầu)** of China?

Why did we popularize the strange writing style (Latinized) of Colonialist Alexandre de Rhodes, brought to our nation, from Nam Quan Pass to Cà Mau Cape?

No! Our compatriots should completely eliminate that Western-style writing – even though it is a really clear quick writing style (2). Let us return to our ancestors' written language, which was also traditional Chinese.

Chinese people are our friends - perhaps our teachers too. No shame to acknowledge it – is it the first civilized nation in the world?"

"Chinese people are our friends - perhaps our teachers too. No shame to acknowledge it – Is it the first civilized nation in the world?"

What about the medical science from the West? They only cut, drill, gouge, grate! That's all!

Trường Chinh in Chinese VIP outfit. (Image source: qdnd.vn)

Dear fellow countrymen! Let us dismiss methods of medical treatment from the Western Empire from our country!

Let's dump their labor/delivery clinic and hospital. Let's use our inherited ancestors' medicine patches, especially the globally popular Chinese medicine.

Let's return to this method: first, support our Chinese friends. Later, eliminate numerous colonial imported methods such as science, inventions...etc out of our beloved Vietnam.

Let's wipe out "intellectuals" who originated from European and American schools, the imperialists and the colonialists! (3).

Wish for a "general counter-attack" and "use all methods to eliminate colonialism".

Trường Chinh

Secretary General of the Labor Party

-After having taken over the South, Le Duan, Secretary General of the CPV did not bother to hide their ultimate goal:

"WE FIGHT THE FRENCH. IT IS A FIGHT FOR THE SOVIET UNION AND CHINA"

How would Truong Chinh's dreams be achieved?

Note that the measures applied were cruel and bloody, a Stalinist style of terrorism with Leninist techniques to achieve this goal.

After seizing the entire North Vietnam in 1954 and the South in 1975, Ho chi Minh and his associates applied the brutal, bloody and inhumane measures initiated by the Chinese communists, to wipe out "remnants of the traditional society". Nhân Văn Giai Phẩm (published magazines in North Vietnam in a cultural-political movement in late 1950s by artists and intellectuals) was destroyed as products of the colonial empire and feudalist society.

The communists carried out plans like "campaign attacks to the bourgeoisie class", "restructing the industries and commerce", "wiping out all capitalist seeds." In the countryside, the "land reforms campaign" was the most obvious destructive action. The violent public denouncements and humiliations (**đấu tố**) of the landlord class were typical scenarios, directly orchestrated by the Chinese communist advisors. People recall the case of Mrs. Nguyễn thị Năm, a rich landowner who owned large plantations in the Northern Highlands. This elderly lady contributed so much to the "revolution" during the French resistance. She provided foods and assistance to prominent Communist Party leaders such as Truong Chinh, Ton Duc Thang, and many faithful members of the Party Central Committee, and Ho associates, at her plantation, protecting them from being arrested by the French Secuirty Services.. Her son joined the Viet Minh armed forces, to fight against the French. He was a regiment commander. She was prosecuted for being a landlord, subjected to public denouncement and humiliation, and killed. Some communist members were resentful of such immoral acts, expressed dissatisfaction to Ton Duc Thang, a close associate of Ho. And Thang came and voiced his complaint to Ho. Ho only observed that "it is pitiful to kill a woman" and stayed silent. Why did Ho keep silent? Ton Duc Thang replied that the order on killing of Mrs. Năm directly came from a Chinese adviser of the Land Reforms Team.

About 40,000 party members were exterminated under the land reform program during the preriod of preparations of building of socialism, just because they had been either landlords or related to the later or intellectuals.

When the party started the campaign of resistance against the Frenh Colonialists, the party had no resources. They called upon rich landlords to contribute money, wealth. Many joined as fighters besides donating their wealth, in the movement of resistence for indepedence.. They fought along side with the party. With their intellect they led, directed the fightings throughout the country, helping win the war. Most of them became party members. Now, the party began a process of builidng socialist regime. Socialism is idiologically a system built on the proletarian class. It does not tolerte people coming from such other classes as rich land lords, bourgoisie, intellectuals etc. One among others is the land reform campaign to implement socialism in the country side. This aims at wiping out all other classes and bringing members of the proletarian class to power, besides depriving the rich of all wealth they have through a "people court", then dividng the wealth to members of the proletarian class.. Every is equal. This is implemented by brutal means of Chinese methods. Now the problem of 40,000 persons who were previuosly landlords and intellectuals, had participated in the campaign to fight the French under the leadership of the party and had become party members had to be solved. Of course, there was no room form them the new society. In order to prevent them from active opposing the party in the furtue, the solution was that they were brutally eliminated through the measures applied in the land reform program. **See also Nguyen Van Canh," Peasants of North Vietnam, 1954-1960", Center For Vietnam Studies, 1987.**

Ho was known to obey his Chinese masters, to eandover to do what ever Red China asked him to do, in order to move Vietnam to socialism.

In accord with these programs, Hồ wanted to completely eradicate all traces of the traditional culture. Books, documents, national customs, lifestyles, families, religions, ceremonial worship, personal thoughts were to be eliminated. Historical monuments such as temples and shrines were destroyed. At the same time, he worked to impose a new culture: a socialist culture with new people, people of a collectivistic society. The individual was not to be recognized and must be dissolved into a collective, as a new unit of the social order. Therefore, Ho laid out a task of reversing tradiional national culture and morality, to erase traditions of a nation, so that future generations will have a shallow knowledge of Vietnam's historical past. His clear goal was to use all measures possible to detach people from the past, to penetrate people's minds with "new" thoughts, and to destroy all the people's strength. With such moves, hopefully the people of Vietnam would merge into a "World of Great Unity" (thế giới đại đồng 大同, Socialism in One Country). However, "a world of great unity" is only a disguised ideal, concealing a secret plot for the Sinicization of Vietnam.

New education has been introduced into Vietnam to shape new socialist men. Through community activities lead by Party, children are trained in schools and adults are shaped for new ways of thinking. Today, when observing the lifestyles and activities in Vietnam under communist Party rule, we could see signs of Sinicization (Hán hóa): clothes worn by Ho chi

Minh and high-ranking officials, languages used in daily activities, organizing styles in the military, government and the populace etc.. Everything has followed the Chinese model. This Sinicization mission was carried out in parallel with the surrendering of Vietnam to China. The goal is to render Vietnam a province of China. To achieve this goal of communist China, the CPV must play a major role. Moreover, Vietnam territory is also intended to serve as a staging base for communist China to advance further South.

----

(1) The daily newspaper Tiếng Dội No 462, (3rd year, August 24, 1951, lunar calendar, July 22, year of the Cat. Selling price was one đồng, editor Trần Chí Thành, alias Trần tấn Quốc, Managing Office at 216 Gia Long Street, Saigon). This newspaper had an article titled "Viet Minh advocated a campaign for Vietnam to be Chư hầu , (a vassal state) to China". It was printed in a flyer signed by Truong Chinh. At that time, when after having a military force under their command, Vietnam leaders did not hesitate to show that they are willing to be subordinate to China, and even wanted to be Sinicized (culturally assimilated).

(2) Now, after 66 years of the Socialist Republic of Vietnam in pwoer, the CPV leaders is a stirring movement preparing to apply the project "New Vietnamese Language Version", which Bui Hien claimed as its author. It is allowed by the Communist Party of Vietnam, officially published in November 2017 to replace the "strange writing style of Alexandre de Rhodes" (using Latin alphabet, instead of Chinese characters as before) that Truong Chinh requested to abolish, even though it has existed for over 300 years. This new Vietnamese written language is considered a transformed Han Chinese, transcribed into Beijing Chinese. It has been approved by Vietnam's Ministry of Education, to be implemented in Vietnam's education system. Some schools began to teach Vietnamese young children the new reformed written laanguage. Someone further revealed that this is the Reformed Vietnamese Language Version prepared by the China's Department of Languages, headed by Prof. Tu Huong Hoa. This project was completed in March 1998, to be utilized in Socialist Vietnam, in an attempt to replace and abolish the current Vietnamese language. That way, the Sinicization of Vietnam advocated by Truong Chinh would be successful.

Remember that in 1951, when Truong Chinh called for elimination of the present Vietnmese written Latinized language as Vietnmese have used, the call cleary did not come from the CPV themselves. It had to be from Red China. Truong Chinh was just a spokesman for the project. Red China has records on it and sttill is working on it. And now some 70 years has past, the Red China Minsitry of Education found an opportunity to have the CPV leaders execute what Red China wants them to do to erase the Vietnamese language presently used.

The Chinese never forget these things. Over a 1000 years, they have continued to invade Vietnam though they were defeated many times..

(3) ER The following article related to this scheme:

Conference on Annexing Vietnam into China: A Province Or Autonomous Region? between China Department General of Intelligence and Department General 2, Vietnam Ministry of Defense , Dec. 2009.

Ninh Cơ reported, C/N 2009/12

http://www.nationalistvietnameseforum.com/Nationalist%20Vietnamese%20Forum/Audio/0
61509.wma

Conference on Annexing Vietnam into China: A Province or Autonomous Region? (Recorded by Ninh Co. Excerpt from an audio recording document in a secret meeting, between representatives of the South China Intelligence Department and Vietnam's General Department 2. For archives under strict confidentiality).

"The return of Vietnam to the great country of China is first and foremost. Sooner or later. But sooner is better than later. Historically, Vietnam was once a district of China, a branch of a big Chinese tree. China and Vietnam were one. That is the eternal truth. That was also the view of comrade Ho (HCM) when he took a oath at a ceremony to join the Chinese communist party. Respected comrade Ho also taught: "China/Vietnam are like lips and teeth. Opened lips cause cold teeth". That means that the two countries are two parts of the same body. Comrade Nông Đức Mạnh had once proudly claimed to be a Zhuang ethnic member, when meeting with the State Council members. The Zhuang ethnic group is a part of the people of China……"

2. ACTS OF SUBMISSION TO THE NORTHERN EMPIRE

During the period of Chinese colonization in Vietnam, China sent Chinese rulers to Vietnam. Those rulers were called Thái Thú ("Governor")". Today, Han descendants are smarter. They don't use Chinese as rulers, but recruit the local faithful communist Vietnamese to handle this job. Vietnamese people are ruling the people of Vietnam on behalf of China. They are called Sino Puppets. Interestingly, the local Sino Puppets or Henchmen have applied brutal bloody measures against their own compatriots. Peopler could not complain about cruel foreign rulers as in ancient times, used these as eveidence to mobilize people to wage a war against foreign aggressors. Bloody massacres happened during the Land Reforms in 1952-1956 such as killings of Mrs Năm, or 40,000 party members or extermination of a total of 5% of the 17 million North Viet nam people at that time. Is there anyone who dare declare that this was Chinese act, or could accuse and condemn Mao Zedong for them, though those horrible killings were actually authored by Maoist cadres? The confiscation or seizing of the total assets of rich people in north Vietnam, who would say those acts were masterminded by the Chinese communists -- even though those acts originated from Red China's policies and were directed by the Chinese communist cadres? The tax policies, the ruling of Vietnam according to Mao's strategies etc. were plotted by La Quy Ba (China chief adviser and ambassador to Vietnam) during the 1950s. Ho Chi Minh was just an executor.

Vietnam's borderlands, a part of the Gulf of Tonkin, and Vietnam's territorial waters were transferred to China, and who could accuse China of invading Vietnam and robbing land from her? Beijing easily acquired Vietnam's assets, without being blamed as during the Chinese domination period for those crimes such as: **"forcing Vietnamese people to dive to the bottom of the sea in search for pearls or go deeply in the forests in search for rhino horns"**. Now, the local Sino puppets are performing this task to serve Red China.

What do those Sino puppets do?

2.1. **Suffocating Students Protests**

During Ho Chi Minh's time, orders from Beijing issued to Ho were kept secret. Nowadays, the situation has changed. The CPV leaders' submission to China has been made public even by Beijing though this leads to discredit their Vietnamese puppets. There is no need to protect Puppets ' prestige among the Vietanmese general public. An important reason for this is that Beijing has recruited and could employ some among **a hundred may be more of this type of leaders** (as General Truong giang Long of the Secuity Ministry disclosed this figure in Oct. 2027) who are currently "long sleepers" in the party and endeaover to compete for these positions. Vietnamese leaders therefore do not hesitate to openly accept China's demands, despite the humiliation of doing so.

2.1.1. Viet Youth's patriotism: a challenge to the CPV leaders as servants of Foreign aggressors..

Photo courtesy of Dũng Đô Thị's blog. (Trà Mi, RFA, June 16, 2008)
Lê thị Kim Thu, December 16, 2007, Hà Nội
Django, Hanoi, December 9, 2007.

Banner "Get Up and Go! Oh compatriots!

AFP PHOTO/Le Thang Long

2.1.2. Orders come from Beijing:

In November 2007, when State Council of Minister established Sansha district to formally annex Hoang Sa and Truong Sa into Chinese territory, Anti-China Vietnamese college students demonstrating on December 9 in Hanoi and Saigon, demanded defense of those archipelagos. Hu Jintao, China Communist Party's Secretary was angry at those protests, considering these as 'disrespectful crimes'. On 11 December, 2007, Hu asked his clerk to call Nông đức Mạnh, the General Secretary of the Communist Party of Vietnam, demanding Mạnh to **"suffocate"** all students' anti-China protests against the Chinese invasion of Paracels and Spratlys. Nông đức Mạnh pledged to Hu Jintao's secretary: *"Because of the everlasting friendship with China, the Vietnamese leaders are ready to make a total sacrifice to China"*. TK, Reporter, December 12, 2007.

In addition to Hu Jintao's clerk's warning directly to Nông đức Mạnh, Chinese Foreign Ministry spokesman Qin Gang publicly issued the same order from Beijing Ministry of Foreign Affairs to Vietnam.

BEIJING (Reuters) – "China **chided** its neighbour Vietnam on Tuesday (Dec.11), saying the Southeast Asian country was straining ties by asserting claims to a chain of islands that may be rich in oil." (Note: Reuters used the verb "chided" (mắng chửi), meaning: to reprimand, scold, with disdain.

In a press conference on December 11 (BBC), Qin Gang continued: "Several times, Chinese and Vietnamese leaders exchanged views on the issue of sovereignty over the islands. They agreed to continue resolving disputes together, through negotiation and dialogue, to maintain stability in the South China Sea and for *the mutual benefit of both parties*".

BBC,December 19, 2007:

On January 18, 2007, Chinese Foreign Ministry spokesperson Qin Gang spoke at an international press conference (no direct contact with Vietnam communist leaders): *"China pays close attention to the anti-China protests in Vietnam"*. Qin Gang reminded Vietnam's leaders: "We hope that the Vietnam government will take responsibility, at the same time having **effective measures to prevent such matters from harming our bilateral relations**". Regarding sovereignty over the islands, Qin Gang said: *"China has indisputable sovereignty over the islands and nearby maritime region, in the South China Sea"*. The angry statement of the communist China State Department's spokesman Qin Gang from Beijing, warning Vietnam communist leaders about allowing the college student protests in Hà Nội and Sàigòn, with chanted slogans, raising banners to demand the defending of the Paracels and Spratlys, and opposing Beijing and Chinese invaders, with the demonstrations on December 9 and 16, 2007.

Le Dung, spokesman for Vietnam's Ministry of Foreign Affairs, denied the allegation, when Beijing implied that Vietnam's government supported those protests. He replied to Qin Gang: *"Those demonstrations occurred spontaneously"*. Immediately after that, Vietnam's leaders rushed to utilize tactics previously learned from communist China, such as mobilizing secret police, security forces and Party members to suppress protesters and actively disperse demonstrations intended for the following weeks.

To show loyalty to Beijing and to act on Beijing's orders, Vietnam leaders have openly acknowledged Beijing's claim that "the Paracel and Spratly Islands are territorial waters of China". Even though being publicly "insulted", the Ministry of Education and Training did not hesitate to officially issue a written order to ban the students protesting, and to require affiliated units to block anti-China protests. Many calculated measures such as arrest, imprisonment, threats, prosecution, school expulsion, pressure on each student's family, isolating each student at home, or on the streets leading to the Chinese Embassy in Ha Noi or the Chinese consulate in Saigon -- were used to paralyze the student protests.

Vietnamese Communist authorities exerted their best efforts, and really fulfilled the duties demanded by the Northern Dynasty. They have succeeded.

Nowadays, that foreign nation has no longer paid attenton to saving face for their team of local Sino Henchmen (太守). In doing so, Beijing leaders knew the consequences of their acts and also knew who were their Vietnamese puppets. Especially in this case, these Sino puppets now have an evil reputation. They convince no one. Their words are not trusted or listened to. To rule or hold power, the Sino puppets can only continue to use violence, to terrorize in order to stabilize the unrest. That is how the Chinese masters are pushing Vietnamese leaders into submission by depending on China for survival.

This regime now has succeeded in assisting the Chinese invaders to dominate Vietnam though indirectly. Historically, Vietnam was ruled by the Han Dynasty for about 1,000 years, but never successfully. Nowadays, the local Sino puppets have surrendered plentiful lands and seas to China. They join hands with the Chinese invaders, to occupy *Hoàng Sa* (the Paracel Islands) and *Trường Sa* (the Spratly Islands). After fully occupying the South China Sea, the entire Vietnamese territory will easily become a province of China.

2.1.3. How to execute orders from a foreign nation?

2.1.3.1. Government agencies: in charge

Since the anti-China forces are mainly college students, The Ministry of Education and Training have issued a number of notices to order Party leaders and school administrators to carry out the duties of suppressing students:

Directives from the Ministry of Education and Training to Presidents of colleges, schools and heads of Training Centers re. suppression of students demonstrations against China' invasion of the South China Sea.

BỘ GIÁO DỤC VÀ ĐÀO TẠO   CỘNG HOÀ XÃ HỘI CHỦ NGHĨA VIỆT NAM

Số: 13587/BGDĐT-HSSV   Độc lập – Tự do – Hạnh phúc

V/v: Tăng cường công tác đảm bảo
an ninh, trật tự an toàn xã hội

Hà Nội, ngày 21 tháng 12 năm 2007

Kính gửi: - Giám đốc đại học, học viện; Hiệu trưởng trường
đại học, cao đẳng và trung cấp chuyên nghiệp
- Giám đốc sở giáo dục và đào tạo

HỎA TỐC

Tiếp theo công văn số 12914/BGDĐT-HSSV ngày 09 tháng 12 năm 2007, Bộ Giáo dục và Đào tạo yêu cầu Giám đốc các đại học, học viện, Hiệu trưởng các trường đại học, cao đẳng, trung cấp chuyên nghiệp, Giám đốc các sở giáo dục và đào tạo triển khai một số công việc sau:

1. Tiếp tục phối hợp chặt chẽ với các đơn vị có liên quan quán triệt cho tất cả học sinh, sinh viên, cán bộ, giáo viên nhà trường tuyệt đối không được tham gia tụ tập, biểu tình, tuần hành trái quy định của pháp luật.

2. Triển khai các biện pháp nắm bắt diễn biến tư tưởng của học sinh, sinh viên, cán bộ, giáo viên nhà trường thông qua các hoạt động, diễn đàn, các website, nhật ký trên mạng … để chủ động xử lý và báo cáo kịp thời.

3. Xây dựng phương án triển khai cụ thể và có mặt tại hiện trường để phối hợp giải quyết khi vụ việc xảy ra.

4. Phối hợp chặt chẽ với cấp uỷ, chính quyền, công an các quận, huyện, phường xã trong việc phòng ngừa và xử lý khi vụ việc xảy ra.

5. Chịu trách nhiệm chỉ đạo thực hiện các công việc nêu trên, đặc biệt lưu ý các ngày thứ bảy, chủ nhật, ngày lễ, tết, kỷ niệm và báo cáo kết quả triển khai về Bộ Giáo dục và Đào tạo.

Mọi thông tin xin liên hệ: Vụ Công tác học sinh, sinh viên – Bộ Giáo dục và Đào tạo, 49 Đại Cồ Việt, Hà Nội. Điện thoại: 04 8694984, Fax: 04 8681598, E-mail: ndmanh@moet.gov.vn. Di động: 0913 319904, 0912 609907.

UBND tỉnh Hà Tây
Sở Giáo dục và Đào tạo

Số: 1854/SY-GDĐT

Hà Đông, ngày 21 tháng 12 năm 2007

SAO Y BẢN CHÍNH

Nơi nhận:
- Lãnh đạo Sở
- Các phòng ban Sở
- Các trường THPT, TT GDTX
- Các phòng Giáo dục
- Lưu VP

KT. GIÁM ĐỐC SỞ GD&ĐT HÀ TÂY
Chánh văn phòng

Kiều Văn Minh

KT. BỘ TRƯỞNG
THỨ TRƯỞNG

Phạm Vũ Luận

Written Directive from Minister of Education and Training dated Dec. 12, 2007 to heads of Universties, Colleges & ssubordinate agencies re. banning students'protests.

BỘ GIÁO DỤC VÀ ĐÀO TẠO   CỘNG HÒA XÃ HỘI CHỦ NGHĨA VIỆT NAM
Số: 423 /BGDĐT- CTHSSV   Độc lập - Tự do - Hạnh phúc

Hà Nội, ngày 19 tháng 9 năm 2008

TỐI MẬT

CÔNG ĐIỆN KHẨN

BỘ TRƯỞNG BỘ GIÁO DỤC VÀ ĐÀO TẠO ĐIỆN:

HỎA TỐC
- Giám đốc các đại học, học viện khu vực Hà Nội
- Hiệu trưởng các trường đại học, cao đẳng và trung cấp chuyên nghiệp khu vực Hà Nội

Tiếp theo nội dung cuộc họp với lãnh đạo các trường ngày 10/9/2008 về công tác an ninh trật tự; Căn cứ tình hình thực tế và ý kiến của Uỷ ban nhân dân thành phố Hà Nội; Để góp phần đảm bảo an ninh trật tự và an toàn giao thông trên địa bàn thành phố Hà Nội, Bộ Giáo dục và Đào tạo yêu cầu các đồng chí Giám đốc, Hiệu trưởng các nhà trường:

1. Có biện pháp cụ thể, bằng các hình thức phù hợp tổ chức cho học sinh, sinh viên của nhà trường học tập, sinh hoạt tập thể tại trường trong ngày chủ nhật 21/9/2008 để quản lý học sinh, sinh viên. Chỉ đạo, phối hợp chặt chẽ với tổ chức Đoàn TNCS Hồ Chí Minh, Hội Sinh viên để triển khai hoạt động này.

2. Chủ động phối hợp với cấp uỷ, chính quyền địa phương và các cơ quan chức năng trên địa bàn để phát hiện và xử lý kịp thời các nguy cơ gây mất an ninh, trật tự.

3. Tổ chức tốt việc trực ban lãnh đạo, bố trí cán bộ để sẵn sàng giải quyết các sự việc phát sinh.

Đề nghị các nhà trường tổ chức thực hiện nghiêm túc các nội dung trên.

Trong trường hợp có vấn đề phức tạp xảy ra cần có báo báo ngay về Bộ theo số điện thoại: 04.8694.916 hoặc 0913.319904. Email:nnhuy@moet.gov.vn.

Nơi nhận: KT. BỘ TRƯỞNG
- Như trên;   THỨ TRƯỞNG
- PTTg. Bộ trưởng (để báo cáo);
- Bộ Công an, Cục A25;
- Thành uỷ, UBND TP. Hà Nội;
- TW Đoàn, TW Hội Sinh viên VN;
- Lưu VT, Vụ CT HSSV.   Phạm Vũ Luận

Urgent Message dated April 14, 2008 from Minister of Education and Training re. HOW TO HANDLE students'protests agaisnt China

A directive dated Dec. 7, 2007 from the President of the College of Industries, Hanoi to students, staff and employees .

Subject: Forbidding to gather in frant of China Embassy in Hanoi re. Paracels and Spralys.

ĐẠI HỌC QUỐC GIA HÀ NỘI | **CỘNG HOÀ XÃ HỘI CHỦ NGHĨA VIỆT NAM**
TRƯỜNG ĐẠI HỌC CÔNG NGHỆ | **Độc lập - Tự do - Hạnh phúc**
Số 42/TB-HCQT | -------------------
(V/v không tham gia tụ tập tại ĐSQ Trung Quốc) | *Hà Nội, ngày 7 tháng 12 năm 2007*

Kính gửi: **TOÀN THỂ CÁN BỘ, SINH VIÊN TRONG TRƯỜNG**

Thời gian vừa qua, Quốc Vụ viện Trung Quốc phê chuẩn việc lập thành phố cấp Huyện Tam Sa thuộc tỉnh Hải Nam để trực tiếp quản lý 3 quần đảo trên Biển Đông gồm hai quần đảo Hoàng Sa và Trường Sa của Việt Nam. Trước diễn biến này, Bộ Ngoại giao Việt Nam đã có tuyên bố: Việt Nam có đầy đủ bằng chứng lịch sử và cơ sở pháp lý để khẳng định chủ quyền đối với hai quần đảo nói trên và coi hành động trên đây là vi phạm chủ quyền lãnh thổ của Việt Nam, không phù hợp với nhận thức chung của lãnh đạo cấp cao hai nước, không có lợi cho tiến trình đàm phán tìm kiếm biện pháp cơ bản, lâu dài cho vấn đề trên biển giữa hai bên. Quan điểm của Việt Nam mong muốn tăng cường quan hệ láng giềng hữu nghị với Trung Quốc, chủ trương giải quyết hoà bình mọi tranh chấp giữa hai nước trên cơ sở tôn trọng pháp luật quốc tế.

Gần đây, trên mạng Internet xuất hiện một số lời kêu gọi sinh viên tập trung trước Đại sứ quán Trung Quốc để kích động, phản đối Trung Quốc thông qua sự kiện trên trong khi Nhà nước Việt Nam đã chủ trương giải quyết sự việc này bằng con đường ngoại giao chính thống.

Vậy, Nhà trường yêu cầu cán bộ, sinh viên, học viên cao học trong trường thực hiện đúng chủ trương của Đảng và Nhà nước đối với sự kiện này tránh bị kích động, lôi kéo thực hiện những hành động đi ngược chủ trương trên.

Đề nghị thủ trưởng các đơn vị phổ biến và nhắc nhở cán bộ, sinh viên trong đơn vị thực hiện tốt công văn này.

KT. HIỆU TRƯỞNG
PHÓ HIỆU TRƯỞNG

Nơi gửi:
- *Như kính gửi (để thực hiện)*
- *Lưu HC-QT*

PGS. TS Hà Quang Thuỵ

197

2.1.3.2. **To mobilize the Party/Groups/Unions, security armed police (under-cover or not), and military members in civilian clothes, for the duty of suppression:**

To implement the Party and government's executive orders, party members, uniformed policemen, security forces and military... are mobilized to suppress students on the streets: Uniformed policemen are responsible to maintain public order on the streets. But the ruthless oppression -- including beating techniques adopted from Nazi Germany for North Vietnam communists--is the duty of the police and army in civilian clothes. They infiltrate into public groups, pretend to be protestors, identify leaders, suddenly t\ake action: arresting student leaders, then disappeared. Barbaric measures are used at police stations Victims are tortured including being brainwashed.

The following photos show how do the escurity and police forces together with the CPV apparatus deal with student protestors in compliance with Beijing demands in Hanoi in 2008

Police forces show off, are deployed in Hanoi streets and are ready to violently suppress the demonstrators. A police unit is marching into the area where studenta are staging a demonstration.

Police is surrounding student demonstrators.

RFA: Security forces and police blocked and arrested writer Nguyễn Xuân Nghĩa and teacher Vũ Hùng, in front of Hanoi's Đồng Xuân Market on April 29, 2008, shortly after the beginning of demonstrations.

RFA: On January 20, 2008, reporter Điếu Cày's arms were bent to his back, his body lifted up by six police officers amid his continuous resistance.

Photo: On April 29, 2008, college student Nguyễn Tiến Nam was assaulted by police disguised as civilians. He was arm-locked, strangled and arrested in front of Đồng Xuân Market, Hanoi, after joining the protest against China occupying Hoàng Sa (Paracel) and Trường Sa (Spratly) Archipelagos, while the Beijing Olympic torchlight being welcomed in Vietnam.

Large police task forces in uniform.

The SRV secret police force overwhelms and suppresses the college student protests.

In Hanoi, many policemen and soldiers disguised as ordinary people are involved in suppressing college students. They outnumbered by three times the college students on the streets. In Saigon, reports said the Communist authorities were also worried about unpredictable events, and unsure how they could explode on the streets. So they assigned over 2000 undercover agents, security forces, 1000 policemen, and a regiment of soldiers ordered for active duty. A thousand members from Ho Chi Minh Communist Youth Union, together with students from military schools, security forces and military intelligence are disguised as curious bystanders. In addition, the communist party members were mobilized everywhere to control young people right at their school, or where students lived, even preventing ordinary people from going to locations considered to be gathering places. Other measures applied were to threaten school expulsion, to ban schooling, to terrorize parents and siblings of students protesting China occupying ancestral seas...

2.1.3.3.   **To honor those who contribute to the surrender of lands and sea to foreign nations**

Surrendering lands and sea is a shameful crime. To strengthen the spirit for those criminals who sold the nation, to express loyalty to Chinese communist Party, and to set examples for others, CPV leaders publicly promote their achievements, by awarding the regime's most prestigious medals to the senior party members who actually gave away Vietnam lands, in a solemn ceremony. They were not afraid nor ashamed of what they have done (1).

RFA January 22, 2008: Vietnam's Communist Party decided to award the Gold Star Medal to former General Secretary Le Kha Phieu and former Vietnam President Tran Duc Luong, at a sensitive time when this matter of the Paracels and Spratlys was seriously being discussed in Vietnam. Meanwhile, there were striking opinions from Hanoi accusing Mr. Luong and Mr. Phieu as those responsible for the 1999 and 2000 Treaties with China, while they were in office.

They, together with Do Muoi and Le Duc Anh, are the symbolic loyal followers of the Chinese communist Party. Medals were awarded to them, while Red China was openly annexing the Paracel and Spratly islands into Chinese territory. The CVP leaders wanted to show that *"Vietnam-China relationship was quite good"*, regardless of opposition from people of Vietnam, or of Qin Gang's rebuke towards Vietnam's Communist Party, or of Hu Jintao's anger at students protests. The Gold Star medal awarding ceremony took place solemnly, with Do Muoi's presence. (This is a method of personnel management that Chinese General Chen

Geng 陈赓 used when teaching the Vietnamese communists in 1950: *"Reward those with merit!"*)

Photo by RFA. Do Muoi (CPV Secretary General) is behind Le Kha Phieu (former CPV General Secretary) during the Medal Awarding ceremony. Do Muoi is still dressed in traditional Chinese ranking party style of 1950s, that now Chinese leaders have given up..

(1) Besides, there are other methods in preventing them from escaping Red Chinaa control: a) Ideological indoctrination (training when becoming a member: for example: 'to love the country is to love socialism'), b) Red China helps placing them in powerful postions, c) Money (a blogger said: if you can't buy Prime Minister Nuyen tan Dung by money, you can buy him by a lot of (a huge sum of) money), d) Penalty: death (Global Times has repeatedly reminded Hanoi leaders of it)

2.1.3.4.   Suppression Techniques:

2.1.3.4.1.   Overview

Vietnamese Communist leaders have strictly applied what Lenin called "**organization weapons**" in this situation. The communist party sets up different groupa or orgnizations through out the country. They are either social, political, professional, or charity…, .even governmetal agencies or commercial or industrial corporations are included in on group, It is called the **Fronts organization** in which the parrty plants "a cell" to lead and especially to contol its members. Two organizations that play a core role of leardership in the front organizaton are the communist party and Ho chi Minh Youth Union. In communist Vietnam, the front organization is the Fatherland Front.

Every citizen must be a member in one or many organization of the Fatherland Fatherland Front.

How does China run the show of direction of suffocating Vietnamese protests?

In the old days, there were one or a few people who served as puppets for foreign powers. Today, with Lenin's tactics, they are a large group of people- organized, commanded, disciplined, salaried with special favors. They are well trained, equipped with techniques as to how to carry out this mission. This is the mission of the Communist Party of Vietnam. This Party, especially, is reinforced and imbued with 'Ho Chi Minh's thoughts'. They only are taught to absolutely obey orders, not knowing the difference between right and wrong. Ethical integrity is obedience to their party. They are taught that fulfilling their duty as assigned by the party is noble and and is considered a duty to serve the country. " To love the party has a same meaning with to love the country". With the same pattern of thinking, Do Muoi, Secretary General of the CPV, a top cmmunist leader, publicly declared re. land dispute with China, in the third meeting of the Communist Party Central Committee (3rd plenum) in June 1992, that *"we must maintain socialism led by Communist Party of China. Socialism is an extremely important matter. The land issue is less significant, and could be "sacrificed" in exchange for Socialism".* Nong Duc Manh was not ashamed to speak to Hu Jintao's secretary as quoted: *"for the everlasting friendship between Vietnam and China, the Vietnamese leaders are willing to render all [to China]".* etc.

Therefore, anyone who protests China occupying Vietnam lands, will be liquidated by all means, including violence.

2.1.3.4.2. How do native Sino Puppets suppress demonstrations?

The party just gives a diretive to the Fatherland Front (properly the party cell that leads the concerend organiation) to suffocate all demonstraions against China, the Front just executes it. The entire Party network will be mobilized to carry out the order. The party networkin this case the Fatherland Front broadly spreads out in the entire country, everywhere, in all corners of the country, in hamlets and villages, in city wards and districts. It penetrates into the social strata, agencies, schools, companies, with a network of secret policemen deployed everywhere, in every social agency and in the military, etc.. In addition, the Hukou 戶口簿 (hộ khẩu) system or "household registration", is to control every member of each family living within a small geographical area throghout the country under the control of a local secret security team..

It is the cell that has aduty to identify who is who. So the party knows who is actively involved in organizing anti- China demonstrattions. Every means possible the party has, is used to neutralize those who would be involved and who is the leader: harrassments, arrests, isolations, pressure to be put on their family (parents or siblings), landlords who rent a shelter to the subjects, workplace (firing from jobs). Another tactic is to derange young people, dividing college students, creating suspicions and hatred among each other.

To prevent protests that Hu Jintao feared, the CPV ordered numerous policemen, security forces and military to control the rallying groups. Victims were arrested, then went through physical and mental torture. As a result, after being released from prison, victims no longer have the will to oppose the Party. At prison, the party uses Pavlovian brainwashing techniques, to cause damage to the victims' mental health, False creating a crime, such as "disturbed the public order", "violated national security",)... was used for prosecution. Another example: blogger Điếu Cày was prosecuted on tax evasion, even though this victim paid his tax. There were cases of school expulsion, threatening parents, wife, children, brothers and sisters. Authorities could pressure employers for job dismissal ...

Anyone determined to join the protests has to deal with many difficulties from the Party's police network. They have to use tricks to deceive or mislead the police. They have to have a courage to deal with methods of physical and mental oppression. Young Vietnamese are brave (dũng) in face of terrorizing threats while Vietnam's communist government is determined to protect the invaders.

Writer Nguyễn xuân Nghĩa talked about his case, when he intended to go from Hai Phong to Hanoi for demonstrations there on April 29: *"We were only nervous of the location leaking out. If so, police had already surrounded the area before we showed up. However, we had to escape first from home, before we could announce it. Friends joining the protests already knew what was going on. But for the international and overseas media, the news had to be out at the last minute".*

RFA: Mr. Nghia said he tried many times until to leave home in Hai Phong for Hanoi. According to him, every morning while doing exercises, a few security officers rode on motorbikes behind him. On the morning of the 25th, as usual, he jogged near his home, along with motorbikes following. Suddenly, Mr. Nghia jumped on the Hai Phong - Hanoi bus. The bus ran away about 3 km, from home, then it was followed by a security police car, with siren and lights blaring. This was a sign forcing the bus to stop. He then jumped down, and continued to run home… **(Thiện Giao, RFA correspondent, 04-29-2008)**

Other examples:

The following are cases of dissidents being detained by security police of the Communist regime and receiving harsh Staliinist measures in protests against the occupation of the Paracels and Spratlys:

Security police pressured a relative of a young man' who left Saigon for Hanoi to participate in anti- Chinese demonstrations:

- Young Lương Tuấn said he was fearless when expressing his political opinion, especially in matters related to the national territory. He said, while he was in Hanoi, his wife in Saigon was interrogated by police about her husband. (Thiện Giao, RFA: April 29, 2008)

Examples :Leninist/Stalinist measures used by police forces:

A Vietnanese communist secret service agent is using Judo technicks to deal with a young protester. **Any one dares to say that it's a Chinese who oppresses a Vietnamese?**

In front of everyone, the public witnesses brutal treatment of college student demonstrators. However, in prison, Vietnamese police authorities' actions are even more cruel. One victim is beaten until dying of a broken neck. Have the victims or the public ever resented the Chinese invaders for such cruel barbaric acts to that extent? This is a sophisticated tactic of the modern-day Chinese invaders, because they use the local Sino puppets to carry out that task.

Protests in front of Hanoi Dong Xuan Market:

-**Mr. Túc:** "They grabbed hands and legs, they carried, they pulled, they tore, they grabbed the head of Nguyễn Tiến Nam, some held his arms, some grasped his legs, some pulled his hair. He was carried like an animal. They took these people to another place, and now we don't know where they are jailed, how they were detained, we don't know at this moment. I see some people here. I have come here, wanting to telephone people, but now after coming here, I am unable to contact him ... (response to RFA, Viet Hung correspondent, April 29, 2008).

The police surrounded the protesters in front of Đồng Xuân Market, Hanoi, April 29, 2008. Photo provided by local activists in Vietnam.

-Example: police setting up ambush to trap student demonstrators.

 Mr. Đỗ Duy Thông: I have just been at Đồng Xuân market since this morning. I was there from one a.m. with everyone, disguised as motorbike taxi driver, or general laborer lying there till morning to wait for activists. When it was time for us to take action, Nghĩa, Hùng, and Tiến Nam raised up banners, while I was taking three photos, then the security police quickly appeared. They locked arms of three people behind their backs, bringing them to Đồng Xuân police station for crime check. So I took three photos (Việt Hùng, radio correspondent RFA 2008-04-29)

- Example of demanding the landlord to evict students, not allowing renting rooms for schoolers.

College student Kim Duy: Yes. When being bothered so much by police about their rental home, even if compassionate landlords wants to protect their beloved college students, they are afraid of security police's pressure. A college student temporarily resides at the rental place, the landlord has to abide by the laws: he has to obtain a temporary residence permit; he has to

report to the local security agency even if the student is absent one day, though the demand by security police to report continuously is an illegal act. Through it, these activities by the government have directly or indirectly impact on students education, because they have to move to another plcae. This is a threatening pressure from the government and police. Many college students have ost their renting privileges. *"During over 4000 years of history, Vietnamese people have strongly opposed to **assimilation** scheme by China. The torchlight politicizing needed to be boycotted and condemned so that the world is aware of."* (Viet Hung, April 29, 2008)

Hanoi plainclothes police and security forces blocked and arrested the anti-China demonstrators, while Beijing's Olympic torchlight was carried across Vietnam.

-Writing an anti-Chinese article, people could be arrested and prosecuted in court:

- Attorney Lê chí Quang wrote the article **"Beware of the Northern Empire"**, so he has been imprisoned since 2002. Many years later, Quang was brought to trial, imprisoned and tortured for 5 years in prison. It is said that he was barbarically tortured while imprisoned, his mind has been broken down.

- Reporter Điếu Cày Nguyễn Hoàng Hải was hunted because of writing blogs to protest China invading the Paracels and Spratlys. He fled to Da Lat, followed by police into his hidden place, and was finally arrested in April 2008. Two months later, the security police announced his detained location, while Reporters Sans frontières (RSF) called for the victim's unconditional release. Reason for the arrest? It was tax evasion. He was prosecuted in Court and punished with a 30-month prison sentence

- Nguyễn Anh Tuấn, a high-ranking party member, lost his position as Editor-in-chief of VietnamNet (March 26, 2008) because he published an article on Hoang Sa (Paracel) and Truong Sa (Spratly) Islands;

- Examples of protesters' arrests, at the scenes of street demonstrations or sit-in protests at home:

College student Bùi văn Toản of the University of Industries was arrested on September 13, 2008, detained for nearly two months and released on October 28, then placed under house arrest in Thai Binh.

College student Phạm Hồng Vỹ was arrested on December 6, 2008, for protesting against China spending US $29 billion dollars to search, explore and drill oil in the Spratly archipelago of Vietnam.

College student Phạm Thanh Nghiêm asked for protesting against China's invasion of Hoang Sa. Not successful, she was arrested at her home in Haiphong during a sitting in protest with a banner 'Paracels & Sprtlys belong ton Vietnam", without trial.

- Teacher Vũ Hùng, writer Nguyễn xuân Nghĩa, college student Nguyễn tiến Nam and many others (April 29, 2008) were arrested in front of Đồng Xuân market in Hanoi for protesting against China invading the Paracels and Spratlys. They were also brutally maltreated.

- Examples of economic control: the Party orders employers to cancel the job contracts, or not allowing the victims to work for a living.

Producer Song Chi lost her contract for making TV series TFS at "Ho Chi Minh City TV Station" (in Saigon) because of protesting China invading Hoang Sa-Truong Sa (May 10, 08). Producer Song Chi made the following statement in an article entitled "**Sadness With the Name of Vietnam**" "*Yet, a peaceful demonstration, moreover, a protest to oppose another country's aggressive act of invasion against our own country, is perfectly normal in any other nation. But in Vietnam, demonstrations are not allowed, even though they are peaceful....You already know that expresing such ideas is very tiresome*" (Tra Mi, RFA reporter, 2008-05-10)

RFA file photo - The Party succeeded in using barbaric repression measures, to eliminate the spirit of patriotism among Vietnamese college students who organizied or participated in the demonstrations opposing China invading the Paracels and Spratlys.

So what kind of government is it when it suppressed its college students protesting against a foreign nation occupying the Paracel and Spratly Archipelagos, as presented in this book? <u>**Do they represent people of Vietnam, or represent the invaders?**</u>

Blogger Măng and Blogger HT calls the CPV "**China's local Sino puppets** ruling Vietnam. Student Kim Duy implies the conspiracy **of Sinicization**, an **assimilatIon** of the people of Vietnam into the people of China, to be carried out by the CPV. These thoughts were also raised by Bloggers and journalists Người Buôn Gió, Phạm Doan Trang and Mẹ Nấm. They were later arrested for protesting China invading Hoang Sa (Paracel archipelago) and Truong

Sa (Spratly archipelago), and for denouncing General Secretary Nông Đức Mạnh, President Nguyễn minh Triết, Prime Minister Nguyễn Tấn Dũng, and National Assembly Chairman Nguyễn sinh Hùng who gave away to China Vietnam's Bauxite mine in the Central Highlands. It is those leaders who helped China set up a bridgehead in this strategic area from there she could move and take the Southern part of Vietnam..They are **real Sino puppets.**

The relationship with China presents a sensitive problem. The communists used shrewd tactics to suffocate all protests that relate to that relationship, even though a protestor just wears a blue T-shirt reflecting the spirit of protection of Paracels and Spratlys against Red China. Blogger Mẹ Nấm wore a blue T-shirt and was arrested. She was isolated from her 3-year-old daughter --despite the young little child need care and milk from a mother. Responding to AFP, on September 13, 2009, Ms Nguyễn Ngọc Như Quỳnh, owner of Mẹ Nấm blog, said that she was just released, after being confined twelve days in prison. Ms. Như Quỳnh was set free, after being arrested and jailed as a member of the group of three journalists and bloggers. Blogger Người Buôn Gió and female journalist Phạm Đoan Trang were held a few days, then released. According to AFP, Ms. Như Quỳnh also confirmed that the police asked her to stop writing the blog and she would be reunited with her daughter. And she obeyed.

Before being detained, blogger Mẹ Nấm had written extensively on Vietnam-China relations, including project to exploit bauxite in the Central Highlands, as well as the sovereignty issue on the Paracels and Spratlys archipelagos in the South China Sea. Như Quỳnh told AFP: the main reason for which she was arrested together with blogger Người Buôn Gió and journalist Đoan Trang, was that they advocated wearing blue T-shirts, calling for the suspension of bauxite mining project and confirming Vietnam's sovereignty over the Paracel and Spratly Islands. According to Như Quỳnh's mother, she herself wore that T-shirt in last July. According to an anonymous foreign diplomat in Vietnam, those three people were arrested for planning to produce more of those T-shirts.

2.2. **Being inactive, submissive, not daring to protect people against a killing by foreigners**

Afraid of China's threat, Vietnamese authorities chose not to take any action against harrassments, killings of fishermen in the Paracels, inluding sinking their boats by Chinese naval vessels No measures are used to prevent such things from happening, except for making the same statements for the past over two decades: "Historically, Hoàng Sa and Trường Sa have been within Vietnam's territorial waters".

a. Roger Milton, The Straits Times, Singapore, July 28, 2007 wrote: Senior Vietnamese military officers have now confirmed that in the July 9 clash, which was first reported in The Straits Times, one Vietnamese fisherman was killed and six were injured. One boat was sunk...Initially, it was understood that the skirmish had occurred near the Spratly Islands, but military sources now say it was further north in waters around the Paracel Islands. Asked why the Vietnamese navy had not defended the fishing boats, a military commander in Danang said: 'You must ask Hanoi's leaders about that'.

b. Hanoi (dpa) – August 30, 2007. Two Vietnamese fishing boats have been captured by the Chinese navy in waters near the disputed Spratly Islands and the 28 crew members are being held until their families raise money to pay a fine, Vietnamese authorities said Thursday.

c. The two boats were captured on August 21 just north of the Spratly Islands. "They said the Chinese navy told them they had violated Chinese waters and would have to pay a fine,"

d. Roger Milton, The Straits Times, July 19, 2007, Singapore

Tensions are rising between China and Vietnam on the sovereignty rights over the Spratly archipelago (quần đảo Trường Sa), after another violent clash, in this oil-rich offshore area. On September 7, Chinese naval vessels fired on several Vietnamese fishermen's fishing boats in the maritime waters near the Spratly islands, 350 km from Ho Chi Minh City. Military sources said a Vietnamese fisherman boat was sunk in this attack. One fisherman died and some others injured.

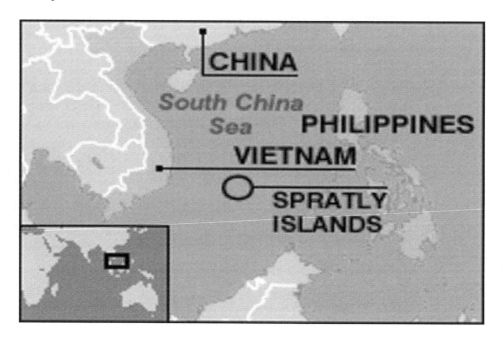

Professor Carl Thayer, an expert on Vietnam at the Australian Defense Academy, said: "Vietnamese naval officers say Chinese ships engaged in aggressive action for a while". Vietnamese officials also said there were minor clashes, when Vietnamese [fishermen's] boats encountered Chinese boats in the disputed maritime waters. Professor Thayer said: "China's actions are part of a common strategy to assert sovereignty, and to prevent Vietnamese fishermen from encroaching on their waters"

e. In first six months of 2007, *"five other ships with 60 fishermen have been seized by the Chinese and then returned."* In addition, Vietnam made a formal protest in July after the Chinese military fired on two Vietnamese fishing vessels, reportedly killing two fishermen.

f. Killing Thanh Hóa fishermen, January 8, 2005. China shot and killed 9 people, and captured a number of Vietnamese fishermen who were fishing in Vietnam's territorial waters, in the Gulf. Some boats were sunk. That incident scene was situated in the west of Gulf's delineating line, according to 2000 Agreement; i.e., it was within Vietnam's territorial sea. A nearby fisherman saw a colleague suddenly shot, and fled to Thanh Hóa, chased by a Chinese naval ship all the way to the Vietnam coast. The fisherman's boat was shot hundreds of times before the Chinese naval ship left.

g. The Chinese captured three Vietnamese fishing boats.

BBC, April 2, 2007. News from Vietnam: China seized three Vietnamese fishing boats of fishermen from Ly Son island district, Quảng Ngãi province. The three Vietnamese boats were seized by the Chinese while fishing in the Paracels on 3/25. A total of 41 people were on those three fishing boats. China sent three ships to Woody Island (đảo Phú Lâm) in the Paracels. A fishing boat owner, Mr. Trần Văn Rỡ was fined 6,000 yuan. Each of the remaining two ships was fined 140,000 yuan. It is not clear why China imposed those penalties. Later, China released Mr. Rỡ 's boat with 32 fishermen, so they could pay fines. Currently, China still holds two boats.

h. Vietland: News from Vietnam: at about 1:47pm on January 15, 2008, a Vietnamese fishing boat, number 91234-TS in Phú Yên province, was chased and sunk by Chinese Navy vessels. Via radio, they called for help, on channel 16 (156.8 Mhz). Before being sunk by a Chinese vessel, the boat owner reported the sinking location was at 12o50 North latitude and 113o40 East longitude, offshore of Nha Trang, 42 nautical miles northeast of the Spratly Islands. The Vietnamese Communist authorities, after having learned of rescue message, disseminted it on the emergency frequency, which was heard by many people. About bout two hours later, the Vietnmese media with the fake news reported on line that the Vietnamese fishing boat was sunk by the Chinese ship, at different location, at coordinates of 12o50 North latitude and 109o40 East longitude. It was about 80 nautical miles southeast of Đại Lãnh cape, off the coast of Ninh Hòa. An article in Tuổi Trẻ (Youth) newspaper reported that the Vietnamese fishing boat was sunk by "stranger ships".

i. The Straits Times, Jan 23, 2008: Qin Gang accused Vietnam's fishermen in the Spratly area of "violating China's territorial sovereignty, national sovereignty and China's right of governance". "China expressed serious concerns about this matter, and **has severely dealt with Vietnam". The statement of China's spokesperson was made while Vietnam's National Assembly Chairman Nguyen Phu Trong was on an official visit to the country.**

Usually, when fishermen of a nation infringe on another nation's territorial waters, the host nation never commit such barbaric acts as shooting and killing or sinking their fishing boats. In civilized nations, only fines are paid and violation citations issued. In this case the Chinese communists committed barbaric acts towards Vietnam's fishermen, deliberately ignoring the Socialist Republic of Vietnam. Vietnam's leaders apparently considered those matters as normal. Therefore, tt encouraged China to continue those acts and the killings of Vietnamese fishermen have continued.

2.3. At Beijing's request, Vietnam stopped humanitarian projects and cooperation with USA and others

Some specific cases:

a. Hospital Ship USS Peleliu: Accepting Vietnam's invitation, this ship came to Đà Nẵng on July 16, 2008. In two weeks being here, the ship offered charitable medical services, helping poor families who could not afford medical treatment. This hospital ship left Đà Nẵng on July 25, before the deadline, since China did not want the USA presence with such activties in Vietnam, though it is purely humanitarian. One report mentioned the bewildered surprise of over one hundred doctors and medical hospital staff on board, when it was suddenly ordered by Vietnamese authorities to leave Da Nang before the deadline. China did not allow foreigners to do such humanitarian work in Vietnam, though Vietnam's leaders have always talked about independence and sovereignty but silently submitted to China.

b. The Straits Times, Jan 23, 2008: Early last year (2007), there was a proposal to set up a Maritime Affairs Ministry to manage a public policy concerning maritime resource exploitation and the protection of sovereignty. But the proposed ministry has yet to materialize, a point that illustrates how tardy public policymaking can have important national consequences.

- Vietnam's leaders did not establish the Ministry of Fisheries, since the Sansha City 三沙 was already formed (2012). It is China's new governmental unit, to manage this territorial sea transferred from Vietnam. Therefore, the establishment of an SRV agency at the ministry level was no longer necessary.

c. Vietnam Spratly Tourist Agency (BBC April 19, 2004) was officially established. It was terminated after Beijing's objection.

To compete with China for tourism on Paracel Islands, Vietnam announced they organized a tour to the Spratly archipelago before March 30, 2008. In early April, Duong Xuan Hoi, Deputy Head of Traverling Tourist Department, a Vietnam Navy agency in Nha Trang who was also present on that 8-day trip with Gen Phạm van Tra, Minister of Defense, stated that next trips will be organized and they garanteed the trips will be safe, because those tourist attractions are on islands under Vietnam's sovereignty. Vietnam authorities announced another tour to take place in early April.. However, right at the beginning of the month, China reacted strongly to Vietnam bringing tourists to the Spratly Archipelago 南沙群岛 (Nansha/Nam Sa). A week earlier, Vietnam ambassador Tran Van Luat was called to China's Ministry of Foreign Affairs for criticism. Shortly after Vietnam's HQ996 tourist ship left the port, a Chinese Ministry of Foreign Affairs spokesman reiterated that China was unhappy about that trip, since Vietnam was still taking tourists to the Spratly islands despite China's strong opposition. Later, Vietnam Navy's Travel Agency in Nha Trang was asked: when would the next trip be? Answer: there was no intention to do so. Since then, the project is no longer mentioned.

2.4. Accepting China's acts of invasion, a participation in a crime:

The Paracel Islands: In 1956, communist Chinese military forces invaded Amphitrite (Tuyên Đức) area, east of the Paracel archipelago, belonging to Vietnam, while Ho Chi Minh was silent. Being silent is to consent. This is an accomplice to a crime.. Such acts are self-accusatory, and confirmed the previous scheme planned by Ho and his accomplices to sell-off Vietnam territorial waters to China, as they did officially in September 1958.

Then in 1974, Chinese invaders moved to occupy the west part of the archipelapo: Crescent Group. This area consisted of many reefs, and is situated west of the Paracel archipelago. and the Republic of (South) Vietnam navy bravely fought against the invaders. They shed blood to defend the islands, but failed. Ho and his associates once again sided with the hegemonic Beijing invaders.

About this Chinese invasion it should also be mentioned:

The Republic of South Vietnam Navy sent battleships to Drummond Island (đảo Duy Mộng) to recapture lands that had been seized by China.

Reports from Beijing: On January 17, the South Vietnam Navy landed on đảo Kim Ngân/Vĩnh Lạc of the Crescent Group and stormed Robert Island (đảo Cam Tuyền/Hữu Nhật) to remove China's flag. On the 18th, South Vietnam warships directly struck Chinese battleships 402 and 407, etc. Next morning on the 19th, the South Vietnam Navy occupied Duncan Island (đảo Quang Hòa/Sâm Hàng). The battle actually occurred on this island. When the battle started, the South Vietnam Navy swiftly attacked and sank a Chinese battleship. Later on, The Republic of South Vietnam Navy (RSVN) could not resist a large Chinese naval force, so they retreated to Triton Island (đảo san hô Tri Tôn), Money Island (đảo Quang Ảnh), Robert Island (đảo Cam Tuyền/Hữu Nhật)-- finally sailing home to Đà Nẵng, Vietnam.

China announced that South Vietnam had 4 deaths, 20 injured, over 100 missing, and 48 captured. The South Vietnam Navy also lost a battleship. That was information from Beijing.

A noteworthy fact is that, according to Chinese information, on February 1, 1974, when reporting the Paracels incidents, the Soviet radio station in Moscow blamed the Chinese leaders. While the Soviet Union responded to China's aggression, Vietnamese communists remained silent. The Communist Party of Vietnam has been criticized for missing an opportunity-- the support of Soviet Union in opposing this invasion. The archipelago was awkwardly sold. What can people say? Maybe it is best is to be silent.

(See Nguyễn Văn Canh, Communism on Vietnam Lands, Volume II, Pages 354-356, Kiến Quốc, 2002)

There was disdainful silence. To illegally transfer lands to enemies is a seriuos offense.

2.5. Accepting Beijing's public disdain is a diplomatic humiliation, but the CPV leaders considered it a normal matter.

Accepting this type of disdain is a challenge for any human conscience, and certainly a challenge for the people of Vietnam. It expresses a spirit of foreign dependence, though all the times they shout the slogans of **independence and sovereignty**. Clearly, Vietnam's leaders don't respect national honor. The notorious corruption case of PMU 18, or the East-West Highway construction with Japan's aid is an example.. This causes disrespect from the international community towards Vietnamese leaders. In annual Conferences of the financial sponsors, this subject is openly repeated. However, nothing changes. Japan representative of the group demanded Vietnam to take appropriate action to corret the problem or Japan will cut off all its aids. It was a painful warning. However, Vietnam's leaders kept silence, with no desire to change. Finally, Japan officially announced to cut off the aid to build the highway.

An other example; In 2001, Vietnam received a grant of $US 400 M from IMF to do preperartions for the free market economy to function properly. It has to produce all related legislations, setting up a system of insurance, retructuring the economy etc.. This is a grant in aid for four years, e.i. Vietnam doesn't have to pay back. Until 2003, IMF has disbursed $170 M to Vietnam, the IMF representative in Vietnam told the Vietnam Governor General of the National Bank that per contrach, IMF have hired a third party auditing corporation to do auditing the expenses. The Governor replied that in Vietnam we have a law that protect state secrecy, Vietanm could not release any details of the exepenses. The IFM representative said, per contrach when you signed, you knew that condition. He refuse the auditing. The IMF changes his idea, saying that now you just write down how you spent the money. It is enough for me to convince the IMF Board to approve and continue to release the money. The Governor still refuses to requirments and finally, IMF cut off the aid and withdrew the remaing 230 million..

Why did such a thing happen? **Answer**: the "moral values" pursued by CPV are completely different from the common values accepted by ordinary people and also in civilized countries. What happened is merely a reflection of a basic principle of Marxist-Leninist ideology that guides Vietnam communist leaders in action. They have been taught that, in any social relations, including such personal relationships as those of members of a family: husband and wife, father and son, brothers and ssters… , there is always a "**struggle**" in which "**Who wins over Whom**" is a guidance. When you just think of winning in a fight, any means and any tactics are considered good, applicable, so long as you win.. That is the value to be promoted and every one is encouraged to follow. As a result, any treaty that a communist nation signs with a opposing country is just a tactic to call off the war temporaily. When they become strong, they will tear off the document and launch a counter attack.

The communits do not accept national honor as a value to be followed. In this case, CPV leeaders just rely on Red China for support to hold power, though they are ill treated.

Chinese foods and products contain toxic substances. The Straits Times, Singapore 28/8/2007. The Vietnamese ambassador to China was called in by the Foreign Ministry earlier this month and lectured about Beijing's unhappiness over how the Vietnamese media has highlighted the furor over tainted food and counterfeit goods from China. Diplomatic sources say Vietnam's Ambassador Tran Van Luat replied that his nation's media reported the tainted food and forged products scandal objectively without maligning China. But Beijing disagreed and indicated that any recurrence could lead to Vietnam's exports encountering problems at the Chinese border.

Nguyen Khanh, RFA correspondent, 22 August 2007, talked about this issue as follows:

Information experts in Hanoi added: the Vietnamese Ambassador to Beijing is continuously under pressure from China. It was reported that after midnight, China's Ministry of Foreign Affairs arrogantly asked Vietnam's Ambassador to come over, for questioning on issues that could adversely affect their bilateral relations.

Top Vietnam leaders are scorned disdainfully, even during official visits (as guests):

This is the case of Vietnam President Nguyễn minh Triết while officially visiting China. In May 2007, Nguyễn minh Triết went to Beijing for a pre-announced official visit. Before that, during April, the Chinese navy shot and killed Vietnamese fishermen while fishing on the Spratly Archipelago, because of their violating China's sovereign rights over territorial waters. Triết remained silent, with a big smile, eyes closed, and stepped forward in greeting, with no opposition, no postponing or canceling of trip, to preserve his honor -- and while China made no apology on that matter. The Vietnam communist leader expressed no opposition.

The same thing happened with Nguyễn phú Trọng, National Assembly Chairman, visiting China in January 2007 while Vietnamese fishermen were killed by the Chinese navy.

Such incidents were not accidental, including Qin Gang's public statements regarding the anti-China student protests.

In the relationships between nations, never were such disrespect acts of public disdain committed at that level. In the history of Chinese colonial rule, there is no mention of such disrespected behavior from China's Empereur toward Vietnam's Kings. No disrespectfull treatment even occurred with Vietnamese envoys. People witnessed the subumissive spirit of CPV leaders. The past hidden relationships between Chinese leaders and Ho chi Minh and affiliates did not reveal such bad behavior and treatment from China. It was only later that information shows the Chinese leaders's disdain to Vietnamese leaders. During the Land Reforms, while the Chinese advisers were directing Vietnamese local group to brutally persecute and kill Vietnam's land lords, Ho Chi Minh remained silent, even though he knew of this matter. Party leaders such as Nông đức Mạnh, and state leaders such as Nguyễn minh Triết, Nguyễn tấn Dũng etc... have publicly accepted that ill treatment. They were smiley, and even declared that the relations between the two parties and the two countries are *"raised to a new height"*.

2.6. Chinese in Vietnam acted as living on China

They were protected by Vietnamese police, while raising banners "Hoang Sa and Truong Sa belong to China". On the other hand, young Vietnamese living in Vietnam are suppressed and harassed by their own government, when advocating that the Hoàng Sa 黄沙 (Paracel) and Trường Sa 南沙 (Spratly) Achipelagos belong to Vietnam.

2.6.1. A Blogger's Statement

A blogger in Saigon wrote this following report, during the Olympics torch relay in Saigon:

"China announced sending troops into Vietnam to protect the Olympics torch relay"; "Alert our compatriots of China's campaign of invasion".

"For many years, China has conspired to invade and occupy Vietnam. China has flooded a million militia members into Vietnam. They occupy areas and turn them into military bases, and also control many critically important regions in Vietnam.

The Vietnamese communist originated from "Minh Hương 明香" (Ming dynasty descendants) are ruling Vietnam, in the role of the local Sino puppets. They are carrying out an open door policy, allowing Chinese to freely travel everywhere, snooping around, freely doing business and freely accumulating merchandise for sale.... Meanwhile, Vietnamese people cannot freely travel, but are strictly controlled by hộ khẩu/hukou 戶口 system (family registration) copied from China. Building trans-national highways across Vietnam, and promoting open border crossings help Chinese civilian people and troops penatrate into Vietnam. (Allowing) Killings of fishermen and attacking their boats openly and freely in coastal areas, with no objection from Vietnam's government,. instead, setting up a Vietnam-China comprehensive cooperation program is to formalize the presence of Chinese in the armed forces, in security agencies and Chinese civilians spread out inside Vietnam with the purpose to transfer the management of the country with respect to the economy, markets, schools, natural resources, lands, etc. to Chinese administrators…

"The announcement of the presence of China Security forces to protect the Olympics Torch Relay, is to formalize the presence of China's military on Vietnamese territory. An evidence shows that previously while Vietnamese protested against China seizing the Paracels and Spratlys, Han Chinese officials ordered a bunch of Chinese security forces to arrive in front of China Embassy, holding flags and banners declaring "Hoàng sa (Paracels), Trường Sa (Spratlys) are blood of China" (blood of robbery and invasion).

"Evidence?- the unfairly oppressed Vietnamese people (Dân Oan) across many provinces have submitted complaints and protested against being constantly oppressed, harassed, terrorized, beaten and strangled by the outlaw gangsters. Those violent and wicked people are Minh Hương Chinese among the Chinese gangsters and Chinese security forces. In decades, they have learned how to speak and write the Vietnamese language as a Vietnamese".

Vietnamese people shouldn't be misled by those Vietnamese communist –sino lackeys (Việt Gian CS) or local Sino puppets ruling Vietnam. They are destroying our country., destroying our natural resources, market economy, environment, waters/rivers, food, healthcare, etc. ..Their orders are to firmly safeguard a consolidated united China (including Vietnam, Tibet, Laos, Cambodia, Burma, Malaysia, Korea, Australia ...)" -- Blogger HT

2.6.2. Vietnam police in uniform protecting Chinese Communist Youth during the Olympics torch relay

1). Uniformed policemen protected those young communist Chinese demonstrators. They called for defending China's Paracels and Spratlys in December 2007, and during the 2008 Olympics torch relay in Saigon, in April 2008.

Vietnam authorities allowed the Vietnamese uniformed policemen to publicly protect 30 young Chinese who demonstrated in front of the Chinese Embassy. They blatantly carried the banner *"the Paracels and Spratlys belong to China"*. Vietnam police even protected hundreds of young Chinese dressed in white sportswear, with Beijing Olympics badges and carrying red China flags, blatantly and arrogantly marching on Vietnam's streets. They noisily spoke the Chinese language, as if walking on Beijing streets. Vietnamese Communist leaders have assisted young Chinese to carry out activities in Vietnam as ihey do in mainland China.

Under the protection of Vietnam Police, this Chinese Parade on Saigon's streets has posed a challenge to the Vietnamese people. China's presence has been blatant in Vietnam. Meanwhile, Viet college students have been chased, arrested, harassed, terrorized, hunted, and blocked on many streets. They were prohibited to gather or demonstrate. Vietnam communist leaders are afraid of those anti-China protests that upset Beijing's invaders.

Dan Oan danoan@voiceofvietnam.org: **An ironic event on January 8, 2008**: About 30 Chinese citizens carrying flags and banners "The Paracels and Spratlys are Drops of China's Blood" in front of the Chinese Embassy, to affirm their sovereignty over these two archipelagos belonging to Vietnam. Those Chinese demonstrators were solemnly protected by Vietnam's security forces. They demonstrated with no difficulty.

On January 4, 2008 and January 8, 2008. Vietnam communist authorities allowed Chinese tourists carrying China flags to demonstrate in front of their communist China Embassy, yelling out the slogan *"Hoàng Sa and Trường Sa are China's flesh and blood"*. It is an act of selling off the nation, which had never happened in history of Vietnam and the world. It only derived from the acts of the treasonous CPV.

2). On 4/29, communist Chinese youth swamped Saigon. A blogger called it chaotic.

RfA news on December 12, 2007. A large crowd of 150-200 Chinese from youth to middle age people were standing at a corner of the Rex Hotel. They held dozens of large China flags, singing and dancing. They all wore their white Olympic uniforms with bloody red letters.

A blogger reported: "They displayed their fangs and claws to our Vietnamese people. My anger was as like fire burning. I almost ran my motorbike through this barbaric crowd, no matter what..... But the inherent fear pulled me back. I called. Five minutes later, the police force dissipated them from the Rex Hotel. The entire group walked along Le Loi ave, shouting out loudly, waving flags. The security forces continued to walk behind them. They gathered at the park on 9/23 next to Bến Thành market, to continue dancing. The security police continued to guide them toward Trần Hưng Đạo Ave.

"In the afternoon. at 14:00 on April 29, 2008, wandering around..... ..."

Chinese Youth from China came over and rallied, guided and protected by the Socialist Republic of Vietnam uniformed police forces.
Photo by Ho Lan Huong

2.6.3. Raising banners demanding to unify with China, at the former Republic of (South) Vietnam Natioal Assembly Building in Saigon

Blog Mr. Dohttp://blog.360.yahoo.com/blog-i6NVJtsyc6fL1iElqBL11pf3_ao-?cq=1: "At the torch relay in Saigon on April 29, 2008, in front of the former Republic of (South) Vietnam Ntional Assembly, Blog of Mr Do questioned: Chinese people stood in the middle of Saigon and publicly yelled: *"Firmly maintain a unified nation"*. What does it mean? Meanwhile, the Vietnamese are not permitted to say: "The Paracels - Spratlys belong to Vietnam". The answer is, if we look at a Chinese map, there are three blue and yellow lines under Hainan Island. These lines are symbols for Hoàng Sa 黄沙 (Paracel), Trường Sa 南沙 (Spratly) and Trung Sa

中沙 (Zhongsha). The Chinese Youth informed Vietnam's communist leaders of China's determination to unify this fatherland".

Blogger HT explained: the banner "Unify Fatherland" that the Chinese Youth raised up in front of the old National Assembly building in Vietnam means: **Vietnam is in the plan to be unified with China.**

"堅決支持祖國統一"= "Firmly support the unification of the fatherland".

2.6.4. Communist Chinese Youth blatantly live in Saigon as a 5th army, publicly in front of the Vietnamese people and communist authorities.

Thanh Tin wrote:

"Alert: A newspaper notified that Chinese are disguided as employees of travel company. They brought Chinese soldiers into Vietnam. They rented hotels and provided robes for the tourists who then are disguised Buddhist monks. They traveled everywhere in the city, seeking information on the topography of Vietnam, in preparation for a massive invasion".

"Communist Chinese officers hold the yellow Buddhist robes, preparing to disguise themselves as monks ..."

Monday 4/21/2008 A group of Chinese travelers rented hotels on Lê Duẩn street, Hà Nội. Every day they wear religious Buddhist robes, walking throughout the city, begging for food. Hanoi police recently discovered that group of suspicious travelers. They rented Tuấn Hương hotel on Lê Duẩn street, but did not report their temporary residency. The Chinese visitors were sponsored by Nam Long Travel Company to enter Vietnam beginning 4/10. The Vietnamese 'authorities" levied administrative fines on the Tuan Huong hotel, and also requested the Nam Long company to control and clear-out those "special" visitors.

2.6.5. Chinese People and China Flags on Saigon streets

Nguyễn Khanh, Radio RFA correspondent, 2008-05-02: The sacred Olympic torch of 2008 had already left Vietnam. It went to Macao within a few hours, then returned to mainland China, to start a new journey before entering Beijing stadium, in the opening ceremony organized on August 8, 2008.

Photo Ho Lan Huong

Photo Ho Lan Huong

To prevent anti-China demonstrations, security was maximized for the Beijing Olympics torch relay at "Ho Chi Minh city" on 4-29-2008.

The torch traveling across many different countries drew great attention to everyone. This is important not because of the roadmap, nor the meaningful sport, but the massive anti-China demonstrations in several places to protest Beijing authorities suppressing the Tibetan people. China failed to improve human rights, as committed to with the international community, seven years ago, when they awarded China the honor to organize the Olympics, the world's largest sports competition.

In only two places did the torch pass without any obstacles: Pyongyang and Saigon. The first place was Pyongyang, North Korea's capital. Under government directives, from early morning, hundreds of thousands of people lined up along both sides of the streets, waving flags to welcome the sacred torch. The second place was Saigon city in South Vietnam. Here, all plans to protest against China occupying Hoàng Sa and Trường Sa islands were suffocated by Vietnam's government. Several people were arrested. Some were released. Some were imprisoned in hidden plcaces, somewhere.

The Beijing Olympic Torch arrived and left Saigon, leaving behind a dark red trail on Vietnam territory: a massive display of red China flags, and thousands of Chinese people parading on the streets of Vietnam, surprising the Vietnamese people. This remarkable event is the topic chosen by our Vietnamese Language Department, sent to our listeners as part of our Magazine's Weekly Story on Current Affairs. This week's magazine was arranged in collaboration with Nam Nguyên in Bangkok, and Nguyễn Khanh and Trà My in Washington. This article was read by Thiện Giao:

"Only Chinese people"

People, flags, and China maps flooded Saigon streets, in the Beijing Olympics torch relay on 4-29-2008. The 2008 Beijing Olympics Torch entered Saigon, was carried across several streets in several hours then on the journey to Hong Kong. That torch was not in Saigon long, but it has left many thoughts and grievances in the hearts of Saigon residents.

It was right in downtown of this city. On the evening of April 29, people only saw China flags and Chinese people speaking Chinese language. All are Chinese whlle a very few curious Vietnamese as outsiders observed in silence.

"Very crowded. The majority are Chinese. They hung flags and cheered loudly. No Vietnamese people there. I saw that all flags were China flags. I know they were Chinese, but I don't know whether they were Chinese residents or Chinese from China".

A Vietnamese woman saw the Olympic torch relay ceremony on April 29, and related it to Tra Mi, reporter of Radio Free Asia. In a hastily written e-mail from Saigon, a journalist recalled:

"Friends, I see Vietnamese people looking at the torch as a strange object, while thousands of Chinese people cheered. There were Chinese security police also. When my friend used his camera to take a photo, he was interrupted by a security guard. He objected in Vietnamese, and that guy yelled back in Chinese".

The success of the torch relay campaign was the first effort of premier Nguyen Tan Dung. Dung flew to Saigon for a few days in advance, to arrange a plan, then gave it to Truong hoa Binh, a deputy prime minister for implementation.

2.6.6. The Chinese criminal gangster activities of killing people are also protected by Vietnam police. Vietland June 29, 2008:

"A Chinese gang member beat someone to death in the middle of Hanoi. This incident was ignored.

(Photo of a Chinese gang member)

On the evening of June 29, Nguyen Van Ha transported engineer Phung Luu Trung (born 1975, residing at Water Resources University Complex) by motorbike. At the three-way intersection of Luong The Vinh & Nguyen Trai, a collision occurred with a motorbike Best BKS 29L6-1010, driven by a young Chinese. Then both parties quarreled about the collision. According to witnesses, at the start of quarreling, the Chinese biker used his mobile phone to call his gangster members, speaking Chinese. Then six Chinese gangsters flocked to the scene with pistols and iron bars, attacking Phùng Lưu Trung. Seeing the crowd of aggressive Chinese people, Nguyễn Văn Hà fled the scene. Phùng Lưu Trung was slow to flee, so he was beaten to death at the scene, with a fractured skull, by those Chinese thugs.

Hanoi police investigated this matter in one week, released the news, but concealed the fact that Phung was dead, killed by six Chinese gangsters right on Hanoi streets. People in Hanoi have been upset with the flood of aggressive Chinese residents, who ruthlessly disrespect Vietnamese citizens and blatantly view Vietnam as their own country. Meanwhile, Vietnamese citizens do not have the privilege of legal protection".

2.6.7. China demands change in textbooks.

With no hesitation, China even directly demanded that the CPV education be changed, preparing for total Chinese domination. China wants to lay a foundation for this project. So education is the most important thing to do. With such move, Sinicization will be gradually realized.

Being aware that education provided to young gnerations in the elementary and secondary schools about Vietnam history, is to strengthen the spirit of patriotism, China demanded Vietnam to rewrite Vietnam history lessons in textbooks, about Vietnam-China relations. They hope to kill the spirit of patriotism in Vietnam. Lessons on the anti-French colonial period, periods of fighting against Chinese invaders from the 10th century starting from the Ly dynasty and recent Vietnam history, the border Sino-Viet battles in 1979 need to be altered.

Author Edward C. O'Dowd, in his book "*Chinese Military Strategy In The Third Indochina War: The Last Maoist War*" Routledge, London and New York, 2007 wrote:

"On January 27, 2001, during a reception in Hanoi at 33 Pham Ngu Lao (Hanoi), China Ambassador Qui Jianquo and Chinese Military Attaché Colonel Han Yujia told Phạm văn Trà, National Defense Minister of Vietnam, that they received direct orders from Beijing saying: China was offended by Vietnamese textbooks discussing the hostility between China and Vietnam in the Third Indochina War, about China attacking Vietnam, about China supporting the communist Khmer Rouge. Beijing opposed the descriptive view of Chinese leaders as a solidarity team…. with an intent to jeopardize the warm relations between two nations.

In February 2002 on the occasion of Lunar New Year (Tết), Jiang Zemin, General Secretary of the Communist Party of China visited Hanoi. Jiang pressured Vietnam leaders Mạnh and Lương to change the terms used in Vietnamese history textbooks. Jiang demanded to re-examine the views about China's border operations (Sino-Vietnam war) in 1979, to alleviate China's role in supporting the communist Khmer Rouge. Jiang even told Mạnh and Lương to gently describe China's invasion during the imperial periods (before 1909), and to cherish China's support to Vietnam during the Indochina War II (Vietnam War)..."

2.6.8. China's Orders and Vietnam's Media

CPV policies on media are clear: communication is an important tool, to serve the Party, to serve the interests of China's expansionism. Media has the communication power that shapes the thinking of Vietnamese people toward their enemies. It is a tool for Sinicization. The Party does not hesitate to admit that the CPV's media has become an extension of the People's Republic of China, openly advocating for China, on Vietnam lands. The Chinese communist Party provides scuh a guidance to the media of the Socialist Republic of Vietnam (SRV).

a. A blogger in Vietnam wrote: "February 17 of 2009 marked 30 years of the Vietnam-China northern border war in 1979 (Sino-Vietnamese War/Third Indochina War). It is also the 30th anniversary of the deaths of thousands of our fellow countrymen and soldiers, defending our lands and borders. But nearly a thousand Vietnam news agencies nationwide were ordered not to say a word. It is unfair to not write a word to mention this fact, unfair to not recall the tragic and noble sacrifices of our fellow countrymen and soldiers, in this battle to defend our nation! Meanwhile, a publisher at naional level even published a translated Chinese book, praising Chinese soldiers for having come to punish Vietnam! Wow, just to please the Chinese leaders, to seek a support for the (CP) party. Thus, we show ingratitude to. and insult to the soul of the fallen who sacrificed their lives to protect the country. The (CP) party aspires to survive by this means and how could I continue to adhere to it?

The Du Lich magazine (Tourism) - The Kỷ Sửu New Year issue was suspended for a few months, for **printing articles to show gratitude to our soldiers who sacrificed to defend the Spratlys**. The magazine was suspended. Some people said those articles touched on a "sensitive" matter", **RFA, October 30, 2009**. More important are the following two articles, mentioning the patriotism of Vietnamese people fighting against the "Northern invaders" in history. During that time, they were published in this magazine:

1) *"Tản Mạn Đảo Xa"* (Scattered Stories About A Far Island). This article was written by reporter Trung Bảo, son of Nguyễn Trung Dân, deputy editor-in-chief of Tourism magazine, to celebrate the spirit of patriotism expressed by college students and young people of Saigon, after China established Sansha 三沙 district in November 2007 on Hainan Island to manage the two archipelagos of Vietnam.

2) An article entitled *"Kịch Thơ Hận Nam Quan"* (Poetry Script on the Sorrow of Nam Quan Pass) by poet Hoàng Cầm. This article highlighted the spirit of patriotism of scholar Nguyễn Phi Khanh (1355-1429). He advised his son Nguyễn Trãi to return home, and support the King's revenge, instead of crying. The Chinese invaders captured Phi Khanh made him a prisoner, and took him to Kim Lăng city, China. Tearfully saying farewell to his father at Nam

Quan Pass, Nguyễn Trãi was advised to return home, to fight for revenge and be patriotic. Later, Nguyễn Trãi became a scholar, a nationalist, a strategist for Lord Bình Định Vương Lê Lợi. Under their leadership, the people of Vietnam defeated Ming Chinese invaders at Chi Lăng Pass in 1427. Chinese general Liễu Thăng, the commander in chief of the invading Chinese armed forces was killed in this battle. Vietnam regained its independence after ten years of Resistance War.

Those two articles expressed gratitude to those Vietnamese soldiers who died in battles against China. Tourism magazine expressed an anti-China spirit, so it was suspended. Nguyễn Trung Dân, deputy editor-in-chief of this magazine had his business license withdrawn. His job was suspended. Dozens of employees were fired, including Nguyễn Quốc Thái, his assistant Nguyễn Trung Dân.

To eliminate people's spirit of patriotism in Vietnam society is to execute what China has demanded. It has been executed by the highest agency controlling Vietnam's media. In January 2001, Chinese ambassador Qui Jianquo, together with Jiang Zemin, in February 2002 demanded changes in Vietnamese history on Sino-Vietnamese relations.

The CPV leaders are unashamedly executing this policy. They try to take side with China, even though they face huge challenges from the people of Vietnam.

b. Vietnam media plays a spokesman role for the Communist Party of China, to propagandize China's military operations on Vietnam territory.

The CPV's Electronic News has eagerly transmitted news for China's propaganda, promoting the idea that the Spratly islands is China's territory. This "Electronic News of the Vietnam Communist Party", is an official propaganda agency of the Party's Central Committee. On September 4, 2009, it translated and printed an article from communist Chinese newspapers: "Global Times" and "Pheonix" to publicize Chinese Navy military exercises on the Paracel and Spratly Archipelagos, with a tacit recognition that these archipelagos belong to China. This Electronic News is controlled by editor-in-chief Đào Duy Quát, deputy Head of the "Central Committee on Thoughts and Culture". The following is the article:

http://www.cpv.org.vn/cpv/Modules/News/NewsDetail.aspx?co_id=30127&cn_id=358460

(Vietnam Communist Party) - 8/16/2009. After carrying out the maritime escort duty, the Chinese escort fleet entered the South China Sea, to conduct exercises, with a horizontal line-up of supplies. It was in the spirit of "take a step, practice a step, study a step". On the way back while returning to the bases, the escort fleet conducted military drills and studied combat methods, focused on testing, and improved capabilities of combat command, security distances, and mobile defenses.

On 8/18/2009, the escort fleet consisting of 100 officers and soldiers, reached Fiery Cross reef (đá Chữ Thập) in the Spratly Archipelago, to proceed with supplies and logistics, and to review facilities and soldiers' activities on the island, also, to bringing two helicopter transporting ships "Shenzhen" and "Huangshan" to the island where drill exercises were conducted for helicopters taking off and landing, and the airborne task forces' landing.

In a statement to soldiers on the island, the escort Nam Hai Fleet's deputy commander emphasized: "Regardless of being soldiers escorting or defending the island, they have the same mission to protect the national interests. Hopefully, soldiers are trained to well defend the border on the southern sea of the Nation. At 9:30, on 8/18/2009, the fleet left the island, and continued its journey returning to its military bases.

On August 24, 2009, the Chinese Navy began a two-month period of parachute training. These exercises were kick-started from an airport runway on the Paracel archipelago. It is considered to be a training activity, to practice aircraft landing for the Chinese navy. One of the new noticeable military training activities in 2009 is the parachute training with helicopters, from an airport runway on the Paracel archipelago".

c. RFA 12/22/2009 -- PLA Posters in Saigon

In early December 2009, a large size poster in "Ho Chi Minh City" (Saigon) was installed to mark the anniversary day of the Vietnam People's Army on 12/22/2009. The poster in front of the Red Cros Office s in Phú Nhuận district, Sàigòn, had a symbolic image of China's Liberation Army, not carrying the traditional AK to represent soldiers of Vietnam People's Army. The drawing image was identical to China's photos in Sina.com. It was discovered by a blogger, so HCM city government took down this poster. On December 12, a similar poster was erected in front of the People's Committee headquarters in District 4, Saigon. Another was erected in front of the Center for Advanced Politics of the District Party Office. Interviewed by RFA Radio, the Director of the Department of Culture, Sports and Tourism Nguyễn thành Rung replied: any wrong-doing employee would be "reviewed".

d. Vietnam bloggers arrested over China shirt protest

- HANOI (Reuters) - Vietnamese police has arrested two bloggers and a journalist for their involvement in a plan to print T-shirts opposing China's investment in a bauxite mining project and its claims over disputed islands, sources said. The arrests underscore how sensitive Vietnam considers relations with China while Hanoi faces the challenge of keeping public opinion in check as Internet usage blossoms -- and where it draws a line for dissidents to follow.

Nguyen Ngoc Nhu Quynh, 30, who blogged under the name "Me Nam", or Mother Mushroom, was arrested on **September 2** for "abusing democratic rights" and harming national security, her mother said by telephone from the beach town of Nha Trang.

"About 10 or 15 police came to arrest her at around midnight," said the mother, Nguyễn Thị Tuyết Lan - *by **John Ruwitch**.*

RFA: "Arrested for wearing patriotic slogans"

Hà Giang, RFA reporter, 2009-07-23

Blogger Quỳnh Như was detained by the security forces, because of wearing a T-shirt with the slogan "SOS, Keep It Green, Security for Country".

Photo courtesy of blogger Dũng Đô Thị

Young Vietnamese wearing advocating T-shirts "Keep It Green, Security for Country" on Hanoi streets 7-18-2009.

We were informed that blogger Quỳnh Như, a young lady from Nha Trang, owner of blog "Mẹ Nấm" was detained and interrogated by security forces: wearing such a slogan would jeopardize the national security.

-Last Friday (September 09), police in Hanoi arrested Pham Doan Trang, a journalist with the pioneering online news portal Vietnamnet, saying she had "violated national security", editor-in-chief Nguyen Anh Tuan said.

Those two arrests followed the detention of Bui Thanh Hieu, who blogged under the name "Người Buôn Gió" *(Wind Trader)*.

Like many Vietnamese, the three opposed China's claims of sovereignty over the Spratly and Paracel Islands in the South China Sea. They were also critics of a government plan to partner with a Chinese state-owned company to exploit bauxite reserves in Vietnam's Central Highlands.

e. In May 2009, Vietnam's Ministry of Industry & Trade cooperated with China's Ministry of Commerce to publish a bilingual Sino-Vietnamese electronic newspaper. It posted an article in the Vietnamese section about the statement of Qin Gang, spokesman for China's Ministry of Foreign Affairs from Beijing, asserting that the archipelagos of Paracels and Spratlys indisputably have belonged to China. It was translated from Chinese media. Officials from Vietnam's Ministry of Commerce explained that the website with ".vn" is the domain and responsibility of Vietnam's government, but "managed and produced" in Beijing.

f. Two managers of Dai Doan Ket newspaper of the Vietnam Fatherland Front (VFF), were removed from office because of "violating the Media Law".

Mr. Dinh Duc Lap, member of the Central Committee of Vietnam Fatherland Front, confirmed with BBC that Mr. Ly Tien Dung, editor-in-chief and Dang Ngoc, Deputy editor-in-chief received official discipline letters.

This newspaper printed a controversial article

In February, Thái Duy wrote an article openly stating that, after 1975, "a foreign model of

socialism is still unfamiliar with Vietnam, but the National Assembly unanimously supported it. From this serious mistake, platform and policies are no longer derived from the people's interests. The relations between the Party and people are no longer attached as before".

7. Arrested because of the slogan "PARACELS & SPRATLYS BELONG TO VIETNAM"

http://thongtinberlin.de/thoisu/bibatvikhauhieuhsts.htm

Blogger Điếu Cày Nguyễn Văn Hải, a former soldier from North Vietnam, was brought to trial on the morning of September 10, 2009 after being imprisoned nearly five months, on a criminal charge of "tax evasion". He was arrested in April because of his article against China's invasion.

(RFA) Police suppressed journalist Điếu Cày.

g. In 2001, after writing the article *"Be Alert of the Northern Empire"*, attorney Lê chí Quang was arrested and sentenced to five years in prison.

2.6.9. The security forces openly suppressed individuals who speak out: Hoàng Sa (Paracel) and Trường Sa (Spratly) belong to Vietnam.

They were arrested, beaten, and their properties confiscated. They were evicted from their homes, losing their jobs, and prosecuted at court.

a. "On the morning of 11/27/2009, dozens of multi-level security officials from Ministry, citiy, Hai Bà Trưng ward and Bách Khoa town policemen swarmed into the Ta Quang Buu neighborhood, near the Minh Chau bookstore, to arrest five workers at a coffee shop.

Reason for this arrest: since 11/9, some banners "The Paracels & Spratlys belong to Vietnam" were hanging in two coffee shops. The shop owners refused to remove them. Security forces confiscated two banners which had been rolled up, hung on the wall, and because of being exposed to the weather , the banners would be rolled out by themselves and people look at them.

Those arrested included Mr. Võ Đức Toàn, 40 years old, Ms. Trương Thị Lan, 33 years old, Ms. Nguyễn Thị Thêm, 65 years old, Mr. Trương văn Phòng, 30 years old, Mr. Trương văn Thành, 32 years old. The entire group of people above were detained at Bách Khoa police station. Until midnight, they were released on 11/27. The security police constantly summoned and threatened them for imprisonment for several years. Van, Bách khoa police station's deputy chief, seriously swore to put them in jail. If not, he would sexually harass their sons. Two coffee shops' assets were completely confiscated -- including tables, chairs, bowls, trolleys, goods, etc., worth nearly 5 million dong.

Mr Trương Văn Phòng was brutally beaten by security forces, when he brought the outdoor canvas with printed slogans to the police station. Police swarmed the renting residence of Ms Nguyễn Thị Thêm at Phương Mai town, searched her home, and ordered the landlord to evict her immediately. Ms Thêm had no place to live. She alternately stayed overnight at her relatives. Dozens of security officers ransacked Mr. Võ Đức Toàn's family home, and took away many of his valuable belongings. Mr Võ Đức Toàn admitted constructing and hanging the two banners mentioned above: "The Paracels & Spratlys belong to Vietnam". Mr. Toàn and Ms. Lan have two small children, a 6-year-old granddaughter and a 3-year-old nephew. His family was prohibited to sell sweets, thus having no livelihood, while their assets were completely confiscated. They endured a very difficult life, being threatened with imprisonment solely for expressing patriotism.

We strongly condemn the communist security police's behavior towards those patriotic citizens, and urgently demand the media and individuals, in Vietnam and overseas to condemn this barbaric repression as well as help the patriotic Vietnam citizens through extreme hardships, under the communist dictatorship. Contact Mr Võ Đức Toàn +84956791436. Email:

nguyendinhthang2009@gmail.com

b. Ms. Phạm Thanh Nghiên, the sit-in protester in Hải Phòng with ta banner *"The Paracels & Spratlys belong to Vietnam"* will be brought to trial in Hải Phòng city court on December 17, 2009. She was the last one in the group struggling for 'democracy" arrested during the months of August and September last year in Hà Nội and Hải Phòng. Their banners expressed the spirit of patriotism, but irritated the two communist governments of Vietnam and China. Phạm Thanh Nghiên, 32-year-old, a sistership partner with activist/attorney Lê Thị Công Nhân, was imprisoned on September 17, 2008. For a year, her family was prohibited from seeing Nghiên, and had no information about her whereabouts or her health. In countries respecting human rights, the laws of criminal procedures toward the inmates and their families do not allow such treatment. At that tine, she was arrested and imprisoned on September 11, 2008, then released the next day, but was placed in house arrest with security agents' presence before her home, until September 17, 2008, while sitting-in in protest in front of her home with two banners: *"The Paracels & Spratlys belong to Vietnam"* and *"Denouncing Phạm Văn Đồng's diplomatic note to sell-off our nation"* she was arreted again.. To arrest a skinny girl under one meter and a half tall, with no intention of violence, the Hanoi regime mobilized nearly 30 multi-level police officers to surround her home. They read the arrest warrant at her residence at Đông Hải town, Hải An ward, Hải Phòng city. Previously she submitted an application for a permit to organzie a protest but it was declined, although complying with the law (September 14, 2008). Before her sit-in protest, Phạm Thanh Nghiên published on the Internet a letter. *"I have no other choice, than a sit-in protest right in my home, to voice the right to express my viewpoint. This right is clearly written in article 69 of the Vietnam Constitution. This time, if the government suppresses, harasses or uses violence against me, or even jails me, at least through the risk of safety of my life I show to the world a truth that in this country there is no freedom of expression, even in my own home, and also. with this sit-in protest, I oppose this government's coward acts in dealing with the northern nation, but it has brutally suppressed every voice, every patriotic demonstration of Vietnamese citizens. This is the only small task that I, as an individual, could do at this moment"*. Phạm Thanh Nghiên was arrested, jailed, assaulted on the streets, terrorized, threatened many times. However those tactics did not frighten or deter this frail girl on the battle for human rights, freedom and democracy for herself and her compatriots. She and a few others were arrested on April 30, 2008 while peacefully demonstrating against the Beijing Olympics torch relay. She was jailed for a few days, without being prosecuted. On June 17, 2008, she petitioned for a protest, but was denied by the communist government. She was punished for a daring petition unwanted by the communist government. The security forces terrorized her and her entire family. Nghiên was threatened and placed under house arrest, until July 16, 2008.

2.6.10. A low-rank employee of China Embassy officially interferes in the Vietnamese Communist Party's leadership.

Thanh Quang, RFA reporter, 12-07-2009

"It is increasingly clear that Vietnam leaders seem to avoid offending China, even though Beijing has increased its aggressive acts of dominating a disadvantaged Vietnam. More Vietnamese democracy activists are increasingly suppressed, especially those anti-China patriots.

Most noticeably, Vietnamese leaders seem to be very weak in their reaction. Ho Toa Cam, a Chinese diplomat in Vietnam, only a counselor on economy and trade at he Chinese Embassy in Hanoi, bluntly asked the Vietnam givernment to issue warnings – even including exerting disciplinary measures– to those Vietnamese newspapers that "disrespectfully" wrote about the quality of Chinese merchandise. He called it "a lack of friendship".

Ho Toa Cam: some Vietnamese newspapers published unfriendly statements toward China.

Ho Toa Cam, the counselor on economy and trade, was authorized by the China ambassador in Vietnam to issue a warning referring to recent articles in some Vietnamese newspapers mentioning Chinese merchandise.

Ho Toa Cam said there are many types of Chinese goods –"Chinese merchandise of poor quality is flowing into Vietnam, because Vietnam has such needs. A buyer on this side has a helper on the other side".

Ho Toa Cam criticized Mme Phạm Chi Lan, a prominent Vietnamese economist, vice president of the Vietnam Chamber of Commerce and Industry (VCCI), and scholar Nguyễn Minh Phong, who made "unfriendly" statements.

Ho said that he had been a correspondent for Xinhua news agency, for a few years in Vietnam. He was surprised to see Vietnam's government allowing such offensive articles, disrespecting the "16 golden words" 黄金字 motto set by China for Vietnam *(long-term stability, future orientations, friendly neighborhood, comprehensive cooperation)* and "4 goods" 好 *(good neighbors, good friends, good comrades, good partners)*. He expected the controlling agency, the Vietnam Ministry of Information and Communications (Bộ Thông tin và Truyền thông/TT&TT) to pay attention to, and remind and warn those newspapers of it. Ho emphasized that the press must act in accord with the agreements of the two governments.

Replying to Ho, Ms Quản Duy Ngân Hà, head of Vietnam International Cooperation Department of the Ministry said:

- Those articles reflect the perspectives of Vietnamese scholars, not the viewpoints of Vietnamese governmental agencies/organizations.

- The editorial offices should be responsible and be disciplined for wrongdoing. It is incorrect to say Vietnam's government allowed the publishing of those articles.

Ha affirmed positive Sino-Vietnamese relations. Ho's concerns were submitted to the Ministry of Information and Communications, to be reviewed by her "comrades".

Ho added: "Learning from experience is necessary, for the absolutely correct moves. Such articles should not be posted, then later on' they will be reviewed.' Need to control them tightly". "Both sides mentioned a Chinese press management team coming to Vietnam, to assist the Vietnam Ministry of Information and Communications with valuable experience, to the control of media."

2.6.11. Weakening daily under increasing pressure from China

2.6.11.1.   A young Chinese in Hanoi challenged Vietnam police:

Tue, February 9, 2010 9:38:14 pm

"That Chinese guy did not wear a helmet, parked his bike against oncoming traffic, acted arrogantly, smoking in congested traffic".

One afternoon, at the intersection of Tôn Đức Thắng and Quốc Tử Giám (Hà Nội), a young foreign biker with no helmet was questioned by Police. He parked his motorbike right in the middle of the street, disregarding the busy traffic.

About 15:30, according to some witnesses, a young man with dyed red/yellow hair, with no helmet, was riding his Wave bike on Tôn Đức Thắng street going toward Nguyễn Thái Học. When being asked by police to pull-over to check ID, he pretended not to understand Vietnamese.

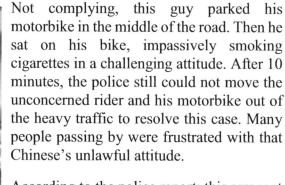

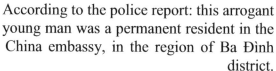

Not complying, this guy parked his motorbike in the middle of the road. Then he sat on his bike, impassively smoking cigarettes in a challenging attitude. After 10 minutes, the police still could not move the unconcerned rider and his motorbike out of the heavy traffic to resolve this case. Many people passing by were frustrated with that Chinese's unlawful attitude.

According to the police report: this arrogant young man was a permanent resident in the China embassy, in the region of Ba Đình district.
"The young Chinese guy worked in the China embassy. His attitude was arrogant and disrespectful to the Vietnamese people. This is a life lesson for the Vietnamese communists being enslaved by the Chinese invaders, restrained in the "16 golden words" and "4 goods" mottos. He was just an ordinary Chinese worker in the China embassy, daring having such a disdainful attitude. Probably, Chinese officials or governors of Chinese origins would have badly treated VCP leaders. The coward Vietnamese communist newspapers dared not publish the workplace of that Chinese guy, just only identifying him as a resident in China embassy, in Ba Đình district".

2.6.11.2. **About such acts as the harrassing of Vietnamese people**

and killing, beating, and robbing the fishermen in the Paracel archipelago, the Socialist Republic of Vietnam government has remained inert and complicit.

232

Quảng Ngãi fishermen were harassed while fishing near Lincoln Island. They were imprisoned on Woody Island (đảo Phú Lâm), being demanded for ransom. The Red China navy confiscated their fishing tackle and tools. Another 200 fishermen were not allowed to shelter on Robert island (đảo Hữu Nhật) during storms. Risking their lives, they entered the island to avoid the storm, despite being shot.

Quảng Ngãi fisherman bowed down pleading for mercy....for fishing on Vietnam's own waters.

When the storm was over, the Vietnamese fishermen was ready for leaving. Suddenly, Chinese soldiers jumped on each boat, confiscated assets/fishing gear, beating the fishermen, searching for valuables. No action was taken by the Socialist Republic of Vietnam (SRV) government, to deal with that situation.

Vietnamese fishermen were clasping hands, raising their arms to surrender, in front of guns pointing at them--- from Chinese soldiers. The Vietnamese fishermen bowed to the Chinese soldiers, asking for mercy. People who see such scenes on the Internet feel indignant. It is heartbreaking.

How could Vietnamese communist authorities have a courage to ignore it, without any reaction? When Vietnamese fishermen were attacked by a "stange ship" (1) , they called the SRV coastguard forces. No response. No rescue! They were afraid to make China unhappy, or afraid to be killed. They even ignored the task of "rescuing" fishing boats being sunk by "strange ships". Vietnam's government only advised that fishermen find ways to assist each other, and the government would compensate them by providing oil for this.. This policy has existed for a long

(1) Department of the Education and Propaganda of the CPV Central Committee instructs all media not to name "Chinese Naval Ships" that sink Vietnamese fishing boats, or kill fishermen, but to say it is a "strange ship"

time. In July 2007, a similar incident happened. Some Vietnamese fishing boats worked near the Spratly Island (đảo Trường Sa) within the Spratly archipelago. They were fired upon and sunk

by the Chinese navy. A fisherman was killed and the Chinese ships left. This incident was witnessed by a Vietnam communist navy ship. Vietnamese naval ship quietly left, neither protecting nor rescuing the victims. An international journalist at Đà nẵng questioned a Vietnam Navy Colonel, a coastal commander in this maritime area: why did the Socialist Republic of Vietnam (SRV) Navy ship neither protect nor rescue the victims? The Vietnamese communist commander replied: "*You should go and ask leaders in Hanoi*".

Meanwhile, the Vietnamese socialist government has been silent, as if nothing happened. The fishermen, victims of Quảng Ngãi province, responded by establishing a "Fishery Association" to protect each other. Regardless of the diplomatic protocol, the secretary general of the Association sent a letter directly to the Chinese Embassy in Hanoi, "petitioning" China to cease all acts of killing, harassing, suppressing, arresting, and beating Vietnamese fishermen.

"Vietnamese fishermen must have their rights to work for a living, on Vietnam's territorial sea, inherited from their ancestors for generations." This incident occurred before the eyes of Vietnam communist government leaders. No action! China's Embassy in Hanoi is the communist Chinese administrative agency, to place Vietnam under their ruling. Such a foreign Ambassador is also the Governor-General. The Communist Party of Vietnam has been truly the Local Sino Puppet, to play a dummy role, to enforce China's rule over the Vietnamese people. The acts of "ignoring" China shooting and killing Vietnamese fishermen offshore, on the territorial waters of Vietnam, make the Vietnamese leaders accomplices to the criminal offenses.

China has prohibited Vietnamese fishermen from fishing, by cruel and inhumane measures, as mentioned above, regardless of the international law requiring humanitarian action to save people endangered at sea, including escaping from storms. By these measures, Red China think that they assert their sovereignty over South China Sea. The Socialist Republic of Vietnam (SRV) keeping silent, not protecting their citizens in this situation is an act of acknowledging sovereignty of a foreign nation over our inherited territorial sea. In reality, it is an act of surrendering Vietnam's Eastern Sea to Red China, pursuant to the "cow's tongue map" published by China a half century ago.

- SPECIAL REPORT FROM VIETNAM: VIETNAM LEADERS SUBMISSIVE TO CHINA AT ASEAN MINISTERS CONFERENCE

In a special report from Vietnam, the Saigon Broadcasting Television Network (SBTN) correspondent reported that many people were upset with images of Hanoi's communist leaders cowering in front of their communist Chinese masters. Please join us with the following news...(video insert).

This photo went viral online, from the ASEAN National Defense Conference, organized in Vietnam (Oct. 2010). Patriotic Vietnamese people criticized Vietnam's leaders slavishly yielding to Red China. In reality, it is similar to the image of that shameful photo. Vietnam's leaders were alarmed by China's anger over the US intervention in the South China Sea, as well as the reappearance of Russians in Cam Ranh Bay. Nguyễn Chí Vịnh, Phùng Quang Thanh, and the most high-ranking Vietnam leaders took turns appearing on the domestic and foreign media, to clarify what happened, and vowing to be loyal to Beijing on behalf of the rest of the Vietnamese communist regime.

Conceding to international pressure, Beijing released nine Vietnamese fishermen, to lower the pressure on the Chinese General Luong Quang Liet (Liang Guanglie) who went and attended the conference. Vietnam happily released the news, but Beijing was angry. China forced Vietnam to delete the information, until the conference was over. It was General Phùng Quang Thanh, Vietnam's Minister of Defense who released that information to media (before the date dictated by China). Vietnam's online media released the news, but then withdrew it. According to some sources, at China's request, the news on nine freed Vietnamese fishermen was only reported after the Conference. Witnesses at this conference also said Hanoi's leaders were cowed and afraid in front of the Chinese leaders. This caused much criticism within the Vietnam Communist Party. It was revealed that during a meeting, Nong Duc Manh, the CPV's General Secretary, happily rushed to embrace Chinese General Liang Guanglie, in the salute style of socialist leaders. But ironically, Luong just smirked in response, and did not put his arms around Nong. Embarrassed, Nong turned away and started talking to someone nearby.

For many years, China has increasingly captured several Vietnamese fishing boats and fishermen working in the disputed South China Sea waters, between the two countries. Over one hundred families in Quảng Ngãi Province had to sell-off their houses, or borrow money to pay fines to China, to rescue their family members. According to Asia News online, some Vietnamese fishermen said they are frightened every time they go offshore fishing, because Red China regularly sank the Vietnamese fishing boats, or arrested the fishermen. The victims told stories of being abused by the Chinese communists. They were forced to stand all day. hands on head, kicked or beaten with electric batons. (SBTN)

Posted on 13 Oct 2010

2.6.11.3.   Being enslaved even in faith, to please China

2.6.11.3.1.   A Vietnamese Cultural delegation

Was sent to attend a ceremony at the temple where the Chinese General "Phục Ba Tướng Quân 伏波将军" (Mã Viện/Ma Yuan馬援) is worshipped. During October 2008, a large group of Vietnamese musicians attended the Chinese festivities at the temple of general Ma Yuan at Phòng Thành, Đông Hưng, on the other side of Móng Cái. In the Vietnam delegation, there was a male Vietnamese playing the role of Thi Sách, and two female officials performed as the two Trưng Sisters. They joined the commemoration, dancing and singing. During the first century, Queen Trưng Trắc (older sister), Thi Sách (her husband) and Trưng Nhị (her younger sister) led Viet people, raised up and heroically fought against the Han Chinese and overthrew Chinese rulers, liberating the Viet people from the yoke of Han. Later on the Han sent an army of sòme 20,000 men commaned by Ma Yuan to retake Vietnam. The Trưng Sisters lost a final battle against General Ma Yuan in the year 40 (AC). The two sisters jupmed to Tây Hồ Lake and drowned themselves. During this era, Vietnamese were indigenous Bai-Yue (Bách Việt) people living on South of Yangtze River. Under the Han ruling, Chinese rukers erected a huge and tall column, made out of bronze with the purpose of destroying all the Viet people. The hollowing words were inscribed on the column " Đồng Trụ Triệt, Giao Chỉ Diệt" *"Column collapsed, Viet people externinated". If the bronze column falls, the entire Viet people will be exterminated.*

2.6.11.3.2.   Cemeteries honoring "Chinese Fallen Heroes"

In some border provinces. Vietnamese authorities established 'monumental' cemeteries along the border, to "honor" those Chinese invaders who were killed by the Vietnamese army when invading Vietnam. They were part of the 56,000 Chinese soldiers who invaded Vietnam, and were killed in the border battles of 1979. Meanwhile, "Vietnamese communist fallen heroes" cemeteries such as the one at Vị Xuyên are neglected, isolated. Did they die in protecting their homeland, fighting against foreign invaders? Were they punished for that? At a Lạng Sơn, there is a cemetery containing the remains of Vietnamese soldiers killed by Chinese invaders. At the cemetery entrance, the written words "Vietnamese Heroes" on a wall were removed by the Vietnam government.

In short, Vietnam Communists "honor the Chinese heroes" who died at the border when invading Vietnam in the 1979 battles.

CEMETERY OF THE CHINESE HEROES

Entrance to Cemetery for "Chinese Fallen Heroes" in Lạng Sơn, on Vietnam soil.

The monument of "Chinese Heroes" in Lạng Sơn Province has these written words: "*Nhân Dân Việt nam Ký Công*" (Vietnamese people in appreciation).

An official letter from the People's Committee of Lang Son province "totally agreed" to invite China's government to join the "incense offering ceremony" during Thanh Minh (memorial day), in memory of those "Chinese Fallen heroes" who came and nvaded Vietnam in the 1979 war.

Mời Đoàn đại biểu Trung Quốc dự Lễ Dâng hương tưởng niệm các liệt sỹ Trung Quốc CV 218/UBND-KTTH).

Thứ Sáu, 26/03/2010 - 03:47

Kính gửi:

- Các Sở: Ngoại vụ, Lao động, Thương binh và Xã hội;
- Ủy ban nhân dân huyện Hữu Lũng.

Sau khi xem xét Tờ trình số 21/TTr-SNgV ngày 22 tháng 3 năm 2010 của Sở Ngoại vụ về việc mời Đoàn đại biểu Trung Quốc tham dự Lễ dâng hương tưởng niệm Liệt sỹ Trung Quốc nhân "Tiết Thanh minh", Ủy ban nhân dân tỉnh Lạng Sơn có ý kiến như sau:

1. Nhất trí chương trình mời và đón tiếp Đoàn đại biểu Đại sứ quán Trung Quốc tại Việt Nam và đại biểu cựu binh Trung Quốc vào dự Lễ dâng hương tưởng niệm Liệt sỹ Trung Quốc tại huyện Hữu Lũng theo đề xuất của Sở Ngoại vụ.

2. Giao Sở Ngoại vụ làm đầu mối liên hệ mời, chịu trách nhiệm về công tác Lễ tân trong việc đón tiếp đại biểu Trung Quốc vào dự Lễ dâng hương.

3. Giao Sở Lao động, Thương binh và Xã hội chủ trì, phối hợp với Ủy ban nhân dân huyện Hữu Lũng và các cơ quan liên quan chuẩn bị nội dung, cơ sở vật chất tổ chức Lễ dâng hương và thực hiện chế độ báo cáo theo quy định.

Ủy ban nhân dân tỉnh chỉ đạo để các Sở, ngành, đơn vị liên quan biết và thực hiện./.

MEMORIAL WREATH had these written words:

First line: People's Council, People's Committee, Fatherland Front Committee ....

Second line: Forever in Remembrance of the Chinese Heroes.

3) For people to better understand how the communist Vietnam leaders have treated their people sacrificed in battles against Chinese invaders, consider the case of 64 Vietnamese sailors who died in March 1988, while on the water near Johnson Reef (đảo Gạc Ma). They carried supplies on shoulders or heads for their compatriots stationed on this reef. They were unarmed. They were surrounded by four Chinese destroyers from four sides, firing heavy artillery on them. They sacrificed their lives to protect the country, in a very touchy situation (see photos below, in the *"Protest against China's Hegemony, with collusion of the Communist Party of Vietnam"*). The Party and State never mentioned and commemorated them, lest they offend Beijing. In a similar case, four Vietnamese coast guards were shot to death, and two seriously wounded, only because they were near the HD 981 Oil Rig, recently in May 2015. Their sacrifices are to protect their communist leaders who on the contrary betray them by doing all what they can in order to earn trust and benefits from the enemy.

Vietnam's Communist leaders, then and now, across many generations, are cold-hearted, insensitive, ungrateful individuals -- even towards their comrades who sacrificed for them. A typical example is Mrs. Nguyễn thị Năm, who wholeheartedly supported and protected the top Vietnam communist leaders, provided them shelters at her plantation to avoid arrests by the French rulers, including Ho Chi Minh. She fed them, and offered her substantial fortune in assisting the Vietnamese communists fighting against the French colonialists. But, as a "sinful" land owner, she was executed by Ho Chi Minh's team of Land Reform Campaign, in the horrific "public trials" of denouncement and humiliation *(đấu tố)*. Even dogs are kind and faithful to their owners. Not the communists.

There is a very deep level of dependence on China: The plan of domination of the Red Chinese empire in Vietnam is very sophisticated. Plenty of information has revealed that China's influence has penetrated into the district level of the Socialist Republic of Vietnam. China's influence is capable of replacing the provincial or district officials, and the Communist Party of Vietnam will facilitate this. Currently the Vietnamese Communist Party is preparing for a greater plan, which is, members from the Communist Party of China (CPC) would constantly train the CPV cadres in great numbers to carry out China's objectives.

If we compare the present situation to that under feudal Chinese domination of Vietnam during the 1,000-year period, we will find out that the CPV treats its citizens worse than the Han rulers did to the Vietnamese people. In first century, Governor Su Ding 蘇定 (Thái thú Tô Định) was a greedy, brutal Han Chinese official. Similarly, Vietnamese communist authorities have acted brutally to their own Viet people. In the past, the Chinese rulers ordered Vietnamese people to search for pearls under the sea and rhino horns in deep forests. It was acually at great risk. However, their treatments was not so harsh or brutal as those of the CPV. In this era, the Chinese communists act smarter. They have selected the most faithful diligent local Sino puppets in Vietnam to serve China's interests:

Economically, right after the bilateral relationship was re-established in November 1991, Vietnam leaders assisted the two Chinese landlocked provinces, Yunnan and Guangxi in exporting their goods to the South by opening the border and re-building the two railroads: one from Lao Cai and the other from Lang son to to Hai phong. The products produced by people living in the two provinces could go to Vietnam and to South East Asian countries. After few years, their standard of living doubles. The people of Vietnam must pay dearly for that wealth. Did any Chinese ruler demand the enslaved Vietnamese people to search for pearls as in the times under the Chinese domination?

Geographically and politically, Vietnamese authorities, playing the role of local Sino puppets have tried to secure a tightened domination of Vietnam, with harsh measures and actions listed in the Section II of this Dossier. It is expected that Vietnam becomes a territory of Red China, serving as a staging base for China's expansionism, advancing towards Southeast Asia nations, as intended by Mao since the mid-1950s.

In the role of a Sino puppet/Han Chinese official, the CPV leaders officially stand together with the Chinese invaders. They obediently execute orders from their Chinese masters, to brutally suppress their compatriots, without feeling ashamed.

There have been protests by the patriotic Vietnamese at home and overseas, most aggressively on the matter of the Paracels and Spratlys. On the occasion marking the establishment of the 60-year bilateral relationship between Vietnam and China, in a rare press conference on 01/06/2010, the ambassador of China Ton Quoc Tuong warned the Vietnam communist leaders: *"The most valuable experience in the process of the 60-year Sino-Vietnamese relations is that cooperation is to develop, opposition is to fail"*. Ton emphasized: *"Vietnam should temporarily put aside its dispute with China, wait for a ripe time to resolve it"*. What did Ton say to Vietnam's leaders? – *You guys should cooperate with China, for many good things*. If you choose fight against China, you will be executed. The "dispute" here is the sovereignty over the Paracels & Spratlys. This matter must be put aside, until the times is ripe.

When is the times? - China has already surrounded the South China Sea, with well-established military bases. And later, when Vietnam becomes a part of mainland China.

Why did Ton hold a press conference at that time? Nowadays, the people of Vietnam are well aware of the Chinese invasion. The threat is real. To deliberately keep many things secret, Vietnam communist leaders have used all of the government apparatus to suppress movements demanding to defend the Paracels and Spratlys. These movements have increasingly threatened China, to the level of making it impossible to achieve its goals. Therefore, Ton organized this press conference in Hanoi to threaten Vietnam's leaders. Of course, it aimed directly at Vietnam leaders Nông đức Mạnh, Nguyễn tấn Dũng, Nguyễn minh Triết, Nguyễn phú Trọng, Trương tấn Sang...China has an urgent need to delay the disputes to be solved, preparing for a "ripened" situation, to accomplish her plans. This is a time-delay strategy, so that the resistance movement could not be strengthened in time, before achieving the Chinese plan to annex Vietnam into China, as *"mountains connected to mountains, rivers connected to rivers"*. This is the pursuit of Ho Chi Minh's dream, under the leadership of Mao Zedong.

Vietnam's leaders have tried to be submissive to China, but still Ton publicly warned them. Vietnamese fishermen were shot to death, beaten and robbed by China's navy on the Paracel waters, for example in June and September 2009: Vietnam's leaders made no objection. From May to August 2009, China prohibited Vietnamese fishermen to fish on the waters at latitude 15, with the reason of "protecting the Chinese fishing grounds". Vietnam leaders dared not to respond. In October 2009, China conducted military exercises on the Fiery Cross Reef, on the Spratly archipelago. and clearly stated it was "to protect China's sovereignty" over this archipelago. Vietnam's leaders had no objection. Vietnam media even voluntarily acted as a "propaganda mouthpiece" for the Chinese military exercises "to protect China's sovereignty". When China opened up the tourism industry on the Paracel archipelago, on December 31, 2009 Nguyen Phuong Nga, spokesman of Vietnam's Ministry of Foreign Affairs objected to it. Then on January 5, 2010 Chinese spokesman Jiang Ju responded: *Actually, nothing new. They claimed sovereignty over those islands.* I think, their statement did not interfere with China's development plan in the region, nor cause any significant damage to the bilateral relationship between the two neighboring nations. Vietnam was silent.

***

2.6.12. The Central Highlands' Bauxite Project

"Long Story of Expansionism"

This ia a long story about Chinese expansionism through exploiting Bauxite in the Central Highlands of Vietnam.

In the article "**Warning of China Expansion**" posted on DCV Online on 10/06/2008, the writer remarked on China's disturbing acts, causing disadvantages to Vietnam, as follows:

There are ongoing aggressive disturbances from China, especially in this period China views this current situation as very favorable for them to be more aggressive, while only dealing with insignificant reactions from the outsite world.

Knowing difficulties Vietnam is facing : economic difficulties, loneliness in the political arena, social unrest, especially, internal conflicts within the ruling Communist Party, China arrogantly carried out their ambitions: to seize the borders, lands, waters, islands and sea of Vietnam, without fear of any reaction.

Every year, they arrogantly prohibit all navigation on the South China Sea. including the Spratly and Paracel archipelagos, during two months (June and July) for their military exercises. They even forbid Vietnam to exploit the oil fields in the South China Sea (Eastern Sea/Biển Đông of Vietnam).

For decades, China has adopted a strategy of persistant "nibbling" at the territory of Vietnam (land, waters, air), until she feels that she has a capability to reset the national borders for land, and the territorial waters (including the islands) between the two nations. The communist government of Vietnam is only slavishly yielding to Red China.

Allowing China to exploit Bauxite in the Central Highlands is no exception. It is totally within China's dark intentions. According to the U.S. Bureau of Mines and U.S. Geological Survey, currently there are about 43.3 billion tons of Bauxite being mined in the world, and about 15 to 20 billion tons are still intact underground. Also according to the U.S. Bureau of Mines and U.S. Geological Survey, currently, 50 countries in the world have Bauxite ore, and about 211 Bauxite sites contain over a million tons of reserves. Worldwide, those reservesa are capable of producing 30 billion tons of Bauxite, of which Australia accounts for 23.7%; Guinea 19.5%, and Brazil 14.4%. One third of this reserve belongs to the mines being exploited, 2/3 belongs to the sites in the feasibility exploration process. According to some experts, such Bauxite reserves plus this presnt mining rate would provide a plentiful supply to the global aluminum industry for 170 years.

The natural resources of Bauxite currently in Vietnam are found in the Northern provinces such as Hà Giang, Cao Bằng, Lạng Sơn, Bắc Giang, Sơn La, Nghệ An and also in the Southern provinces of Kon Tum, Quảng Ngãi, Phú Yên, Đắc Nông, Lâm Đồng, Đồng Nai and Bình Dương. Originally, Bauxite ores in Vietnam have two main types. The first type are derived from sediments (some were transformed). They are concentrated in the Northern provinces. The second type of Bauxite is derived from "Laterite" (a soil and rock type rich in iron and aluminum), formed by extensive chemical weathering of Basalt, (an igneous rock from volcanoes). They are concentrated in the Southern provinces.

According to old documents from the Soviet Union, the Central Highlands of Vietnam has the largest Bauxite reserves of about 8 billion tons.

According to scientific resources, Bauxite is a type of sedimentary ore of a pinkish brown color. Its main components include Aluminum hydroxide Al(OH)3 mixed with other elements such as iron, and silicon. Alumina (Al2O3) can be extracted from Bauxite, which is the main raw material for aluminum smelting in electrolytic furnaces.

On November 11, 2007, communist Vietnam's Prime Minister signed Decree 167 to approve the zoning plan for exploration, mining and processing, to use Bauxite ore from the period 2007-2015, which could be reviewed in 2025. Currently, Vietnam National Coal and Mineral Group has explored and invested in construction for Bauxite mining and metallurgical projects for Alumina in the Central Highlands. However, this project faced fierce opposition from the public, at home and abroad, because there are risks of destroying the environment, as well as endangering the cultural and social life of people in the Central Highlands.

They ignored the public opinion. They even ignored the evaluations of scientists. They ignored the opposing voices of those high-ranking CPV members, such as retired communist general Võ Nguyên Giáp and Nguyễn Ttrọng Vĩnh, former communist Vietnam ambassador to China from 1974-1989. The CPV Politburo insisted that the exploitation of Bauxite ores in the Central Highlands is a major, important government project. The Politburo already decided to approve this project.

Facing that authoritarian decision, scientists at many levels strongly opposed it. The political and military specialists warned that our "National security would be jeopardized because China is advancing deeply into the Central Highlands". The social and cultural experts said "the endangered cultural diversity of the Central Highlands could be destroyed". The environmentalists said "It will destroy the environment, pollute the soils and waters. Also, the rich Central Highlands will fall into complete destruction" etc..... The media did not dare to criticize the exploitation of Bauxite in the Central Highlands.

As Vietnamese people, whether inland or overseas, we are concerned about the survival and destiny of the Vietnam nation. We cannot ignore this major event that will have long-term impact in all aspects, for our beloved Vietnam. For different views, I would like to quote the following opinions of Nguyễn Tấn Dũng, Prime Minister of the Socialist Republic of Vietnam (SRV), a member of Vietnam Communist Party's Politburo, on the issue of exploiting Bauxite in the Central Highlands. Also, <u>a Letter of Nguyễn Trọng Vĩnh</u>, a retired Vietnamese communist Major General and Vietnam Ambassador in Beijing 1974-1989 sent to the Vietnam Communist Party Politburo. And an article on reasons why the Vietnam Communist Party's Politburo decided to allow China to exploit Bauxite in the Central Highlands:

Perspective of Nguyễn Tấn Dũng through The Politburo

The exploitation of Bauxite ores is a grand policy of our Party and State, mentioned in the Resolution of the 10th Congress. The Politburo also reviewed the Bauxite development strategy three times. The Government has approved the plan for developing Bauxite in the Central Highlands, efficiently and with sustainability.

We don't have many mineral resources, including some important minerals which are in small reserves, or already exhausted. The Bauxite in the Central Highlands has a reserve of about 8 billion tons which need to be carefully considered for strip mining.

For scientific and technical development, together with the Government's awareness, the strip mining would be done effectively to produce Bauxite, for aluminum. At the same time, to ensure the environmental protection and sustainable development ...

The Government assigned Deputy Prime Minister Hoàng Trung Hải to this location, to preside over a conference together with scientists and journalists concerned about the Bauxite exploitation. At the conference, there will be presentations on the matters concerned, such as environmental protection, methods, technology... to reach a consensus.

Letter of Nguyễn Trọng Vĩnh

Dear respectful comrades,

For a long time I had no information, until recently reading a letter from General Vo Nguyen Giap, and hundreds of disagreeing opinions from scientists, officials and people everywhere in the North – Central – South. Then I knew that we had agreed to Chinese to exploitation of bauxite in the Central Highlands. This is too dangerous! Like other people speaking out, I also see the hazards: destroying the ecological environment, damaging the primary forests, endangered the lives of Montagnard people, and toxic waste dumped into rivers originated from or flowing through the Central Highlands. It will badly impact the lives of South Vietnamese people inhabiting the Đồng Nai River banks. It could also impact hydropower construction in the South. The most worrisome of all is national security. We all are aware that

China has built a mighty naval base on Sanya (Tam Á), Hainan Island (đảo Hải Nam). Frankly, the base is built, not to fight any invading enemies, but to threaten Vietnam. China is ready, waiting for a chance to seize our Spratlys, after quickly seizing the Paracels from the Saigon government. Now if we allow China to exploit Bauxite in the Central Highlands, there will be five, seven or ten thousand Chinese workers or soldiers arriving to live and engage in activities here. They will establish a "China town", a "military base" on this very crucial strategic area of our nation (bringing in weapons is not hard). In the North, China has a strong offshore naval base. In the Southwest, she has a fully equipped army base. So how would our independence and sovereignty be? Previously, to protect our independence and sovereignty, we had lost a miilion lives!

Vietnam has sufficient historical and legal evidence for the possession of the two archipelagos, Paracels and Spratlys, but China has none. Yet the Chinese media created evidence, and always openly claimed those two archipelagos as their territories. China's Council of Ministers publicly and officially announced their decision to establish Sansha 三沙 district. . China has conducted such actions opeenly, whole she wants us to be silent, and not to discuss this subject. So unreasonable! We want to live in peace and have friendship with China. Even in friendship, we must also fight appropriately, to protect our Fatherland's legitimate interests. If not yet convenient for our leaders to officially speak up, then let the media and history scientists present facts and reasons. Why not allow people to peacefully protest, when our national territory is violated? Why suppress the spirit of patriotism?

Comrades, even though you have the right to do whatever you want or decide, you should also pay attention to public opinion. You should listen to analytic voices about the benefits, hazards, rights or wrongs, so you can carefully think and consider. The same with any dynasty, either past or present, if government policies were beneficial for the nation and people, then people would support them. If government policies were wrong and harmful to the people and nation, then people would be upset. If the people are upset, and mistrust the government, then it is difficult to have a stable and prosperous nation. "The king exists for some time, people are for long-term".

Dear respectful comrades,

Those were the straightforward honest words of a 70-year-old party member with a hope that these opinions be considered.

The reasons why the VCP's Central Committee Politburo decided to allow China to exploit Bauxite in the Central Highlands (Excerpt from Central Highlands Bauxite - Mạnh, Dũng and General Giáp)

This project emerged during Prime Minister Phan Van Khai's tenure. With his reserved nature, he did not promote it. To please Mạnh, Khải delayed the research process proposed by the authorities. He did not oppose it. When taking office in mid-2006, Dũng continued to extend this delaying tactic even more. By the beginning of 2008, Vietnam's economy fell into crisis amid the Party's internal conflicts. In early June, Mạnh visited China to seek solutions for Vietnam's economic problems. Two weeks later, Dung visited the U.S. for similar reasons. China told Manh that **they would supply funds to save Vietnam's economy, with a**

condition that China be allowed to mine/extract bauxite in the Central Highlands and send as many as 20,000 Chinese workers here. As for the USA, they promised with Dung to provde a fund of $US 20 billion. And Vietnam doesn't need to call World Bank or the International Monetary Fund for help..

Dung rejoiced when returning home, and boasted about the results and his achievements. Manh was frustrated with such demands from China. How could he convince the CPV Central Committee Politburo to approve China proposal? Hu Jintao pushed Manh' by saying that "so long as you have a determination, you will achieve your goal". Both parties agreed to set up a hotline, to keep "each other" informed in a timely manner. Shortly thereafter, China's Ministry of Foreign Affairs repeatedly asked Prime Minister Nguyen Tan Dung to officially visit China, but Dung found ways to decline. At that time, Dung obviously was leaning towards the United States and expecting help from the USA. He looked to the USA for empowerment, especially for his corporate economy. However he kept waiting without any results as promised by the USA. Only different groups from the USA began coming to Vietnam to sign MOU's, to reserve places for future ventures. Vietnam's economic situation became worse daily in August, September and October last year (2,007) at that moment, like tight strings near their breaking point. The time was ripe for China to act. Dung had no choice. He was forced to passively submit to China.

Before the trip, China rejected all solemn official diplomatic ceremonies. Dũng had no choices. He accepted the invitation to visit China. But surprisingly, the most solemn diplomatic welcome ceremony actually did occur in China, similar to that reserved for a chief of state. The results of that visit were announced as unexpected successes. **China got a promised approval for the bauxite project in Vietnam's Central Highlands, before the end of the year 2008. Besides bringing Chinese people into Vietnam, China still was granted a special status for management of workers and contrrolling mining and processing sites in the mining areas, with all privileges for China under its own diplomatic status and characteristics. On the contrary, China was willing to pre-finance " quietly" this bauxite exploitation, so Vietnam could have resources to deal with the economic crisis. How much financing? So far, no one has revealed it (1). When I "praised" China for a smart move, Manh's former assistant said:** *"It's not difficult to handle a greedy man like Dung. For him, benefits will cover everything"* **(2)**

The research work proposed by the government authorities was quickly completed with simplicity, with a majority approval. The government immediately submitted it to the Party's Central Committee Politburo. Then it was approved with the absolute majority vote. The Standing Congressional Committee approved it, without going through full Congress. Such rapid approval has created waves of discontent among many classes of people, including the military. Military strategists know well: Vietnam's Central Highlands is narrow but critically important. Early in 1975, during the "spring operation", North Vietnam controlled the Central Highlands, leading to the quick fall of South Vietnam on 4/30. Whoever could occupy Vietnam's Central Highlands, could control the entire Southern region. It is easy to divide Vietnam in half, at the narrow Central Highlands. Some military generals are upset with this *"selling off of the nation"*, but unable to do anything. They sought help from General Vo Nguyen Giap, although knowing about his fragile health, and avoiding a dramatic impact.

There were no other choices. Hopefully his reputation could change this matter. Indeed, general Giap was really shocked by this situation. Vietnam's leaders unexpectedly gave up the Central Highlands so easily.

His letter sent to Dung, posted on Vietnamnet, was only one of numerous public opinions. General Giap's entire letter clearly analyzed the critical risk of the loss to the Vietnam nation, by permitting China to mine Bauxite (the principal ore of *aluminum*) in the Central Highlands. His letter was sent to the entire Central Committee Politburo of the CPV, not just to Dung. Everyone knows the results: that condemned Bauxite project is still being carried out, regardless of objections from this patriotic general and others. Due to this stressful situation, Giap's health further deteriorated. Several times he was admitted into the hospital that year. Some people said he would have been blessed to pass away prior to witnessing the decline of a nation that he helped to establish, with his love for the nation and people. He luckily survived his last serious illness.

Unexpectedly, prime minister Nguyen Tan Dung turned from being "cold" to supporting and accelerating of this Bauxite project. To "conciliate" with Giap, Dung allocated Vietnam's lucrative investment projects to Giap's children. To predict it in advance, Giap reminded his children to carefully safeguard themselves. General Giap's children have not pursued political careers. They are businessmen. Not sure whether Võ Điện Biên and Võ Hồng Nam could guard themselves under several financial privileges, a close friend (in the military) said those good kids could preserve Giap's family reputation. This person also said, Trương Gia Bình, FPT chairman is no longer Giap's son-in-law. If not, it would be easy to bribe this guy, causing an impact on general Giap's family. General Vo Nguyen Giap died in October, 2013 (he was a prominent military commander in the First Indochina War 1946–1954 and Vietnam War 1955–1975).

According to some information, during that visit to China, Mạnh received a hard blow from Chinese leaders. A high-ranking Party member told another high-ranking anonymous leader in the Vietnamese delegation to China: "**if Vietnam would not satisfy China's demands, then very likely China would publish some documents related to Ho Chi Minh's agreement with Mao Zedong on Vietnam's borderlands and territorial sea. If so, it would be disastrous to the Vietnamese Communist Party's reputation. Mạnh had no other choices**?

Knowledgeable people said there were already over 10,000 Chinese workers in Vietnam's Central Highlands, even though the mining process was only in the preparation phase.

For Bauxite mining in the Central Highlands, besides various disadvantages such as damaging the living environment, and the social culture, there are also economic risks such as the complete destruction of cultivated areas for coffee, pepper, rubber, etc. Another big disadvantage is to permit foreigners to exploit mineral resources while Vietnam's government has no knowledge of this subject matter.

According to experts, to get Bauxite, the sedimentary rock/material with high aluminum content, the topsoil must be stripped for cultivating. Then the strip mining can continue by transporting rocks and soil materials into the factory. The Bauxite production is processed first into Alumina, then into Aluminum by electrolysis. On average, two tons of Bauxite rocks/topsoil could be processed into one ton of Alumina Al2O3 (Aluminum oxide). Two tons of Alumina will produce one ton of Aluminum. According to the contract, the Bauxite mining in Dak Nong will only process Bauxite ore into Alumina, then sell it to foreign countries, rather than extracting the metal Aluminum for industrial use, or selling it at high prices. Currently, the market price of one ton of Alumina is 370 US dollars. To extract Alumina from Bauxite rocks/soils, a huge amount of electricity power must be used, for all phases of production. It also requires a huge amount of water, for each phase of production, along with the chemicals needed for metallurgy. Of course, after that, it will release water containing toxic chemicals, including the highly toxic Red Mud, contaminating the surrounding soil and water.

Most important is the national security of Vietnam. For the interests of Vietnam's communist government, the Party and individuals, Vietnamese leaders have allowed a dangerous Chinese "expansionism" scheme into the heart of Vietnam. Our national security is in danger, due to China's presence in the Central Highlands of Vietnam.

Let us question Vietnam's communist government: why permit China into the Central Highlands to mine Bauxite ore?

- Why does China firmly want the rights to mine Bauxite ore?

Will the exploitation of Bauxite ore in the Central Highlands actually bring significant economic benefits to the people of Vietnam? Did China bribe Vietnamese communist leaders, to gain its legitimate presence in the Central Highlands? (1)

- Why did the Party's Central Committee Politburo ignore public opinion and the evaluations of scientists? -- Why did they ignore the opposing voices of those high-rank Party members, against allowing China to exploit our Bauxite ore?

- Is China's Bauxite exploitation in the Central Highlands just the tip of an iceberg?

(1) Trinh xuan Thanh, President of PetroVietnam Construction Corporation, after having escaped to Germany denounced that China provided a US$ 10 billion aid to Vietnam and the amount was released through Ban Viet Bank, of which Nguyen thanh Phuong, Nguyen tan Dung's daughter, was chair of the Board. (2) People talked much about US 300 million dollars for Nông đức Mạnh, 150 million dollars for Nguyễn Tấn Dũng awarded by China.

Report of Major General of Police Forces
Lê văn Cương

Hanoi, March 3, 2009

Institute of Strategy and Science of Public Security

ABOUT THE PROJECT OF BAUXITE MINING AND PROCESSING in DAK NONG and LAM DONG, by TKV

After attending the scientific conferences organized by VUSTA and the Party Central Committee Office, also surveying the facilities of strip-mining and processing Bauxite in Dak Nong, Lam Dong, I have some initial ideas as follows:

1. The project of mining and processing Bauxite in the Central Highlands, invested by TKV incorporation, is economically inefficient because:

The TKV project submitted to the Prime Minister has a few problems:

a). First, the Vietnam National Coal and Mineral Group (TKV) has not calculated the rising costs such as: the problems of transporting the ore, selling products, chemicals used for strip mining, processing and exporting (for a distance of about 250km) the cost of using electricity, water ....

b). Second, China has transferred its backward technology into Vietnam (China has advanced technology, or could buy advanced technology from developed countries, but they don't transfer it into Vietnam).

c). Third, TKV has chosen China as the only partner for production - which is extremely risky and dangerous.

Does TKV know or not know? Did it deliberately not report it completely? I believe both.

There are many other problems, but with the above 3 problems one could predict: economically, the Bauxite mining and processing by TKV in the Central Highlands certainly is ineffective. It could lead to huge financial losses.

2. In the long run, the TKV project of Bauxite mining and processing in Vietnam's Central Highlands will cause environmental and ecological disasters.

- First, the reservoirs containing red mud in Dak Nong and Lam Dong could be safe for 10 - 15 years to come. However, after 20 years, no one can be sure. The rainy season in the Central Highlands could last several months. Heavy rains could last 5-7 days, even 10 days. In that condition, the reservoirs of red mud on the plateau very likely could lead to incidents: lakes overflowing, landslides, broken dams, cracked lakebed...).

- Second, Bauxite mining and processing sites in Dak Nong and Lam Dong are situated in the upstream rivers of Dong Nai and Serepok (flowing into Cambodia and the Mekong River). No one can guarantee that Bauxite mining and processing will not pollute (toxify, contaminate) the water sources of these two rivers. About 15 million people use water from the Đồng Nai river system (daily life, industry, services, production...). The TKV corporation has no ability whatsoever (financially, technologically...) to overcome problems of wastewater treatment or handling pollution for the Đồng Nai and Serepok rivers.

The costs to overcome environmental disasters will rise to tens of billions of dollars, ten times greater than the benefits from Bauxite mining and processing.

3. Bauxite mining and processing in the Central Highlands is seriously violating our national security.

The threats to Vietnam's national security happen gradually, and are not easily noticed, such as the economic efficiency and risk of environmental catastrophes. Our national security is severely jeopardized by:

-First, this project is economically ineffective, and could lead to financial losses. From there, it could cause a great impact on Vietnam, socially and politically. People have already lost confidence in the Party leadership, and State management.

- Second, such environmental and ecological disasters will cause great impact on Vietnam's stability, socially and politically. Over ten million people will suffer severe environmental consequences, that could not be overcome for a long time.

- Third, China has entered our Central Highlands, to further advance and control all three nations: Vietnam, Laos and Cambodia. Currently, China already leased a large region at Munbunkiri province, along the border of Dak Nong, for 99 years. China owns the large economic projects in the A-Ta-Pu province, the southernmost province of Laos, bordering on Vietnam and Cambodia (at the Indochinese three-way intersection). This is an immeasurable threat to Vietnam's national security. Are the decision-making Vietnamese leaders aware of this serious matter, when allowing China to control our Central Highlands?

4. Petition

4.1. Proposing the Prime Minister to directly listen to scientists' opinions, on the project of Bauxite mining and processing in the Central Highlands.

4.2. Allowing a small-scale trial (about 300 tons of aluminum/year). Decision for large-scale mining will come after 5-10 years.

REPORTING PERSON

Major-General, Associate Professor Lê Văn Cương, PhD.

After the project of exploiting Bauxite was revealed, Vo Nguyen Giap and hundreds of Vietnamese intellectuals opposed it.

China Reactions:

On the webpage youyiguan.com (China) on February 7, 2009, there was an article titled: *"Vietnam Prime Minister Nguyễn Tấn Dũng highly evaluated the Sino-Vietnamese cooperation for various Bauxite works in the Central Highlands".*

At a conference on the government work development in Hanoi, Vietnam's prime minister made a statement: **"The Sino-Vietnamese cooperation to establish the projects for bauxite ore in the Central Highlands is <u>a major policy of Vietnam's Party and government"</u>.**

Bauxite ore reserves previously reached several billion tons, due to insufficient exploration. There are limitations on Vietnam's finance and technology, that make it impossible for mining. It was proposed by various Chinese companies to exploit Bauxite, in the Central Highlands of the South. Finally, this project has started. In addition, the transporting route connecting Bình Thuận port and the Central Highlands, at different levels to serve the Bauxite exploitation as reported, was completed in June. 2008.

However, in Vietnam, there are some villains talking wildly, and unreasonably demanding the suspension of various Sino-Vietnamese projects. Our national companies (China) have invested a large amount of money, and step-by-step executed the construction. Even early this year, someone initiated a petition for *"the suspension of various Bauxite works in the Central Highlands"*. The petition was sent to the prime minister's office. They even invited a high-rank Vietnamese military leader signing the petition, to represent them".

This project is huge, but few people knew of it, until half a year ago, when the chief company, Vietnam Coal and Minerals Company, organized a consulting conference with the experts, preparing to start the construction. Even Congress did not discuss this matter.

The process of research, consulting, evaluating impacts, assessment, informing, collecting opinions before making decisions -- none of that was carried out seriously. Perhaps the mining project at Nhân Cơ was previously planned with a Chinese company. Therefore, there were confidential assessments of the environmental impacts, economic benefits, impact on the ethnic culture in the Central Highlands, and national security.

- Aluminum Corp. of China Ltd. or Chalco, are two Chinese companies cooperating with Vietnam Mineral Company. This company lobbied the Lam Dong Provincial Committee, to support the project allowing China to exploit (meaning there are both levels, upper and lower, sharing benefits from China)

- **Surface Area of Bauxite Mining Region in Central Highlands**: According to information from Vietnam National Coal and Mineral Group (TKV), July 2007, Dak Nong has six regions having Bauxite ore, with a total surface area of 1971 km² occupying 1/3 surface area of Dak Nong province at the following locations:

Tuyên Đức: 354 km²; Đắc Song: 300 km²; Bắc Gia Nghĩa: 329 km²; Nhân Cơ: 510 km²; Quảng Sơn: 159 km² of Bauxite ore are also found in Bảo Lộc, in Lâm Đồng province, and currently are being exploited, although not at as large a scale as in Dak Nong province.

- **British newspaper Financial Times reported** on Nguyen Tan Dung's Bauxite Gift to Beijing, Sunday, May 10, 2009

London - After a series of articles in the international media about the controversial bauxite mining in Vietnam, England's Financial Times said bluntly: **it was actually a gift to China, from Prime Minister Nguyen Tan Dung**. In his article, David Pilling looked at how a rising Chinese nation is finding ways to overshadow Japan, and assert extra pressure on its neighboring nation. But in the situation of Vietnam, this author highlighted bauxite mining as a significant issue, showing the reality of the Sino-Vietnamese relationship. For the first time, a major Western newspaper in the West used the term **"client state"** to describe this relationship. According to the author, Vietnam's prime minister Nguyễn Tấn Dũng recently visited China, paying tribute to the Chinese leaders. Of course, it did not reveal anything on Dung as an individual. The important point is, Vietnam's Prime Minister brought the gift from Vietnam to China – a natural resources used to make aluminum. Author David Pilling called it a way of paying tribute to China. He discussed the relationships between the two parties. The China-Vietnam trade deficit was also an issue raised by several international newspapers -- such as the Wall Street Journal, New York Times, The Economist and Asia Times. This was a reason why the Vietnamese communists were so determined to promote the bauxite project. David Pilling said Vietnam was completely helpless when China pushed ExxonMobil out of the joint project with PetroVietnam. Meanwhile, nobody in Vietnam rushed to welcome the Chinese investments. Historically, Vietnam was occupied and dominated by China in 1000 years.

SOME PHOTOS:

(Bauxite), a military base (the Trojan horse). It is this place where, Vietnam communist leaders have allowed the admission of 20,000 Chinese workers. This is a restricted area. Vietnamese police and security forces are not authorized to enter for security checks. At any given time, Chinese workers could become self-armed soldiers to take over Vietnam's government. Many similar suspicious centers have appeared in Quảng Ninh, Hải Phòng, Đà nẵng, also in Rạch Giá, far deep in South Vietnam.

Photo by GEHO: Red mud reservoir at a bauxite mining site in India.

Chinese engineers reside in this secluded fenced area, and a zone closed to Vietnam security forces. It is very convenient and extremely effective as a commanding headquarter for the 5th army to direct the war, if and when China wages the war.

2.6.13. Assisting foreign invaders to establish military bases all over Vietnam: to lease Vietnam's forests and strategic locations for the long-term: 50 years.

Earlier, several retired Vietnamese generals condemned the Hanoi regime for quietly leasing (long-term renting) our strategic forest lands on upstream rivers to companies from China, Taiwan and Hong Kong. Those forests are located in 10 mountainous provinces of Vietnam - - for planting cajuput trees to provide raw materials for paper manufacturing. Vast forest areas of up to 300,000 acres have been leased to Chinese companies for the long-term. As a result, the environment is devastated, as the downstream areas are flooded during the rainy season. No water is available during the dry seasons.

This presents a great danger for Vietnam's national security. The threat to Vietnam for a thousand years, domination by northern China, is still here.

As revealed, the ten provinces leasing forests to China are Lạng Sơn, Quảng Ninh, Cao Bằng, Nghệ An, Hà Tĩnh, Quảng Bình, Quảng Nam, Bình Định, Kon Tum and Bình Dương (north, central and south of Vietnam). Other information revealed leasing in Hà Giang, Thanh Hóa, Khánh Hòa, Đồ Sơn and also Đà nẵng seaport. No one clearly knows about other provinces.

Regarding the provinces that leased long-term use of upstream lands to foreigners (China), to plant forests for raw materials

"Lieutenant General Dong Si Nguyen, was in charge of Program 327 for seven years, aiming to cover bare hills and mountains with green plants, to protect forests and the ecological environment. Also, Major General Nguyen Trong Vinh, is the former Ambassador of Vietnam in China (1974-1989). These two senior revolutionary nationalists sent to "Bauxite Vietnam" the following article, to highlight the danger of land leasing to China, Taiwan and Hong Kong

for a period of 50 years, with over 264 thousand hectares of forests containing the upstream rivers. 87% of those forests are within critically important provinces along the borders.

Bauxite Vietnam

General Đồng Sỹ Nguyên
Major General Nguyễn Trọng Vĩnh

Following the executive orders from Prime Minister Nguyễn Tấn Dũng, Cao Đức Phát, Minister of Agriculture and Rural Development sent an inter-departmental delegation to directly inspect the two provinces of Lạng Sơn and Quảng Ninh. Also, they collectively reported on eight provinces: Cao Bằng, Nghệ An, Hà Tĩnh, Quảng Nam, Bình Định, Kon Tum and Bình Dương. The results: 10 provinces [only 9 provinces listed, missing one] have issued fifty year leases of upstream forest lands to 10 foreign enterprises for the afforestation for raw materials, with total surface area of 305,353 thousand hectares. Hong Kong, Taiwan, China occupy over 264 thousand hectares. 87% of them is in the critically important provinces at the border.

This has greatly jeopardized Vietnam's national security on many fronts. This serves temporary interests, but sets thousand-year damage pouring onto our children and descendants. Lost wealth can be recovered, but lost lands are completely lost. It is potentially hazardous to allow Hong Kong, Taiwan, China to exploit Vietnam's forests on upstream rivers. These renters have the right to destroy trees and lands irresponsibly. When the forests at the upstream rivers are destroyed, the irrigation reservoirs will no longer have water sources. The hydroelectric plants will lack water, and no longer be effective. Floods and flash floods will be disastrous. Last year, many Central provinces suffered such disasters. Is this a serious warning, or not?

Provinces selling forests are causing suicidal harm to our nation. Nations who rent our forests could intentionally destroy our nation, bringing deadly disasters to our people. It is an ill-judged, cruel and reckless move. If Vietnam exerts no effective measures, foreigners could come over to exploit, cultivate, construct houses for 50 years, and propogate, to create "Taiwan villages", "Hong Kong villages" or "China town". So we could lose part of our national territory, while facing danger in our national defense.

We agree with five remedial proposals from the Ministry of Agriculture and Rural Development. We wish to clarify the first 2 proposals:

For those provinces which have already mistakenly signed leases with foreign enterprises, especially the critically important provinces at the borders, we need to convince renters to contract with local residents for cultivating plans. For those provinces that haven't signed leases, all moves should be suspended immediately. Instead, Vietnamese enterprises must be motivated to invest. To carry this out, we should combine their money with a part of the fund allocated to reforestation of five million hectares.. If not, these forest lands are lost. Date: Wednesday Feb. 10, 2 010, 5:41 pm

Nguyễn Hữu Anh

Urgent Letter of Major General Nguyễn Hữu Anh sent to the National Assembly's Standing Committee

Together, the two generals Đồng Sĩ Nguyên and Nguyễn Trọng Vĩnh, the communist senior "revolutionary" veterans sent their letter to the National Assembly's Standing Committee, via the website "Bauxite Vietnam", from the Internet to readers. Their letter requested the urgent resolve of the 10 provinces **selling** upstream forests to China. The website "Bauxite Vietnam" highly recommended this letter to readers.

Bauxite Vietnam

THE SOCIALIST REPUBLIC OF VIETNAM
Independence – Freedom – Happiness

To: National Assembly's Standing Committee

In a short time, in a large area, the 10 provincial regions of the North, Central, Central Highlands and South Vietnam, including the critically important localities for national defense, security, and economy – those 10 provinces have allowed over 10 foreign enterprises, mainly from China, Taiwan, and Hong Kong, to lease our forest lands for a long period (50 years). These are upstream forest lands. Their businesses are to plant trees, on a large surface area over 305,000 hectares = 3050 square kilometers, comparable to the area of Hà Nam province.

Vietnam's territory is narrow and people are overcrowded. In a few dozen more years, Vietnam's population could reach 120 million people. Where would the highlanders or plateau rural farmers obtain land to cultivate?

Selling strategic national land is a shocking matter! How could the People's Committee leaders and director of Lạng Sơn Planning and Investment Department dare to loudly say: nothing to worry about!? Have they thoroughly considered the benefits or harms? Are they not violating Vietnam government policies?

Let us question those leaders of Lạng Sơn and the 10 provinces who sell our forest lands: Can you assure the citizens of your provinces and all citizens of Vietnam, that those foreign enterprises won't blindly pursue super profits? That they won't devastate our invaluable forest lands? That they won't cause significant impact on our water reserves, reservoirs, rivers or flood intensity? That they won't take advantage of Vietnam, by excessively bringing in Chinese workers, propagating, and multiplying the Chinese villages here? That they won't create conflicts of interest with local people, on our forestlands? That they won't affect our national security and social order, short term and long term?

As a senior citizen, a voter, a military officer 46 years in the army, I have dedicated nearly my entire life, my mind and physical energy to contribute my small part, together with our people, our army. We have maintained each tree, each inch of soil at the resistance bases. We have extended the liberated areas, advanced to reclaim all airspaces, sea, land, islands and mountains and forests of our beloved Fatherland of Vietnam.

My heart was pained when hearing about ten provinces being leased in long term (50 years). Over 305,000 hectares forestlands!

I earnestly ask the Standing Committee of the National Assembly, in the best interest of the nation, with the responsibility of the highest powerful government body, to please form a special Congressional team, to conduct an urgent investigation of the leasing of forest lands in those ten provinces. Please provide conclusions with accuracy and directions to the Government and those ten provincial authorities, to seriously and appropriately handle this matter, to minimize dangerous risks for our country.

Respectfully, with confidence in Congress.

Hanoi, February 27, 2010

Major General Nguyễn Hữu Anh
Senior revolutionary veteran, retired at town Hàng Mã.
Phone: 38432021,Posted by boxit.vn on 03:13
Tag: Borders, Environment

General Đồng Sĩ Nguyên warned about leasing Vietnam's forestlands to foreign nations (see photo)
Author: Thu Hà

General Đồng Sĩ Nguyên opposed the long-term leasing of the upstream forestlands to foreigners, at some regions.

"With Vietnam, do not think the strong would defeat the weak".
Thinking about the collective strength of the people.

Be Responsible to speak up

-I know that you have recieved letters that were sent to government authorities, warning about the dangers of long-term. leasing forest lands on upstream rivers to foreign countries Why do you disagree on this matter?

I don't know who did it, but I feel responsible to speak up.

Vietnam is distinctively smaller than a Chinese province, with narrow width, elongated length, and short mountains slopes down to the ocean. Floods travel as swiftly as sounds, and natural disasters occrur continuously. Our environment is getting worse daily. The rising sea has engulfed more river delta areas. This has posed a grave threat to Vietnam's national security in many ways.

Besides the problem of destroying forests at upstream rivers, causing flash floods, I also wonder about several leased locations having geopolitical and strategic importance. During the resistance eras, all provinces had armed bases in the mountainous areas. During the Anti-French Resistance War in Vietnam, we had the Việt Bắc area. Against the United States, we had the Trường Sơn forests and the Southwest Region. Those forest lands at upstream rivers are situated in the armed bases or border areas. Examples are: Nghệ An already leased lands in Tương Dương, Quỳ Châu, Quỳ Hợp, the three strategic "national fences" localities. Also as with Lạng Sơn.

In the era of renovation, it is necessary to say that our Party and State utilize lands for various purposes, but they must carefully consider the scale, the location, and calculate each meter of land. While our people still lack land, houses, and jobs, we absolutely should not "sell-off or long-term lease" land to foreign countries for business, planting raw materials, real estate, golf courses, or casinos.

Although it's late, from right now all authority levels must respect each inch of lands belonging to our nation. If we have a temporary interest, a thousand-era damage is pouring onto our children and descendants. Lost wealth can be recovered, but lost lands are completely lost.

Amid numerous objections, the provincial governments still signed the leases!

- Some people said that my proposal originates from inaccurate information. Therefore such a reaction be somewhat radical.

General Đồng Sỹ Nguyên

I have information, not only hearsay. I have information from brothers at the provincial military headquarters, reported by the security forces. Immediately after receiving these reports, I called the local authorities to inquire. The provincial chiefs also acknowledged those matters are happening.

At some localities, the security forces and the provincial military headquarters voiced their opposition, but the government still signed the leases. Even some provincial chiefs signed the leases with foreign countries to rent the forest lands at upstream rivers.

Deputy Prime Minister Võ Văn Kiệt assigned me to be a special envoy for two jobs: First, to stop the forestry burning. Second, to temporarily suspend the timber exports. Till end of his life, Kiet was still concerned about those two matters.

In an authorized letter, he clearly assigned comrade Đồng Sỹ Nguyên the right to handle on-the-ground matters without report. Seriously, this was to guard our forests and lands. To empower people for the afforestation, Kiet also transported rice from the South to support them.

I was assigned by the Party and State, to supervise the program 327 for seven years. Together with local authorities, I have traveled extensively to forests, coastal areas and islands. I have climbed several 1000m mountain heights, on foot, and through binoculars, directly witnessing the destruction of forests for cultivation or cutting down precious trees for timber use and export.

People could clearly see how dangerous it is to destroy forest lands at the upstream rivers. Therefore, upstream afforestation is important for survival. It is a matter of life for citizens. We must not just plant forests; we must also protect them.

Already leasing over 300,000 hectares of forests (one hectare=2.47 acres)

- Until now, have you received any response to your petition?

When I submitted the petition, I received a call from the Prime Minister. The Prime Minister told me he had received the letter, and it was passed to the Ministry of Agriculture for field investigations. The Ministry of Agriculture carried out the order of the Prime Minister, completed the investigation, and sent me a letter.

- *What were the investigation results from the Ministry of Agriculture?*

The Ministry of Agriculture agreed with me: It is true that 10 provinces have leased the upstream forest lands to foreign countries. The Ministry directly investigated the two provinces of Lạng Sơn and Quảng Ninh (north Vietnam). In addition, there were reports collected from the eight provinces of Cao Bằng, Nghệ An, Hà Tĩnh, Quảng Nam, Bình Định, Kon Tum và Bình Dương. 10 provinces permitted 10 foreign enterprises to lease the upstream forest lands for 50-year terms, for the afforestation of raw materials. The total surface is over 300,000 hectares. There are enterprises from Hong Kong, Taiwan, and China. They occupy over 264,000 hectares, 87% is in the critical provinces at the border.

"I don't know who did it, but I have the responsibility to speak up".

It is short-sighted!

- *Local officials, when interviewed, dismissed the concerns. Their reason? They said the projects were carefully considered for the community benefits. What do you think about this reason?*

This is not convincing.

Right in the reports of the Ministry of Agriculture, facts are confirmed, that some places have reclaimed people's lands which actually were owned by someone in order to be leased to foreign entities.

Naturally, people living on the plains must have agricultural fields and the montagnards must have forests. To rent out forest lands, how could people make a living? That needs to be addressed. Many of our resistance wars were only for this purpose: peasants having agricultural land, and montagnards having forests. People supported that purpose, and the revolution was successful.

Caring for citizens must be the first priority, even before collecting money for the budget. We must rely on arguments like increasing budgets, to make decisions. Allowing foreigners long-term leasing of the upstream forest lands, is very short-sighted!

Why not ask ourelves: why did foreign businesses choose lands leased mainly at Lạng Sơn, Cao Bằng, Quảng Ninh, especially Nghệ An, Hà Tĩnh, Quảng Bình -- **where highway 7 and highway 8 lead to Lao and the Central Highlands?** Clearly, those are critically important provinces near our borders. They are critical strategic locations. Our people have a lack of job opportunities. When foreigners lease lands, will they use Vietnamese workers, or send their own people over?

Let us take **Đồ Sơn** as an example of leasing land to foreign nations. I investigated directly around that area. **They installed landmarks as big as boundary markers**, prohibiting Vietnamese people from entering. My bodyguard was refused when requesting for entrance. Then I got out of the car, pressing hard for entrance. Finally, I got in.

Some local authorities said there have been places that could be leased out because it has been unused for a long time. That is irresponsible. If a land under your control is left unused , it means that your duty is not fulfilled! When I worked for Project 327, I was well aware that our people always had a land shortage. I wanted to work on a project, but there was no land available for me..

The petition to immediately suspend the unsigned projects

"Lands are sensitive properties through many generations. For the sake of presence and future each inch of land use must be calculated carefully. So in your regards, what we must do in this situation?

For those provinces which have already mistakenly signed the leases with foreign enterprises, we need to convince them to contract with local residents for plaanting Particularly at the critically important provinces at the borders, if local authorities have not signed a contract with foreigners, stop it immediately. Instead, we must mobilize Vietnamese enterprises for investment, by cooperatively using part of the 5 million hectare afforestation project fund.

The provincial authorities could direct the district leaders and forestry leaders to establish specialized units. Within a year, lands and forests could be officially allocated to each family unit. The "red books (ownership titles)" could be issued for the purpose of forest protection and economy promotion, combined.

From here, I propose to extend "the poverty reduction program" in the mountainous areas, into "the get-rich program" for the highland compatriots, combined with the arranged resettlement of projects. Conditions to get rich in the mountainous areas are better than on the plains.

Forest leasing to foreigners halted after the general's wake-up call.
Last updated: 3/13/2010 18:37

Dong Sy Nguyen, one of Vietnam's longest-serving and most respected military men, launched a sharp verbal attack on local governments leasing land. Vietnam's prime minister has asked provinces not to rent out forest land to foreign investors as critics say the practice is jeopardizing national security and the environment.

"Provincial People's Committees are not allowed to grant new investment permits to foreign projects in forestation and seafood breeding. They have to wait until the government is done inspecting the situation," PM Nguyen Tan Dung said in a statement posted on the government's website on Wednesday.

The Prime Minister's statement came after the Lieutenant General visited northern and central border areas two weeks ago.

A total of 10 provinces including **Quang Ninh**, Lang Son and Cao Bang in the north, Nghe An, Ha Tinh, Quang Nam, **Khanh Hoa** and Binh Dinh in the central region, Kon Tum in the Central Highlands and Binh Duong in the south, have permitted foreign firms to rent 305,353 hectares of forest land in total, according to figures from the Ministry of Agriculture and Rural Development (MARD)

Many of the plots had been leased for 50-year terms, and 264,000 hectares, much of which in border provinces, has been leased to companies from China, Taiwan and Hong Kong.

A Tuoi Tre newspaper report on Thursday cited a source as saying that the Hong Kong-based Innov Green Corporation had won permits to rent forest in the north-central province of Thanh Hoa. The company now has the rights to a total area of 349,000 hectares in six provinces, though the land has only been committed and is not yet fully leased.

In some places, the forest being rented out had been previously owned by local residents who were expropriated from their land, said PM Dung, echoing Lieutenant General Nguyen's grievances aired in late February and earlier this month. Dung also said some rented areas were important to national security and the national economy.

In two interviews two weeks ago, Lieutenant General Dong Sy Nguyen said all plans to lease forest lands to foreign companies should be canceled and concerned provinces should persuade their foreign partners to re-lease the land to locals.

He noted that the recent trend by which foreign firms, many of whom are Chinese, engage in deforestation in Vietnam's relatively untouched hinterlands was fueling flash floods and he lamented that "many politically important locations" had been leased.

"This is a huge national security disaster," said Nguyen, according to VietNamNet, a local newswire.

Nguyen, who last month received a medal from PM Dung for his 70 years of service to the Communist Party, of Vietnam is the former vice chairman of the Council of Ministers, the cabinet of the Vietnamese government, and has also served as Deputy Minister of Defense, Minister of Construction, Minister of Transport and Commander of the Hanoi High Command.

"Although it is late, we still have to honor each decimeter of our national territory," said Nguyen in the VietNamNet interview.

"Wealth can be retained once it is lost, but losing lands is losing everything," Nguyen told the newswire.

The 87-year-old Nguyen, former head of the state afforestation program 327 and ex-supervisor of the Ho Chi Minh Highway project, also told VietNamNet he had inspected a leased area in the northern port city of Hai Phong's Do Son District, only to find that a foreign company had set up landmarks that resembled national border markers and banned all Vietnamese from entering certain areas.

Tough questions.

In both interviews, Nguyen specifically criticized Nghe An Province for leasing forests in Tuong Duong, Quy Chau and Quy Hop districts, saying they formed a protective "national fence."

He told VietNamNet it was necessary for the Party and government to use lands for certain purposes during the reformation process, but he argued that land in sensitive areas shouldn't be leased out to foreign companies for business purposes like planting material forests or building casinos and golf courses.

"It's only natural that delta residents have farms and highlanders have forests. How can they earn a living [without their lands]?" said Nguyen.

"Our countless revolutions were made so that farmers could have farms and highlanders could have forests. The revolutions succeeded because the people pursued these causes," he said. "Taking care of local residents should come first, and before national revenue benefits".

Source: **Thanh Nien Agencies**

Reader's letters: Respectfully sending to Seniors Đồng Sỹ Nguyên, Nguyễn Trọng Vĩnh, Nguyễn Hữu Anh!
Posted by bxvnpost on 03/11/2010, NH

The forests being cut for foreigners to lease at Lộc Bình district, Lạng Sơn province.

I am a woman, having less knowledge of national defense and national security than you do. When I was young, I lived during those glorious days of great heroism, when "the sound of gunfire echoed across the sky at the borders, calling our people into a new battle…". so I absorbed the ideal of "a noble life for everyone: "INDEPENDENCE – FREEDOM". I am the daughter of a soldier, one of your teammates. He died in 2006. My father was the Political Commissar of a Division. Often, I heard him talking about the importance of national defense, national security, the costs of war, peace, independence, freedom ... Therefore, when reading about your devoted petition on the web *VietNamNet, page Bauxite Vietnam*, I am very impressed. Although of old age, with limited health, you are highly responsible for our nation and people's destiny, for the future of our Vietnamese descendants.

Dear elders! 10 provinces leasing forest lands to foreign nations for a 50 years term, is it the last number ? Will it pose grave danger later, to lease our coastal lands for a 50-year term, as renting out Vietnam's forestlands for 50 years? Đà Nẵng Seaport is an extremely important stategic military position, so that the French colonialists and the United States imperialists chose for landing, to invade Vietnam. Yet currently, Đà Nẵng's coastal lands are also leased to foreign countries (including China, Taiwan…) for a 50-year term. I ask that any provinces or cities permitting foreign countries to lease 50-year term of the coastal lands – which are critical localities for national defense, security, and economy – be investigated and statistically surveyed by the Central Government. It is for timely prevention, since the South China Sea has been a *"very hot"* issue.

Leasing forest lands and coastal lands to foreign nations seems to bring super profits for the economy. Therefore, national security is not considered a serious matter, for provinces and cities. Is there any other reason for which they rushed to lease so much land? A top leader of a city that is under the direct command of the central government, must answer to voters who raise questions as to why this city is leasing so much coastal land to foreign nations for 50 years.: *"We don't have to do anything, while collecting money from land leasing and from their business services. It is so wonderful! So why complain? The city only leased it for 50 years. Nothing was sold! So why be afraid of losing the Nation!"*. I found that leader's answer/analysis too simple. It seems not satisfactory.

I only ask for permission and boldly voice my worries and concerns. That's all. Because I am just a woman, as the poet Xuân Quỳnh wrote:

> "We are just nameless ordinary women
> Used to having the daily small kitchen jobs
> We don't have submarines, missiles, aircraft
> Nor having atomic nuclear power

We only have pots and pans with fire
Having love and lullabies".

I wish you elders good health. You elders are the pivots, the beliefs, the pride of the Vietnamese people!

N.H

Note: The following Lạng Sơn villages are in the areas being leased to China, and the company renting forests is Innov Green Lang Son (Vietnamnet):

This company is a member of Innov Green Lạng Sơn, belonging to Invov Green Incorporated (company registration No.198 issued by Ministry of Trade, Kingdom of Cambodia, 2/25/2004. Wu Gwo Wei is the legal representative, a Chinese citizen). Investment certification No 14104300056. First certified on 2/21/2008; First change of investment certification on 3/12/2009, signed by Nguyễn Văn Bình, deputy chair of People's Committee (UBND), Lạng Sơn province.

The investing project of "Planting forests for high-grade timber in Lạng Sơn province" on a large scale, expected to be 63,000 hectares. The investing area covers 49 villages belonging to 7 districts: Văn Quan, Tràng Định, Lộc Bình, Chi Lăng, Cao Lộc, Bắc Sơn và Đình Lập.

Investment funding project of 800 billions đồng. The time frame to carry out the project is 50 years, since the date of issuance of the investment certification. (Source: Department of Planning and Investment in Lạng Sơn).

The terrifying massacre at Tổng Chúp, Hưng Đạo village, Hòa An district. Chinese army used bamboo stakes and wood-chopping hammers beating 43 women and children to death, then tossing them into wells.

In 1979, China's army swept across the Vietnam border, and massacred many women and children. DIAGRAM TO LEASE FOREST LANDS

MAP OF LEASED FORESTS

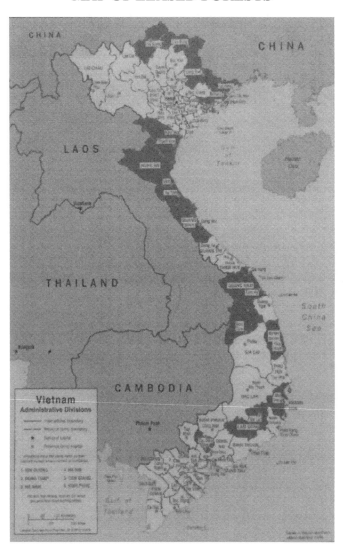

Notes on Maps:

A). The following 14 provinces already leased forests to China, at least since 2004:

- Quảng Ninh, Lạng Sơn, Cao Bằng and Hà Giang in the north; Nghệ An, Hà Tĩnh, Quảng Bình, Thanh Hóa in North Central Region; Quảng Nam, Khánh Hòa and Bình Định in the central region; Kon Tum, Lâm Đồng in the Central Highlands and Bình Dương in South Vietnam.

B) Some details:

- Đà Nẵng Sea port also was leased for the long-term.

- Lạng Sơn: 63,000 hectares. Locations allocated for the projects: at 49 villages belonging to 7 districts: Văn Quan, Tràng Định, Lộc Bình, Chi Lăng, Cao Lộc, Bắc Sơn và Đình Lập; leasing to Invov Green company.

- Nghệ An: leasing lands at the districts:Tương Dương, Quý Châu and Quý Hợp. They built fences as "defense areas".

- At Đồ Sơn. "they installed landmarks as big as boundary markers, and forbid Vietnamese people to enter. My bodyguard was refused when asking for entrance. Then I got out of the car, pressuring them for entrance……..". General Đồng Sỹ Nguyên recalled.

Hong Kong-based Innov Green Corporation already owned 349,000 hectares of lands in 6 provinces.

Annotated Maps of leased forests:

1) In history, the forest-dense mountainous areas like Nghệ An Hà Tĩnh, Quảng Bình and Bình Định etc.. are where King Lê Lợi established the resistance bases, in 10 years fighting the Chinese invaders. Now, it is offered to our enemies. No more resistance bases for Vietnamese forces exist if China dominates this time.

2). Vietnam is cut into four pieces, no longer interconnected for protection and national defense.

Piece #1 in North Vietnam: the boundary is cut-off in the four provinces of Thanh, Nghệ, Tĩnh, Bình.

Piece #2 in North Central: it is cut off in Kontum going to Quảng Nam Đà Nẵng.

Piece #3 and #4: Lâm Đồng down to Bình Dương (dividing South Vietnam into 2 parts). In June 2010, Vietnam major general Nguyễn trọng Vĩnh reported 10 provinces leasing Vietnam's forests (actually 18 provinces, not 10).

ILLUSTRATED MAPS of THE RESISTANCE BASES OF NAM ĐÀN and
CẦN VƯƠNG

Illustrated maps and information provided by researcher Hà học Lập. The Nam Đàn resistance base in Nghệ An was established by Lord Bình Định Vương Lê Lợi, to fight the Chinese invaders during Ming dynasty (1424) for ten years -- while the entirety of Vietnam was under China rule (1418-1427). The resistance base (1893-1895) of Cần Vương movement was established by the revolutionist Phan đình Phùng in Hà Tĩnh, to fight the French colonialists.

The gray color is the Hồng Lĩnh 99 -mountain range. This historic rugged mountain region consists of two historical resistance bases. Now, Vietnam communist party leaders leased this entire area to China for afforestation for a 50-year term. Would any Vietnamese resistance forces be able to shelter in any bases, in future uprisings in case of being dominated by

264

foreigners? (*Hồng Lĩnh mountainous area is also called Hồng Sơn, consisted of three districts: Đức Thọ, Can Lộc and Nghi Xuân, of Hà Tĩnh province*).

The scheme of leasing Vietnam's forests has divided our nation into four pieces, as shown in the map. On each piece, there are military bases of China's 5th army. They have become Chinese Headquarters. Those northern Beijing invading soldiers are stationed there, ready to deploy, to eliminate the uprisings of the Vietnamese people, after the complete establishment of Chinese rule.

These are dense rugged areas at the upstream rivers, used as militia bases, to revolt against foreign invaders -- by King Lê Lợi and the wise senior compatriots in the Cần Vương resistance movement against the French colonialists. Now, these upstream locations are "leased" by Vietnam's communist leaders to foreign nations. What if China launches a war to invade Vietnam and then how could our patriotic national forces have any bases for resistance. If so, China's domination in Vietnam could become permanent, and the sinicization would be easy.

An answer for the reason to lease forests/lands:

A letter wrote: "...we don't have to do anything, while collecting money from land leasing and from their business services. Wonderful! So why complain? The city only leases it for 50 years. Nothing is sold! So why be afraid of losing the Nation!" NH.

2.6.14. Chinese Workers and Reality

Hundreds of Chinese workers in Nhân Cơ

http://www.bbc.co.uk/vietnamese/vietnam/2010/02/100228_bauxite_update. shtml

Nhân Cơ Alumina Producing Manufacturer is the second aluminum production project in Vietnam. This second aluminum production plant from bauxite ores in Vietnam started on 2/28/2008 in Nhân Cơ, Dak Nong Province.

The management of Nhân Cơ aluminum joint venture said this project will have **600-700 foreign laborers at peak time, mainly from China.** Nhân Cơ alumina production project, invested in by Vietnam Coal and Minerals Group (TKV), consisted of two plants, built on a surface area of 850 hectares, not yet including the strip mining section.

It is a bauxite ore refinery, with the first phase capacity of 1,65 million tons of dry refined ores per year. The aluminum production plant has the capacity of 650,000 tons per year.

The total investment for the two plants is approximately 12,000 billion đồng.

Specifically, the aluminum plant had a total investment of nearly 9,000 billion đồng, built and supplied with equipments by CHALIECO contractor (Chinese), expected to finish on October 2012. A large number of foreign workers in Vietnam, especially the unskilled Chinese workers in key projects, has caused frustration to the public.

For Nhân Cơ project, Vietnam authorities affirmed to tighten their management of foreigners.

Tuổi Trẻ (Youth) Newspaper quoted Trần Phương, vice chairman of Dak Nong People's Committee as saying: "our province is well experienced in managing foreigners, since most of the hydropower projects implemented in this area have bought equipment from China. The Chinese experts instructed us how to install and operate".

Bùi Quang Tiến, chief executive officer/ CEO of Nhân Cơ Aluminum Joint Venture told the Voice of Vietnam Radio: *"Nhân Cơ alumin project is funded with 100% capital from Vietnam, not associated with any other country"*.

"After two years of construction, the entire group of foreigners would return home, so this project would be completely managed by Vietnamese people".

Tiến affirmed that this company has many "strict regulations" for foreign workers.

Controversal Project.

This is a second project to exploit bauxite and Aluminium producing plant, after the Tan Rai, Lam Đồng project. This is also owned by TVK. Bui quang Tiến, CEO of the Nhân cơ Aluminium Joint Stock Corporation. TVK provided only 20 to 30 % of the capital. The rest will be loans from either inside or outaside sources.

Ministry of Industry and Commerce affirmed that both projets, Tân Rai and Nhân cơ are "at the testing stage.

At period 2011-2015, the three Groups 1, 2 and 3 at Dak Nong will be in operation Their output is projected at 4,5 to 6 milliom tons a year.

Ministry of Indutry and Commerce estimates that the bauxite ore reserves in Vietnam are 5,4 billion tons.

The Nhan cơ Management hopes that the income will be $US 211 million /year, employing directly 1,350 people and indirectly over 12,000 others.

Exploitration of bauxite in Central Highlands is a very severe controversial issue in Vietnam.

Some retired generals, inlcuding Gen Vo nguyen Giap, Gen. Dong sy Nguyen petitioned to suspend the project. One of the reason is that the highland area occupies a very important strategic position. When there is a great number of foreign workers, national security will be threatened.

Another Chinese corporation has just won a bid to buld a large size Electricity Plant in Quang Ninh: More Chinese worlers will enter Vietnam.

The Mao Khe (Dong trieu) Electricity Plant with $US 500 million capital is an element to kick off the economy to prevent the economy slowdown.

On July 7, Media from the country reported that the TVK has chosen Kaidi from China to build the Mao Khe Electricity plant.

The contract for construction is signed persuant to guidelines of EPC (Engineer, Prcourement and Construction). This means that Kaidi does a complete work until the plant produces Electricity. Vietnam Press reported that Kaidi will do engineering survey, planning, provision of equipment and machine, construction work, testing. In addition, The Chinese corportion will experiment, train, maitain machine and equipment....

Kaider has 36 months for plant 1 and 42 months to complete both plants..

TVK is the main player of the Mao Khe plants.

" For the past few year, the number of Chinese workers coming to Vietnam has increased dramatically. The consequences leads to fightings: Chinese attack Vietnamese, Chinee despise local security and authorities. Just yesterday, a news from Vietnmnet reported that a hundred Chiense worlers cuased "disturbances " in areas surrounding the Cement plant 2, Nghi son, Thanh Hoa.

What did Vietnamnet report actually begian 6 months ago. On Dec, 28, 2008 there was a final Football game AFT beween Vietnam and Thailand. Nguyễn văn Đen and his wife Le thi Nghi who were directly invloved on this matter, said that after the game was over, 6 Chinese workers entred their shop, buying cigarettes. They opened the box without paying. Then they were involved in scuffle with Nghi, and Đen chased them out of his shop. Immediately they attcked Đen. Đen and wife used stick to defend. After that they came back with some 40 Chinese. Đen had to call for help from his neighbours. However all of them wre ferociously attaccked. Then, some 200 Chinese came in, blocking all lanes of the area, and beat whoever they met. They borke windows, did daamge to houses in the neighbordhood.

Duong thi Dao, Đen's neighbor said:" They broke in houses with lights on and destoyed things inside", while Dao thi Minh said " they were so great in number. Any one who was on the street had to run away."

A video showed that a hunded Chinese workers rushed out, hands holding shovels, sticks, spikes ...destroying every thing. After they withdrew, the scene was so devastating. Quite dilapidated is a scene created by Chinese workers. Senior Lt Col. Nguyễn như Thân, Deputy Chief, Economy Security Services of the Thanh Hoa province said that there have been a number of serious disorders caused by Chinese workers in this area. For example, on September 24 last year, inside the campus of the plant run by the Chinese management, two local residents were arrested for being thiefs. After being notified of the fact, members of the Nghi son security office were sent in to bring them back to the office for investigation. However the Chinese management did not release them to the security team. In addition, they allowed some 50 workers to suppress the secuirty force and required the secuirty force to take action as they demanded. And, in November 2008, some Vietnamese climbed the wall to get inside to steal some pieces of steel. They were detected. They were arrested and beaten. The local security office demanded that they be handed over to them, but the Chinese management refuesed and tried the case by tighing them up, then hanging them at the entrance gate over night. They were released the next day. Another story was told by Lt. Col Thân: In April this year while workers of the Hanoi Construction Co. were working on a scaffold, below it Chinese of the CNBM were assembling machines. A Vietnamese worker accidentally dropped a string and hit a Chinese who fell down. The Chinese got lightly injured. The Hanoi Connstrution Co. sent him to a hospital for treatment and paid all mdical expenses. The Chinese corporation still asked for a extra compenstion of 1,200 yuan and the Hanoi Constrution refused. The Chinese CNBM mobilized all its employees with sticks, pipes to encircle the Hanoi Construction Co. management…

Chinese workers are so disruptive evrywhere At the Cong Thanh Cement Plant, in Nhân Trach District, there are a lot of disturbances. Aftter work, Chinese workers usually come to coffee shops, restaurants where there are fughtings beteen Vietnamese and Chinese. An owner of a grocery store, also renting bicycles in front of the plant said.: one day, my mother rent to a Chinese a bicycle at $50,000/day. Three days later, he come back, without paying and intended to do damage to the bicycle. Under the situation, I reduced the amount to $100,000. He still did not want to pay. In addition, he beat me, and run after me inside the shop" A Chinee worker who rented a bicycle, carrying 3 persosn, without wearing helmets, hit a local then run away. When he was stopped, he was impetuously opposed to it, causing chaos in the entire area. Recently, a Chinese brought in ecstasy into karaoke shop at the Ninh Xa, Bac Ninh. He raised the volume of the sound, danced at midnight, causing chaos in the area. A local security unit came in, bringing him to their office, then released him without doing anything.

On the night of Dec.28, 2018, a hundred Chinese workers at the Nghi Son Cement Plant rushed out to the street, equipped with sticks, disrupting the area, beating passengers, yelling, breaking in homes of neighorhood, created a devastating area, before withdrawing.

On June 21, a Vienamese female worker living in the My Đinh area got into an elevator. She was sexually harrassed by a Chinese worker. She quickly hit a button and the door is open, she got out safely. The perpetrator was arrested and no body heard about how the security office dealt with.

The above stories are some created by thousands of Chinese workers present in this country. A question is if 5 or 6000 Chinese workers are brought in the Nhan cơ area, what happens then? This doesn't include security or national defense that has been raised by public figures.

One weird thing is that the Nghi Son story occurred 6 months ago and until now somebody raised it up. Another weird thing is that when Chinese workers create disturbances, local security forces seldom appear quickly and arrest those Chinese, while with Vietnamese, they dealt wiith barbaricly, including inhuman measures, even they are patriotic intellectuals.

This situation preplexes me vey much, liivng under the Vietnamese communist regime. And the security force is really stupid.

Le Minh

June 23, 2009.

Chinese worlers ceuse disturbances at the Nghi Son, Thanh Hoa Cement Plant

by Xuan Hoaang-Vũ Điệp-Nhật Tân

Vietnamnet.vn/xahoi/2009/06/854202

Bustling- Chinese villages in Hai Phong

07-2424/06/2009 (GMT + 7)

http::://vn/xahoi/2009/06/854563/

Residents of Hai phong call the area where Chinese workers conentrate at Ngũ Lao " Chinese village". Not far from this place, in Thuy Nguyên District, there is a slum where a thousand undocumented Chinese workers live. In Hai Phong, a newly formed a China town with restaurants, karaoke shops, massage parlors to serve Chinese in the area.

Chinese Village in Ngũ Lão.

Before the Hai Phong power plant starts, the area reserved for building apartmeents for Chinese workers is an agricultural zone with pools where fish is raised by local residents.

Chinese Village at the Ngũ Lao village, Thuy Nguyen, Hai Phong:

Though it is a place where Chinese workers of the power plant concentrate, it includes different sections: Administrtion Section that has three offices: Hồ Bắc, Đông Phương and Quảng Tây.

In front of each unit, there is a seperate gate with its own guard team. Each office has its own separate apartment area for its workers to reside., with a kitchen and a numbers of amenities. The apartment area for the Quang Tay group wiith a largest number of workers includes 130 rooms, enough to accomodate 1,000 workers. The area for each room is about 10 square meters with insulated walls, containing 8   2-story bunk beds. 8 workers live in one room

A Chinese street in Thuy Nguyen

rvnaf2002@yahoo.com , Monday Jun 15, 2009 at 2:06 pm, rvaf

Chinese workers in Lam Dong doing exploitation of bauxite

What do you **Hear and See**: It is dreadful!

by Vang Anh

What do you see: At the Lam Dong Bauxit Ore Exploitation site, in Bao Loc, you see a sign with TKV, and around the entire site, so much flag of the Nhât An Corportation, written in Chinese characters is displayed. Asked as to who is building this site, residents replies briefly: China! At the Nhan cơ site, people **just hear Chinese music**. These are disks or tapes used for Chinese customers to enjoy when they come.

Chinese workers at the Tan Rai Bauxite Mines

At the Lộc Thắng town, besides this restaurant (about 1 km from Tân Rai) there is an other Chinese restaurant situated at the end of the town, owned by a local Chinese Vietnamese open to serve Chinese workers. Mrs Phuong said that about 800 Chinese are working there.

Few local workers.

We found that those who work at the site are Chinese. Only few of them are Vietnamese coming from Nghe An-Thanh Hoa provinces.

Apartment

Chinese worlers 'jobs are digging wells, building pillars. Vietnamese are builders' helpers or carry sand and mortars for the construction. Tiền, a Nghệ An resident, said that a work day salary is 80,000 đồng, minus $25,000 đồng for foods. Net is 55,000 đồng/day. If he works overtime, he will get an extra 40,000 đồng/ day. Lang, a Chinese through an interpreter said that a Chinese receives150,000 đồng/day. He refuses to answer a question as why the corporation doesn't hire a Vietnamese because of low pay. Lang has been in Vietnam for 10 yers. He had been a manager for Song Thần corporation, Ho chi Minh City. When Tan Rai started the bauxit, he got a job here.

Mr. Nguyễn tiến Long, a local resident confirms that very few local residents are recruited to work at this project . They only recruits members of the household that has received money as compensation of land expropriated. Locals who work there are women. They carry dirt or sand.

30 Chinese workers at Quảng Nam

Updated Friday 24 April, 2009 (GMT +7)

On April 23, The Electronic News of the Voice of Vietnam reported that the Alumin Nhan cơ-the TKV has completed an evaluation of environmental effects re. exploitation of bauxit, and aluminum metallurgy at Nhân cơ. It will submit the project to the Dak Nông People's Committee for review and approval withiin 4 days. At the same time, the corporation prepares to construct the plant with an output of 650,000 tons/year. The total capital is 12,500 billion đồng. Mr Bui quang Tiên told VOV that Chinalco, a Chinese corporation is studying the laws and regulations o Vietnam, then bring Chinese in to work for the project.The projection is that some 2,000 Chinese will work at the project. In a MOU, both sides, the Nhan cơ Jont Stock Co. and TVK confirms that they only recruit technicians from a foreign country and unskilled laborers will be locally recruited. Foreign workers will live in a 2 heatare area, not far from the plant.

At The Nhan Trach, Đong Nai
Updated at 07.47, Tuesday June 23, 2009 (GMT +7)

VIETNAMNET. 200 unskilled Chinese workers have been detected by inspetors of the Labor, Disabled soldiers and Social Department of the Dong nai Province as undocumented workers at the Nhan trach Cement factory. The fines will be 5 million đồng/person and they are to be deported.

Perplexicity.

Present at hamlet # 3, Phuoc Khanh village in the evening of June 19, at the time when 200 unskilled Chinese undocumented are deported, we see a lot of Chinese workers riding motor cycles or walk on streets leading to coffee shops or restaurants.

Thousands of Chinese workers come to Vietnam.

In a talk about construction on March 27 organized by The Vietnamese Federation of Construction Orgnanizations, Mr. Tran ngoc Hung, Chairman of the orgnanization confirmed that Vietnamese contractors are worried because most large economic projects offered in bidding go tho foreign corporations. He said that Chinese contractors got most of such projcts as eledtricity, cement, chemistry. " the thing worth paying attention to is that Chinese contractors used to bring in thouands of workers and equipment, while the equipment could be produced locaally." Mr. Nguyen cong Luc, Director of Economy Office of the Prime Minister Office who went to visit a power plant in Quang Ninh with Deputy Premier Hoang trung Hai confirmed that "in one plant, more than 2,000 Chinese workers have been brought in", while Mr. Trần văn Hạnh, President of Vietanmese Construction Association said " One speical thing is that Chinese contractor do not hire Vietamese labor, but hire Chinese, even those workers come to Vietnam as tourists.

Martha Ann Overland, Time 16/4/09, Phạm luu Quỳnh translates:

Mr. Nguyn văn Thu, President of Vietnam Mechanic Entrepreneur Association warns: " the danger is that China has been awarded in most bidding to do chemical, elcticity and cement projects. They gnaw every thing, nothing left".

Vietnam in danger

by Vu hoai Nam

.....We know that, recently the government of Vietnam has approved a Chinese Corporation that is Xina Pu Dien to exploit bauxite ore and process it into aluminium. It is merely disguised as a commercial corporation. Actually, its leaders are Chinese field officers in different braches: general staff, intelligence, combat Research, map drwaing team....

Prtivate sources from China Main Land notifies that in the 25 km2 area of the bauxite ore exploitation, a PLA company as a special task force with all modern equipment, commo means, Jeep trucks is raising up tents for staging troops. Disguised as an unit to protect the explo

itation site, the company is commanded by a brigadier general, 4 colonels and a number of compny level officers of such branches as intelligence, cambat, civil mobilization, engineer... In order to safeguard Secrecy, they wear no insignias. They have posted signs "No Entry" so that no one is allowed to come near their base, including Vietnam government authorities.

They are waiting for construction materials to be shipped in to build fortified structures.

Besides, China will send thousands of people of the Han origin to this Cenral Highland area to resettle down and lie in wait.....

Some photo re. Chinese workers in the Central High Land.

Minh Hanh Photos

Are you ready?

Nguyễn tấn Dũng's reaction to individuals who opposed the exploittion

Gen. Vo nguyên Giap called for abolishment of the project.

After having sent 3 letters opposing the project, Vietnamese communist Prime Minister Nguyen tan Dung paid a visit to him, bringing in flowers on the occasion of his 99th birthday. The bauxit project does not cease its operation. Early 2010, Gen Giap passed away.

Recently Major General Dong sy Nguyen raised his voice against the long termed forest lease project. Prime Miinister Dung awarded him a highest medal. Will the lease be stopped?

Why did other retired generals not voice about these two projects? And the active generals serving under the CPV flag- do you agree with the policies and keep silence?

ATTENTION: Hong Kong, Tawain and Red China are one

….. Until now, we just see some "progress" in Red China ambitions. However, the contributions made by the CPV to the goal as expected by Truong Chinh who declared in 1951 are so lmited . As a result, Red China has endeavored to push the CPV into position to be more active. The road is still long. Red China may be need more time, 50 hay 100 years more.

(Road leading to Beijing)

Ngạo Nghễ electronic newspaper, October 3, 2010.

Ngạo Nghễ: This photo describes the cowardice of Vietnam communist leaders to their masters in Beijing.

Symbol of Submission: China's puppet Nong Duc Manh, General Secretary of the Communist Party of Vietnam, illegitimate son of Ho Chi Minh is respectfully bowing to welcome Hu Jintao.

CHAPTER IV: PROGRESSION OF AN ACTION PLAN TO CONTROL and TO ENSLAVE THE PEOPLE OF VIETNAM BY A FOREIGN POWER

This chapter will summarize events and acts by Ho chi Minh and the CPV in assisting the Chinese Communists to gain control over Vietnam and put the Vietnamese people under the yoke of domination by Red China., throughout the two periods of Vietnam's recent history. **Period I:** Resistance against French Colonialism until 1979 and **Period II**: Submission to communist China since 1990

1. PERIOD OF ANTI-FRENCH RESISTANCE: SEEKING LEADERSHIP

Ho chi Minh solicited Chinese Imperialists to direct anti-French war efforts and to establish a political structure in Vietnam.

Since Ho Chi Minh established his government, on January 1st, 1950, at the Sino-Vietnam border, Ho needed Chinese Communists' leadership and assistance for the "proletarian revolution" to be successful. Professor Qiang Zhai in the book "*China and the Vietnam Wars, 1950-1975,*" North Carolina Univ., published in 2000, wrote that Ho asked Mao to send "advisors" to Vietnam to lead the war efforts and to provide military equipment and materials.

On January 18th, 1950, People's Republic of China was the first nation to recognize Ho's Democratic Republic of Vietnam. In April of that year, Ho Chi Minh requested China to send military personnel to Vietnam as "advisors" at Viet Minh headquarters and at divisional level, and as "**commanders**" **at regiment's and platoon's levels**. China did not agree to the proposal of sending "commanders." On April 17, 1950, the Chinese Communist Party set up a military advisory group consisting of 79 advisors, together with some assistants...

Beijing's insertion of itself into Indochina matter should to be viewed under the historical relationship between imperialist China and its neighbors. Chinese emperors always considered Vietnam within its sphere of influence: an imperial power and its vassal state. To Mao, this tradition obviously had to continue. Some Vietnamese still look to China as a political model and for inspiration. It is not a surprise then that Ho Chi Minh's decision to seek support from Mao not only stemmed from ideology, but also from the habit of seeking leadership from China.

To battle the French army in Cao Bằng, besides asking China to send assistances and a military advisory group to Vietnam, Ho also suggested that Mao send a **high-level military advisor to direct border operations.**

Accordingly, **Chinese General Chen Geng** 陈赓 was sent to Vietnam on July 7, 1950 to **direct the war** efforts. Chen Geng launched the tactic of "to siege outposts and destroy rescue forces" (*công đồn đả viện*) aiming at taking over Cao Bằng and some posts near Lạng Sơn. As a result, the situation in the areas of Việt Bắc and North Vietnam changed dramatically. Viet

Minh expanded its theaters of operations; Viet Minh is abridged for Viet Nam Cach Menh Dong Minh Hoi, or Communist-dominated Vietnam Revolutionary League). Consequently, French troops had to withdraw from Lào Cai, Lạng Sơn and Hòa Bình. They finally abandoned almost the entire area north of the Red River Delta.

The French withdrawal from Hòa Bình also opened up roads for communication between Việt Bắc and North Vietnam's '*liberated*' areas, forming an area controlled by Viet Minh.

Chen Geng set up training for Viet Minh military leaders and improved military corps, which included setting up merit and demerit system, implementing techniques of treating war prisoners, method of conducting victory celebrating activities for propaganda purposes, implementing methods of choosing candidates to promote acts of heroics, techniques for troop mobilization, programs to recruit from captured Vietnamese prisoners, programs to "re-educate" French nationals and Moroccan nationals prisoners before releasing them back so they could subvert the French troops, and organizing "review meetings" for commanders above the platoon level. On behalf of Viet Minh, Trường Chinh presented reports on "border campaign" evaluations.

By the end of 1950, communist advisor Chen Geng returned to China, despite Ho's wish to retain him.

Chinese advisors offered plans to increase the efficiency of the leadership structures. They helped to reorganize Vietnam's general staff, political commissars, military logistics, and divisions. Division-level Chinese advisors organized training courses for Viet Minh cadres to educate them on communist ideology, which Chinese advisors referred to as "correction training" (*chỉnh huấn*). So Viet Minh officers could follow correct "political thoughts" in order to achieve, "correct political actions."

So, under the title ADVISOR, Chen Geng actually was a commander of Ho army.

The victory of the battle at Điện Biên Phủ in 1954 was (partially/ in large part) due to (the) Chinese Communist Party's (Chinese military's) strategy and command. **Chinese General Wei Guoqing** 韋國清 and three Chinese divisions were mobilized to direct the siege and attack on this French military post. Chinese communists built a road from Mengzi city (Southeast of Yunnan province), about 30 km from the Sino-Vietnam border. On this road, thousands of vehicles transported military supplies materials for this battle. As a result, the Viet Minh achieved victory.

Mao appointed **La Kuiba** (La Quý Ba) to be China's **supreme representative** to direct Vietnam's political activities. Along with implementing ideological education for Vietnamese armed forces, La Kuiba assisted Ho chi Minh in formulating policies for social reforms, including the so-called Land Reforms Campaign, Industry and Commerce Reconstructing, destroying and eliminating National bourgeoisie among other things. He helped setting up the legal system, and financial and taxation policies; controlling radios and the press; programs regarding the treatment of various minority groups; and establishing agricultural taxation. The new tax system was copied from China. Vietnam's State Bank was established with the launching of a new currency, which was printed in China.

The "social reform" policies designed to push society to socialism followed closely the Chinese counterpart model. Pursuant to these policies, Trường Chinh, who was later General Secretary of the Communist Party Vietnam, personally directed the Land Reform Campaign. Under direct instructions of Chinese communist cadres, the campaign was carried out in extremely oppressive and bloody manner. For purposes of carrying out this campaign, Ho sent his loyal communist cadre Hồ Viết Thắng to China for training. Upon his return to Vietnam, Thắng directed a secret training center in Cao Bắc Lạng to train the communist cadres on how to conduct it. These communist specialists implemented this terrifying campaign throughout all Vietnamese villages and hamlets under their control, under close supervision of the Chinese communists attached to the campaign cadres. The extermination of landowner's class, in extremely brutal and Chinese communist cadres decided barbaric manners. With this operation, Ho's communists destroyed Vietnam's traditional social structure, eliminated completely the elderly rural leadership, and wiped out Vietnamese traditional culture, including historical sites, among other things, in order to build a new socialist society.

The programs to "reform Industry and Commerce" and to "attack national bourgeoisie class" were led by Đỗ Mười. Those campaigns and other measures were no less oppressive.

Next was the construction of a new socialist society following closely Chinese socialist model. The policy of establishing "agricultural cooperatives" was implemented extensively. Throughout North Vietnam, cooperatives 合作社 (hợp tác xã) were established, where everyone was mandatorily assigned into teams and were made to be part of cooperatives. Through this program and other measures, the Party tightened its control over the population. All private property were confiscated or nationalized and came under the control of the "State." The Party has sole and complete power and authority to make decisions in all facets of social life, under the claim of acting on behalf of all citizens. A new educational program was carried out to create a new citizenship, as Ho advocated.

The following were examples of the manners through which many Vietnamese people underwent re-education in order to be citizens of the new society. Instructors and administrators of these campaigns were Chinese communist cadres.

Photos illustrate scenes in Reeducation Camps

Excerpted from Pham Van Thanh's sources, providing factual descriptions of hard labors imposed in "re-education" camps.

2. After 1990: THE ERA OF SUBMISSION TO CHINA's POWER ON VIETNAMESE SOIL

From the mid-1980s, the Soviet Union began to change its approach to relationship with the West. The new approach was to reduce confrontation between the capitalist and communist blocs. Once there was no more need to defeat capitalism, it was no longer necessary for the Soviet Union to provide financial assistance to its satellites in exchange for their international support. Therefore, no more assistance was forthcoming to the Communist Party of Vietnam.

For the 4th 5-year Economic Plan, which began in 1986, the Party received $14.5 billion in assistance. On the average, it received US$2.9 billion per year. But by the fourth year--1990--financial assistance was down to $100 million. By 1991, the Soviet Union cut off all assistance. Forced to adapt to the new circumstances, the Party had to implement the *Đổi Mới* (or Renovation) program in 1986. In addition, the Party received annual Soviet Union assistance up to US$1 billion for its war efforts to invade and to control Cambodia, which began in 1980.

To deal with the abandonment by the Soviet Union, the Party leaders looked for a new master. The era of submitting to China began.

How did the Party manage to return to China's sponsorship while pro-Soviet Union leaders of the Party were still in powerful position?

Some Party leaders were secretly guided by China's Embassy in Hanoi, through its military attaché, and in a sophisticated plan of contacting China via the Foreign Affairs Committee of Vietnam's Ministry of Defense and of assisting said leaders to submit to Red China. The submission to China marked the debut of an obedient regime bowing to the Sino Imperialism and of a concrete plan to impose Red China's imperialist control on the Vietnamese people. Vietnamese communist leaders have become in effect the local Chinese puppets in a role of administrators and also enforcers serving the interests of this foreign power.

After contact with China was successfully made, and blindsiding the pro-Soviet Union faction in the Vietnamese Party in the process, Chinese leaders publicly invited Vietnamese communist leaders to formally visit Beijing. On August 28, 1990, the Chinese Embassy received an order from Beijing suggesting Truong Duc Duy (Chinese Ambassador in Hanoi) to convey an invitation to Nguyễn Văn Linh (General Secretary/Communist Party of Vietnam) as following: *"China's General Secretary Jiang Zemin and Prime Minister Li Peng will welcome comrades General Secretary Nguyễn Văn Linh and Đỗ Mười, President of the Council of Ministers, to visit China from September 3 to September 4, 1990, also will welcome Phạm Văn Đồng, advisor to the Party's Central Committee."*

Because the Asian Games were held in Beijing, in order to maintain confidentiality, China arranged a meeting venue in Chengdu, Sichuan. On the following day, Duy came to the Vietnamese Communist Party's Central Guest House to convey the invitation by Jiang Zemin and Li Peng to Nguyễn văn Linh and Đỗ Mười. These two people accepted the invitation and informed the Politburo of Vietnamese Communist Party of the invitation. But the arrangement and advocacy for the visit to China was kept completely secret, so as to avoid alerting the pro-Soviet Union faction in the Politburo.

On the 30th, China notified its Embassy to arrange for a general "working" agenda. On the morning of September 3rd, a Vietnamese airplane left Hanoi, arriving in Chengdu at 1:00 pm. In the afternoon, leaders of both sides engaged in discussions. That evening, the Chinese invited the Vietnamese to a dinner. On the morning of September 4th, the summit conference continued until the evening when the Vietnamese left Chengdu to return home. Truong Duc Duy had accompanied the Vietnamese delegation to Chengdu for the summit conference.

After returning from Chengdu, Duy stated that two nations' top leaders met to mainly discuss how to settle the political conflicts in Cambodia, and the normalization of Sino-Vietnamese relations.

Regarding Sino-Vietnamese relations, both sides advocated maintaining a forward-looking attitude and letting go of old disputes. At the end of the meeting, the two countries' leaders signed a "Memorandum of the Summit." Pointing to deeper implications, Jiang Zemin cited two following verses from Jiang Yong's poetry from the Qing Dynasty:

Độ tận kiếp ba huynh đệ tại
tương kiến nhất tiểu mẫn ân cừu
度盡劫波兄弟在
相逢一笑泯恩仇
Which is translated as follows: "Through turbulent waves, brotherhood still endures. After one meeting, just a smile, all feuds and grievances are gone."

Overtaken by emotions, that night Nguyễn Văn Linh penned the following four verses:

"Huynh đệ chi giao số đại truyền;
oán hận khoảnh khắc hóa vân yên;
tái tương phùng thời tiểu nhan khai;
thiên tải tình nghị hựu trùng kiến,"

Roughly translated as follows.

"Brotherhood through many generations, animosity quickly fading like departing clouds,

Laughing together at reconnecting meeting, reviving the thousand-year-old relations."

The pro-Soviet Union faction was not notified of other secret plans.

A year after the Chengdu summit, in November 1991, Đỗ Mười, Vietnamese Communist Party's then General Secretary, and Võ Văn Kiệt, then President of the Council of Ministers, visited China. Leaders of the two nations declared Sino-Vietnamese relations normalized. In February 1999, leaders of China and Vietnam in the "Joint Statement" affirmed a framework for developing bilateral relations in the new century. In short, it is the widely hailed slogan of "16 golden words," roughly translated as follows: *long-term stability, orientation toward the future, friendly neighbors, comprehensive cooperation."*

Dealing with the Soviet Union's abandonment, what did the Vietnamese communist leaders give up in exchange for the bilateral relationship with and for assistance from China? There were not many details disclosed at that time. But the following is instructive. A short time after Linh's delegation returned to Vietnam, the Vietnamese communist authorities searched and located 72 former Chinese rice mill owners remaining in South Vietnam; others already had fled overseas during the period when then new communist regime had struck down the commercial bourgeoisie class. The communist authorities announced the return of those rice mills and factories to the former Chinese owners. However, those owners declined and said:

"When you confiscated our factories, they functioned well. Now, those factories are ruined." Vietnamese communist leaders had to order said mills and factories repaired before returning them to the former owners.

When the relation was normalized, it was discovered that the two parties had settled the border dispute and many other issues. Then the border was redrawn in 1999, with large Vietnamese territories at the border were transferred to China. The sovereignty of the Gulf of Tonkin in 2000 was renegotiated, and Vietnamese communist leaders transferring 11,000 km² of maritime waters to China. Finally, the common fishing grounds arrangement and what transpired subsequently in the Spratlys are also the consequences of the Communist Party of Vietnam capitulating to China.

Nguyễn văn Linh, Đỗ Mười and Phạm văn Đồng received their due "credit" for laying the foundation ominously, it is a relationship predicating on Red China's exercising imperialist domination of the Vietnamese people through their local puppets i.e. the Communist Party of Vietnam.

The entire 7th Central Executive Committee of the Communist Party of Vietnam and the subsequent Committees in early 1900's were responsible for implementing the above-mentioned long-term plan of action. It is impossible to understate the importance roles of the Party's general secretaries Đỗ Mười, Lê đức Anh, Lê Khả Phiêu, Nông đức Mạnh, and Trần đức Lương in the said congresses in establishing and strengthening this Chinese imperialist domination of Vietnam.

Recently, Vietnamese communist leaders ceded national sovereignty to China to large extent on Vietnamese soil and have attempted to turn Vietnam into a political department of China. Among others, they in policy and practice have allowed Chinese nationals coming and going freely in Vietnam without visa control, allowed Chinese government-linked business operating in certain areas of Vietnam the right to self-rule, allowed Chinese currency circulating freely in lieu of Vietnamese currency in certain areas, abolished any reference in high school history textbook to past Chinese subjugation of Vietnamese people, and tried to replace existing Latinized Vietnamese writing system with Chinese-influenced writing system, though the traditional writing system has been extensively used through centuries in the press, in laws and regulations, in literature, in education, in science and technology, in commerce and in vernacular usage. Many Chinese nationals living in Vietnam are not subject to Vietnam's laws and regulations.

During the historical one thousand years of Imperialist Chinese's subjugation, exploitation and oppression of Vietnam, the Han Chinese gained relatively negligibly when compared to said gains on behalf of China by Ho Chi Minh and by the Communist Party of Vietnam, and more remarkably said gains were made only within the last few decades. The domination and brutal exploitation of Vietnam by Imperialist Han China were accomplished by force and occupation, whereas the offers and surrenders of Vietnam's sovereignty, territories and domestic concessions to Imperialist Red China by Vietnamese communists were made through formal treaties, publicly and willingly, and where they would be more difficult to overturn later.

PART III

APPENDICES

**VIETNAM, A STARTING POINT FOR CHINA TO CONQUER 'THE EARTH':
ONE WORLD ONE DREAM ONE CHINA.
That is the Century of China**

PROCLAMATION of the *Committee on Protection of Territorial Integrity of Vietnam* about Pham Van Dong's diplomatic note on September 14, 1958

According to media in Vietnam, on September 15, 2008, China Embassy in Hanoi published a diplomatic note from Vietnam Prime Minister Pham Van Dong sent to Zhou Enlai, 50 years ago. It stated that the Democratic Republic of Vietnam (communist North Vietnam) acknowledged that the Paracels and Spratlys were Chinese territories.

On this occasion, the **Committee on Protection of Territorial Integrity of Vietnam** (the Committee) expressed its opinion on that diplomatic note.

LEGAL:

1. A transfer of the territorial land or sea must be decided by the people. People's intent on that issue must be stated publicly and freely. Congress has the utmost responsibility to formally express this people's intent, in an official format described by the Constitution. Therefore, this is an authority of the Legislature.

The Executive branch is a part of the government responsible for executing People's decisions. The Executive branch, i.e. the Vietnam government has no authority to make such a decision.

On behalf of the Democratic Republic of Vietnam (DRV), communist Prime Minister Pham Van Dong sent this diplomatic note on September 14, 1958, to the communist Chinese Premier Zhou Enlai to acknowledge China's territorial waters, following China's statement 10 days earlier. Pham Van Dong acted beyond the power of the Executive branch. He had no right to do it, and was not permitted to do so. Such an act had no legal validity.

2. Zhou Enlai claimed the 12 nautical miles, including the Paracel and Spratly Archipelagos. It is an act of invasion, because these two archipelagos were never owned by China. But with Zhou Enlai's statement, they were China's territory. This is an act contrary to the international law.

Pham Van Dong's act was an abuse of power. As a head of an exectuvie branch, he was not allowed to do it. Moreover, he recognizes Zhou Enlai's act which was illegitimate, So, what did Dong do was not valid. In this situation, enforcing Pham Van Dong's statement, China (People's Republic of China/PRC) is merely a hegemonist.

3. In the diplomatic note, absolutely there was no mention of the transfer of Vietnam's Paracels and Spratlys to Communist China. This note only refers to the recognition of 12 nautical miles from the Paracel and Spratly Archipelagos, as Zhou Enlai unilaterally stated. This piece of paper cannot be used to justify this transfer of a property from one entity to another.

4. When recognizing these two archipelagos as China's property, Pham Van Dong did it on behalf of the Democratic Republic of Vietnam (DRV) as the 'owner' of those two archipelagos.

In fact, under the 1954 Geneva agreemnt, they belonged to the South Vietnamese government. Pham Van Dong transferred something that North Vietnam did not have. Such a transfer was not valid because there was no **cosideration**. When there is no "object" or properly or no consideration for exchanging, the contract is void.

If Dong did so in exchange for Chinese aids to invade South Vietnam, it was a "false promise", something to deceive China.

Using Pham van Dong's note is just a pretext for Red China to take Paracels in 1974 and then some reefs of the Spratlys by force. In 1979, Pham van Dong sought ways to avoid respomsibilty for Red China's invasion by admitting that **because of "the war", he had to make such a decision**. Later, Foreign Minister Nguyen Manh Cam repeated the same explanation as a defense. However both of them forgot that at that time the CPV enjoyed the most "peaceful period" in order to build socialism in North Vietnam by harsh measures with support of the whole socialist block. There was no threat from imperialism.

Meanwhile, China cited other "evidences" of sovereignty over the two Paracel and Spratly archipelagos:

First: In 1956, Vietnam's deputy Foreign Minister Ung van Khiem told Chinese diplomat Li Zhiman, a "chargé d'affairs" of the Chinese embassy in Hanoi: historically, the Paracels and Spratlys were China's territory.

Such a statement had no legal basis, **if it existed**, especially when it occurred in a private office, not at a public place or a press conference. Often, after a meeting of diplomats, a joint statement is published, about issues of mutual concern. However, the joint statement was formed at a higher level. In this case, even with a joint statement, it does not help to transfer and assert sovereignty.

Second: China cited that student textbooks for 9th graders in Hanoi before 1974 stated that the Paracels and Spratlys formed a security belt protecting China against the 'imperialist plot'. Vietnam has intended to honor Master China, by forcing north Vietnamese students to study about the national defense for "fatherland China". However, Hanoi textbooks' teaching does not imply that Ho Chi Minh already surrendered these two archipelagos to China.

In summary, the diplomatic note recognizing China's sovereignty over the Paracel and Spratly Archipelagos has absolutely no valid legal basis.

DECLARES:

China relied on this diplomatic note to enforce the "promise" by North Vietnam leaders: in 1956, China deployed troops to occupy the Amphitrite Group (Tuyên Đức) and in 1974, the entire Crescent Group (Nguyệt Thiềm) in the Paracel Archipelago.

Later, they advanced deeper southbound, seizing a number of reefs in the Spratly archipelago. China enacted laws and made new maps to occupy the entire South China Sea. Chinese military have built islands from 8 reefs in the Spratlys, on which fortified sttructures have been erected for military purposes. Sansha district is created, to formally annex Vietnam's islands into China.

Thoughout history, China has always had a dream, to take over Vietnam, to annex it to China as a province.

Under this serious situation, the Committee demands

1) China:

a) To abolish China's statute promulgated in 1992, claiming the rights of China to control all navigations in the South China Sea, aiming at peventing the scientific ships and military vessels of foreign nations from coming to the sea.

b) To revoke the Chinese Map redrawing the boundary of the South China Sea, re- published in June 2006. That boundary is too close to Vietnam coastlines, obviously to deprive Vietnam's "Survival Space", to "strangle" the vitality of the Vietnamese people, in order for China to advance into sea for expansionist purpose and therefore forcing Vietnam to become a "province" of China.

c) To return to Vietnamese people the entire Paracel and the Spratly archipelago' Islands where China has illegally occupied.

d) To remove all Chinese military bases illegally built on the islands of Woody (đảo Phú Lâm), Triton (đảo Tri Tôn), Drummond (đảo Duy Mộng), etc. including China's command posts, seaports, airports, etc... built on the Paracel archipelago.

e) To destroy at least four Chinese fortified structures on the Fiery Cross Reef (đá Chữ Thập) and a three-story fortified structures on the Mischief Reef (Vành Khăn).....

f) To demand China to order their naval ships to stop shooting and killing Vietnamese fishermen, stop wrecking Vietnamese fishing boats working on Vietnam territorial waters. To end Chinese military exercises with live ammunitions, threatening lives of Vietnamese fishermen. To abolish the ban on Vietnamese fishermen fishing on the Paracel and Spratly Archipelagos. To abolish the Tam Sa/Sansha 三 沙 district established by the Chinese Council of State Affairs in November 2007.

2) the Communist Party of Vietnam (CPV)

To order the Socialist Republic of Vietnam (SRV) as an independent nation with full rights of self-determination

a) To publicly abolish Pham Van Dong's diplomatic note to Zhou Enlai on September 14, 1958.
b) To reject Pham Van Dong's "confession", and then repeated by Nguyen Manh Cam, citing "because of the war" to justify the plot to sell Vietnamese land..   c)
To order the Socialist Republic of Vietnam Navy to protect Vietnamese fishermen to fish in the Eastern Sea, including the Tonkin Gulf, instead of just being motionless, in watching the

enemy (China) killing our own people as in July 2007 in the Spratly Archipelago and in the Gulf of Tonkin in January 2005.

If Red China does not satisfy the above demands, Vietnam leaders could order Vietnam Navy to use explosives to destroy the Chinese military facilities on the Fiery Cross and Mischief Reefs... just as Philippines did in 1994 to a Chinese structures on an island near their coast. Don't be cowards anymore!

If China does not satisfy the above demands, then Vietnam is obligated to bring this matter before the Permanent Court of Arbitration (PCA) at The Hague, to request settlement of this dispute. Only the Socialist Republic of Vietnam has the standing and the right to raise that issue. No one can. Let me repeat that only the Socialist Republic of Vietnam as a legal entity has a right to do this before this international court. The Communist Party of Vietnam must be responsible to the Vietnamese people for this. There is no way to escape this duty. The Socialist Republic of Vietnam government must straightforwardly raise this issue. It is one way to atone for the crimes committed by Ho Chi Minh and his VCP members. Interestingly, the Socialist Republic of Vietnam has become a non-permanent Member of the United Nations Security Council (UN Security Council). In this position, the Socialist Republic of Vietnam needs to raise the banner of 'law and justice' to maintain world peace and security. This issue is directly related to the protection of the interests and the vital rights of the Vietnamese people. It is also noted that the international support for the Socialist Republic of Vietnam in the UN Security Council seat as a representative of the Vietnamese people to raise a voice for the oppressed people including the Vietnamese people in the international community, not to serve the hegemonist.

Few months ago, President Bush announced that the United States supported territorial integrity, when Nguyen Tan Dung came to Washington DC. The US Deputy Secretary of State Negroponte arrived in Hanoi, publicly calling for the South China Sea disputes to be settled according to the Law of the Sea. Thus, it is clear that there is no small US interest in regional stability, indirectly warning the hegemonists who cause instability to the world. In June, at a security conference held in Singapore including the United States, Japan, Australia, India, etc..., people called for the same. The free world would support the South China Sea dispute on that basis of the laws. That means, they will stand by Vietnam on this matter, against China aggressor.

The Committee demands the SRV government to act. For this dispute, the Committee also emphasizes legal documents be submitted to the International Court of Arbitration, including the Land Border Treaty signed in 1999, and the Tonkin Gulf Treaty in 2000.

Made in California September 15, 2008

Prof. Nguyen Van Canh

1. DISCUSSION ON PHAM VAN DONG's DIPLOMATIC NOTE AND CONSEQUENCES:

Forum on January 19, 2014 from 12:00 pm to 3:15 pm (edited)

Father Pham Son Ha, in Germany, introduced:

Thank you Ladies and Gentlemen, participants to the Forum.

Currently in Vietnam, there are serious discussions from intellectuals to ordinary citizens, including the state-controlled media about the Paracels battle in 1974 against the Chinese communist naval forces that invaded Vietnam. China launched a powerful fleet of 11 battleships and about 30 other supporting ships and vessels to invade the islands of South Vietnam. The RVN Navy only had four battleships to defend their islands. In this book "Dossiers on the Paracels & Spratlys and National Sovereignty", published for the third time, April 2010, page 69, Ptof. Canh wrote *"In the very first minutes of this battle, the RVN Navy forces sank Red China's Flagship 274. The entire operation command was under the direction of Admiral Phuong Quang Kinh, Deputy Commander of the South Sea Fleet, and the Front Commander, along with four Colonels, six Lieutenant Colonels (among them four were ship captains), seven juniot officers and a number of crew members were killed. China Patrol Craft Escort 271, and two Torpelleurs 389 and 396 were badly damaged and were later scrapped. Four fishing boats were sunk..."* 74 heroic navy soldiers of South Vietnam were sacrificed, including the Captain of Nhật Tảo battleship HQ-10, Major Nguy văn Thà and Vice Captain Nguyễn Thành Trí. 42 others were captured by China as prisoners of war. The HQ-10 naval battleship was hit, was pulled off the battle, and sank. Captain Nguy văn Thà decided not to get off from this ship, despite his injury. The captain died with the ship...

This is an example of a heroic sacrifice of the RVN Navy soldiers, in the mission of national defense, to protect Vietnam territorial integrity. This noble patriotc sacrifice must be upheld, honored, recognized forever in the heart of everyone. The Vietnamese people are proud of the noble sacrifices of the heroic officers Nguy văn Thà, Nguyễn thành Trí and 72 soldiers of the RVN on that maritime battle to defend Paracel Islands. On the contrary, the Vietnam communist leaders have quietly blocked the movement to commemorate those sacrificed soldiers in order to avoid China's anger. Admirable courage and determination of the soldiers of the Republic of Vietnam! A shining example. It is a sharp contrast to the coward attitudes of the CPV's leaders who assist the enemy invaders. Their People's Army were motionless when Chinese troops invaded Vietnam sea. One amusing point: when the battle started, another Vietnamese Communist Party's big brother, the Soviet Union through the Moscow Radio. condemned the Chinese invasion. And Hanoi leaders did not seize this opportunity to call on the Soviet Union for help to defend Vietnam's territory.

To day, January 19, 2014 is the 40th anniversary of the loss of the Paracels to Red China.. It is a day to honor those heroic warriors, who sacrificed themselves for defense of this beautiful nation that our ancestros have left to us, though they had shed so much blood to preserve It.

On this day, many Vietnamese groups/associations inland and overseas hold meetings to commorate this mighty Paracel battle. With us, to day I propose to talk about some other related issues with a hope that they could help glorify our heroes' sacrifices

They are:

I. Several issues related to Bien Dong/Eastern Sea/South China Sea, specifically related to the Paracels and Spratlys: **the diplomatic note of Pham van Dong, and the current situation of Bien Dong.**

II. What is the United States intention to help block the current China's scheme ofexpansionism? **This deals with the United States and Asia Security. See Appendice 7.** Now, the Forum once again welcomes Prof. Nguyen Van Canh.

First, we would like to introduce Professor Nguyen Van Canh.

Before 1975, Mr. Canh was Professor of Law and Politics, Saigon Faculty of Law. He was also a Lecturer at the National Defense College, and Command and General Staff College of the Republic of Vietnam Armed Forces.

In the United States, Professor Canh is a former Scholar of the "Hoover Institution on War, Revolution and Peace" at Stanford University, California.

He is Chairman of the Committee on Protection of Territorial Integrity of Vietnam (Uỷ Ban Bảo Vệ Sự Vẹn Toàn Lãnh Thổ Việt Nam).

Before starting the conference, Professor, please briefly introduce **about the Committee** that you represents. Three years ago, in January, you launched the "Global Paracel Day" to **commemorate soldiers of the Republic of Vietnam Navy sol**diers who lost their lives in the Paracel Battle in 1974, also **to assert Vitenam sovereignty over the Paacles and Spratlys**. Here in Germany, we responded to your call, and on that occasion, I had the pleasure of knowing you. I am very impressed with your knowledge and background, and see that the Committee on Protection of Territorial Integrity of Vietnam has played a very important role, with important contributions to people of Vietnam.

Prof. Nguyen van Canh:

"Around April 1994, scholar/professor Nguyễn Khắc Kham in San Jose, CA called me, saying : "I have an article written in Chinese about a conference in Taiwan, including 10 scholars from mainland China and about 100 local scholars. They met for two days, then declared that the Paracels and Spratlys belong to China. They called upon overseas Chinese around the world to help seek evidences, to prove China's sovereignty over the South China Sea. Please come and see me on this matter"

Scholar Kham was my professor years ago. So I visited him. Professor Kham said: "the Vietnamese communist government is quiet on this matter, because it has transferred lands and sea to China. The intellectuals inside Vietnam can't speak up. The Nationalist Chinese

(Taiwan) and Communist Chinese (China) usually are against each other, but they collaborate on this issue. Overseas, we can't sit still". Professor Kham said we must raise our voice on this.

I asked Professor Kham to lead the campaign. He refused and told me thad "You must do something about it."

So following his recommendation, I convened a meeting with 30 overseas Vietnamese intellectuals on June 22, 1994 at a conference room of the Hoover Institution on War, Revolution and Peace, where I worked. This group is known as the Overseas Vietnamese Intellectuals. The group made a public objection to the Chinese scholars statement arguing that the Paracel and Spratly Islands have long belonged to Vietnam legally, historically and geographically.

Soon after this, there were news from Chinese media saying a scholar found a piece of a broken bowl on a certain island, and an other person picked up a broken vase or pottery on another island. So I thought of having a permanent organization to deal with this problem. A year later, the Committee on Protection of Territorial Integrity of Vietnam came into existence. This Committee is composed of Professor Vu Quoc Thuc, Professor Nguyen Cao Hach, Attorney Vu Ngoc Tuyen, Attorney Vo Van Quan and me.

The Center For Vietnam Studies, established in 1987, becomes an arm of the Committtee, charged with a mission to collect and archive concerned materials. In 2007, when China established Sansha district to govern the two archipelagos of Vietnam, the Committee created a Sub Committee on Paracels

The purpose of this Committee, is to collect, evaluate, analyze, summarize, interpret the collected relative documents and resources, also to disseminate them to different places, especially a number of Research Centers for anyone who need to use them now or in the far future like in the next 100 years ffrom now. About disstribtion, the Committee provides documentary resources to the United States government officials. The Committee has eight channels of communication using various means, including electronic, to Vietnam. The Committee knows that many places have got our materials safely. The people in Vietanm need to be well informed, provided with well researched documents, so that the srtruggle for freedom and democracy in Vietnam will be more effective.

- Two books were published:

1) Dossiers on Paracels & Spratlys and National Sovereignty,

2) Territorial sovereignty and China Expansion. Over 30 maps drawn from the 16th century, mostly ancient, have proved Vietnam's sovereignty over this sea. Over 100 photos show omilitary facilities built on the Paracel archipelago. About 40 photos of fortified military fortresses have been built on 8 reefs, emerging from the water surfcae among some 16 islands in the Spratlys that China occupied since 1988.

-Publishing a White Paper, 2008, entitled " Red China's Expansionism over Paracels & Sprstlys with the collusion of the Socislist Republic of Vietnam."

- There are related research documents, such as "Protest against China's hegemony with Collusion of the CPV". There are maps showing Chinese expansion all over Asia (except Japan) as their territory, and maps showing Red China's intention to occupy the western part of the Pacific. These documents have been sent to the leaders of the United Nations.

-From 1994, about 60 statements related to Vietnam's Sovereignty over the Eastern Sea and on land have also been published.

 -Father Son Ha: Prof. Canh, now please start talking about the proposed topics.

-Prof. Canh:

1.1. THEME I: THE DIPLOMATIC NOTE OF PHAM VAN DONG AND STATUS OF THE EASTERN SEA (SOUTH CHINA SEA)

PHAM VAN DONG's DIPLOMATIC NOTE ON PARACELS - SPRATLYS:

The only important evidence that China relies on to prove its sovereignty is the letter of Pham Van Dong transferring the Paracels and Spratlys to China. That is the source of all problems in the South China Sea today. This piece of paper was used by China to justify its position in South China Sea, publicly, repeatedly, internationally. On September 14, 2008, the Chinese Embassy to Vietnam held a solemn ceremony right in Hanoi, celebrating the 50th anniversary of signing that diplomatic note. China reminded Vietnam leaders and Vietnamese people about that material evidence.

1.1.1. CONTENTS OF DIPLOMATIC NOTE

As Prime Minister of the Ho Chi Minh Government, Pham Van Dong sent a note to Zhou Enlai on September 14, 1958 to recognize of the decision of the People's Republic of China 10 days earlier, declaring China's territorial waters is 12 nautical miles, inluding the two Vietnam arhipelagos, i.e. China has sovereignty over the islands.

First of all, I read the diplomatic note of Pham Van Dong, Prime Minister of the Democratic Republic of (North) Vietnam.

Dear comrade Prime Minister,

We would like to bring to your knowledge that:

The Government of the Democratic Republic of Vietnam recognizes and supports the declaration of the Government of the People's Republic of China, dated September 4, 1958, about decision of the Chinese territorial waters.

The Democratic Republic of Vietnam Government respects this decision and will give instructions to its State bodies to thoroughly respect the 12-nautical-miles width of the territorial waters of China in all their relations in the maritime field with the People's Republic of China.

Best regards, comrade Prime Minister./.

September 14, 1958

This letter was voluntarily written by Pham Van Dong in response to Zhou Enlai's unilateral Declaration.

What does Zhou Enlai's statement on September 4 say? This Statement consists of 4 articles, and article I is written as follows:

Statement of the Government of the People's Republic of China on the Territorial Sea

(1) The territorial waters width of the People's Republic of China is 12 nautical miles. This provision applies to the entire territory of the People's Republic of China, including the Chinese land on the mainland and offshore islands, Taiwan... and adjacent islands, Penghu archipelago, Dong Sa archipelago, **Xisha islands (Paracels**), Zhongsha archipelago, **Nansha Islands (Spratlys),** and other islands belonging to China.

The coastal nations usually declared the border limits on the territorial water. China also did. By this Statement, China publicly claimed the sovereignty over the Xisha 黃 沙 (Hoàng Sa/Paracels) and Nansha 南 沙 (Trường Sa/Spratlys) of Vietnam. In response to that unilateral statement, Prime Minister Pham Van Dong of the Democratic Republic of Vietnam (communist North Vietnam) sent a note to Chinese Premier Zhou Enlai 周恩来 written as such: "The Government of the Democratic Republic of Vietnam respects this decision".

Thus, North Vietnam leaders admitted that China has sovereignty over the South Vietnam's archipelagos!

WHAT IS THE CAUSE THAT LEADS TO THE 'TRANSFER' OF SOVEREIGNTY TO RED CHINA?

This is clearly an act of selling a part of the nation. Why did Vietnam communist Leaders have such a decision?

According to the Far Eastern Economic Review issue dated March 16, 1979, because the public is surprised at the recognition of Chinese sovereignty over the Paracels and Spratlys, Pham Van Dong argued that "*It was at war times and I had to say that*". That excuse raises even more question because there was no war during that time in the region.

It was not until 1992, under the pressure of the public about this act, Nguyen Manh Cam, Foreign Minister of the Democratic Republic of Vietnam further developed the Pham van Dong's word of war, in a press conference on December 2, 1992. It was reported by Vietnam News Agency on December 3, as follows:

"The previous statement of our leaders was published in the following circumstances: With the Geneva Agreement of 1954, the southern territory of the 17th parallel, including the two archipelagos of Paracels and Spratlys was administered by the South Vietnam Government. Moreover, Vietnam must concentrate all forces at the highest priority to counter the American aggression in order to protect national independence. Therefore it seeks support from friends all over the world. Meanwhile, Vietnam-China relations are very close and the two countries trust each other. China has agreed to provide Vietnam with **massive support and priceless aid**. In this context and stemming from that urgent need, our **leadership's recognition** of China's sovereignty over the Spratlys and Spratlys **per China's demanding**, this was essential to preventing the US imperialists from using the islands to attack us; because it directly served the fighting for national independence and freedom.

Such recognition was not related to the historical and legal basis of Vietnam's sovereignty over the two Paracel and Spratly archipelagos."

Thus, Nguyen Manh Cam has explained more clearly about the "war" that Pham Van Dong: mentioned. It was the war of American aggression. In what was called the protection of national independence, Ho ordered Pham Van Dong to transfer those two archipelagos to Mao in the name of preventing the US imperialists from using those islands to attack Vietnam.

On the Far Eastern Economic Review, issue of March 16, 1979, in an article entitled "End of the Battle but Not of the War" **Nayan Chanda** commented on this matter: "**What has happened today in respect to the two archipelagos in South Vietnam, is the result of the "shady settlement" between China and North Vietnam, the two communist brothers. No one in the world community wants to step-in to help settling the current disagreement between the two communist nations of Vietnam and China. The reason is clear: the diplomatic note and recognition of the Vietnamese Communists cannot be erased by Vietnam, a small country who used a 'trick" to deceive China. Moreover, it is impossible for the Vietnamese Communists to escape China. In addition, Vietnam has to follow the communist China footsteps of ' renovation' to advance to socialism".**

"Though exuberant in creating a catastrophic war for both North and South, and greatly contributive to international communist movement, Ho has promised without self-respect and knowledge, to give China a portion of Vietnam's land that he will have in the future, though he knows that he is not sure whether he could swallow South Vietnam.

 "So, Who created the Vietnam War? Who were so willing to do everything possible to seize South Vietnam, even including selling land? Selling Land during wartime and even when Vietnam War ended, Pham Van Dong denied it, by blaming the war?".

Frank Ching, in the Far Eastern Economic Review, Feb 10, 1994, "Paracels Islands Dispute" wrote: "It is clear that there were times when the Saigon administration in fact stood up for Vietnamese interests far more staunchly than did the government in Hanoi. A case in point is the dispute over the Paracel Islands in the South China Sea. The Paracels, like the Spratlys further South, are claimed by both China and Vietnam. But when Hanoi was receiving aid from Beijing, it muted its claim to the Paracels. The islands were seized by China after a military clash in January 1974, during which Chinese troops beated the South Vietnamese defenders. Since then, the islands have been under Chinese control"…... "For as early as 1956 the Saigon government issued a communique reaffirming its ownership of the Paracels and the Spratlys. Saigon also issued decrees appointing administrators of the Paracels. Up until its defeat by Chinese forces in 1974 (only months before South Vietnam itself fell before the communist onslaught from the North), the Saigon government continued to assert Vietnamese sovereignty over the Paracels".

"It was very clear that Mr Ho Chi Minh, through Pham Van Dong, gave PRC "a big pie" because at that time Mr Ho Chi Minh was preparing for invading South Vietnam. Mr Ho needed colossal aids and closed eyes to accept all conditions of Beijing. It was easy for him to sell "only on paper" two archipelagoes which still belonged to South Vietnam by then".

Ho chi Minh, an evil man, sly and effective in using deceitful tricks, encountered China as an evil master in cheating. China knew well that Ho had no rights on those two archipelagos, at that time. The Han Chinese having a tradition of world expansion, can patiently wait, "ambush for long-term". Even if waiting for 100 years, for a convenient opportunity to seize the "object" they want. Being shortsighted, Ho only knew and used to use tactics to achieve temporary victory, such as seeking only little profit in the immediate future, so he was stuck in this case. Later, he explained " **because of war**", and " because of the **need to protect the country against the American imperialist aggression**", "**respect for Mao's decision**". That was a criminal act, reflected Ho's stupid mind. There was no shadow of war, no American imperialist activity lurking for invasion.

However, with *"massive support and priceless aids"* for Ho chi Minh regime, Mao Zedong achieved both goals:

a) Obtaining these two archipelagos peacefully. No blood loss for Mao to become "the owner" of South China Sea. Meanwhile, Ho chi Minh and his accomplices were also excited to receive great aids and seeing no loss..

b) Attacking and taking over South Vietnam. Unable to deploy his Chinese troops to conquer South Vietnam, Mao used Ho and his accomplices as vanguards to realize his ambitions..

Indeed, the explanations of Pham Van Dong and Nguyen Manh Cam prove that. After having occupied the North in 1954, Ho designed a plan to expand the communist power into the Indochinese peninsula, preparing to advance farther. Ho divided this region into 4 theaters of operations: A, North Vietnam; B, South Vietnam; C, Laos and Cambodia; and D, Thailand. Ho chi Minh was a pioneer in his mission to carry-out this destructive war. This was a "noble" duty of a serious international communist.

In this plan, B is South Vietnam, the first target to be taken. Ho urgently needed from Mao "massive support *(needing support from friends all over the world)* and priceless aid *(money, guns and other military necessities...)*, because it was an "**urgent need**".

Under Mao's plan to take all nations in the South East Asia region, South Vietnam is a staging base for China to further advance its hegemony. The anti-China Vietnamese patriotic nationalist forces still remain strong in South Vietnam. Mao knows that a foreign aggressor like Mao can't do it. Over 1,000 years of dominition is a lesson of experience of humiliation for China. The best way is to use local natives. Mao was clever to turn Ho and his communist affiliates into "mercenaries", unaware of their role as puppets who were serving Red China's interests.. It was Ho and his accomplices who were going to create a **terrible bloody fraternal war**, assisting Mao Zedong to annihilate the **patriotic Vietnmese nationalist forces**. In this war, in the name of safeguarding of independence and autonomy of the nation, Ho and his accomplices did not mercilessly slaughter their compatriots, destroying the fundamental values of nationalism and other forces against Mao.

In summary, all what has been happening throughout Vietnam from the 1950s to the present from culture, society, territory, economy, politics,... , has proven that Ho and the PCV have contributed priceless contrtibutions to the Chinese Communist Party's plan of expansion.

1.1.2. VALIDITY OF THE DIPLOMATIC NOTE

Does Pham Van Dong's note have any legal value to help China claim sovereignty over the Paracels and Spratlys?

A. In terms of content, the 'transfer' in the diplomatic note must be based on the spirit of freedom (no coersion), transparency, equality, uprightness,... even the motivation of this acknowledge must be legitimate. If not, this instrument will be considered as containig defects and will become worthless.

a) No one can transfer to someone else something that he does not have. The two archipelagos of Paracels and Spratlys at that time were owned by the Republic of Vietnam. North Vietnam did not have the legal ownership of those islands, how could it transfer them to China? Such a transfer is considered as a fraud. Ho chi Minh intended to deceive China in order to receive aids. On the other side, China knew it was a deception, but now still demands North Vietnam to acknowledge this territorial transfer. In addition, it was an abuse of power-an illegitimate act. The Republic of (South) Vietnam was the legal owner of the property, and had never granted it to Ho chi Minh, his accomplices or their communist regime.

b) Ho and his accomplices signed this recognition in a state of ignorance. Pham Van Dong excused himself "because of the war, then say so". Then communist Foreign Minister Nguyen Manh Cam added: *"We are focusing our efforts on fighting the American invasion"*. The war was so obsessive in their minds, so they lost the ability to judge. Cam said: " **such recognition was not related to the historical and legal basis of Vietnam's sovereignty over the two Paracel and Spratly archipelagos."** That time was the thriving era of Vietnamese communists, since there was no "American emperialist lurking for invasion". No "shadow of war" to threaten North Vietnam. Because of their lack of knowledge and confusion, Vietnam communist leaders lost their abilities to perceive the actions and consequences of that land transfer. An average person can see what is happening in the South China Sea today. It was like a blind faith to believe that "China approved so much aid". Nguyen Manh Cam emphasized: *"China agreed to provide us with massive support and priceless aids..."* for North Vietnam to meet the "urgent need" to fight *"against the American imperialist aggression, to defend the country"*. Because of that, they get so excited, then volunteer to play the role of the henchman in the international Communist conspiracy for Mao without knowing it.

c) Vietnam leaders are confused in trusting Red China. Nguyen Manh Cam praised that relationship as *"a warm Vietnam-China relation, and two countries trust each other"*; Ho gang has been mistaken in the belief on China 's "massive valuable aids". China's aids are not for free. Their mission, as a communist brother, is to build socialism/communism in North Vietnam, to prepare for invading South Vietnam, then to gradually take over Southeast Asia at their costs. It has been an international obligation. Ho chi Minh has been gravely mistaken, lacked intelligence and understanding. He gave up the sovereignty to China and could believe Vietnam "still has historical and legal sovereignty" on it ?

d) Inequality in this behavior: "Massive support and priceless aids" from big brother China was a debt trap for the poor communist Vietnam! Poor and greedy, North Vietnam had an "urgent need" to invade South Vietnam. In this condition, Ho was forced to accept the Chinese "demand" to recognize the Paracels and Spratlys as Chinese territory, in exchange for such aids.

e) Motivation to recognize "China's sovereignty" is also criticized. Ho and his accomplices exchanged South Vietnam's archipelago for aids in order to purssue a non- transparent or illigimate goal which is to expand of the International Communist Movement. The aid is used as a means to wage an aggressive war against South Vietnam. It was a terrible bloody fraternal war. And this event was confessed by Pham Van Dong and Nguyen Manh Cam. To be more specific, journalist Nayan Chanda of the Far East Economic Review mentioned above, said this was only a "shady settlement" of the two Communist brothers...

In short, the recognition of Vietnamese communists expressed in this Diplomatic Note is considered bearing so many defects. Therefore, it has no ltgal value.

And Vietnam's sovereignty over these two archipelagos remains unchanged.

B. With repect to procedure, a diplomatic note is only an "administrative letter" to exchange views between two governments (executive branches). Could such an administrative letter be considered official words to recognize national sovereignty? No! The transfer of sovereignty, land or sea, is not legitimate in this case. To transfer a territory, international law requires a treaty. For a treaty to take effect, both partners must first sign a transfer document. When it comes to this, it must be made clear between parties that the exchange is like buying or selling something. Of course, a land transfer must be legitimate and open for the public to understand and comment. Vietnam's National Assembly must approve that "document" or initiative on land transfer. Finally, the head of state must promulgate it.

In some countries, a referendum is needed. Territory sale is a serious matter, requiring a government procedure, to honor the will of the nation. If it is not done so, that act is flawed, and invalid.

C. Chinese Act is illegal. In the statement, Zhou unilaterally and implicitly claimed to have owned those two archipelagos. Unilateral declaration of ownership of two such archipelagos is an illegitimate act. China has never legally acquired ownership of these two archipelagos. Vietnam has been the owner for thousands of years and is the owner. Pham van Dong's recognition of Zhou's declaration is not valid, because Zhou has never been owner of the two archipelagos..

D. To declare 12 nautical miles of territorial sea, according to the Law of the Sea and the nine-dash line map. The 1982 Law of The Sea allows an island to be extended into the open sea, which is the " continental shelf", and the "exclusive economic zone" of 200 nautical miles, beyond the "territorial sea of 12 nautical miles". For an island to have this sovereign right, it must have all the conditions defined, such as the self-sustaining (economic) condition, to earn the status of an island. The reefs in these two archipelagos claimed by Chnia are not eligible, as defined in the 1982 Law of the Sea (Công Ước LHQ về Luật Biển 1982). On the other hand, geographically, these two archipelagos of South Vietnam are very far from the mainland China. Especially, the Spratlys is over a thousand kilometers away from the mainland China. So how could they be Chinese territory? When Zhou Enlai claimed sovereignty over the Paracels and Spratlys, with the 200-nautical-mile expanded into sea in order to draw a 9-dash map in the South China Sea, China could not rely on that, to justify it. It is the arrogant behavior of the powerful expansionist that disrespects the law and the world order.

In summary, legally, the Pham Van Dong's diplomatic note is not legitimate. Therefore the China's invocation of that diplomatic note as a proof of her sovereignty is only an unjustified excuse of a "strong hegemonist."

It is Pham Van Dong's Diplomatic Note used as an excuse for China to occupy these two archipelagos. Currently, China already has an aircraft carriers and several military fortitied installations on the two archipelagos to protect their assets illegally seized. They have established an administrative agency to manage them, and thus formally annex the entire South China Sea into China. So, the communist Vietnam must be responsible for this problem. As a government, the Socialist Republic of Vietnam leaders under the leaderhsip of the CPV has a duty to reclaim the Paracel and Spratly Archipelagos.

1.1.3. SOLUTION TO RECLAIM THE PARACEL AND SPRATLY ARCHIPELAGOS

The Communist Party of Vietnam must take great responsibility for losing the Paracel and Spratly islands to China. This is a serious crime, because they are deeply involved in a conspiracy to sell Hoang Sa-Truong Sa to the enemy of the nation, and can never be forgiven.

At the risk of the Chinese Communist's permanent possession of the archipelagos as everyone witnessed, in order to atone for this crime, at least, the Vietnamese Communist Party and the Socialist Republic of Vietnam must do some works, as to lay a **legal and political foundation** for presnt time or future generations to reclaim soverignty.

Only the Socialist Republic of Vietnam has a standing to do this.

a). The Party must give an order to the SRV goverment to publicly denounce Pham Van Dong's letter is *"null and void"*. There is no need to send such a Statement to China. This behavior may or may not cite the reason, and I emphasize that unilateral public declaration is sufficient.

If the Vietnamese communists wants to cite a reason, it could say that the leaders were seduced and promised by Red China to have abundant financial and military aids, to invade South Vietnam; or that being extremely fascinated by the socialist ideology, shortsighted or over excited by victoies few years ago, or were stupiid, the previous Admisntration of Vietnam blindly agreed; or that they was deceived by China conspiracy, therefore they could not know that this is a debt trap and Red China now asks to transfer the archipelagos to her. A reason that Nguyen manh Cầm raised could be used to invalidate Pham van Dong's note: *"Recogniton of the 12 miles has nothing to do with the legal and historic sovereignty"*...

b) This matter must be brought to the Permanent Court of Arbitration at The Hague, to accuse China of invading by forces, taking the Paracel archipelago in 1956, in 1974. Also China is occupyng 6 reefs in the southern Spratly archipelago in 1988, and others in 1992. China has built so many fortified military structures to protect their occupation. This lawsuit, to be submitted, is the beginning of the mission to reclaim Vietnam's sovereignty. No matter how long the process would take, at least that is the basic step. *The Committee on Protection of Territorial Integrity of Vietnam* has sufficient documents, maps and photographs as evidences available for this purpose.

Communist Vietnam must stop supporting China for permanent occupation of the Eastern Sea that the Vietnamese people have inherited from their courageous ancestors. Vietnamese communists should not continue their cowardice, or hiding that cowardice by "just saying that Vietnam's legal and historical sovereignty", or announcing that "they are going to purchase weapons (submarines)" to 'defend ' Vietnam's territorial seas.

The Philippines is an immediate lesson to learn.

c). Of course. those two measures above are necessary legal solutions. But this is only the first step to be taken for the purpose of defending Vietnam territory. There are also long-term preparations in all such aspects as *diplomacy, economy, military,...* especially building the **internal strength** such as mobilization of all national forces in this struggle against China hegomonistic ambitions. And stop all helping hands activities provided to the enemy of the Vietanmes people.

The Committee on Protection of Territorial Integrity of Vietnam many times so far has demanded the SRV to do these things.

It was Ho chi Minh's scheme that led to the disastrous situation today in the South China Sea.

So what is the situation in the South China Sea

Pham Van Dong's Diplomatic Note, as mentioned in Part I, is the only pretext for China to justify her act of invasion of the Paracel and Spratly Archipelagos by forces. Communist Vietnam has signed a seller's note, and they have received aids/money. It's a debt trap. The pay-back "items" are the Paracels and Spratlys. Now China, the buyer, has deployed the military or the use of forces to enforce the commitment.

That letter leads to the following situation on Biển Đông/EasternSea/South China Sea.

1.1.4. SITUATION IN EASTERN SEA

On June 23, 2012, the State Council of the People's Republic of China (Red China) approved the establishment of "*Địa Các Tam Sa Thị*", which means the City of Sansha 三沙市 (Tam Sa Thị) and its headquarters located on the Woody Island, part of Vietnam's Paracel Islands. Originally, Sansha was a small area on Hainan 海南 Island. In November 2007, China established an agency to manage three archipelagos, including the Paracels and Spratlys of Vietnam and gave it the name of District of Sansha. Now, China upgraded this administrative unit from the district level to the city level. Also, again to remind the world that China has actually merged the area of nine-dash-line (Biển Đông of Vietnam) into China. To officially govern this maritime area, China has established an administrative system here, even there were no inhabitants and no economic activities (1). The Chinese Congress's Standing Committee of Hainan Province, at the 32nd conference on July 17, 2012, decided to form People's Council for the Sansha City. This is a legislative body, consisting of 45 members (2), located in a two-story brick house (3) on Woody Island. They are responsible for enacting laws for this regional area. A large number of members of the Chinese People's Council makes people mistakenly believe that these archipelagos have a very large Chinese population.

Xinhua News Agency said the first conference of the "Sansha City People's Council" ending Monday July 23, elected Bo Trang, former Deputy Chief-of-Staff of the Hainan Military Region, as Council President and Tieu Kiet was appointed as Mayor, head of the city's administrative agency.

In addition, Global Times reported that China was building a jail and made it clear that it was for detaining foreign fishermen that Beijing accused of illegally infiltrating their waters.

In addition, especially to alert the countries in the region, Red China announces "the militarization of Sansha City". Ministry of Defense spokesman Yang Wuquan said China already established the Sansha Military Headquarters. Colonel Tai Hyhong, was appointed commander of the city, and Liu Chaoyi, a colonel, to serve as political commissar. The representative of the Red China Ministry of National Defense also stated that the mission of the Sansha military agency is to mobilize defense forces, to protect Sansha city and to assist in disaster prevention. About the defense activities at sea (outside the two archipelagos) are still under control of the Chinese Navy (China Daily July 27, 2012).

On the other hand, the International Radio of China reported that on June 28, during a press conference in Beijing, a defense official, Canh Nhan Sinh, said that the military has established a patrol program to "prevent war on the Spratlys waters", within the framework of activities to protect «national sovereignty»..., «the determination and will of the Chinese military to protect national sovereignty and territorial integrity are inexorable." China creates a situation, with teams of patrolling vessels ready for combat. Chinese officer Cảnh Nhạn Sinh bluntly said China will be firmly against "*any military aggression from any neighboring countries*".

Announcing the decision of establishing the Sansha Command and placing garrison under this Command, then its mission meant that the Red China is ready to use forces to protect its sovereignty.

ooo

Since the 1970s, after having taken the Paracel archipelago from the Republic of Vietnam, Red China has built barracks, facilities, airfields, wharves, weapons depots, telecommunication systems... everywhere.

The following are some military structures made of reinforced concrete on:

A) Paracel Archipelago: -Woody is the most important center, with a runway of 2700 m long, 120 m wide for jet aircrafts. Since Woody Island was a small island, (about 1.3 square kilometers) China filled in more cement and conglomerates at both ends of the runway for extension. In the 1970s, the runway length was 1,000 m, for propeller aircrafts. There are two seaports for battleships, two 2-story buildings, helipads, four 5000-m3 reservoirs for rainwater (each year, up to 140,000 tons of rainwater collected for military use), telecommunication facilities, meteorological stations, radar systems. The barracks were constructed for a thousand Chinese soldiers (marines) to station. In the northeast, a small dune has an access road. Here are the ammunition depots. Woody Island is one of the four islands where the Chinese Army has arrested, detained, beaten, looted and punished for a ransom Vietnamese fishermen in Ly Son Island, who fish in the Paracels area.

There is not a single civilian inhabitant here, nor any economic activity.

-Duncan Island, where the battle against Red China aggression took place in January 1974, is an island with a large command post.

- The Chinese military bases are also built on other Islands: Tree island} Mộc/Cây), Lincoln is;and} Robert Robert (Hữu Nhật), Money Island {Quang Ảnh). On Triton Island (đảo Tri Tôn)/ 123 nautical miles away from Cù Lao Ré, Quảng Ngãi) there is a tele-communications structure. and China built a seaport in 2012,

B. In Spratlys, right nw, 2008 there are more than a dozen military fortified structures, massive towering over the water, at south reefs of the archipelago such as the Fiery Cross (5 architectures), Mischief (4), and Johnson, Subi, Gaven, Hughes, Chiqua, Cuarteron.

In summaary, all of the activities and behaviors listed above which Red China has carried out is a long process to legalize the appropriation of Eastern Sea from Vietnam. This is an evidence that China is merging the Eastern Sea into the territory of China. In this situation, China has considered the Eastern Sea (South China Sea) as her territory and is ready to protect it by force.

ooo

China knows that the occupation was illegal, and it seeks to legitimize (legalize) that territory. How? If China forces communist Vietnam to sign a treaty to transfer, the later dares not to do such thing openly, though it has quietly supported the enemy to achieve this goal. The best way under this situation to assert soveingnity over the Eastern Sea and then protect it, is

-to use political influence of a great power in placing Vietnamese communist cadres who are pro-Chinese in key government positions as it has happened in the present frame work of the two-party sistership relation. Om one side, the leaders positively pevent (or eliminate) any opposition to China's activities to exercise its rights as owner of the sea and on the other China carries out continuously such activities as patrol, arerest of Vietnamese fishernen for fishing illegally in their "waters", military exercise from May to August every year ......, In a long run, the sovereignty will become an acceptable reality.

-to bribe the CPV leaders with a huge amount of dollars in exchange for concessions. The bauxite ore mine exploitation case in the Central Highlands or the Ha Tinh project of metalurgy are examples.

Such continuous activities could be extended for a long period of time, even a decade or more if necessary. At first it will be a defacto recognition, then it is a "fait accompli".

These methods are used for the time being i.e. when China is still weak. However, when it is strong enough, it will use force to attain the goal.

Re. the two areas of China activities: exercise the sovereign rights and defend the claimed sovereignty, see Appendice 4: RED CHINA USES FORCES TO LEGITIMIZE SOVEREIGN RIGHTS OVER THE SPRATLY ARCHIPELAGO

In January, 2014, Beijing announced that it would deploy a 5000-tonne surveillance ship to be stationed in Woody Island for patrol.

With this plan, China will extend its operation for ten or even a hundred years. Vietnam's Eastern Sea will become the territorial sea of China; like Guangxi and Yunnan/ Those two Chinese provinces, once belonging to Vietnam, are now something that exists in the memory of very few Vietnamese people.

The contributor of this present achievement to the Chinese Communist Party is Ho Chi Minh and the successive generations of leadership of the Vietnamese Communist Party. In the past, when the Vietnamese people lost Guangxi, Yunnan, they had to make a way to the south. Now, **Biển Đông, the Eastern Sea is the last survival space for the Vietnamese people**.

Losing it is to lose everything.

In one of my articles, I wrote: there are ten million Vietnamese fishermen living along the coasts from Thanh Hoa (north) to Ca Mau (south). Under Vietnamese communist ruling, those fishermen could not make living except that they become Chinese or "Sinicized" (assimilated into Chinese), and flying the Chinese Red flags on their fishing boat, they are safe offshore. And also the entire nation of Vietnam will gradually becomes part of the Great Han Chinese Empire

Note:

1) Chinese military has built rainwater reservoirs along the edges of the runways. Immediately after publishing Part I, an alumni from Saigon College of National Defense called, asking me about potable water in Woody. I told him: drinking water is a serious disadvantage of China's military, while building the fortified structures on Vietnamese islands. That alumni *"demanded Vietnam Prime Minister Nguyễn tấn Dũng to act immediately, not just talking out loud on this matter. Prime minister Nguyen Tan Dung should "bravely" announce the defense for Vietnam sea. Dung said "he does not exchange sovereignty over the islands for unrealistic, vaguely peaceful friendship". With Kilo submarines equipped with the state-of-the-art missiles from Russia, and the supersonic missiles purchased from India, Vietnam could destroy China's military structures and eliminate all Chinese troops occupyng here, by launching a series of rockets at once. Particularly at Woody Island, if we just launch six rockets into the middle of the runway on Woody Island, the water tanks will be broken and as a consequence, the defending troops will have to surrender... The "National Self-Defense" troop, formed by Vietnam Communist National Assembly three years ago, will acquire those islands"* I told him that what did Dung state is just a "joke".

(2) The 45-member City Council is a hoax, to deceive the world. This is a propaganda. It is to give to the world an impression that about a 'million inhabitants' are living on the island, with such many "delegates" representing them. In fact, on Woody Island, there are only barracks with flat houses builtt for troops. On the other islands, there are only soldiers. There are no regular houses for ordinary inhabitants. Very few roads for traffic, because the island are too small.

(3) The "City Hall" is located in a two-story building, in the military base. It is one of the two similar buildings, announced to be "the administrative office to serve civilian people".

(4) The same thing happened in the past. In 2000, the communist Vietnam and China signed the Treaty on Fisheries in the Gulf of Tonkin, to divide it into two different sections. But greedy China demanded extra 'joint fishing area'. Each side gathered its own fleet of fishing vessels to go fishing with the other. Both of them go fishing together and the catch will be divided in half. After signing the Treaty, Vietnam's National Assembly hesitated to ratify it, because China had too many large fleets of ships with 200 horse powers, well equipped, with better fishing nets of 60 nautical miles at length, managed by two trawlers at the net's ends. Only China had those ships. Vietnamese fishing boats are made of wood, more fragile at sea. Everyone knows that such steel ships are owned by China. Large Chinese fishing fleets navigating freely on the South China Sea will be exposed internationally. Vietnamese could find out such a cooperation with Chinese and oppose to the party. Therefore, the National assembly dared not pass it. Because of the long delay, in February 2002, Jiang Zemin came to Hanoi to pressure Nong Duc Manh, to have it approved by the National assembly. It was finally

passed in June, two years later comparing to the Land Border Treaty: it was passed only in 6 months.

1.2. THEMES II: THE USA AND ASIA SECURITY

Please see Appendice 7

1.2.1. SOLUTION TO THE DIPLOMATIC NOTE PROBLEMS

Nha Tran, RFA correspondent

2008-09-17

Communist Prime Minister Pham Van Dong's diplomatic note in 1958 expressed his approval of China's decision on Vietnam's territorial waters. It was about the two archipelagos Paracel and Spratly in South Vietnam. It caused waves of frustrated discontent and indignation, in the Vietnamese communities, national and international.

Nhã Trân (RFA) interviewed Dr. Nguyen Van Canh, Chairman of the Committee on Protection of Territorial Integrity of Vietnam, a scholar on international laws, on his perspectives for a solution to solve this problem based on international laws and the United Nations Convention on the Law of the Sea, UNCLOS).

Administrative letter

Asked about how do international laws or UN Convention of the Law of the Sea deal with China behaviors regarding attacking and killing Vietnamese soldiers and fishermen for decades in the Paracel and Spratly Islands, right in Vietnamese territorial waters?

AFP photo: Chinese Marines Drills

Dr. Nguyen Van Canh answered:

According to the international Law of The Sea, as well as the general principle of law, China's action of invading the territory of another country, as the case of Vietnam will never be allowed nor never accepted. It is really an aggression.

Nha Tran: Doctor, also according to international laws or the UN Convention on Law of the Sea, Pham Van Dong's diplomatic note issued in 1958 supports the Chinese declaration of their territorial sovereignty within 12 nautical miles, at that time. Within the legal framework, is the occupation of both archipelagos of Paracels and Spratlys of Vietnam by China legal?

Dr. Nguyen Van Canh: Pham Van Dong's diplomatic note only recognizes 12 nautical miles that the Chinese government at the time declared was not valid in tetms of a transfer of the islands. The diplomatic note of a prime minister, or from an executive branch is only an administrative letter in the field of diplomacy. On the issue of territorial transfer, the constitutions of most states require a treaty which is then ratified by Congress. It represents the will of the people on the transferring of territory. The Executive is not authorized to do this job. Besides, it is important tto note that when Zhou Enlai declared "those 12 nautical miles", he implied that China had been the owner of the islands. However, in reality, they still belonged to Vietnam. So when Zhou Enlai's claim was illegal, Pham Van Dong's regconition of what the Chinese leader declared was not valid either.

Nha Tran: Doctor, did you just say both of their acts are illegal?

Dr. Nguyen Van Canh: Yes. All are not valid. As Zhou Enlai's statement was illegal, Pham Van Dong's act acknowledged that illegal declaration. In the end it was of no value. It is a general principle of law.

Territorial Concessions in exchange for aids

Nha Tran:. While these two archipelagoes were officially under the management and control of the South, the Republic of Vietnam Government has asserted that sovereignty since the signing of the 1954 Geneva Agreement. What do you think about the motivation for the former Prime Minister of the Democratic Republic of Vietnam when he approved the 1958 claim sovereignty of the People's Republic of China over the sea including Vietnam's Paracels and Spratlys.

Dr. Nguyen Van Canh: This is something like the Frank Ching of the Far Eastern Economic Review saying in 1979 that Mr. Pham Van Dong sold what he didn't have, or in other words, he wanted to deceive China in exchange for China supports and aids for Hanoi authorities to bring troops to invade the South Vietnam.

Unfortunately, when Hanoi authorities won the war and occupied South Vietnam, it became a big problem. Red China now uses her power to enforce that promise. That's the reason for which Vietnam has to deal with to day.

Nha Tran: The diplomatic note from the former Prime Minister of the Democratic Republic of Vietnam was also used by Beijing to support her activities of invading Vietnam's sovereignty over the Paracels and Spratlys. Therefore, in terms of legal requirements, in this situation, what should Vietnam do to invalidate that diplomatic note? And to reassert her sovereignty over the two Paracel and Spratly archipelagos?

Dr. Nguyen Van Canh: The Socialist Republic of Vietnam has many ways to do. **First** , the SRV can make a declaration publicly and solemnly to reject Pham van Dong's note. The SRV just makes a public statement. This is e-noguh. The don't need to cite reasons.

Second, the SRV demands Beijing government to abolish a law enacted in 1982 on the "exercise of sovereignty" over the South China Sea. China announced that anyone passing by this sea, must be authorized by China. The law specifies that oil research as well as military ships passing by must ask for permission from Beijing authorities. The 1992 law was just based on that Pham Van Dong's statement.

Third, the SRV also requires China to destroy all military structures on the Paracels and Spratlys.

Intervention of The International court?

Nha Tran: Sir, in recent years there is ample evidence that one of China's top goals is becoming hegemonic in the South China Sea. So is there any hope to prevent it? If Beijing ignores Vietnam objection, can Hanoi bring the matter to the International Court of Justice?

Dr. Nguyen Van Canh: If Red China's government continues her path, Vietnam could as a sovereign, independent country, bring the matter to the Permanent Court of Arbitration at The Hague, because her rights are violated. Private persons don't have a standing to bring that matter to the International Court.

The government of Socialist Republic of Vietnam must be obliged to bring the matter to the International Court. Recently, we have published the "*White Paper on Vietnam's Sovereignty over the Paracels and Spratlys*", asking for an international intervention. 192 members of the United Nations as well as many Heads of State must come forward to support Vietnam with a purpose to help resolve the South China Sea dispute, not allowing a blatant abuse by "a srong who oppresses a weak".

Nha Tran: Has there been any case like this before the International Court of Justice?

Dr. Nguyen Van Canh: Like Vietnam, there are no cases. The case of Vietnam is very special because the Vietnamese government itself has tacitly transferred the territorial sea to China, and quietly allowed China to invade her Eastern Sea. It is the behavior of a government to sell a nation.

Nha Tran: Thanks to Dr. Nguyen Van Canh, Chairman of the Committee on Protection of Territorial Integrity of Vietnam, for today's discussion.

Dr. Nguyen Van Canh: This is a very important issue. More details are needed to explain the whole problem. The short answers do not fully explain it. For more information, please visit our website www.vietnamadvisory.org.

Nha Tran: Yes. Good Bye Sir.

(1) On May 5, 2014, Le Hai Binh, spokesman for the Communist Vietnam State Department, on the occasion of the HD 981, spoke out that Pham Van Dong's diplomatic note was not legitimate.

1.2.2. VIETNAMESE COMMUNIST LEADERS TALK ABOUT VIETNAM LANDS AND TERRITORIAL WATERS?

- On September 23, 2008, the *Văn Hóa* (Culture) Magazine interviewed Lê công Phụng, Vietnam Ambassador in USA. The following is summary of main points.

(www.vanhoamagazine.com)

RFA 25 September, 2008- Journalist Lý Kiến Trúc... "Thirdly, regarding Paracels-Spratlys disipute with China, I asked him as to how to solve this problem. Lê Công Phụng cited words of the American Deputy Minister from a recent press conference in Hanoi, affirming that US companies have the right to exploit and do business offshore where Vietnam has sovereignty. President Bush also announced that USA will protect the territorial integrity for Vietnam.

Asked about proposed dialogues, Phung says Vietnam has always advocated for dialogues and is determined to defend Vietnam's land and sea. Phung affirms that Paracels and Spratlys are indisputably territories of Vietnam, though Paracels is now completely occupied by China. He said:

"Regarding the Paracels and Spratlys: Vietnam has sufficient evidences, legally and historically to assert Vietnam's sovereignty over the Paracels and Spratlys. Many people suggest that Vietnam take this matter to the International Court, or to the United Nations to fight for sovereign rights over Bien Dong. **We are planning to do so**. We also see that our country Vietnam is next to China. Our ancestors have placed us there, we must be there. We are living next to a big nation, so must know how to survive.

We defeated the Chinese feudal lords, then we provided rice, food, gold, horses, carts, and even rolled out red carpet for them to go home. It is our father's experiences of living next to a vast neighboring country. We have learned this from our ancestors.

Now that China is such a developed nation. We can't stop them for being a strong country, so we must learn how to co-exist with a big strong nation. Honestly, if China is in trouble, we would not be at peace neither. We definitely must guard our own sovereignty, lands, territories. We must know how to co-exist with them".

INTERVIEW ON TERRITORY AND TERRITORIAL WATERS

Translated by Do my Thien, Ph.D

Orange County, 26-10-208, *Văn Hóa* interviewing Prof. Nguyen Van Canh.

Editor's note: Prof. Nguyen Van Canh has edited the answers in this interview and provided additional details and illustrations.

* Prof. Nguyen Van Canh's Response to Ambassador Le Cong Phung's statements

* A Vietnamese Motto:' when the country is in danger, it's every ordinary citizen's responsibility...'

Ly Kien Truc: Greetings, Professor, firstly on behalf of the Vietnamese Diaspora's TV station Freevn.net and Van Hoa magazine, we are honored to receive you and thank you for having agreed to grant us this special interview today, and may we wish you the best of health, so you could continue with the work for the benefit of our future generations. Please refer to *www.vanhoamagazine.com*

Prof Nguyen Van Canh: Greetings to Journalist Ly Kien Truc and to all audience, it is my honor to be here today to answer questions Mr. Ly Kien Truc might pose in relation to the Gulf of Tonkin, Hoang Sa and Truong Sa (the Paracel and Spratley Islands) as well as issues related to a certain point on the Vietnamese territory. I will try to answer each and every question you might raise.

LKT: Professor, prior to our interview with the Socialist Republic of Vietnam's Ambassador Le Cong Phung in Washington, D.C., we managed to contact a few officials and were informed that a White Paper you authored has been sent to various important American legislative and executive authorities, and to the General-Secretary and 192 members of the UN.... Because of the very effect of this White Paper, some embarrassment has been felt by the current Hanoi government, as the White Paper expresses everything that Vietnamese at home and overseas could possibly get hold of as the truth related to the Sino-Vietnamese border issues, to the Gulf of Tonkin, to Paracel and Spratley islands.

Consequently Ambassador Le Cong Phung through some intermediaries organized for us an interview, where Mr. Phung talked about negotiation process between Vietnam and China on the Sino-Vietnamese border. Throughout this process of negotiation, starting from 1991 as the year Vietnam reconciled with China, since you have been following this negotiation process between Vietnam and China, has there been anything new arising that you have noticed?

Prof Canh: The negotiating process did not start from 1991. These negotiations took place prior to 1979, a period before the time Communist China (CC) attacked Communist Vietnam (VC) in that year. Both sides already had discussions. In the beginning, the VC still took the Franco-China Treaty that is the 1885 Tien-Tsin agreement, together with its 1887 Convention as basis for negotiations, while CC refused to recognize it as a fact. The strange thing is whatever the CC demanded; the VC later abandoned their previous position and yielded to

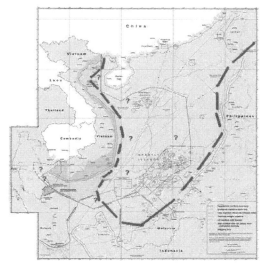

those demands. It means the border determined by the 1887 Convention was no longer used as basis for negotiations. The inability to keep to that border determination results in making territorial concessions, therefore legitimating the Communist Chinese expansionist occupations.

LKT: Professor, in Mr. Le Cong Phung's interview on the negotiation process, he stated that what did Hanoi agree on is based on the 1885 Tien-Tsin agreement and its 1987 convention, together with clauses of the 1982 law of the sea. If those legal bases were used as they said, why would you think there has been further and further retreat in the face of such Chinese Communist encroachment?

Prof Canh: I think the gradual retreat and concession to CC have been due to the VC leadership who has become the CC's lackeys, and in the White Paper, I call them missionaries. As time goes on, the extent of their servility to China becomes greater. It would earn them the name indigenous governors (puppets) who reign Vietnam on behalf of foreign aggressors. It is them who carry out the hegemonic ambition of Communist China over the Southeastern region.

You have enquired about the Tien Tsin agreement signed in 1885. This agreement had been recognized and gone into effect for more than one hundred years that the VC quoted in their negotiations with CC, for which I can hardly consider it as a sound foundation. Thus in negotiations, the VC have yielded to CC's demand and tacitly abandoned that agreement while making concessions for a new border line to be set up. That is their 'mission' of selling out our land and sea.

In addition, they also assisted in a tacit way the inclusion of a portion of Vietnamese land into Chinese territory. It could also be added that their action is tantamount to assimilating Vietnamese to Chinese ethnicity, akin to what Truong Chinh announced in 1951 in the name of Lao Dong Party Secretary-General...... And the new borderline that CC has drawn over the Vietnamese part of South China Sea which has been dubbed "the dragon's tongue" on the new map, redrawn and published by CC in June 2006, is an example of how the Communist Party of Vietnam (CPV) tries to help CC achieve their hegemonic objectives.

Up to now, the CPV has not taken any active action against this CC move. That Vietnamese students' demonstrations against CC at home about the Paracel and Spratley issues in recent months having been savagely crushed is another instance. The new South China Sea borderline gives CC a right to ownership of the territorial waters as close as to Vietnamese coastline and therefore bloc off Vietnamese Survival Space, and I shall come back to this issue later:

LTK: Yes, Professor. Back to the negotiation on land borders, Mr. Le Cong Phung said he has been accused of selling off land near the border area between Vietnam and China. He asserts however no precious square kilometers are lost, and the Nam Quan pass is there, still intact, so is the Ban Gioc waterfall. Professor, do you agree with these statements Mr. Le Cong Phung made on Free Asia Radio recently?

Prof. Canh: Incorrect, completely incorrect, and I can even say that those are lies really. In listening to that interview, I think he confirms that the Socialist Republic of Vietnam government has used the Franco-China Agreement of 1885 or the Tien-Tsin agreement signed between Patenôtre and Ly Hung Chang as legal basis for the negotiation. It turns out that the agreement was eliminated completely. If we compare Phung's statements with a main document issued in 1979 by the Vietnamese Communist Party, which is, entitled "The Question of Border between Vietnam and China", we will find that the above stated points are totally incorrect.

I will take for example the Trinh Truong area adjacent to Mong Cai. This area stretches six kilometers along the border and 1.5 km deep inside Vietnamese territory. The CC side has 'swallowed' all that area and annexed it to the so-called Dong Hung commune. So what does it mean by saying not a single square kilometer has been lost? Likewise there are 40 similar spots along that border, and at many of those spots, the CC have come over to chase Vietnamese inhabitants away and occupy their land and houses, then brought in CC settlers before formalizing the situation. There are other places with 9 km in length and 1.5 km in depth, and therefore "the difference of only one square kilometer between two sides" stated by Mr. Phung is completely fallacious. I have documents authored by the government of the Communist Vietnam that denounced the Chinese over this matter. There are so many details, and I cannot discuss it fully here.

I will include a summary to make it more comprehensive.

The more important issue presently is the question of the Spratley islands: the consequences of Ho Chi Minh's decision on the transfer of the Spratleys and Paracels to Red China and an extremely huge potential danger arises for all Vietnamese people's rights and interests. This also involves what you have referred to as effect on peace and stability in the Southeast Asian region. In reality, the potential danger to stability can spread even further.

LKT: Professor, I would like to return if I may to the issue of the Spratleys and Paracels. To continue with our conversation today Professor, there is a rather important point Mr. Le Cong Phung appears to be very concerned about and has expressed some personal frustrations over the issue of Sino-Vietnamese border. What did Mr. Phung reveal to me is that from now until the end of December this year, conflicts over some high grounds along the Sino-Vietnamese border are to be solved. About those high spots, I asked Mr. Phung if they are strategic routes that Chinese armies had used over thousands of years to invade Vietnam, he said that they would be. Those six high spots are still under contention between Vietnam and China, would you, Professor, you have a definitive appraisal of those six spots, and in your opinion, what importance do those high spots play in the present context of Sino-Vietnamese relations?

Prof. Canh: First of all, for many years Beijing has pressured the VC to complete quickly the border pegging and marker building. Why? To make it a "fait accompli" and therefore render irreversible whatever the VC have pledged in the 1999 border agreement. Remember that the CC have never trusted VC leadership, always consider them as a treacherous group. And therefore, the Chinese demanded that this work is to be done by the end of 2008. The VC is chasing that deadline. After the border has been pegged out, Beijing will publish a map of the new borderline. We will know by then where and how much land we lose. The VC dare not publish the map, which is supposed to be attached to the 1999 agreement.

Next, I am pretty sure the issue is related to those high spots. There are two significant routes the Chinese armies had used in invading Vietnam. One is the Nam Quan pass area in Lang Son, and the other area is north of Ha Giang province.

Concerning the Nam Quan pass area, if we look north, there are two mountain ranges in Quoc Khanh village, Trang Dinh district, to the left. These two ranges being adjacent to Nam Quan pass look over the route from China to Vietnam. I know they are now completely occupied by CC. They are now inside CC territory. And to the right, there is a region called Binh Do 400 (of Cao Loc district) the location of which is behind the border marker no. 26 (based on Tien-Tsin Agreement). Binh Do 400 is also in the Chinese hands. The two high ground areas flanking both sides of Nam Quan pass which helped defend Vietnam, are now lost. From ancient times, whenever China invaded Vietnam, their armies were defeated at that pass.

Now that rugged mountain area which serves to protect our fatherland has fallen into CC hands.

The second point is another other strategic position situated on the Ha Giang border. In Ha Giang during the 1979 war, the CC sent 3 armies, plus two independent infantry divisions from Kunming (14 divisions in total) to invade the northern Ha Giang border area. The route for advancing troops into Vietnam in this area with rugged mountains is no longer in Vietnamese territory. It was exactly the area where our ancestors stopped the Chinese advances to invade our country. At present the CC troops have occupied and held tightly on to that area which has been annexed to CC territory. The CC has changed the names of two of those five ranges of mountain to Lao Son and Giai Am Son (see attached summary).

In the future, if CC brings its armies over to occupy more land, with these two areas in their hands, the invaders will march over at their leisure.

LKT: Dear listeners, in the first part of our interview with Professor Dr Nguyen Van Canh on borders between China and Vietnam that we have just concluded, the Professor has clearly presented his views and at the same time his reaction to Mr. Le Cong Phung's recent statements. As we know this is a response from a professor who has done many careful studies on the issues concerned.

Professor, we have just discussed the situation of Nam Quan pass and when we mention Nam Quan pass, we Vietnamese do not fail to recall Ban Gioc waterfall, which forms possibly the most picturesque scenery of Vietnam in the North, and as everyone knows at present and also according to Mr. Le Cong Phung, half of Ban Gioc belongs to China, is this true?

Prof Canh: I cannot be quite certain about verification as the VC Party covers everything up. However I think the loss of Ban Gioc fall is true. Previously Ban Gioc fall lay deep in Vietnamese territory, but today half of it lies in CC, and especially since CC built a reinforced concrete dam over a section of Qui Thuan River, half of Ban Gioc fall belongs to China exactly like Mr. Le Cong Phung said. Consequently, if pegging and mile posting are to be done, Ban Gioc Fall must be on a new line and they have planned the border line to go through the middle of Ban Gioc fall, instead of being way up north according to the Franco-Chinese border map, and not along the midstream of Ban Gioc waterfall like what Phung talked about. The picture/illustration in the attached document can say more clearly about the situation of that waterfall.

LKT: Professor, however, Mr. Le Cong Phung stated that based on the two maps issued by Vietnam and China respectively, according to that Franco-Chinese map the border peg was situated in the middle of the river at that time, is this correct?

Prof Canh: I do not think so. I am sure that the Ban Gioc fall area in particular lies deep in our territory, and according a VC's document released in 1979, CC sent 2000 soldiers over the border to cast a reinforced concrete curtain along a tributary river bordering Vietnam in order to change its course, and the Ban Gioc fall previously is inside our territory; now the border has been moved so close that we have lost half of the Ban Gioc waterfall. Only a few days ago, a Vietnamese correspondent reported that three years ago the CC embassy in Hanoi organized an excursion from Vietnam to visit Ban Gioc waterfall. Among the invited guests were Viet Communist Party officials, also news agencies etc. What for? To prove that part of this waterfall belongs to CC. The famous scenic resort is now named in Chinese 'Detian, Premier Spectacular Scenery'. That was also a signal to the CPV, to Vietnamese people, and to the world that the situation is irreversible. Certainly, the CPV's mouth will shut up again like they have been doing so far. Please see the illustrations in the appendix.

LKT: Now we talk about the Gulf of Tonkin and Sansha District matters as well as the Decree on Fishing between Vietnam and China. According to recent presentations in conferences that you conducted, the Gulf of Tonkin is now considered almost a conspiration between Vietnam and China, which allows China to control that Gulf. Could you please describe how the Gulf of Tonkin is controlled and how the Gulf of Tonkin is carved up for fishing, with respective economic rights and benefits for Vietnam and China?

Prof Canh: The listeners and audience would be aware that in December 2000, the VC and CC signed an agreement concerning the demarcation in the Gulf of Tonkin region. In addition, they appended another agreement called the agreement on cooperation of fishing in the Gulf region. About these matters, Le Cong Phung stated that the 1887 Convention was the basis for redefining the Gulf area and the loss of area was negligible if at all, and Vietnam's gain amounted to several thousand square kilometers according to the law of the sea (1982). Phung has denied all losses.

And so let me demonstrate how much has been lost, and what is the present situation of the Gulf of Tonkin.

The map we use here is that of the Gulf of Tonkin as defined by the 1887 Convention and was drawn in an agreement by both sides (see map in appendix). Starting from Mong Cai here, and we can see a **red line** running north-south from Mong Cai down across the mouth of the Gulf, with one side being Huang Liu of Hainan, and the other side, our Con Co island of Northern Vietnam. That is the mouth of the Gulf measuring about 130 nautical miles. Let me stress that this red line is the line drawn in the map of the 1887 Convention signed between the Qing dynasty and France. This red line lies east to Tra Co (T ch'a- Kou) island, running south to the mouth of the Gulf. The part to the west of this line belongs to Vietnam, and that to the east, to China. Before signing the agreement, Ly Hung Chang complained that China had lost heavily, ceding too much territory to France and continuously made requests for "this and that extra bit". At that time Constans, the French government emissary (for signing this convention to divide up the Gulf region) wanted to return to France as soon as possible, and ceded to China a piece of land called Pack Lung Cape, about 20 or 30 km east of Mong Cai. In addition, there was an enclave on the other side of the border called Soc Son village that had belonged to Vietnam, under Father Pierre's administration. Both were also given to China. This leaves only the area west of the red line from Mong Cai downward as ours, otherwise that red line should be drawn from Pack Lung Cape, not from Mong Cai.

And they drew a Red Line like that to divide up the territory. According to that Convention, it is the borderline dividing up the Gulf region. What is the area of the Gulf region? It is about 123,700 sq. km. Based on this Red borderline; Vietnam owns 77,000 sq. km and China the remainder. The Franco-Chinese convention stipulates that 64% belongs to Vietnam, and only 36% to China. Now they have signed an agreement in 2000 to split 54/46, what did they base on? At first, CPV demanded that the Franco-Chinese Convention be basis for negotiation. The CC said no, because that convention was signed under the treacherous oppression of French imperialists, and as a consequence, China had to concede. It was an inequitable agreement. That is why CC now wants to be more equitable. That had been CC's demand since the 1970s, to which the VC had not acceded either.

The CC has reasoned that the Red Line was only a line for the sake of administering the islands, not a frontier demarcation line. The convention therefore should be annulled and the border re-drawn. However, if we look at the imperial Franco-Chinese Convention text to determine whether it is an 'administrative' line or a borderline, we find that this line is clearly defined in that Convention as the border between the two sides. Nevertheless CC exerts its power in bringing pressure to bear on the VC in insisting that this line is an administrative one, and not a border. Today all that CC demanded has been satisfied by the VC. What then, is the situation of the Gulf of Tonkin agreement today?

The CC demanded that a borderline should go from Mong Cai to the middle of the Gulf, then head south to split the gulf in halves. There are 21 reference points starting with point no. 1 at

Mong Cai, as shown on the attached map, that demarcation line curves out to the middle of the gulf ending at point 21. All the part to the east of it belongs to CC, while the western part to Vietnam. As a result Vietnam only occupies 54%, China about 46%. After this re-determination of the border, Vietnam has lost about 12,000 sq. km.

When such an agreement to divide the gulf has been reached, China was still greedy. They said they wanted an agreement on shared fishing. Thus there are two agreements in reality, one agreement on territorial determination, and another on cooperation on fishing. What in effect does this fishing pact involve? This pact determines that from each side of the demarcation line, each country must contribute 30.5 nautical miles to a joint fishing area. This means fishing together. This is a large area, lying south of the 20th parallel occupying 35000 sq. km. The pact is to last 12 years and can be extended for another 3 years, totalling 15 years. That is not all. There is another region north of Bach Long Vy island. This is called the smaller transition area, and its limit is for 4 years only.

The question is: Why, after the gulf has been divided, must there be cooperation on fishing still?

And why did the VC accept such cooperation on fishing arrangement? Don't they have the capacity to fish on their own, or they must co-operate with the CC in order to fish? This is an unimaginable concession to the Chinese communists.

Vietnamese fishermen use only rudimentary tools, wooden boats with small horsepower, how can they engage in joint fishing with Chinese fleets of big ships of 200 horsepowers capable of fishing in deep waters, where each net dragged by two boats extends up to 60 nautical miles from end to end, that is 100 km. How then can this co-operation and sharing of fishing be carried out?

What is more, such fleets will trawl the gulf region, going back and forth, very close to the gulf coastline and thus in 15 years there would be no more fish for us Vietnamese to catch. Besides, Tran Duc Luong has agreed with the CC to establish an "economic belt" in 2005 along the coast. What is left for them to make a living on? At present, some fishermen have to go far south in their wooden boats pursuing a livelihood. In July 2007, a number of Vietnamese fishermen were shot and killed by Chinese naval forces for working in their territorial waters.

Practically, the cooperation on fishing arrangement presents a great disadvantage to Vietnamese fishermen. To work in this joint fishing area, you need a permit. Who issues this permit? On the VC side, it's the local governmental authorities. Many fishermen have to pay fees when applying for a permit. Some cannot afford the high fees. And when they fish in our waters in the common fishing area without a license, CC navy or coast guards, even Chinese fishermen can check to see if they have permits. If a permit is not produced, CC fishermen have the right to "strip" the catch, meaning they would plunder the catch and load it on their ships before turning the Vietnamese fishermen back.

To my knowledge, in the common fishing ground, there is a zone in the middle of the gulf with great depth where a type of fish called Ca Day [sea bed fish] can be found. They live at a great depth. They fetch a high price. Vietnamese have no boat big and modern equipments to catch this fish. The CC does have the means to fish them.

Another point to note is the event of January 8th 2005, a number of Vietnamese fishing boats from Thanh Hoa were at the location which I mark red on the map in the Appendix, working in the new territorial waters, about 12 km west of the new demarcation line for this gulf, at the reference point no. 14 of this line. While they were fishing there, CC navy ships of the steel armored type approached, and with CC flag lowered, fired a volley of shots. A number of fishing boats sank. At least 9 Vietnamese fishermen died on the spot. A fisherman working nearby, seeing the shooting and what was happening tried to make an escape back to Thanh Hoa. A CC navy ship chased after, and fired many shots on the victim's boat right up to Vietnamese coast before sailing off.

Such is the situation of the division of the gulf area and the common area of shared fishing. Another thing has also been observed: Those two agreements were signed in 2000, but not until 2002 were they ratified by the VC national assembly, while the land agreement was ratified within 6 months (June 2000). Why is this so? The answer is that the VC did not dare ratifying it right away for fear that CC fishing ships being very big, and such a fleet in operation could not escape international notice. On closer observation, the international community recognized that the VC has given up too much of their people's rights, and also for fear of adverse public reaction at home, they let it drag on. That was why in Feb. 2002, Jiang Zemin came to Hanoi demanding early ratification. The VC then had to take some action, and not earlier than in June 2002, it was ratified by the Vietnamese national assembly!!!

LKT: Professor, you have just described an extremely huge disadvantage for Vietnam in the Gulf of Tonkin, at the same time the second agreement, the so-called Decree Paper (protocol) on cooperation on fishing, has clearly shown that this joint fishing area not only brings in economic income for China but also the effect of big Chinese steel ships sailing to and from right next to Vietnamese coast line. In your opinion Professor, what is the situation concerning national security around the Gulf of Tonkin?

Prof Canh: Alas, this is another danger, as half of the Gulf has been given up, CC navy can come right close to Vietnamese coast line. Also conceded to CC is the right to check and control right up to the coast. The CC demanded that "now you and I must patrol together." The VC and CC agreed to establish navy boat squadrons to share-patrol in the Golf region. What does share-patrolling purport to do? Merely to control the VC. CC is so big and their naval power predominates. They can bully the VC, but there is no way for the VC to bully them. Shared patrol means CC ships can go right into our coast to check and control Vietnam. As in reality within the Gulf zone, there are only two parties: VC and CC. And neither other third country nor any pirate group coming from far away would dare cause instability for CC. Of course as far as security is concerned, the VC just sit idle, tacitly letting the CC control natural resources under the sea bed, allowing CC scientific ships to go prospecting occasionally for oil deep into our Gulf territorial waters even in the new frontier zone.

LKT: And so according to this map Professor, North Vietnam today lies right close to Hainan Island where CC is building a nuclear submarine base. From there to the Gulf border, it is not at all far. What is the reason for establishing a nuclear subs base on Hainan after this agreement was signed?

Prof Canh: This is another issue. In this context, CC has considered she has already taken the Gulf area. However, concerning the Sanya base, the nuclear sub base, CC signals that she wants to occupy the whole Spratly archipelago in the south and all the South China Sea will be used as a stepping stone in the advance towards Southeast Asia.

LKT: So, the agreements including on the joint fishing one in the Gulf of Tonkin constitute the first launching pads for gradually advancing to the South, aren't they?

Prof Canh: Correct. There has been news about CC navy headquarters moving to this region already.

LKT: Professor, advancing gradually south, then the nearest point is the Paracel archipelago; then from your perspective Professor, what situation the Paracels find themselves in now?

Prof Canh: About the Paracels, we know that up to 1974, the South Vietnamese Navy had been fighting to protect the remainder of the territory being the Crescent (or Nguyet Thiem) group. In the context of the Paracels, may I take this opportunity to praise the sacrifice of Republic of Vietnam Navy who had valiantly defended the fatherland? There was information we did not know of until recently revealed by some documents, that an Admiral named Phuong Quang Kinh, second in command of the South Sea fleet, then commander of the battle front had lost his life together with the whole battle command at the Paracels. In addition, 4 colonels, 2 lieutenant colonels, all commanders of battle ships, also suffered the same fate.

The Republic of Vietnam naval force consisted of only 4 ships, not equipped with missiles like CC ones, and had to fight against a great Chinese fleet of 11 battle ships and 30 others.

On the South Vietnamese navy side, the highest-ranking officer, Navy Major Nguy Van Tha together with 58 soldiers heroically sacrificed themselves in the defense of the island that we have inherited from our ancestors.

From then on, the Paracel islands have fallen into CC hands. And not until now Le Cong Phung has admitted this truth. There, CC has built many military bases. The most often cited base is a base on Phu Lam island, or internationally known as Woody. From the 1980s at this base, CC has erected many military establishments capable of housing several thousand troops, fresh water reservoirs, helicopter pads and even an airstrip. This airstrip has been widened and lengthened to 2,600 m to allow bombers to take off and land. There is a fuel depot. At first it was an advance outpost to move southward, linking with the Spratleys and further locations. In addition there is a second island called Pattle. In 1974, this island still belonged to the Republic of Vietnam.

Many military bases are now found on this archipelago. There are many photographs of military installations. This one is on Tri Ton Island, which lies nearest to our Da Nang. This is the military headquarters on Tri Ton. This is a photo of another military base. This is the border marker on Tri Ton Island. This island is called Dao Cay or Cu Moc (Tree) Island. This is the CC military headquarters on Quang Hoa Island of the Paracels. This island is in the Crescent group...

LKT: So all the Paracel islands are controlled by Chinese army command. Thus apart from our loss of islands and of national security, we also sustain economic losses, Professor, what do you think of?

Prof Canh: They have taken the whole archipelago. In June 1992, they signed contracts with the US Crestone Company to prospect for oil in the 25,000 km area south of the Paracels. Thompson, President of Crestone, stated that CC has promised to use its armed forces to protect the oil prospecting and drilling. Even the guano that South Vietnam had developed and the fishing are controlled by CC. They forbid our fishermen to come and if anyone happens to stray into the area, CC would shoot to kill, or at least imprison and fine them for transgressing Chinese territorial waters. Naturally, the military bases there indicate that they permanently threaten Vietnam.

LKT: Speaking of the Paracels, by the way Professor, we have learned of a few matters from current affairs. That is we have read in a recent news report that CC is prepared to invite Vietnam to participate in a joint development of resources at the Paracels, what would be your opinion Professor, if this were true on the Chinese part?

Prof Canh: If that were true, it would only be an amusing statement, because they have now controlled all the Paracel archipelago, as Le Cong Phung has now finally confirmed when he said, "The Paracel islands have completely been taken by China and the Paracels in legal and historical aspects always belong to Vietnam." Once this archipelago is in CC hands, they would never give it up. I do not believe that report is true.

LKT: All right Professor could you then envisages that there is another reason for China to suddenly invite Vietnam to participate in joint exploitation of resources on the Paracels?

Prof Canh: No, I do not think so. Otherwise, that is only a propaganda tactic. Even right on the Chinese Vietnamese border region, CC has sent troops to chase Vietnamese inhabitants off their homes to allow Chinese citizens to move in. Some Vietnamese protested because their houses were burnt down. After the houses were burnt, they let CC migrants come over and rebuild to live on the same property. In that spirit, how can they talk of inviting the VC to joint-develop resources? On the contrary, in December 2005, VC met with CC in Beijing, then they circulated information about co-operation in prospecting for oil in the Spratley archipelago. This has happened. It means the VC invited CC to collaborate with the intention to divide the profit maybe. The reverse case where CC invites VC to collaborate in business to share profit could never exist, once CC owns the archipelago. The joint cooperation in fishing in the Gulf of Tonkin is another example.

LKT: Yes, right, to come back to the Chinese southward expansion, they are approaching the Spratley islands and in fact the Spratley archipelago ocean region is many times larger than the Gulf of Tonkin and its natural resources can be said to be tremendous for Vietnam. At the same time it is also a disputed area between six Asian nations. And so Professor, what do you think about the Spratley islands sprouting so many issues at present, for instance, the oil company Exxon Mobil has been chased away by CC and currently there is movement of the US naval force closer to the Spratleys?

Prof Canh: Ah, we know that when Nguyen Tan Dung went to see Mr. Bush, he intended to invite the US to enter Vietnam so as to auger in some area for some economic benefit. As thus, the US will defend economic interests and therefore protect the VC as well. Such would be their calculation. Whether that scheme is feasible or not, it would not be as simple as they think. If we look at the new border drawn by CC along the nine-dash lines on this map, some people call it the "dragon's tongue" map. The CC territorial waters as such cover all the South China Sea. Would the US be able to expel CC from the Paracels and some islands of the Spratleys that have been occupied by them, in order to help VC preserve her territorial sovereignty?

As for saying "there is movement of US naval force closer to the Spratleys," this is not quite correct. The US Fleet has been permanently present in this ocean region. The US has said they will not relinquish their presence here. Surely it is in their interests not to abandon the South China Sea, especially when the value of two-way transport of goods and trading amounts to trillions of dollars annually. Obviously, has CC threatened US interests yet or how far has the threat gone? That is a question for the US in defense of their interests. As for the ExxonMobil Company, the US State Department stated that ExxonMobil would be protected. This company has informed it will continue to prospect and drill for oil. On this knowledge, BP has also announced it will return to the area, though it already left the area after being threatened by CC.

LKT: This means the "dragon's tongue" map covers the whole South China Sea and the Spratley islands.

Prof Canh: The total area covered is three and a half million square kilometers. Le Minh Nghia of the Committee for the Continental Shelf of the VC prime minister's office stated early in the 1980s that of the whole South China Sea covering three and a half million sq. km, an area of three million sq. km is occupied by them. If we look at the new map then the area occupied by CC is bigger than 3 million sq. km, as it spreads closer to the Vietnamese coastline. And so we ask what is the distance between its boundary and Vietnamese coast? I do not have the co-ordinates to determine how close it lies along the Vietnamese coastline. However, let's compare to the distance from the mouth of the gulf being less than 130 nautical miles. Divided in halves, each side is about over 60 miles. Consider this distance from Cam Ranh to the new border against the half-distance to the gulf mouth, and then the former is shorter than the latter. It may measure only about 40 or 50 nautical miles. This indicates how vast the CC plot is, and how gargantuan their ambition is.

They still plot to go further than this, not just staying limited to the Spratley. From Hainan Island, the CC has already built the **Sanya base**. This "secret" naval base was only disclosed in April 2008. This is an extremely important base for advancing southward.

The Sanya base has two parts. **The first part** is a secret base with a capacity to host 20 nuclear submarines of the 094 type. At present, it is known that CC already possesses 5 of these submarines. They can carry intercontinental ballistic missiles with a 10,000 km range with multi-nuclear heads. The US Defense Department predicts that there will be 5 more produced within the next five years. In addition, CC currently has about 57 subs, a number of which are of the Song S20 type with German Diesel engines. They hardly make noise while running submerged, and therefore cannot be detected by satellites when they are at a great depth. Some of these are equipped with long-range missiles capable of reaching 1000 miles. The subs are equipped with Yingji-8 missiles, which can be fired underwater to destroy aircraft carriers on the surface. Sanya is an extremely dangerous base and to the left of it is a sea region with a 5000 m depth, an excellent place for parking submarines. **The second part** is related to 3 docking jetties. This is a type of jetty designed for aircraft carriers and is equipped to allow 6 carriers to dock here and all equipment or troops and missiles can be loaded onto the carriers. At present an 800 m-long jetty has been completed, two more are about to be built. The question is: When docks for aircraft carriers are built like this, has CC come to possess any aircraft carriers yet? The answer is 'not yet', but they are now preparing for their arrival.

In 1995, I released a paper saying that CC plans to have a fleet called Blue Ocean fleet operate in the year 2000 in the South China Sea. This fleet would have at least one aircraft carrier by 2000. They were negotiating with Ukraine to purchase a Varyag worth 2 billion USD. I have shown a picture of the Varyag in the White Paper. However nothing had been spotted in 2000, and not until now one document is found to refer to that aircraft carrier. Deng Xiaoping had ordered to suspend the purchase of aircraft carriers to **save money for the production of bio-chemical weapons.** If the Blue Ocean Fleet was activated now with that aircraft carrier, it would not still be strong enough to fight the US and would be eliminated. Therefore, the project was postponed. The latest news is that a wrecked USSR Kuznetsov or Varyag that they purchased previously is being repaired and will be ready in a near future.

LKT: Professor, in our interview with US Ambassador to Vietnam, Michael Michalak, he said that in the search for MIAs lost in Gulf of Tonkin during the Vietnam War, they have now activated the search and the search activation has been excellent, and so Professor, of what significance would this say about security issues in the Gulf of Tonkin?

Prof Canh: Ah! I did know something about this. For a long time, right from the 1980s, there has been the issue of discussing with the VC about searching for Americans Missing In Action everywhere including those American MIA's in the Gulf of Tonkin. There, when US planes entered Vietnam to fire on North Vietnam, there were a number of planes crashing into the Gulf of Tonkin. Now, to search for American MIA's there, both sides have agreed in principle on a number of conditions to search for those downed airplanes there. This means the VC will expedite in assisting the US, satisfying more US demands about MIA's. In being able to help the US, the VC hopes that the US will help maintain security for the VC.

I think however, that is very difficult, and nebulous, because the CC's influence on VC leadership is too great. I call the present VC leaders, missionaries for CC in realizing the CC's ambitions. Therefore it is difficult for that eventuality to take place in the near future.

LKT: Professor, also in our interview with Ambassador Michael Milachak, we asked a question about Mr. Le Cong Phung's statement that at present Vietnam has a plan to bring the Paracel & Spratley islands issues to the international court based on the 1982 law of the sea in San Francisco. When I asked the US Ambassador for his opinion he said that such a thing should be developed that way. They should just go ahead with it. What would you think Professor, about both the statements of Mr. Le Cong Phung and Ambassador Milachak?

Prof Canh: In my view, those statements by Michael Milachak are only normal. There are international structures responsible for solving international conflicts. They are International Court and the 1982 law of the sea (not in San Francisco). Le Cong Phung said the Socialist Republic of Vietnam (SRV) is planning to bring this matter to the International Court. That is a very positive step. According to you, you have said that due to the White Paper and the public dissemination of the White Paper, as well as the announcement of the Committee on the Protection of Territorial Sovereignty on 15 September this year, as well as my statements on Free Asia Radio, they acknowledge that "the Paracels completely belong to China" and said that "many people demand to bring the matter to the international court and to the UN's attention", and "we plan to..."

For years, many have asked me: what is the solution to the Paracel-Spratley issues? My answer is "the international court", and nothing else can be done apart from the international court at this time. With the international court solution, the question is who has the right to bring the issues up, and who is responsible for bringing them to court. Territory and territorial waters problems are those pertaining to a nation, and only member nations of the UN can raise the matter with the international organization. The nation in case is the SRVN. Before the international court, only SRV has a standing to do so. That is why so many times I have demanded that the SRVN government have the responsibility of raising that matter, and I demand that the VN Communist Party order the SRVN government to do that, as we are merely private individuals, and being those who love the country, we can only demand that they defend the rights and interests of our ancestral land.

To mention the international court solution is to have to play the game of the law of the sea that is internationally proclaimed. To speak up about "national sovereignty" that President Bush points to, and to call for conflict resolution through the laws (the sea law and the international court) like the US State Department and Ambassador Milachak do about playing the sea law game as such, those are not solutions by force.

About this question, last May, while attending the ceremony for fallen soldiers in Hawaii, I had a chat with Admiral Timothy Keating, Commander-in-Chief of the US forces in the Pacific Ocean region about the CC threat and about bringing the matter to the UN to warn them. Afterwards, I sent him some documents. On 30 June, at the Shangri-La Conference in Singapore, he stated that no one can defeat the US, and that if there is any conflict, the law of the sea is there to be used in resolving it. Milachak's statement is also within those limits.

That is what the whole world wishes for. That is the rule of the game of civilized countries and of the international community, wanting to maintain order and peace for humanity that way.

LKT: However Professor, if we may, we would like to quote Mr. Le Cong Phung who said that even if Vietnam wanted to bring the matter up, but CC would not sit down in conference and discuss it, then there is no way it can be done. And so, what does this all mean?

Prof Canh: Yes! That is correct. They may not want to. This should not be an excuse to shirk responsibility however. Even if they agreed to come to the table "in conference," to participate in the international court arising from what the VC pursued as such, and suppose victory is awarded to the "claimant" side – this I am one thousand per cent sure VC would win, with all that is presented in the White Paper complete with historical, legal as well as geographical aspects (although just outlined sufficiently for drafting a document for procedure purposes). Our national assets include the whole of the Paracels even though it is now occupied. As for the Spratleys, they are so far south; the CC has no justification in claiming their rights over them. Even with the Paracels, in geographical context, based on the 1968 National Geographic Society map that has also been used in the book "Dia Ly Bien Dong voi Hoang Sa va Truong Sa" [The Geography of the Eastern Sea (South China Sea) with the Paracels and Spratleys] by Vu Huu San who demonstrates that Paracels is close to Vietnam. For instance the Tri Ton Island that I have often mentioned is so close to our Da Nang coast. That island is only 123 nautical miles from the Vietnamese coast, while an island closest to the Chinese continent is at a further distance. This is not to mention the Paracels lies on the land that is linked to Vietnam continent Therefore the Paracels can never belong to China. Based on that point alone, we could win the case. Let alone the historical aspects, as Prof Tran Huy Bich of the University of Southern California has listed ample documents with diverse sources demonstrating that these two groups of islands have belonged to Vietnam since ancient times. As for legal aspects, I have used a book written by Prof Monique Chemillier- Gendreau of the University of Paris to prove the Vietnamese ownership of those two archipelagos.

Now suppose CC does not agree to the court's decision, what can we do? In reality, the international court's judgment in this case is unopposable except when there is a resolution by the UN Security Council. At the UNSC however, there must be a consensus of the five Permanent Members or 9 out of 15 members. CC, however, is one of the five permanent members. CC will use a right to veto. To lobby for a resolution in this case is not an easily achieved task. Especially the SRVN has neither capacity nor prestige internationally, or perhaps the lowest of prestige even if they sat in the Security Council. Therefore, the decision will not be reached, even carried out. This international organization has no agency to "enforce" the court's decisions. Thus, we can do nothing. At least we can use such basis for future action: to establish an internationally justified course of action. Statement by Bush, the US State Department, by Michalak and as have been reflected at the Shangri-La Conference... are symbolic international support for the Vietnamese people's cause. At the same time international communities' interests in the South China Sea are important factors to help us protect the inherited assets that our ancestors defended with their blood for us and have transferred them to us. Maybe in ten or more years, there will be other actions to be taken. The question is firstly the VC must embark on the course of action; secondly we must create an institution capable of mobilizing the people's power, instead of the present VC policy to terrorize and divide the masses. We need strength in national economy and solidarity... With that I am sure we could regain in strength what has been robbed by the Beijing hegemonic clique with the complicity of the VC.

Demanding the return of lost territory or preventing Beijing's continuing on with occupation that way will attract international support. That is very important, for the sake of world order; nobody can oppose, or contravene the international peace and order objectives as the mad men did in the last century. If that happens, the result is that those mad men will reap tragic consequences.

CC's scheme is to prolong the occupation as much as possible, to create an accomplished fact (fait accompli) and in 100 years, no one would be able to do anything about it. And this is a crime committed by Ho Chi Minh and his Communist Party of Vietnam that have helped CC realize that objective.

Thus at least, the overseas Vietnamese must have a duty do something to lay the foundation for future protection of the fatherland, even in longer terms.

Please look at the images I have illustrated below about the fortified structures erected on islands of Paracels and Spratley, you will get an idea of that danger. Also look at the buildings constructed around in the Ban Gioc waterfall area, you will find out CC's ambitions.

LKT: The detailed overview of Prof Dr Nguyen Van Canh on the Sino-Viet border, on the Gulf of Tonkin, on the protocol on fishing between Vietnam and China, on the Paracels and Spratleys and the current relations between Vietnam, China and the US is very comprehensive. And so Professor, after having been shown such a general picture by you, we as overseas Vietnamese although with no power in our hands, without an exile government, we feel that we have a responsibility, a responsibility of people who love their country. With such a responsibility, in your opinion Professor, what should we do about the question which I quote if I may from you that "**when the country is in danger, it's even every ordinary citizen's responsibility.'**

Prof Canh: This question is extremely difficult to have a good answer under the present circumstances. And everywhere I went over the last decades I have been asked what you can do to restore our fatherland, the Paracels, the Spratleys and etc. My answer has been: 'I am only a refugee from the communist peril. As an intellectual, I know what I must do within my own ability. At least with this White Paper on the Paracels and the Spratleys, we inform and warn the world that this is a great danger caused by Red China. This great danger is not only for the Vietnamese people, but also for the whole world. That is why in the letter that I drafted, which has been sent to the General Secretary and 192 members of the UN as well as to governments all over the world, we raise the alarm to enable them to think about and prepare for the ugliest situation that, I think, would occur. Solving those ugliest situations will entail solving the issues of Vietnam. Vietnamese people's rights and interests go in parallel with those of the whole world. That is the maintenance of peace and order, firstly in the region, and this region is intimately related to the whole world.

APPENDIX:

Below are a few figures and locations extracted from the document "**VẤN ĐỀ BIÊN GIỚI GIỮA VIỆT NAM VÀ TRUNG QUỐC**" [The Sino-Vietnamese Border Issues] published by the Vietnamese Communist Party in 1979 (Nhà Xuất Bản Sự Thật, Hà Nội, 1979; Also see, Library of Congress Online Catalog). This document shows that Le Cong Phung has told complete lies about:

1. The 1 km + difference along all the 1450 km length of border.

Detian waterfall, North side of China. 德天瀑 布 中国侧（北边较大的） Photograph by ExileMoon

a. The Trinh Truong, Quang Ninh area. This area is 6 km long and more than 1 km deep in Vietnamese territory has been taken by CC. This area is now merged into Dong Tam commune, Dong Hung. The border is set back to Khau Truc mount in Vietnam.

Fig.1. The main part of Ban Gioc fall to the north now belongs to CC and its name changed to Detian Fall (Chinese Premier Spectacular Scenery).

b. And so are the Thanh Loa village of Cao Loc district of Lang Son, Kham Khau Village of Cao Bang, Ta Lung, Ta Phu Phin, and Minh Tan villages of Ha Tuyen. The Nam Chay village of Hoang Lien Son (this village is 4 km long and over 1 km deep) also lies within CC territory now. At Nam Chay village particularly, Vietnam lost an area about 300 hectares. In total there are 40 similar locations along the border that have been occupied by CC and their migrants have been brought in to replace Vietnamese inhabitants **Fig. Fig.2. The minor part to the south still belongs to Vietnam. Nguồn bài viết: blogger Măng, Nguồn ảnh: blogger Điếu Cày**

c. Right at the **Nam Quan pass**, in 1955, Ho Chi Minh asked Mao Zedong to extend the railroad from China into Vietnam by 300m in order to join both sides to facilitate communication. Mao agreed and after a while Ho said that the Vietnamese border lays 300m north of the tracks joint as it had existed for hundreds of years. Ho was told that the border is where the two rail tracks are linked together. Ho kept quiet. That was not all. Later CC troops carried the border marker no. 18 on national highway 1 at the Nam Quan pass and put it inside Vietnam by another 200m. Thus ½ km was lost in total.

d. They **moved border markers**, No.136 in Cao Bang, Nos. 41, 42, 43 in Lang Son of the Kum Mu, Kim Ngan and Mau Son areas (9 km length) 2.5 km deep into inland Vietnam. The lost area is 1000 hectares. Also the Na Pang – Keo Trinh area (posts 29, 30, 31) in Cao Bang, 6.45 km long, and 1.3 km deep into Vietnamese territory now becomes part of CC territory. The area lost is 200 hectares.

e. Ban Gioc fall, situated north of the border marker no. 53 in Dam Thuy village, Trung Khanh district of Cao Bang, on the Qui Thuan River was part of Vietnam. CC sent 2 thousand troops into Vietnamese territory to cast a reinforced concrete barrier across the tributary river at the border, redrew the map and occupied part of Ban Gioc fall and also took over Po Thoong of Vietnam.

f. Using armed forces to force the Vietnamese out and occupy their homes and land, they then sent CC migrants over and settle here.

2. The High Grounds

Finally, Le cong Phung stated, "there are six remaining high points" out of 27 points and "we bring the border line to run through those high points."

This statement implies that the above-mentioned 27 high spots belong to Vietnam, therefore lie in Vietnamese territory. CC had occupied all these 27 spots. At present, thanks to our "vigorous struggle" CC has returned them except for six high spots. These six high points are understood as the mountain ranges lying along the border. Now Phung has "succeeded "in bringing the border up to those high spots, thus no land was lost.

This admission, if true, is a self-condemnation of a concession of a land area measured north from the middle of the ridges of those six above ranges.

In addition, how could Phung answer about those following mountain ranges?

The ranges 1250, 1545, 1509, 772 and 233 of Ha Giang province were taken by CC. The 1509 range part of the land of Thanh Thuy village, Vi Xuyen district is known Nui Dat, to have fallen into CC hands and CC have changed its name to Lao Son. The 1250 range was Nui Bac in Vietnam. CC has changed it to Giai Am Son.

These high grounds are Vietnamese strategic spots in the defense against northern armed invasions previously. These ranges are now transferred to CC.

The 820 and 636 ranges of Quoc Khanh village, Trang Dinh district, Lang Son, lying next to Nam Quan pass to the west, adjacent to National Highway 1, also have become CC property. And the Binh Do 400 area of Cao Loc district, Lang Son, behind the border marker no. 26, to the east of National Highway 1 suffers the same fate. These ranges were also essential areas of defense, preventing invaders from the North. Here, thanks to the rugged terrain, our ancestors defeated their enemies. Losing these areas, Vietnam will have much difficulty in protecting her territory.

With the evidence shown above, how could the Vietnamese Communist Party reply to the Vietnamese people that only one km was lost?

THE GULF OF TONKIN AREA

Phung stated:

"We divided the Gulf of Tonkin with China based on international law... When the agreement was signed, if we compared the area between ours and that of China, ours would be larger by eight thousand square kilometres. We did not have any loss. Why did China accept the fact

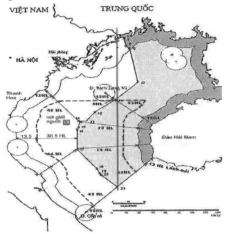

that we gained 8000 sq. km? It is because out coastline is concave, it curves in like this, while the Chinese coast at Hainan curves out like this... To say we lost 10 thousand sq. kilometers (sic) is nonsense, not at all correct. We do not wish to say concretely either how it was divided when it was divided... It may also happen while negotiating; China volunteered to donate us 3000 sq. km elsewhere to take over only 150 sq. km here. But we did not agree, we did not want to occupy water, of what use is the water surface area... We think of what is underneath, which maintains our ownership of the land, at the same time our national interests."

My question: Phung stressed international law as basis for "negotiation". He especially emphasized the 1885 Tien Tsin Agreement as foundation for negotiation to conclude that not only 10,000 sq. km were lost (not 10,000 sq. kilometers as stated above), but also a gain of 8000 sq. km that CC 'donated to VC'. Moreover, CC also volunteered a gift for VC of 3000 sq. km, in return CC only wanted 150 sq. km, which the VC did not agree to... and managed to 'maintain our ownership of the land, and our national interests.'

With the above statement, VC boasted to have achieved 'great success' in negotiating with the greedy Han descended enemy, even though every one knows that CC would customarily crib on inches (not kilometers) of Vietnamese land. Several cases similar to the above have happened and are well-known and the VNCP has denounced it but Phung boldly covered up. There are many areas that the Party forbids people to frequent. They are either deep in the forest or far in the Gulf of Tonkin. In such situations, who would have the means and opportunity to investigate the true situation there?

Phung appeared 'outwardly' pleased, if not proud when he stated that CC have 'donated us' 8000 sq. km., and the CC also voluntarily gave another 3000 sq. km that 'we' did not [want to] take, in exchange for only 150 sq. km.

The question is related to the aspects of dividing the Gulf of Tonkin area originated from the Tien Tsin Agreement signed by France and the Ming dynasty in 1885. To carry out this agreement, both sides signed a document called the 1887 Convention in which the border in the gulf area was defined. In this area, they drew a map dividing the Gulf into 2. On the map, they drew a line straight north-south starting from Mong Cai, running through Tra Co island down to the mouth of the gulf: On the eastern side, at a point on Hainan Island, on the western side is Con Co Island of Vietnam.

That line was named the Red Line. In the Convention it is called the border demarcation line in the Gulf.

The Tien Tsin agreement signed by France's Patrenotre and the Ming dynasty's Ly Hung Chang. Iin June 1887, both sides signed another instrument called Convention of 1887. Both of the instruments constitute international laws. Those documents have been carried out for more than a hundred years. And the Red Line is the border demarcation in the Gulf. Now CC demanded a review of this gulf division with a plot to occupy more of Vietnamese territorial waters. CC wantonly insisted that the red line is merely an "administrative" line that divided the islands in this area, and demanded to cancel it in order to establish a new borderline. The VC had conceded and redrawn that line which now runs through 21 points in the middle of the gulf to divide the gulf in halves according to the 2000 agreement. The VC have given in and yielded a portion of territorial waters to CC.

How much was yielded?

The total area of the Gulf is 123,700 sq. km. And the 1887 Convention stipulated that Vietnam owned 63% or 77,931 sq. km, while China has 37% or 45,769 sq. km. With the new agreement CC gained from 37% to 46% or 56,902 sq. km., and VC have ceded **11,133 sq. km.**

2. COMMUNIST CHINA USE FORCES TO LEGITIMIZE HER SOVEREIGNTY OVER THE SPRATLY ARCHIPELAGO

COMMITTEE ON PROTECTION OF TERRITORIAL INTEGRITY OF VIETNAM

DECLARATION

On the Chinese Communist establishment of Sansha City on Woody Island, August 1, 2012

On June 23, 2012, the State Counil of Ministers of the People's Republic of China (Red China) established "*Địa Các Tam Sa Thị*", that is, the establishment of Sansha/Tam Sa 三 沙 city. Its headquarters is now located on Woody Island, on the Paracel archipelago of Vietnam. Sansha was originally a small area on Hainan Island, and was used as the name of an administratve agenccy at district level that Red China set up here in November 2007, with the task of

managing three archipelagos, including the Paracels and Spratlys of Vietnam. The upgrade of this administrative unit from the district level to the city level is to emphasize its importance and also reminds once more the international community that Red China has actually annexed the nine-dash-map region (Vietnam's Eastern Sea) into the territory of mainland China. In order to formalize the administration of this maritime area, China has established an administrative office, even though there were no civilian people living there. The Standing Committee of Hainan People's Congress (UD), at the 32nd conference on July 17, 2012, decided to establish the Sansha City People's Council. This is a Resolution (legislative) Body consisting of 45 members.

This is one of two buildings with similar structures on Woody Island, now used as the Administrative Office of the city (1)

---

1 The territorial sovereignty and power expansion of Beijing

The two-story brick house on Woody Island is the place where laws on related issues are enacted.

Xinhua News Agency also said the first meeting conference of the "Tam Sa/*Sansha* 三沙 *City People's Council*" ended Monday July 23. It elected Bo Trang, former Deputy Chief-of-Staff of the Hainan Military Region, as Council President. Tieu Kiet was appointed as Mayor, head of the city's administrative agencies.

Global Times reported that China also built a prison to detain "foreign fishermen" being accused of illegally infiltrating this area.

In addition, to alert the regional countries, especially their allies, China announces the militarization of Sansha City. Ministry of Defense spokesman Yang Wuquan said China has established the Sansha Military Headquarter. Colonel Tai Hyhong, was appointed commander of the city, and Liu Chaoyi, colonel, to serve as "political commissar". A representative from the Chinese Ministry of National Defense said: the Sansha military agency has the responsibility to mobilize national defense forces to protect Sansha city, to assist in disaster prevention. For the defense activities on the sea (beyond the two archipelagoes), are still in charge by the Chinese navy (China Daily, dated July 27 - 2012)

On the other hand, the International Radio of China reported that on June 28, during a press conference in Beijing, a defense official, Canh Nhan Sinh, said that the military has established a patrol program to "prevent war on the Spratlys waters", within the framework of activities to protect «national sovereignty»..., ; «the determination and will of the Chinese military to protect national sovereignty and territorial integrity are inexorable." China created a situation with teams of patrolling vessels ready for combat. Chinese officer Cảnh Nhạn Sinh bluntly said China will be firmly against "any military aggression from any neighboring countries".

China announced the decision to establish the Sansha Command post, placing troops under this Command. Its mission is to be ready to use forces, against any challenges, to defend the sovereignty claimed by China.

Since the 1970s, after occupying South Vietnam's Paracel archipelago, China immediately started to build barracks, facilities, airfields, docks, weapons depots, telecommunication systems... everywhere. Particularly on the Woody Island, during that time the international press said that Red China sent a 'thousand' troops to station there. China have built fresh water

reservoirs for military use. There is not a single civilian inhabitant living on the island (2). In Spratlys, more than a dozen military structures, firm, massive towering over the water, on the reefs such as the Fiery Cross (5 architectures), Mischief, Johnson, South, Subi, Gaven, Hughes, Chiqua, Cuarteron.

A structure built on the Mischief Reef.

In summary, all of those Chinese activities and behaviors have been carried out in a long process to legalize the appropriation of Vietnam's Eastern Sea (附件) to annex it into China. In this situation, China already considers the Eastern Sea or the "South China Sea" as its own territory, ready to protect it by forces.

ooo

China unilaterally claims that she is an owner the two archupelaogs. China know that it is an **illegal appropriation**. China sought to legitimize/legalize that territory. In what way? To force Vietnam to sign a treaty like that of the Land Border Treaty. Vietnam communists dare not do it, though silently moved along with China, silently supported China to achieve its goal. The best way for China to do, is China can exercise its sovereignty and defend its claimed sovereignty by bribing with money. Such as the case if Bauxite in the Central Highlands and Ha Tinh. Chinese leasers have calculated and waited for ripe time to act. They threatened, or showed off strength. They have prepared to take over Vietnam from several decades of planning, with their persistent activities. They have demonstrated their presence permanently, for a long time. They got people's attention, to eventually accept the "Chinese" presence in Vietnam. They even yelled, blocked, prevented trespassing, accused Vietnamese fishermen of violating their "territory" even fishing offshore... Further more, in the position of the "owners", when needed, the Chinese leaders can negotiate for benefit sharing with anyone resquested. Various activities can last for years, or even centuries, to make "the invader" becoming the real owner, with undisputable matter. However, those activities should be carried out at when they are still weak. When they are strong enough and times are ripe, they will use that strength to defeat the opponents to become the ultimate final winner!

---

2 Document..., pages 49-52; and Sovereignty .... pages 104-136

The Chinese activities performed on the South China Sea are to assert China's claimed sovereignty.

There are two areas of activities: exercise the claimed sovereign rights and defend the claimed sovereignty

A. Exercise of the Sovereign Rights

This is an illegal act to invade Vietnamese territory. On the other hand, because the international maritime route is running through the South China Sea, that is, it is related to the essential interests of many countries, especially the United States. China chooses to exercise the sovereign rights to an extent only, to peacefully prove their ownership of the South China Sea. It is to avoid military confrontation with the United States and the world. China needs to have a permanent presence in the Eastern Sea.

1. Patrol and surveillance activities by "civilian" measures:

According to the Xinhua News Agency on July 4, the Chinese marine surveillance fleet patrolled the "South China Sea controlled by China", made close observations, in order to "gather evidence and preserve their interests" around some islands and reefs at the center of Spratlys. On the morning of July 3, that marine surveillance fleet passed through some of the reefs in the East of the archipelago.

As camouflage, the maritime surveillance ships are painted in white color (to reduce a character of aggression). They are openly used for patrolling throughout the South China Sea. Currently, China has four such vessels and their base is Hainan Island. AFP quoted Xinhua News Agency: these are four **naval warships disguised** as maritime surveillance vessels. They are conducted by the Chinese National Oceanic Administration, managed by the Chinese Ministry of Territorial Resources. They are not part of China Navy.

The maritime surveillance ships were used to patrol, to monitor, to prevent Vietnamese fishermen from fishing. The Chinese naval soldiers shoot and kill Vietnamese fishermen. They arrested Vietnamese fishermen, confiscated boats, fishing gears and products, robbed money, detained them. Victims were brought to the Woody, Lincoln and Robert islands for custody. They were prosecuted for infringement on China "territorial sea". They were fined, including ransom. They are culprits in many incidents of sinking Vietnamese fishing boats in the South China Sea. They attacked Vietnamese fishermen and then fled. The Vietnam government does not even protect its own citizens, dare not to accuse any criminals at sea. It only said the attack was made by "**strange ships**".

The Chinese naval ships did not hesitate to shoot and kill Vietnamese fishermen.

Those surveillance vessels escort and protect Chinese fishing ships. For example, on July 15, those marine surveillance ships escorted a convoy of 30 Chinese fishing ships to the Fiery Cross, south of Spratly archipelago.

China said it plans to have 500 marine surveillance ships by 2020, to patrol and enforce laws in fishing areas, protect fishing grounds, protect fishermen and national sovereignty, as well as monitor maritime traffic and protect maritime security. **These 500 ships also supported Hainan fishermen in raising tropical fish in cage in Mischief Reef.**

- The People's Daily of China, published on August 1, said that the Chinese government had launched a new patrol ship, 5,400 tons. The ship is specially designed to protect "maritime sovereignty".

Maintaining the marine surveillance ships in the South China Sea is to prove China's sovereignty over this waters.

Sending out a "civilian" fleet from the Chinese Oceanic Administration, or from the Fishery Administration, Beijing leaders consistenly use the policy of "fait accompli" to assert their sovereignty though the ships were equipped with heavy weapons, including helicopters.. This is not "using forces" for asserting sovereignty, thus, China could satisfy the United States.'demand.

2. Directing, guiding and organizing for China fishermen to practice permanently in a large-scale plan in Spratlys.

- Over 1,000 fishing boats departed from Yangjiang seaport, Guangdong Province, as soon as the fishing ban ended. Guangdong Vice President Liu Kun came to the fishing festival to announce: over 14,000 Chinese fishing boats registered in Guangdong Province headed towards the South China Sea from August 1 (China Daily, Aug 2)

- In Hainan Province, at 12 noon on August 1, when the fishing ban ceased in the South China Sea (China called it the "*Sansha fishing ground*"), then a total of 8994 fishing vessels with 35,600 Hainan fishermen simultaneously poured into the South China Sea to practice. Right from the previous day, July 31, many Hainan fishing vessels gathered at fishing ports on Hainan Island, preparing gasoline, accumulating food. An official from the Department of Fisheries and Marine Affairs in Hainan said all the units had been making all their efforts of preparing to support their fishermen going into the South China Sea, from noon 1/8 (Hainan Daily on August 1).

- Xinhua News Agency 新華社 (Tân Hoa Xã) on August 24, 2012 announced a Chinese ship was deployed into the Spratlys to support their fishing fleet. It is a refueling and seafood processing vessel named Quynh Tam A F-8138, with a tonnage of 4,000 tons of Giang Hai Company. The vessel departed from China's Hainan Island to the Spratlys. This large ship is capable to fish, then processing the "seafoods" at once: sliced, dried, chilled them right on board, to provide full services for the Chinese fishing industry. Therefore, with food, water and fuel supplied quickly nearby, the Chinese fishing boats from Hainan could stay working longer in the Spratlys archipelago.

China sent 23,000 fishermen into the South China Sea - figure 1

China sent 23,000 fishermen into the South China Sea - figure 2

3. Other Activities to Exercise The Sovereign Rights

- Red China used the large fishing boat to penetrate deep into the continental shelf of Vietnam and cut the cables of Vietnam oil and gas exploration vessels, such as Binh Minh (180 nautical miles from Vung Tau) and Viking (140 nautical miles from Tuy Hoa) . These happened in May and June 2011, citing "Vietnam violated their territorial waters".

-Announcing bids for oil and gas exploitation within the area of the continental shelf and exclusive economic zone of Vietnam.

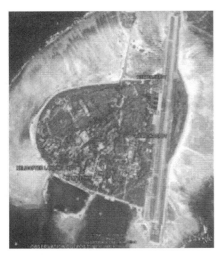

On June 23, 2012, China's Hai Duong CNOOC of Petroleum Group divided an area into 9 lots located on the continental shelf of Central and South Vietnam. Those lots have a total area of over 160,000 km², overlapping lots that Vietnam has numbered from 128 to 132, and from 145 to 156, and Red China invites international corporations to participate in bidding for oil and gas exploration. According to Reuters in the August 1, 2012 newsletter, "Beijing opens this front in order to impose its sovereignty over the South China Sea, parallel to the diplomatic and military fronts." In July, Wang Yilin, chairman of CNOOC Group, said to the press that his call for bidding on 9 lots off Vietnam had attracted many US companies, but declined to tell which companies... On August 28, 2012, CNOOC invited the international contractors to bid for oil and gas exploration on 26 lots. Most of them are situated outside of Biển Đông/Eastern Sea. However, according to Vietnam Ministry of Foreign Affairs, the oil and gas lot 65/12 *"is located about 3 nautical miles from Tree Island within the Paracel archipelago of Vietnam"*

- China has warned, pressured on or threatened several foreign oil and gas companies exploiting oil/gas on Vietnam's continental shelf. China ordered them to withdraw. Particularly the Indian oil company ONGC exploring oil at lots 127 and 128 on the continental shelf of Vietnam, even though this company has been operating here for many years. In the past, China also did put pressure on other companies from the United States, Great Britain, Italy, Russia, etc...

B. Protection of Sovereignty

Red China has officially announced that China has **core interests** in the Eastern Sea (South China Sea). With this statement, China considers the Eastern Sea to be a part of its territory that must be protected, including by force.

So what are they planning to do to **protect the sovereignty** in the Eastern Sea that they have occupied in a situation that the whole world opposes, especially from the United States?

1). The militarization of Sansha and the military main forces in the Paracel and Spratly regions, are placed under the command of the Military Command of Sansha City. Military facilities under the Sansha Command post include: storages, airfields, combat harbors and stationed

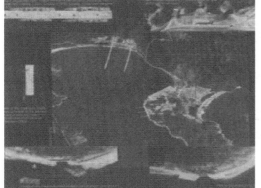

troops on the Paracel islands, fortified structures on the Islands of Woody, Lincoln, Robert, Pattle, Duncan, Triton, Tree... On the islands of the Spratlys, the military structures are built on the Fiery Cross, Mischief and other reefs: Johnson, Subi, Gaven, Cuarteron, Chigua, Hughes.

Woody Island has the largest military installations in the Paracel archipelago, occupied by China. It has played a great role as a "staging base" to control the Eastern Sea.

2). China Naval troops stationed outside of Sansha region is responsible to defend the entire maritime region. Sanya Naval Base(3) in south Hainan Island has long been established, playing a key role to confront any forces.

With two 800-meter piers, already built, enough for eight aircraft carriers to dock at the same time, and three piers for the 094 nuclear submarines, Jin Class, equipped with long-range missiles, carrying nuclear warheads, or Song S-20 equipped with Yingji-8 missiles that can attack enemy aircraft carriers from the water bottom. Sanya base has a cave that can hold 20 submarines 094, used as a staging base to support the shockwaves for the battle.

- In addition, to support its military Sanya base, China formed an 827 rocket Brigade stationed in Guangdong province. According to Taiwan's United Daily News dated July 2, 2012, the 827 Brigade was part of Beijing's strategy to deal with the nations that claimed parts of South China Sea. 827 had the Dong Phong DF-21D and Dong Phong DF-16 missiles. The DF-21D is a type of missile capable of destroying battleships. With a range of 2000 to 3000 km, it can hit any moving target, with high accuracy. The DF-16 is a new missile, with a range of 1200 km, can reach Hanoi in a distance of only 1000km away.

3). Military Activities to Defend Sovereignty

- On the 85th anniversary of the People's Liberation Army, Chinese Ministry of Defense announced the establishment of a "direct attack patrol system" functioning on seas "under the jurisdiction" of China, i.e. the Eastern Sea of Vietnam.

At the same time, Chinese Phượng Hoàng (Phoenix) Television announced that China has different types of fighter jets taking off from the Woody Island airbase, such as the JH-7 and

---

3 Document..., pages 78-80; and Sovereignty .... pages 140-156

Su-30MKK bombers of the China Navy. These aircrafts are used to destroy the targets of "aggression" within the South China Sea. Phượng Hoàng also informed: *with the support of the aerial refueling tanker, these fighter jets' attack range could "reach the US bases in Guam, Australia and Diego Garcia".*

Besides the airbases, the seaports were also built on Woody and other islands, to support large naval vessels (including destroyers), Beijing deployed large battleships in the South China Sea, to safegurd sovereignty and promote her expansion.

A Chinese largest passenger transporting ship, a Roro-class, the "Viking Emerald" also departed from Yantai port (east coast of China) going South. This vessel is disguised as a "civilian ship" with a capacity of 36,000 tons, designed to transport troops and heavy military equipments. The ship is 178m long and 28m wide, can carry 2,000 soldiers and over 300 of military equipments at once. This is the first ship of this class. China is planning to build three more, that year. According to the Military Transport Department's Director, of Jinan Military Region, those ships of this class are capable to transport a large numbers of soldiers and equipments.

The Aircraft Carrier Thi Lang will be deployed to Bien Dong. China also built 3 more aircraft carriers for 2 Blue Water fleets. These aircraft carriers will be stationed at Sanya base in Hainan.

On July 1, 2012, the Xinhua News Agency reported that Beijing deployed four marine surveillance ships at Cuarteron Reef *(Châu Viên)* in the Spratly Archipelago, where Vietnam claimed it has sovereignty. China called it Huayang Reef. The Cuarteron Reef was seized by China Navy in 1988, along with other reefs including Johnson South *(đá Gạc Ma)*, Whitsun *(đá Ba Đầu)*, Lansdowne *(đá Len Đảo)* Reefs. Cuarteron Reef *(đá Châu Viên)* is an atoll, the highest part in the north is about 1.5 m above sea level. Since 2011, China has built durable fortresses and bases that could withstand strong winds of 71 knots/130 km an hour, or 10/12 on the Beaufort wind scale. Beijing has also brought in high-frequency and ultra-high-frequency communications equipment, radars and artilleries and anti-aircraft artillery. China uses this island as a base for their battleships.

Before those arrogant acts of aggression by Beijing expansionists, **the Committee on Protection of Territorial Integrity of Vietnam** solemnly issues this Declaration.

DECLARES

A. For communist China:

1. Vietnam's Sovereignty over the Paracel and Spratly Archipelagos is an indisputable fact.

Indeed, Vietnam's sovereignty over the Paracel and Spratly Archipelagos is proved in the following documents:

a-) "White Paper on the Chinese Communist Party Scheme of Occupying the Paracels and Spratlys with Collusion of the Communist Party of Vietnam", Committee on Protection of Territorial Integrity of Vietnam, published on 10 May 2008, re. sovereignty includes:

- **Geography:** Section II: Geography and Map of Sovereignty (pages 11-12, 15-17 and 33-34)

- **History:** Section III: Sovereign rights of Vietnam over the two archipelagos of Paracel and Spratly in history (pages 13-18)

- **Legal:** Section IV: Legal Sovereignty (pages 19-25)

This White Paper also includes the following three Declarations of the Committee on Protection of Territorial Integrity of Vietnam:

1) The August 8, 2006 Declaration on China's Redrawing of the Borders Map including the South China Sea (9-dash-line) in June 2006, pages 4-7;

2) The December 12, 2007 Declaratio re. Condemning China on Establishment of the Sansha Administrative District, pages 7-8; and

3) The December 21, 2007 Declaration re. Second Objection to the Sansha Issue, pages 8-11

Note: The English White Paper was sent to 192 heads of states who attended the United Nations General Assembly meeting in New York in 2008 by the Federation of Associations of Vietnamese Political Prisoners. Vietnam Research Center also sent to some Southeast Asian Research agencies throughout the world. The Vietnamese Community in Australia distributed 250 copies to the leaders of Australia. Some organizations in the US, France and Europe have also received this White Paper...

b-) Dossiers on Paracel & Spratly Archipelagos and National Sovereignty, 2008, includes:

Maps of Sovereignty, Chapter I:

1) from the 17th century drawn by Vietnamese scholars (pages 15-20);

2) from the 16th century drawn by foreign scholars (pages 21-28);

3) The ancient maps of China with her southernmost Island which is Hainan- the Paracels and Spratlys not inluded in the maps (pages 36-37).

Images of Islands Occupied by China, Chapter II

At Paracels, from pages 45 to 72 and at Spratlys, from pages 73-95.

c-) "The Territorial Sovereignty and China Expansion, Map and Image Records", 2010, including more than 200 maps and photographs.

Particularly in Woody Island of Paracels, from pages 104 to 135, there are 44 images of the bases and 17 pictures of the garrison operations.

In the Spratlys, there are many military structures, fortified, massive, towering out of the water. At Mischief Reef, there are 8 photoes. The Fiery Cross Reef has 5 photos. About 20 other photos on the reefs or dunes located far south of the Spratlys.

Most reefs or dunes have coordinates.

d-) Red China has no evidence of sovereignty:

A fact that needs to be raised is that in June 1994, in order to conduct the conspiracy to annex the Vietnam's Eastern Sea, China sent 10 scholars to a meeting with 100 Taiwanese scholars to search for evidences of sovereignty. This activity was part of a scheme of the Han clan 's expansion.. After the Conference, the Communist Chinese and Taiwanese issued a proclamation saying that China has historical sovereigny over the South China Sea and calling on overseas Chinese around the world to help them to find evidences, to prove Chinese sovereignty over the South China Sea. Later, occasionally a Chinese newspaper posted an article saying that a certain scholar found a piece of ceramic jar on one island, a piece of a broken bowl on the other island, implying that China owned the islands.

Reaction to the Statement of Red China and Taiwan Scholars.

Inside Vietnam, the intellectuals and the Vietnam communist leaders were silent. Therefore, a conference was organized to gather 30 overseas Vietnamese intellectuals, at the Hoover Institution on War, Revolution and Peace at Stanford University, California, USA, on July 22, 1994. The Conference rejected the allegations of those Chinese scholars. The Declaration affirmed that the Eastern Sea/Biển Đông (South China Sea) has belonged to Vietnam, geographically, historically and legally. And Vietnam have "exercised sovereign rights" in many centuries.

Subsequently, the **Committee on Protection of Territorial Integrity of Vietnam**, the successor of "The Elite Group" was formed to continue its activities. On April 29, 1995, the Committee announced the Declaration to denounce the "Legitimacy" of the administrative letter that Pham Van Dong signed on September 14, 1958 sending to Zhou Enlai, about Hanoi's recognition of Chinese sovereignty over the Paracels and Spratlys. **The Committee reaffirmed Vietnam's sovereignty over those two archipelagos** (4)

e-) **Finally,** even among Chinese intellectuals, there are many who oppose China's claim of sovereignty over the South China Sea.

---

4 NGUYỄN VĂN CANH, Communism on Vietnam Lands, Volume II: Communist Vietnam and the World, Section II: *"Relations of Vietnamese communists and Chinese communists"*, Chapter XIV: Proclamation..., Kien Quoc, 2002, 2nd edition, pages 368-372)

On June 14, 2012, a seminar called *"Disputes in the South China Sea, national sovereignty and international rules"* was organized by the Thien Tac Economic Research Institute and the media online Sina.com at the Thien Tac Economic Research Institute. The two main speakers are scholar Li Lenhua, a researcher of China Hai Duong Information Center and Professor Thoi Doan Hoang,

Scholar Li Lenhua said:

"The 9-dash-line on South China Sea is an vaguely unreal line. Our predecessors draw the 9-dash-line, with no specific longitude or latitude, nor having any legal basis...",

"There is no foundation! It was only a one-sided announcement in 1947! In the mainland there are legal scholars, also colleagues in Taiwan sharing the same perception. Back then, some of the coastal countries were not yet independent, and that was only declared by China unilaterally."

On August 13, 2012, scholar Li Lenhua rejected the 9-dash-line. He also posted on his blog a series of articles by another Chinese scholar with the pen name "Bao Phac Tien Nhan" writing on this matter.

Excerpt from "Quanlambao - Even Chinese scholars - Those with knowledge cannot deceive as the allegations by Zhong Nanhai"

- Editor Zhou Fang of Xinhua News Agency also took the same stance:

"Recently, when the Eastern Sea situation has been tense, especially after China acted illogically, denyng the right and the fact such as asserting the"cowtongue map", establishing the so-called 'Sansha city' (三沙市, Tam Sa Thị). Editor Zhou Fang "strongly opposes the use of force in the South China Sea, and also demands the abolition of the so-called Sansha city"...

On July 17, he published the article, "The current situation of Nam Hải (South Sea) will probably pull back the political reform in China" He wrote: "The biggest meaning in creating the 'Sansha City' is to show people the humiliation of China. Also, it will also force the Chinese government and military to turn the cards over, for the neighboring countries and the world to see... Since youth, we have seen the map of Nam Hải (South Sea/Biển Đông/South China Sea/Eastern Sea). A broken line, pink, unsmooth, takes the entire "South Sea" into the Chinese map. So far until today, we know the truth is not so. That national borderline is not acknowledged by the neighboring nations, not recognized internationally, and even our government and our scholars (China) couldnot explain it clearly."

On June 29, Zhou Fang wrote: "To establish 'Sansha City' is an international joke". We strongly demand its abolishment, immediately! To establish 'Sansha City' is an action of China to self-isolate. It is a major strategic mistake that needs to be quickly corrected!"

Sina.com, Zhoufang.blshe.com. Vietnamese version of Tien Phong

2. To annex these two archipelagos into mainland China, through the establishment of Sansha City, by means of showing off forces is <u>**completely illegal**</u>.

The Vietnamese people strongly oppose and condemn this act of Red China. We never accept the invasion by Beijing expansionists. For a thousand years, the Han Chinese failed in their attempt to invade Vietnam. Chinese leaders Ô Mã Nhi, Thoát Hoan,... in ancient times, or Phuong Quang Kinh in recent history (on Jan. 19, 1974) are vivid examples.

This annexation is the result of a series of illegitimate acts in decades, committed by the Beijing expansionists. The Vietnamese people will take **all necessary measures** to reclaim the lost lands and seas, even it is a long-term struggle.

B. For communist Vietnam:

For whatever reason, Ho Chi Minh and his comrades through many generations in the Communist Party of Vietnam are **responsible for** the loss of territorial lands and waters to Red China.

The contribution by the PCV leeader to the eternal enemies of the nation who invaded Vietnam is **a <u>serious crime</u>** and cannot be forgiven. There is no way to justify attitudes and actions against the interests of the nation. The communist leaders are truly Sino Puppet. **The Vietnamese people will never forgive them**. China granted aids, trained and supported the Vietnamese communists to take over the free Vietnam governments by forces. But, could China trust Vietnam leaders who killed and betrayed their own citizens? A lesson from Cambodia is still vivid. Pol Pot had faithfully carried out what Beijing trained him to do. He and his communist Party killed 2 millions people, one-third of Cambodia population of 6 millions people — after 1975 seizing the free government of Cambodia. Pol Pot and his accomplices were bitterly abandoned by their Chinese comrades. Because of the need to cooperate with the United States to resolve the issue of Cambodia, Beijing leaders heartlessly abandoned Pol Pot, its most loyal communist servant. **During negotiations to settle Cambodia problems, the US did not want to punish him for genocide, but recommended China grant him asylum. But Beijing refused. In contrary, China mercilessly abandoned him, just to avoid being blamed for the collusion with a bloody killer, a criminal who committed a genocide — a horrible crime against humanity, condemned by the world, though it was Beijing directed him to do such horible things**.

ooo

The Committee encourages the SRV government to be courageous and decisively side with people of Vietnam, to rescue Vietnam nation. The nation is in grave danger, caused by the Communist Party of Vietnam, since the era of Ho Chi Minh until today. The Vietnamese people do not allow the so-called "**comprehensive cooperation**" with the enemy to continue. Land Reforms in North Vietnam is a lesson. The 1979 war is another. The present situation is clearly disguised. Why do you buy times to **help the enemy** strengthen their physical and moral power to take over the country, even quietly in peaceful ways? The SRV must have a clear stance! Firmly stand-up against the enemy of Vietnamese people! The SRV must seize this opportunity, to speak up, to act, along with all patriotic Vietnamese nationalists, inland

and overseas—to rescue and saafeguar the nation and the people. In such move, we could save the people of Vietnam from a dark future under China's ruling. To liberate Vietnam, the communists will be forgiven from horrible crimes committed.

Regarding the South China Sea issue, the Committee demands Vietnam leaders to start a few small tasks:

1. Publicly and immediately denounce/dismiss that Diplomatic Note of prime minister Pham Van Dong signed on September 14, 1954, under Ho Chi Minh regime ---and to bring the Eastern Sea Dispute to the International Court. In the past, China cited this letter as a legal basis to invade the South China Sea: sending a fleet to occupy the Paracels from the Repulic Vietnam in January 1974. Bring four destroyers in to surround and kill 64 soldiers of Vietnam communist military with heavy artillery, when wading and carrying supplies into Johnson Reef, in March 1988, and occupied 6 reefs then.

The diplomatic note was the source of the invasion of the entire Vietnam's Eastern Sea today. **Destroying that basis will make China no longer to have a reason to justify its aggression.**

As early as April 29, 1995 of the last century, the Committee made a statement that the Diplomatic Note was "not legitimate", having no legal validity . The Committee requires the SRV to cancel the diplomatic note, either by making a public letter to the Red China or the Ministry of Foreign Affairs of Vietnam to announce a unilateral statement declaring that Pham Van Dong's Letter is invalid.

Formally in the international law, such act is sufficient and valid.

In addition, the Committee requires the Socialist Republic of Vietnam to bring the matter of aggression to the International Court.

The Socialist Republic of Vietnam still remained silent on this matter. On September 23, 2008, Journalist Ly Kien Truc, senior editor of Văn Hoá Magazine, in Southern California interviewed Le Cong Phung, Vietnam Ambassador in Washington DC. On this issue, Phung answered: ".. *There are many people saying that this matter should be taken to the International Court, or to the United Nations to fight for it.* **We are also planning**..." *(5)* The Committee reiterated the above statement. In terms of legal procedures, only the Socialist Republic of Vietnam (SRV) government who has the right to fight for this issue, has the standing before the Court. No one other than the Socialist Republic of Vietnam (SRV) government can do, including the Communist Party of Vietnam. The CPV earns a high position" granted by the Constitution of the SRV", even higher than the SRV Government.

---

5 Document... How Vietnamese Communists explains about Vietnam Lands and Territorial Waters, pages 250-262

The Philippines set a good example for Vietnam to follow. even though China only" threatens to "invade" the Philippines in theory with a "9-dash-line map".(6)

2. In order to protect the country against a foreign invasion, the Committee requires that building of people strength be done. Once, the Vietnamese people unite into a firm block, with a strong will to win, the Vietnamese people not only reclaim the Paracel and Spratly Archipelagos, also to safeguard the country. This is the people power.. **The spirit of patriotism displayed by students, young people and the general masses through numerous protests in 2007 when Red China established Sansha 三 沙 (Tam Sa) district to control the South China Sea, Vietnam's Eastern Sea has proven its effect: China annouced abolisshemnt of the project** though it was only in theory to appease the anger of the Vietanmese public.

In order to achieve this goal, Vietnam has to take bold measures necessary to lay down a foundation for freedom and democracy to grow.. **There needs to be a roadmap towards this goal**. The short-term action and the beginning is that the Vietnamese communists must release all those arrested for "speaking out Paracels and Spratlys belong to Vietnam", releasing all prisoners of conscience, ending the persecution for many different reasons, and let people to be free......

Burma is a good example, need to learn.

3. Officially calling upon major powers to support this struggle. The SRV **must create an international coalition in which Vietnam plays an active role**. Thanks to that support, the Vietnamese communists have to respond drastically and practically to each act of aggression by the Chinese, just stop declaring that Paracels and Spratlys historically belong to Vietnam... as repeated for the past decades. Just last month again, when China already annexed the South China Sea into mainland China, Vietnamese leaders had a spokesperson repeat the same statementt. The only exception is that the Vietnamese Fisheries Association was allowed to use **aggresso**r to pinpoint China as a culprit who killed Vietanmese fishsermen in Paracels. This helps the CPV and SRV leaders avoid an act to insult their Chinese Master. The CPV should learn aonther lesson from the Phillippines. Recently, a number of Chinese fishing boats entered the Scarborough Island of the Philippines, escorted by Chinese Navy with aggressive attitudes. . The Philippines responded strongly and firmly. Finally the Chinese Navy had to withdraw, because of the "coming storm". The withdrawal was made because of " a coming strom", not because of the international pressure.

Done in California September 1, 2012

---

6 Document... The Statement on the Diplomatic Note of Pham Van Dong. Nhã Trân from RFA interview, about the Solution for Vietnam, after Pham Van Dong's diplomatic Note, pages 245-250.

Nguyễn văn Canh

Documental resources:

-NGUYỄN VĂN CANH, *"Communism on Vietnam Lands"*, Volume II: *"Viet Cong and the World"*, published by Kien Quoc, second edition, 2002.

- Committee on Protection of Territorial Integrity of Vietnam, "White Paper : Red Chin's Scheme of Expansion over Paracels and Spratlys with Collusion of the Socialist Republic of Vietnam", Center For Vietnam Studies, 2008, Vietnamese Version.

- Nguyễn Văn Canh, *"Documentary on Paracel & Spratly Archipelagos and National Sovereignty"* Center For Vietnam Studies, versions 2008, 2009 and 2010.

- Nguyễn Văn Canh, "Territorial Sovereignty and Red China 's Expansion, Maps and Images, Center For Vietnam Studies, 2010, 2011

2.1. COMPROMISE WITH CHINA TO TRANSFER SOVEREIGNTY OVER VIETNAM' S EASTERN SEA

Committee on Protection of Territorial Integrity of Vietnam

DECLARATION

June 22, 2014

On Red China 's Plot in Securing her Sovereignty over the Entire South China Sea, through installing the Oil Rig HD-981 in Paracels.

On May 1, 2014, China operated the oil rig HD-981 in an area, South of Tri Ton island of Paracels. This was a huge mobile semi-submerged oil rig, largest in the world, 114m long, 90m wide, 136m high, dividing into five floors. It was advertised to be well-equipped for oil drilling at a maximum depth of 3,000m.

China announced that the Oil Rig HD-981 platform would be in operation until August 15, 2014.

To protect the oil platform, China initially sent a fleet of 80 ships. Of these, there were seven naval warships, 33 marine surveillance ships, 40 fishing vessels along with the warship 534 equipped with missiles and a fast attack ship 753, and minesweepers. There was military aircraft constantly flying around the Oil Rig.

Total ships of the Chinese fleet now reached 120. China fleet ordered Vietnamese coast guard and fishing boats not to approach the HD 981 "protection belt". On the first day, they were told not to be within a radius of three nautical miles. Then, the next day, four nautical miles. Phùng quang Thanh, Vietnam's Defense Minister immediately ordered the Vietnamese Coast

Guard to withdraw farther, a 10 nautical miles way, to avoid contact and allow HD 981 to operate.

The Chinese ships used water cannons to attack Vietnamese coast guard ships, even though they were at a distance of seven to ten nautical miles. In the first few days, the Chinese ships directly hit and caused damage to eight Vietnamese fishing boats. Many Vietnamese fishing boats were sunk. On the morning of May 5, 2014, when a Vietnamese coast guard ship approached the oil rig, it was hit by deadly fire from the Chinese navy. Four Vietnamese coast guardsmen were killed and two were wounded.

These are blatant acts of agression by force. To justify it, China announes that the HD 981 Oil Rig operates in an "indisputable" sea under her jurisdiction. To understand such an incident, I would like to review "an agreement on a solution to South China Sea Dispute ", which was agreed to by both nations on June 2011. Why does HD 981 operate in an oil-free area? What do the Vietnamese people expect from the Communist Vietnam's leaders?

2.1.1. THE AGREEMENT BETWEEN TWO PARTIES AND TWO NATIONS ON "SOLUTION FOR THE SOUTH CHINA SEA DISPUTE"

A Treaty was signed in Beijing on June 25, 2011, by Hồ xuân Sơn, Vietnam's Deputy Minister of Foreign Affairs and his counterpart Cui Tiankai 崔天凯, China's Deputy Minister of Foreign Affairs. It was signed in the presence of China's State Councilor Dai Bingguo 戴秉國 (1). This Treaty is called "**Agreement on A Solution to the South China Sea Dispute**", to formalize an Agreement between two communist Parties. It was launched in April 2011 by Chinese General Guo Boxiong 郭伯雄 (Quách bá Hùng), Vice Chairman of the Central Military Commission, China's top military council. This Treaty will bind the governments of two countries.

This agreement is a result of previous arrangements between the two party leaders in Hanoi. From April 12 to 18, 2011, General Guo Boxiong, Vice Chairman of the Central Military Commission and a Chinese Communist Party Politburo member came to Hanoi to confer with Vietnam's Communist Party general secretary Nguyễn phú Trọng, and Politburo member Nguyễn Tấn Dũng….Both parties pledged to cooperate more closely, to seek essential solutions to resolve the issues arising from the South China Sea.

Looking at the Treaty's content, we can immediately see that Beijing has assigned the following **three missions** for Vietnam's leaders to execute, regarding the so-called South China Sea dispute on a basis that the Sea had been transferred to Red China.

a. The first task is 'friendly consultation and avoiding any actions that could aggravate or make matters more complex'.

To show that there an equal footing during negotiations between two sides, the treaty calls for *"Friendly Consultattion"* and avoiding actions that make the situation in South China sea worse.

But pracically, this is an one-way order frrom China to the Communist Party of Vietnam leaders to do anyhting that is contrary to what China wants. China forbids Vietnam to claim sovereignty over the sea. Vietnam leaders are not allowed to make any statement on sovereignty or have any anti-Chniese activity about the matter.

China proclaims that she is an owner of the sea. As a result, she has conducted surveillance ships to patrol in the region.; she has harassed Vietnamese fishermen for "illegal fishing in Chinese waters." The harassments are serious and in some cases barbarous: arrest and imprisoment, fines, robbing victims of cacth, confiscating of equipmen, sinking their boats, killings….

On May 1, 2014, China sent Oil Righ HD 981 to do research in an area south of Tri ton island on Vietnam's continental self with an escort of a fleet at first of 41 vessels including battleships from Chiense navy. On the first days, they sank a Vietnamese police patrol vesael, killing 4 Vietnamese and 2 wounded. Then China sent 39 more ships to the scene to encircle the area. More Vietnamese police were hit.

Huge and furious demonstrations by Vetnamese agaisnt China's aggression occurred in Saigon. The protests became riots. Red Chinese manufacturing plants in Binh Duong were burned down. Some Chinese workers in Ha tĩnh were killed, others were injuried.

The invasion was launched by surprise. Emabarrassed Secretray Genneral of the Communist Party Nguyen phu Trong openly asked for seeing Xi jinping about his problem but he refused. Foreign Minister Pham dinh Minh called Yang Jiechi , but was told that the Oil Rig "is operating in China waters".

The Vietnmese leders were in confusion. They did not know how to deal with this situation. In order to reduce tension among the Vietnanese people through out the country, on one side, Nguyen phu Trong went to meet his electors at the Tay Ho District in Hanoi and Chief of State Truong tan Sang to his district in Ho chi Minh City. Both of them vaguely mentioned the issue of Sovereignty over the Eastern Sea and "there is a need to proetct it." On the other side, Nguyen tan Dung, Prime Minister, on May 11, went to Myanmar for an ASEAN meeting. He talked to the press saying that (China) is a source of instability in the region, danger to the free navigtion on the sea. He dared to go farther saying that " [He] will not exchange the soverignty for a vague friendship." Later on May 21, he went to visit Manila. On this occasion, he leaked to a Vietnamese Correspondent a news that he tailked with President Aquino about the "lawsuit" brought to the Permanent Court of Arbitration against China on her invasion of the South China Sea. He just implied that he consulted the President about the procedure to bring the case to the court.

The Vietnamese leaders in reality had no other choce than just loudly making such hollow statements in order to reduce tension inside the country so as to avoid their responsibilities to their people. They did not intent to deal with the aggression.

Howevrer, it is those statements and because of huge demonstrations in Saigon by the angry Vietnamese against the aggression which made China think that the Vietnamese leaders secretly maneuvered Vietnamese and sponsored these protests, in order to escape from China's control, Yang Yiechi was sent to Hanoi on June 30 for the purpose to keep the situation under control.. Yang reminded the PCV leaders about four Nos. Briefly, there was no friendly onsultation.

b. The second task is "no *outside forces to be involved in the dispute":* The dispute on South China Sea is a problem between China and Vietnam only. It is to be solved by **bilateral negotiations.** China's leaders prohibits Vietnam from allowing "an outside force" to be involved in sovereignty issues. This outside force here is America, a China 's eneny that could be an obstacle to her expansion in the region and in Asia Pacific. After the Regional Security Conference in Hanoi in 2010, China has repeatedly opposed the US involvement in the South China Sea dispute. China has accused the United States of disturbing, creating tension, destroying the peace , and destabilizing this Asia Pacific region. China uses all means possible to prevent Vietnamese leaders from getting along with and forming an friendship alliance with the United States. Under constant pressure, Vietnamese leaders have repeatedly stated they have made no alliance with any nation. When China blatantly invaded Vietnam waters, as the case of the HD 981 Oil Rig, Vietnam dared not call the USA for help. This again is an one-way order from Red China.

c. The third task is "to guide the public opinion and to avoid to make any comments or have any actions harmful to the friendship and trust between the peoples of the two countries".

In this task, China requires Vietnam leaders to:

1. One: Guide the Public Opinion

For the people of Vietnam the territory issue is directly tied to the spirit of Patriotism. To transfer land and sea under these cirrcumstances to a foreign nation, especially China as in this case is a serious matter that sparks a large fire of patriotism to break out nationwide. It fuels a fierce anti-China movement. Large protests broke out in December 2007 when China established Sansha City, in April 2008 during the Beijing Olympics when the Olympic torch was relayed though Saigon, and when Chinese ships entered the Vietnam continetal self to cut off cables of Binh Minh and Viking 2. Those protests were a worrisome concern to China. Such protests have been significant obstacles to China's campaign to occupy Biển Đông of Vietnam. Several Vietnamese intellectuals, community leaders, and journalists (at home and overseas) have continued to oppose the Chinese occupation of Biển Đông with the nine-dash map. China demanded Vietnam's leaders to deal with that anti-China opposition. The Vietnamese people have bitter experiences of 1000 years under Chinese domination. China knows this and continues to pressure Vietnam's leaders to have policies of guiding the public opinion on this matter through the media: newspapers, radio, television, social media, Internet...

Guidance must have two sides: **direction and control. (censure)**

-Direction: Information must be guided and regulated. Do not harm the reputation of China and Chinese leaders. Do not expose any truth detrimental to China and its policy. Do not cause harmful damage to the bilateral friendship between the two nations. Do not distrust the leadership of China towards Vietnam…. For many years, the Vietnamese communists have diligently carried out this task. Chinese naval ships or Surveilance ships used to attack and sink Vietnamese fishing wooden boats in Paracels and sometimes in Spratlys. The CPV Education and Propaganda Depsrtment (EPD) instructed the press that it is a **"strange ship"** that is the culprit, not pinpointing Chinese ships. Not a single newpaper out of some 800 ones dared say by name that the Chinese vessels were involved though every fisherman knew the name and nmbers of such vessels. For example, a Chinese survaillance ship hit a Vietnaese fisherman wooden boat near Lincoln ialand in the Paracels, then quietly left the area though it knew that some vistims were tossed out and swam in the sea. If such a thing is written on the news, the entire world would denounce the evil and barbaric behavior of the Chinese.

In short, no negative talk about "our friendly neighbor" is allowed.

In addition, if some thing that need to propagandize on behalf of the Chinese, EDP do not hesitate to do it even it is hamrful to Vietanm interests. The Digital News, a CPV mouthpiece in September 2009, translated and published a full-text interview from the Chinese "Global Times" newspaper. It was about the military exercises of the Chinese Navy on the Fiery Cross Reef in Bien Dong. That Chinese military exercise was reported as " Defense Operation to protect the Frontier", even though the island belongs to Vietnam .

- Control the source of public opinion. It is called "information censorship". Media must be controlled. No newspapers are allowed to expose any fact about the situation in the Easernt Sea. It could cause "confusion" in public opinion, hence it results in active opposition to China from the public, incites people to take to the streets nationwide in violent anti-China protests. This anti-China movement could break into a anti-china war to protect the territorial Integrity of Vietnam. For example since 2003, when several reefs/atolls in South side of Spratlys were openly reclaimed by Chinese Navy to become artificiall islands on which fortified fortresses were erected, the CPV remained silent. And no mass media were allowed to cover stories about the incident. In July 2007, a Chinese naval ship killed a Vietnamese fisherman and sank a boat operating near the Spratly Island. No media reported it.

2. Two: Be Alert.

Vietnam's leaders must avoid comments or actions that are harmful to the friendship and trust of the "peoples of two nations".

China aimed at whom, when issuing this warning? Chinese media has publicly threatened the CPV leaders for being "ungrateful". Reason? Because they still have intent to protect Vietnam's sovereignty over the Paracel and Spratly archipelagos. Chinese Global Times even suggested the "death penalty" for those leaders for committing the above "crime". In addtion, in a totalitarian regime, the only persons who can make statements or comments are Party leaders. It appears that China aims at the CPV leaders. China threatened them for betraying China. On July 2010 at the ASEAN Conference in Hanoi, US Secretary of State Hillary Clinton suggested the US policy to solve the dispute of the South China Sea by means of multilateral negotiations. Then deputy prime minister Pham Gia Khiem accordingly joined the 12-nation group to support the US stance. This statement is contrary to China policy. China just wants a bilateral rnegotiation. Chinese Foreign Minister Yang Jiechi 杨洁篪 was angry, left the conference room. An hour later, he re-entered the room, insulting Khiem right in the Conference about the position that Kiem took in dealing with the dispute because as a host Khiem did not prevent it from happening. Jiechi insisted: "it must be resolved bilaterally only" i.e. between China and each member of the group. Looking at the Singapore Minister of Foreign Affairs, he arrogantly warned:: "China is a big country. Your nations are small.".

There are two areas where Red China requires Vietnamese Communist leaders **to be alert:** 1) Words or statements; 2) Action.

1) Words or Statements: China demands that Vietnam do not say any word or make any statement that is harmful to the interests and prestige of China. Examples: Support of the USA for multi-lateral negotiations. Support of internationalization of the Eastern Sea conflict;. Alliance with any third nation… As a result, Nguyễn phú Trọng, Trương tấn Sang, Nguyễn tấn Dũng, Nguyễn sinh Hùng….have silently turned a blind eye to such brutal Chinese acts as sinking Police patrol boats killing members of the Police forces, sinking Vietnamese fishing boats when China moved HD 981 with warships to the continetntal self of Vietnam in May 2014. At the same time, Minister of Defense Phung Quang Thanh stated at the Shangri-La Conference about the killings that this is merely a conflict between brothers in a famly. Truly, Vietnam leaders comply with what was dictated in the "Guo Boxiong Agreement".

2) Action: Do not conduct joint oil drills with the United States or other countries. Do not buy weapons such as airplanes and ships. Do not lease the Cam Ranh seaport to the United States or any country opposing China. Suppress all protests against China even by a single person. Any actions to be taken should be in favor of China. When the Sansha District was established, a low-ranking official, Qin Gang, spokesman for the Ministry of Foreign Affairs of China in Beijing on January 18 , 2007 told Vietnamese leaders: "We hope the Vietnamese government will be responsible and take effective measures to prevent anything harmful to our bilateral relations". To repsonse to Beijing demands, Hanoi used all means available to suppress student protests. The SRV government mobilized its apparatuses at all levels to counter mass demontnstratons: secret police, security forces, party members, organizations, military, court, prison system -- including the Ministry of Education and Hanoi University of Technology where the college students play key role in protests. Many were harassed, terrorized, arrested, detained, and imprisoned. When the Oil Rig HD 981 was in Vietnamese waters along with the Chinese navy, Vietnam's top leaders Nguyen Phu Trong, Truong Tan Sang, and Nguyen Tan Dung kept a quiet attitude the first few days, with no action. Then, before fierce and large protests by a great number of Vietnamese in order to "not harm the neighboring friendship" they asked to meet Xi Jinping for a solution, but were declined.

****

Nguyen Phu Trong, Nguyen Tan Dung and others… were given duties prescribed in the June 2011 Agreement. The Agreement really does not include a solution to the dispute on the sovereignty over the islands as expected, but on the contrary stiipulates orders for the CPV leaders to execute a number of tasks on a basis that China has had sovereignty over the sea. The tasks involve what need to done to prevent oppositions for the purpose to safeguard the sovereignty of China.

A question is raised as to how could the jobs be done?

IMPLEMENTATION OF THE AGREEMENT

After the conference of Gao Boxiong with Nguyen Phu Trong and Nguyen Tan Dung, a communique was released, saying: *"the goal of their meeting was to 'promote a comprehensive strategic cooperation with Vietnam'.*

What is the "comprehensive strategic cooperation"? And how to promote it? The two parties are working closely together in all aspects to implement the Agreement.

1). Military Cooperation: Guo Boxiong met Phung Quang Thanh on April 13 to make arrangements for a strategic cooperation between the two armies, 'to become pratically effective and also further to strengthen the cooperation in many other areas'. According to the Beijing Radio, Boxiong instructed three things for Phung Quang Thanh to execute:

a) To tighten strategic contacts. To grasp firmly the correct direction of development of the strategic Sino-Vietnam relations;

b) To respect the tradition of active guidances. To actively create an atmosphere of friendship, solidarity and cooperation between China and Vietnam;

c) To enrich the relations. To actively improve the levels of military cooperation between the two nations.

Phung Quang Thanh was assigned to guide, educate, and unify Vietnamese and Chinese militaries, under the supervision of China. The important purpose is to uncover and eliminate all conspiracies against China by forces, also to propagandize and control the ideological thoughts in Vietnam's military.

2). Security Cooperation: Le Hong Anh, Vietnam's Minister of Public Security paid a visit to Beijing. He met with Minister of Public Security of China, Meng Jianzhu 孟建柱, during the time Guo Boxiong was still in Hanoi. Meng Jianzhu declared: the cooperation of "law

enforcement" is very important in the Vietnamese-Chinese friendship cooperation. He hopes the two countries must cooperate more closely in areas such as "anti-terrorism", increase traditoal cooperations and advance the overall partnership strategy between the two countries. Le Hong Anh pledged: "Vietnam will join China in efforts to strengthen cooperation mechanisms, to prevent crimes, and to maintain social order."

Regarding the role of Security Police Forces in line for "cooperation in law enforcement", after the treaty was signed, in the name of ' maintaining social order', Vietnamese Security Police Forces were mobilized to harshly suppress all protests in Hanoi and Saigon. Hanoi residents witnessed the presence of police officers from China who conduct anti-demonstraion activities and also suppress the demonstrators on July 10, 2011. The reasons were that Vietnamese Police did not fulfill their duties. Demonstratons with slogans "Down with Chinese

Invaders", "'Paracels and Spratlys belong to Vietnam" ... are "actions that do damage to the friendship and mutual trust". Therefore, the Vietnamese communist police had to act harshly to dispurse demonstrations and disable protesters. on Sunday July 17, 2011 A photo showed four Vietnamese Policemen holding one leg and one arm of a protestor. They carried the young patriotic student to a bus waiting on street side. When approaching the bus door, a policeman stepped on the victim's face. That is a symbolic example of the way the Vietnam's Communist regime to deal with the populace, trying to avoid "hurting Beijing's trust".

3. Law and Justice Cooperation: Wang Shengjun 王勝俊, President of the Supreme People's Court of China came to Vietnam to meet with Vietnam's "State President" Nguyễn minh Triết to promote cooperation of "law and justice" between the two countries. After the meeting, Triet said he highly valued the judicial cooperation between the two countries and agreed to strengthen ties, to exchange experiences in the building of a socialist country based on " Ruling By Laws" Wang Shengjun said Vietnam and China are socialist nations, therefore having similar points and dealing with similar challenges. The legal systems of the two countries have played an important role in the economic, social developments and protection of each country 's legal system.

With spomsorship from Wang Shengjun, and in the name of "strengthening the socialist state based on rules by law... protecting the law...". Triet pledged to use the court system to suppress and eliminate those "criminals" causing public disorder which were merely anti-China demonstrators with respect to Eastern Sea invasions.   The Vietnamese court system in the name of maitainng socialist justice operates under Chian's guidances and protection .

In short, in just six days with five urgent meetings, the top leaders of the two communist Parties have successfully laid out a foundation for the "integration" of both parties and governments policies over the South China Sea, including national security, law, propaganda, politics, information, education, organizational structures, military, police forces, court. As a result, the two armies, security, court and propaganda systems become ONE. With such unification, China plays a role of an agency to formulate policies and Vietnam is just an executor. As a consequence, the entire apparatus of the Communist Party and government of Vietnam will be mobilized to carry out China policies and assist her expansion.

China knows that she is not able to take the South China Sea without the practical and active cooperation of the VCP and the Vietnamese government. Therefore, Chinese communists must find every way possible, pay any price and use all tricks available to spur Vietnam's leaders in position to execute China's conspiracy right on their soil. Thus they need to become 'native' powerful governors or puppets to serve China.

What did Vientmaese leaders do internally and internationally when the HD 981 platform moved in and operated in Vientam waters showed that they tacitly complied with China policies. Tha is why Nguyen phu Trong and Truong tan Sang due to strong pressure from the angry general public before an armed invasion by Chinese navy, four weeks later raised a vague voice of protection of sovereignty, while Nguyen tan Dung made a bit bolder bu hollow statement aganst the invasion, though they dared not name Chinese as aggressors and especially no concrete actions were taken to deal with the situation.

This "Guo Boxiong Agreement" has driven top Vietnamese leaders into becoming " China puppets" whose duties are to help China gain control of South China Sea, and the entire Vietnam before going further.

Briefly, the treaty entitled "**Agreement on A Solution to the South China Sea Dispute**" is an extremely unsusual document signed by both Ministries of Foreign Affairs. When we look at the topics, we expect that **both sides has achieved a solution to the sovereignty over the Paracels and Sprtalys.** On the contrary, not a single word was mentioned about it. However, what has been covered is a series of orders from Red China to Communist Vietnam to execute, implying that Communist Vietnam had secretly transferred the archipelagos to China, probably involuntarily. Afraid of reactions from the Vietnames people and also from international communities about the non-transparent transfer of the sovereignty over the islands, China imposes on Communist Vietnam **to do or not to do** anything related to the sovereignty that could hurt Red China's feelings, **on the premise that Red China is already an owner of the islands.**.

As a consequence, for examples, as above presented, all about 800 news agencies received orders from the Party Central Committee Education and Propaganda Department not to pinpoint **China naval ships** that sank Vietnamese fishing boats then quietly left the scene without rescueing victims tossed to the sea, but to say that it it" **strange ships**" that did such a dirty thing; or imprisoning a young fragile female student who protested China as an aggressor by siting-in at home with a banner " Paracels and Spatlys belong to Vietnam"; or communist secret agents who barbaricly attacked students in anti-China demonstrations…

That is all about the treaty.

2.1.2. WHY DID CHINA PLACE THE DRILLING PLATFORM IN SOUTHWEST OF PARACELS, WHERE THERE IS NO OIL?

1. China asserting sovereignty:

China deliberately brought a giant rig to the Quang Ngai coast where it planned to operate for over 3 months. Here, since 1995, Crestone company was allowed by China to do explorations for oil and gas. But no oil was found. So what is its purpose?

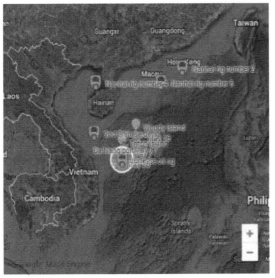

The presence of the oil rig in the Paracels is just an act of "exercice of sovereign rights" on an area that China used forces to occupy illegally in 1974. Because of her illegal occupation, China has regulargely manintained her presence there under different forms with a hope that it becomes a fait accompli in the far future. The area belongs to the Paracel archipelago, an area of dispute between Vietnam and China only. Other countries do not have much interesst in it as the case of Spralys.

Having been controlled by different ways, with a role of puppets as prescribed in the Guo Boxiong Agreement, Viietnamese leaders consisting of numerous top communists have main missions at this time as how to help China become an owner the South China Sea before her next move to South East Asia and later the world. But they need to pass 'tests' in solving any oppositions, primarily those from Vietnamese people themselves inside the country. China thinks that international oppositions will have not much influence so long as she does not use large scale forces in order to create instability in the region

It is China's first step of asserting sovereignty across the region. Next, after the situation is "cooling down", she will move an Oil Platform to other area in the Spratly Archipelago where it is rich in oil and gas.

Photo: Location Map of Rigs in Vietnam's Eastern Sea (South China Sea)

Reuters reported on June 13, that China Sea Services Agency will launch 3 other drilling rigs to the Eastern Sea: Nanhai 2 and Nanhai 5 will operate at a location between Main China and Dongsha, near Taiwan, and Nanhai 9 will be sent to Vietnam continental shelf. In addtion, China will send out 4 others in 6 months. She announces that a toal of 24 oil rigs will be launched out in this stage.

Applying the same tactics, China would mobilize thousand (s) of fishing vessels to surround and protect the rig, with marine surveillance vessels, patrol vessels, and the naval shps in the outer belts. There will be no violence. The Vietnamese Navy will have no reaons to attack, even if it wants, it haa no capacity to meet the challenges, Moreover, the armies of both sides have been "unified" under the guidances of Chinese. In addition, during the period on HD 981 opreration in May 2014, Vietnam Minister of Defense Phung Quang Thanh hinted that Vietam had agreed and considered the case of HD 981 being operated within the Chinese territory legally, though few Vietnamese Coast Guardmen was shot dead and others wounded with a dozen Police patrol ships sunk, not including deaths and damages to fishermen's. He further stated when he participated at a Ministers of Defence conference in Singapore in the same month that what happened there was just a minor conflict within a family. Remember that all active opposiitions to the Chinese invasion from the Vietnamese people had been neutralized. And major powers would intervene only when their interests were harmful. If the oil exploration work is done by Vietnam and China, (bilateral agreement) or they conduct this type of peaceful operation to assert the soveirgnty over the region, can any one could change this situation 50 or a hundred years later?

2. The operation of HD 981 has another more important purpose.

The HD 981 operation drew the attention of the Vietnamese people and the international community from the Johnson South island construction. It caused anger in the Vietnamese populace, and people who paid attention to it. International communities worried about symptoms of instability in the region, and also paid little attention to it now. News on the Johnson Reef appeared after the HD 981 incident occurred a week before. Only the Philippines President voiced his opposition to it. Vietnam's leaders were quiet though the reef is part of their territory, and though China started construction work since late 2012 with transport ships and naval ships equipped with missiles for protection moving back and forth. Vietname leaders pretended not to know it. The artificial island were created and sand banks were raised up to 10 meters high. Now, construction work on a runway was completed .

Now, though knowing what has happened, Hanoi leaders dare not to speak out and take any action against it. Is this because they pledged not to take any action or make any statement that could hurt the friendship relations or the trust of Red China? In addition, they have to guide the public opnion" systematically so as not to create tension or instability in th Eastern Sea. Not until May 16, 2014 at an international press conference in Hanoi, only a journalist raised a question about the case of Johnson South, Le hai Binh, a spokesman of the Vietnam Minister of Foreign Affairs repeated a statement prevously made that Vietam has an indisputable soveingnty over the Eastern Sea. Hanoi has repeated this statemnt for more than two decades.

The Vietnamese people were concentrating on demonstration against Chinese aggressions in Paracels, not to the Johnson South matter.

Is Johnson South Reef important? Johnson South Reef is a part of the coral reefs beneath the sea. Now it has become an island emerged above the water, in the Estern Sea. To date, June 18, 2014 on this island, people can see a runway almost completed. This is a project to establish a very large, 30-hectare military base, with a seaport for naval vessels and a separate seaport for civilian ships. China will build the a residence for fishermen and tourist resorts.

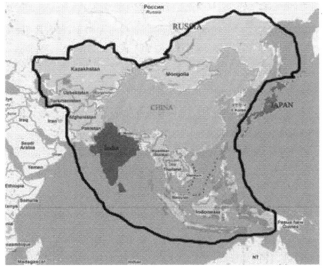

Remarks: Woody Island is a small 1.3 - 2.1 km² command base. Johnson South island has a huge Chinese military base for China to control the Eastern Sea, the Malacca Strait and neighboring countries. At present times, the distance from Woody to Johnson is about 800 kilometers. Chinese fighter jets cannot come from there for their misions, because the jets do not have enough fuel to operate.

Photo: The map of the Great China Empire

Johnson Reef, Mischief and Fiery Cross bases will help China control the corridor extending from Malacca to the North. This sea-lane lies to the west of the Philippines's coastal waters. Military ships of the 7th Fleet navigate on this sea route. Johnson Reef military base could become a type of US Diego Garcia base in the Indian Ocean. It is also a direct threat to Vietnam.

The Oil Rig HD 981 base creation is only a necessary phase for China to assert sovereign rights in the Spratlys, before extending her territory toward all Asia, to become Great China. It then includes: East Asia (except Japan), Southeast Asia, South Asia, Pakistan, Afghanistan and five former Soviet states.

Briefly, with the June 30, 2011 agreement, the Vietnamese communist leaders as local Sino Puppets have carried out the tasks of helping China take Vietnam's Eastern Sea.

The Committee demands:

1. The Communist Party of Vietnam must end a role of Sino Puppet and stop promoting Chinese influence in Vietnam. Top Vietnamese leaders Nguyễn phú Trọng, Trương tấn Sang, Nguyễn tấn Dũng, Nguyễn sinh Hùng, Phùng quang Thanh, Lê hồng Anh, Trần đại Quang, Đinh thế Huynh, Tô huy Rứa....etc.. must not bow down humiliatingly and must not enjoy privilges awarded by the enemy while Vietnaese coast guardsmen risking their lives to defend the border are shot and killed. They said they are committed to protect Vietnamese fishermen while their boats were sunk and many of them were killed and gravely harrassed, doing business in the traditional waters of Vietnam.

We condemn the Vietnamese Communist Party who brought the enemy in, assisted them to occupy the Paracels and Spratlys. Vietnamese communist leaders, Raise your heads up.! Try to live a life with dignity. Don/t continue to serve aggressors and receive their awards at the expenses of your conntry fellows Nguyen Tan Dung had "courage" to accuse China of creatiing an dangerous situation in the Eastern Sea at the ASEAN Conference in Myanmar. Then, 10 days later, on May 21, Dung announced that he would use legal measures, that is, bringing to an international court the Eastern Sea matter, when the Chinese Communist Party placed the drilling rig in the continental shelf of Vietnam. Of course, that statement is contrary to the commitment stated in the Treaty of June 25, 2011. The reason leading to this statement was that because the Vietnamese people were so angry and participated in massive anti-Chinese protests about the Chinese aggression. However it was only a hollow statement. Now being questioned about it, , he said he "is waiting for a 'convenient' time".

2. If all other CPV leaders choose the path of being puppets for the enemy, Nguyen Tan Dung should courageously bring this dispute to the Permanet Court of Arbitration. The court ruling will help Vietnam gain world support, to avoid isolation as at present time, and also will be an evidence proving sovereignty of Vietnam in the judicial process. It is the most explicit and active way of denying the sovereignty of the enemy over the Eastern Sea. Take action, do not wait. Let Nguyen Phu Trong, Truong Tan Sang and his comrades be servants to the enemy.

Finally those puppets would be abandoned by China (like Pol Pot, Hoang Van Hoan, loyal followers of China) when times come. It may not be effective as suggested if Vietnamese leaders send letters to the Secretary-General of the United Nations on China's violation of Vietnam's territorial waters. This issue is political/propaganda matter, while UN is penetrated by China and the Left. China is capable of maneuvering at the United Nations, mainly because they have lots of money to provide aid. China, a permanent member of the Security Council with veto power, is powerful in this institution, and they are smarter than Vietnam leaders..

Done at California, June 22, 2014.

NGUYỄN VAN CANH

PHOTOS

Tian Jing Hao, Dredging Building Ship

Tian Jing Hao as described is a giant mud-dredging 127-meter long ship, weighing 6,017 tons, that can dig 30 meters deep into the seabed and suck 4,500 cubic meters of soil or sand every hour to build artificial islands.

Mien Duong rocket ship to protect construction. There are two ships to protect the construction of five reefs: Johnson South, Cuarteron, Gaven, Fiery Cross and Chigua. They are amphibious transport ships and the Mien Duong ship is armed with missiles 528.

Mien Duong is in charge of patrolling- an anti-ship, and anti-submarine vessel. The vessel is 115 m long, 14 m wide, equipped with four diesel engines, with speeds of 28 knots per hour, and a range up to 4,000 knots.

Weapons include: One 100mm Type-79A two-barrel gun with a rate of fire of 18 RPM, and a maximum range of 22 kilometers; Four 37mm Type-76A two-barrel anti-aircraft guns, maximum firing rate of 180 RPM, and a maximum range of 8.5 kilometers; Two clusters of four YJ-82 anti-ship missile launchers or YJ-83 anti-ship missiles with a maximum range of 180 kilometers; The HQ-7 short-range air defense missile launcher is capable of destroying aircraft at distances of 8-12 kilometers or anti-ship missiles at 4-6 kilometers; Two type-87 anti-submarine rocket launchers (located in front of the main turret) and 2 × 3 torpedo tubes. In addition, the ship also has a landing deck and hangar for Z-9C submarine hunting helicopters.

2.2. OFF-SHORE OIL DRILL HD 981 AND MILITARY BASE ON THE JOHNSON SOUTH REEF

2.2.1. THE OIL DRILL HD 981

Exercise of The Sovereign Rights

On May 1, 2014, China placed the HD 981 rig in Vietnamese waters, 18 nautical miles from Triton Island, 119 nautical miles from Ly Son Island, Quang Ngai, within the Paracel Archipelago, to "explore" oil until August 15. Support for this activity initially consisted of a fleet of about 80 ships, of which, there are seven naval vessels and 33 marine surveillance and fishery ships; the rest are vessels carrying supplies.

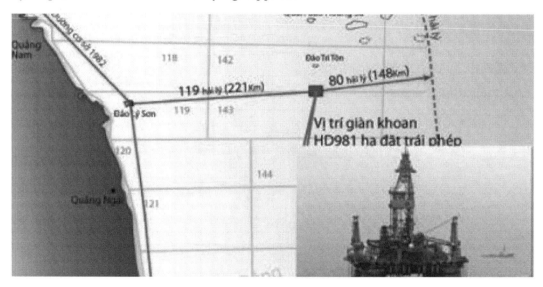

Haiyang Shiyou 981 or HD 9

There are also an armed missile guard ship 534 and a fast attack ship 753.

There were 120 ships at times, operating around HD 981. Aircraft constantly operated around the Oil Rig platform.

China prohibited Vietnamese Coast Guard ships and fishing boats to approach the HD 981 "protection belt", within a 3-mile radius. China ships attacked Vietnam Coast Guard using water cannons, from 7-10 nautical miles away. Right away, Chinese ships rammed directly into Vietnamese fishing vessels. 8 ships were damaged. There were many incidents of sinking Vietnamese fishing boats. On May 5, 2014, a Vietnamese Coast Guard ship was hit by a series of bullets from the Chinese Navy, causing death to four Vietnamese police officers and two wounded. The ship sank.

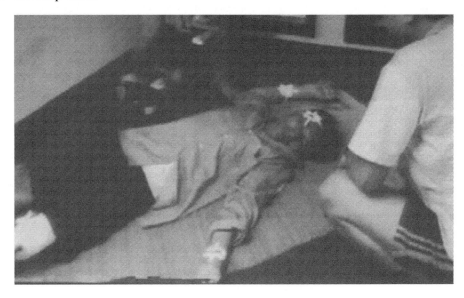

Chinese ships attacked Vietnamese ships with water cannons

Two large Red China ships clamped and sank the Vietnamese Coast Guard ship from both sides, May 24, 2014

The ship is equipped with an HD 981 protection rocket

Clearly, this is an act of invasion by Chinese forces on Vietnamese territory.

In the late 1980s, Vietnamese communists signed a contract for drilling oil with French company Total SA, in the area north of this HD 981 Oil Rig. Vietnamese communists hired the East West Center, University of Hawaii **(1)** to do a research in this area and announced that there were vast oil reserves in the South China Sea and called for investment. After spending about 10 million US dollars to look for oil, Total S.A found nothing, and quietly walked away. Vietnamese communists then let Total explore an area to the south. In the end, Total also failed. Another company, British Petroleum, at this time was allowed to drill in the area to the south of the spot where the HD 981 rig was located, off the coast of Tuy Hoa. They only found oil that contained a lot of sulfur. It could not be commercialized, so they also left, despite losing a large amount of money, like Total. Then in May 1995, the American Crestone Company based in Denver, Colorado, under Chinese direction, exploited oil in an area of 25,000 square kilometers. This area is located to the south of Paracels. Part of this territorial sea overlaps with the area where the French Total previously drilled oil. Randall Thompson, president of Crestone bragged about the fact that China promised to use force to protect oil drilling activities. Sinvce then, after 19 years of sercch, Crestone did not announce any positive ressults..

(1) **Involved in a cheating scheme.**

\-\-\-\-\-\-\-\-\-\-\-\-\-\-

What is the reason for which China moved the HD 981 Oil Rig to a place where there is no oil?

Role of HD 981 in Beijing scheme of expansion

China asserts sovereignty. The operation of HD 981 in Paracels is to justify China's ownership of the entire South China Sea, persuant to international law though this occupation is illegitimate.

1) Political context

The multi-national sovereignty dispute in South China Sea is very tense especially in the Spratlys where there are large oil/gas reserves. Though there is no oil in Paracels, HD 981 presence is an "evidence" that it operates under China jurisdicction. Therefore, moving HD 981 to this area is a first step to assert sovereignty over the whole region, before going further south. China hopes to reduce attacks from ASEAN, especially from the United States because this is an area where there is sovereign rights dispute between China and Vietnam. Moreover, the location is far from the maritime passage corridor from the Indian Ocean via Malacca to North East Asia, so it does not touch much the US national interest as mentioned by Defense Secretary Robert Gates during the Shangri-La Conference in June 2010, and US will protect the sea lane by forces. Those interests are freedom of navigation on Sea and in the air and the Anerican oil companies' exploittation of oil and gas in the Eastern Sea.

In this context, when the rig is located in the Paracels, US and ASEAN countries have less interests to intervene. And HD 981 will play a positive role in the sovereign rights policy for China.

2) Activities to assert sovereignty

In order to become an Eastern Sea owner 'legitimately', especially in the long term, China has prepared and carried out the following series of activities over a long period of times.

a) Enactiing a Law for this Region, China publicizes a new map of China's territorisal waters, drawn by Chen Kai Shek and disseminates the map with nine-dash lines or 'cow tongue' map covering almost the entire Eastern Sea. In 1992, China enacted a law announcing that any foreign vessel, sciencific or miitary, passing through the waters must have a permission from the Chinese govennment, then in 2007 established a local body of administration to manage the region.

b) Annexing The Paracels and Spratlys into Mainland China - In November 2007, they set up "Sansha district" under Hainan province to govern these two archipelagos of Vietnam. Then in June 2012, the State Council of China upgraded this "district" to become "Sansha City" , Hainan., and moved the office from Hainan to Woody Island on the Paracel archipelago. This city has a large government agency staffed with a great number of:personnel. 1. The decision-making body consists of 45 members; 2. The executive body consists of a mayor and a deputy mayor; 3. a military headquarters with the troops to defend the territory (Paracels and Spratlys) and 4. prisons to hold those who violate territorial waters.

Woody (đảo Phú lâm) is a small island with area of 1.3 to 2 km² , has no inhabitants (except for military personnel) and no fresh water. Reservoirs have been built along the runway to collect the rain water for troops.

c). Permanent Possession: building military structures on islands or reefs of the Paracel and Spratly Archipelagos.

d). Use of Military Forces to Defend Sovereignty

China announced a 'divisiom of labor' in using of forces to maintain its claimed sovereignty. Sansha Military Command defends the territory within the two archipelagos, while Chinese Navy patrols and uses the power of the massive Sanya Naval base to protect the remaining territorial waters, i.e. area outside the nine-dash-line region throughout the Eastern Sea. China have available five 094-class nuclear submarines equipped with intercontinental missiles; and have built other bases on the islands of Paracels, and on the Spratlys supported by a fleet with a Liaoning Aircraft Carrier to defend sovereignty.

e. Activities to Exercise the Sovereign Rights

- For many years, China has built many durable structures on most of the islands in the Paracel Archipelago, including airports, seaports, telecommunications and radar centers, facility for meteorology, etc. All are for military purposes. In the Spratlys, many fortified military structures have been erected on eight reefs they have turned into artificial islands.

- The civilian agencies conduct the patrol using fishing vessels, marine surveillance ships, and coast guard, to prevent "violation of territorial waters". Hundreds of Vietnamese fishermen were arrested in Paracels waters and sent to prisons in either Robert, or Lincoln or Woody island for having violated China's claimed territorial waters. They were jailed, fined, and had their fishing gear confiscated. Many fishermen were beaten and some shot dead. Their personal items confiscated, along with fishing gear and seafoods caught , including GPS. In many cases, the Chinese Navy sank Vietnamese boats, then quietly left the scene.

- Other activities include organizing fishermen into groups; providing direction, guidances and support to them; and protecting them by forces. There are thousands of Chinese fishermen from Hainan, Guangdong going to Spratlys for fishing; raising fish in cages underwater in the Fiery Cross area; forbiding Vietnamese fishermen to do business annually from May 15 to August 1 in the name of "preserving sea resources"; forbidding them to come to area when there is a military exercise, using live ammunitions; also comducting miltary operations and drills in Firey Cross area; posing threats and putting pressure on foreign oil corporations from USA, GB and India exploring oil and gas in the area, south of Con Son, demanding them to stop their work and leave; giving warnings to an Indian naval ship navigating in an area 45 nautical miles from Nha Trang for not asking for a permission. In 2011, China survillance shipss entered deeply into Vietnam continental self to cut off cables of the VietPetro 's Binh Minh and Vikings oil reserch ships operating off the coast of Vung Táu and Nha Trang .

- Xinhua News Agency announced on June 15, 2014 that the first school was constructed, on Woody Island *(đảo Phú Lâm)* in the middle of the Paracel archipelago. This is a large school with kindergarten and elementary classes costing about $5.8 million. This school is said to serve children of the families living on the island.

Xinhua News Agency confirmed: "Sansha City (Tam Sa Thị) on Woody island was officially established in July 2012, as the main admininstrative unit for islands in the Xisha Islands (Paracels), Zhongsha and Nansha (Spratlys"

Oil and Gas Exploitation

In this situation, besides assertion of the sovereignty, the HD 981 operation is the first step to gain control of the oil and gas resources in the Eastern Sea. After this step, when the situation is more favorable, with less oposition, then more Oil Rigs will be brought to the oil-rich Spratly

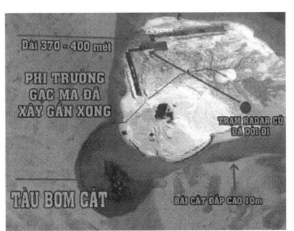

archipelago. Eventually, opposition will not explode out noisily, and China will have a monopoly to control the super oil-rich areas of the Eastern Sea.

If this scheme is no neutralized, it is difficult to prevent Beijing's ambitions, using military strength, under the leadership of Chinese Communist Party with the purpose of establishing the "new world order". I need to emphasize: this is not only a problem that Vietnam has to deal with, but it is also the interests of many nations. Vietnam has an important obligation to seek solutions favorable to all nations in the region and Vietnam must not continue to be complicit with China, the invader.

2.2.2. MILITARY BASE IN JOHNSON SOUTH REEF

China built an artificial island on the Reef, and turned it into a massive Naval Base that helps control of the region.

Photo: Military architecture on the Johnson Reef appeared years before China began to build Johnson artificial island.

On the roof of the concrete building rising out of the sea, there are two satellite communication antennas,- 2.5m dianetter and 2.4m high…. Coordinates: 9°42′N 114°17′E

Johnson Reef is a coral reef located at SW of the Sin Cowe Island, one of the six islands occupied by China on March 14, 1988. It lies in the south of the Spratly Archipelago.

On May 25, 2014, the Global Times reported that China has made Johnson Reef an artificial island in the Spratlys. It could be Johnson Reef, on which there is an airfield and a seaport for battleships for quick response. China declared that the facility is used as a "supply station" for fishermen. There has been offices, motels, farms and a seaport capable to dock large ships of up to 5,000 tons.

Beijing turned the Johnson Reef (occupied in 1988) into a giant artificial island, with a runway for aircraft and a seaport for military ships and civilian vessels (South China Morning Post). There are also residential areas and tourist resorts, all built on this artificial island.

They used sand suction machines that take sand from the sea floor to build the island.

On May 13, 2014, the Philippine Foreign Affairs Ministry accused China of doing construction work at Johnson Reef, including a runway.

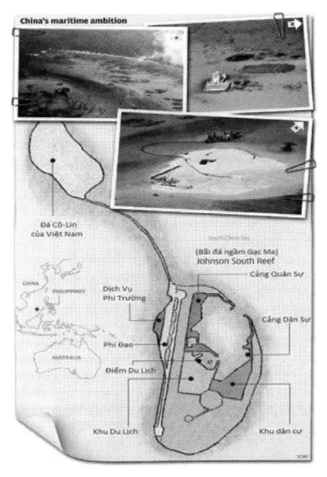

On May 15, Chinese Foreign Ministry spokesperson, Hua Chunying said in Beijing that China has undisputed sovereignty over this area including Johnson Reef, so it has the right to build.

This artificial island will be 30 hectares large. **Note:** The area of Woody base in Paracel archipelago is only around 1.3 - 2 square kilometers.

Johnson artificial island is being formed:

Johnson map with airport and seaport

Photo: Security and Defense Jane Magazine

Note:

Large photo: China's sand suction ship was blowing the sand under the sea to build up Johnson Reef, to become an artificial island.

The four images: from top to bottom from 2012 to now, show a complete change.

The importance of Johnson Reef in expansionism:

Although Woody Island has the main Chinese military headquarters, still, it could not control the Eastern Sea and beyond. The base is too small for the logistics of the air forces and navy. And it is too far to reach Spratlys. The distance from Johnson Reef to Woody Island is about 800 kms, and from the Barque Canada Reef at the 3rd parallel, southernmost of the Spratlys, the distance will be 1780 km. China bought essence air refueling technology to extend the range of their air forces in the Spratlys. Global Times reported that this base can "respond quickly", to help support the military should conflicts arise.

After construction, the giant Johnson base will be as large as the US Diego Marcia base in the Indian Ocean. Connecting the Johnson Reef to the Fiery Cross Reef will make a 44 kilometer long belt. At present, there are five solid structures on the Fiery Cross Reef (please see 2 books: Nguyễn Văn Canh: "Dossiers on Paracels and Spratlys" and "Files and Photo".) On the east side, there is another base called Mischief, where there are also many solid structures, including a three-story structure, like a giant hotel in the middle of the sea, which is used as the Command and logistics base.

Fiery Cross, Johnson South and Mischief Reefs form a triangle to deal with any war situation

This triangle will easily control the sea lane, especially used by the US 7th fleet moving from Malacca to the North East. This lane lies on the west side of the Philippines's coastal waters. A base for China to control and seize the whole of Southeast Asia.

On the Fiery Cross, there is a 116m x 96m platform built for a missile launcher to shoot down a US satellite which is used to control and guide the US aircraft carrier. If the US satellite is shot down, the US aircraft carrier will be disabled.

HD 981 did indeed neutralize international opposition to Johnson Reef construction.

In short, the Johnson South artificial island will cause a great risk in the future, not only for the Vietnamese people but also for the whole region, especially when China carries out the Greater China plot (the whole of Asia is the Great China Empire as the map published in 2010),.

China has flexed its muscles around the Eastern Sea, especially within the last three years since September 2013, she openly and noisily built this artificial island, Vietnam's leaders have continued to keep silent. They pretended not knowing any thing about it, though international press reported on it.. It appears that they continue to assist the Beijing hegemonists in their supremacy and expansionism plan.

We demand Vietnam's government bring this Eastern Sea matter to the International Court.

a) at least to denounce the acts of Chinese hegemony, and thereby call for international support of this difficult struggle.

b) to have evidence in the future to prove that the island is occupied by force, agaisnt the will of the Vietnmaese people, if the island can't be reclaimed now. And this is also to deal with the problem of expiration date prescribed by the statute of limitations, if any.

It should be noted that during his visit to Manila on May 21, 2004, Nguyen Tan Dung impled the use of legal measure related to the current HD 981 activities, and he also made it known that it will be used at appropriate times. However, he has never done it.

I have seen similar delays for decades. That is a communist's tactic. As chairman of the Committee on Protection of Territorial Integrity of Vietnam, I have repeatedly called on CPV's leaders to dismiss Pham van Dong's diplomatic note that China relies on to justify her illegal occupation of the two archipelagos in the Eastern Sea. Dating back since 2011 there have been four statements on this issue: 18 September 18-2011; September 1-2012; December 11- 2012 and January 10-2014. I have emphasized that international custom approves unilateral cancellation, without invoking reasons. Not necessarily a Prime Minister, but only a lower official who makes such statement is sufficient. Not until May 23, 2014, at an international press conference in Hanoi, Trần Duy Hải, Deputy Chair of the National Border Committee, declared that **Prime Minister Pham Van Dong's Diplomatic Note 1958 has no legal validity** to transfer the sea, because those two archipelagos were under the control of the Republic of (South) Vietnam at a time when the letter was sent to Zhou Enlai. **This is a commendable action.** However, concrete actions meed to be taken to implement the statement.

A threat from a military base built on Johnson Reef

China is becoming increasingly aggressive when it plans to build artificial islands in the middle of the South China Sea to serve their military purposes.

A former Philippines national security adviser warned that, if China completes her plan of building a military base on Johnson Reef, it will not be a threat for a single country but to all of Asia Pacific. It will be a dangerous situation. ANC News Channel (Philippines) on June 10 quoted Philippine's former national security adviser, Roilo Golez as saying that, Southeast Asian security will be precarious once China completes her military facilities and runways on Johnson Reef of Vietnam's Spratly Archipelago.

Mr. Golez affirmed that China wants to change the balance of power in Southeast Asia, illegally.

"China wants to consolidate power in the South China Sea, turn it into her backyard pond, with the nine-dash-line map" They want to change the balance of power in Asia Pacific because the United States still holds a dominant position. Red China has begun the challenge for this position", said Golez.

The design of a military base includes an airfield on the Johnson Reef of Vietnam's Spratly Archipelago, revealed by the Chinese 9th Research and Design Institute.

"The base that China planned to build includes a dock that can accomodate destroyers. In addition, we can see the runway more than 1.6 km long. This is dangerous. It can serve as a base for Chinese fighter jets, such as J-11 jets (with a range of more than 3,200 km). Johnson Reef is a round dot in the middle, with radius of more than 1,600 km. This range overlaps many regional nations' territories. So all of our bases are threatened", Mr. Golez emphasized.

Former Philippine ambassador Paranaque said that if the military base is finished, Red Chinese jets could easily reach the entire Philippines, Vietnam and some parts of Malaysia within a radius of 1,000 miles of the facility.

2.2.3. WHAT HAPPENS AFTER HD 981 ENDS ITS OPERATION?

On May 1, China blatantly put HD 091 into operation on the continental shelf of Vietnam with the support of a total of 135 ships. Vietnamese fishing boats and Coast Guards ships were banned within the radius of three nautical miles. They aggressively sank Vietnam Patrol vessels, killed and wounded Vietnam Coast Guards. They sank Vietnamese fishermen boats moving far from the HD 981 site, 9-10 nautical miles away.

Clearly, it is an infringement on Vietnam's territory. This is a serious violation, including use of naval vessels equipped with missiles "to protect HD-981 ".

When the Chinese Navy protecting HD 981 ordered Vietnamese patrol vessels not to approach. Phung Quang Thanh, Vietnamese Defense Minister immediately ordered the Coast Guard vessels to pull out of the three nautical mile belt set by Red China.

The above event, plus the actions of the Vietnamese Communist Party to suppress those Vietnamese who voiced to protect the Paracels & Spratlys, caused a great public outcry leading to large and violent protests. Protestors burned down China's industrial complexes in Binh Duong and Vung Ang, Ha Tinh, including some Taiwanese facilities. In Ha Tinh, several Chinese workers were killed and three were injured.

What happened was a challenge to the Vietnamese Communist Party leaders. This situation has put them in a dliemma: on one hand this clearly shows that they do not defend the country agaisnt the aggressors, on the other, the Chinese thought that they did not intend to carry out what they committed to do as promised in the April 12, 2011 agreement with Guo Boxiong

and so violated the Treaty signed in June with China in Beijing.

Because the pressure from the masses was too strong, and specially to avoid being exposed as country selling lackeys, Vietnamese Communist leaders chose the middle way, meaning not actively keeping the commitment of April 2011. At the same time, Nguyen Tan Dung tacitly got along the protestors: at the ASEAN Conference in Burma on May 11, he. denounced some dangerous acts {of China} caused unsafe maritime traffic. Then, on May 21, Dung went to Manilla and talked about 'the case' at an international court (implying to sue China) that is, taking a legal action against the aggression; while Nguyen Phu Trong and Truong Tan Sang were talking vaguely to angry voters on the issue of sovereignty protection.

China withdrew HD 981back to Hainan on July 15, 2014, instead of mid-August as announced previously.

Could those Puppets escape China;s ccontrol? On June 30, State Councilor Yang Jiechi arrived in Hanoi to meet with the Vietnamese leaders. What did Nguyen Phu Trong, Nguyen Tan Dung and Yang Jiech exhange was unknown. Nothing was published while he was in Hanoi. However after the trip, the Xinhua News Agency reported Yang talked straight to the leaders about 4 "NO's".

1. **Not** to underestimate China's determination and capacity to protect the sovereignty of the islands in the Vietnam's Eastern Sea.

2. **Not** to claim "historical sovereignty" over the islands. Vietnam leaders are not allowed to cite its Vietnamese historical materials/documents to prove "historical sorereignty over the Eastern Sea, including just making an oral statement by a leader. This would lead to misunderstanding by the international community and Vietnam's public on sovereignty over Xisha and Nansha (Paracels and Spratlys)

3. **Not** to entice other countries to intervene in the Eastern Sea matter such as internationalization of the dispute, bringing the case to the international Court; alliance with the US to counter China; allowing a third country to use Cam Ranh Bay….

4. Finally, do **not** break up the Vietnamese-Chinese relations being good after normalization in 20 years.

The Xinhua News Agency also added that Yang (photo attached) told Vietnam: "**Vietnam is a prodigal child, and must return to the country that has suffered much, to be forgiven**". So, Yang Jiechi with threatening words, told Trong, Dung, etc., not to commit treason and return to mother China to be forgiven.

On the Vietnamese communists side, on August 26, 2014, Le Hong Anh, standing member of Secretariat (the second person after the General Secretary) was sent to Beijing to meet Xi Jinping to heal the wounds caused by the protests and find a way to relieve tension between the two sides.

Xi told Le Hong Anh: "A neighbor cannot move away. It is in the common interests of both sides to co-exist friendly"(Xinhua News).

"That General Secretary Nguyen Phu Trong has sent you to China as his special envoy to attend the high-level meeting between the two parties. This shows the Vietnamese aspiration to improve the bilateral relationship".

" [I] hope Vietnam will make joint efforts with China to develop the bilateral relationship."

Directives of Yang Jiechi and Xi Jinping clearly reiterated that the Vietnamese communists pledged to abide by the Treaty signed in June 2011.

Therefore, this "lost/ prodigal child" has tried to become obedient to China, contributing enormously to the Chinese construction activities at the Johnson Reef. The CPV leaders submissively remain silent. China truly controls Vietnam. China has arrogantly exercised its sovereign rights over Vietnam's lands and sea, without any true resistance from Vietnam leaders. They dared not mention Vietnam's historical sovereignty. Nguyen Tan Dung hinted to take legal measures against China for occupying the Johnson Reef. However he took no further action. No seeking support from other nations. Not doing harm to the "existing good neighboring relation". Vietnam communist leaders are seriously enforcing the "4 NO's."

Vietnam , a "prodigal child" has quietly returned to the "Mother China".

ADDITIONAL DOCUMENTS ABOUT JOHNSON REEF

The AISLive Newsletter dated June 20, 2014 describes the giant mud dredging ship Tian Jing Hao and the other two operated from September 2013 between five islands: Cuarteron Reef, coordinates 08 50 N 112 47 E, Fiery Cross Reef: 09 38 N 112 57 E, Gaven Reef: 10 12 N 114 14 E, Collins Reef (Johnson Reef North or Union Reefs North): 09 45 N 114 44 E, Johnson Reef (Johnson Reef South or Union Reef South, coordinates: 09 43 N 114 17 E).

Tian Jing Hao is a giant mud dredging 127-meter long ship, weighing 6,017 tons. It can dig 30 meters deep into the seabed and suck 4,500 cubic meters of sediments/sands every hour to create artificial islands. The other is called Nina Hai Tuo.

From September 2013 until June 15, 2014, three mud dredging ships operated continuously between five islands with considerable distances: about 80 nautical miles in the North-South direction, and over 100 nautical miles in the East-West direction. China sent two naval battleships equipped with rockets to be stationed permanently for defense.

Vietnam's communist leaders have kept silent on these Chinese activities for a long time: from September 9, 2013 to June 15, 2014. How to explain it? By implementing the "Guo Boxiong Agreement", they must NOT do anything harmful to the China-Viet relation, even though the Johnson Reef and other maritime features truly belong to Vietnam —historically, geographically and legally. Yang Jiechi bluntly told the "reckless" son to respect 4 NOs.

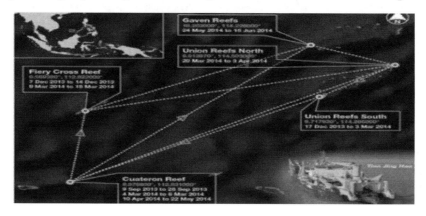

AISLive's article provided important details:

China goes all out with major island 14 building projects in Spratlys.

AISLive tracking of the dredger Tian Jing Hao in the Eastern Sea shows it moved between reefs in the Spratly islands since September 2013. **Source**: Bing/China Merchants Heavy Industry Shenzhen Co./IHS

"China is conducting dredging operations at three reefs in the disputed Spratly islands in the South China Sea, according to data provided by IHS Maritime.

GPS tracking of a dredger using AISLive ship tracking data has confirmed Philippine claims that China has been reclaiming land at five locations since at least September 2013.

The dredging is part of major land reclamation projects undertaken by China on a number of the reefs and shoals it controls in the Spratlys. While such construction is in clear breach of a code of conduct signed by all claimants in the South China Sea territorial dispute, China has rejected any criticism of its activities by saying that the reefs are "indisputably" Chinese territory and so can be modified as Beijing sees fit.

The vessel, Tian Jing Hao , is a 127 m-long seagoing cutter suction dredger designed by German engineering company Vosta LMG. At 6,017 gross tonnes, it is credited as being the largest of its type in Asia. It has been operating on Cuarteron Reef (also known as Calderon Reef, Da Chau Vien, or Huayang Jiao); the Gaven Reefs (Nanxun Jiao and Xinan Jiao, Gaven Reef, and Ladd Reef, Burgos); the Union Reefs (in particular at Johnson South Reef and Johnson North Reef); and at Fiery Cross Reef.

Cuarteron Reef   9-28 September 2013, 4-8 March 2014, 10 April to 22 May 2014

Union Reefs South   17 December 2013 to 3 March 2014

Union Reefs North   20 March to 3 April 2014

Fiery Cross Reef   7-14 December 2013 and 9-17 March 2014

Gaven Reefs   24 May to 15 June 2014

The vessel can deploy its cutter to a depth of 30 m, with an extraction rate of 4,500 m^3 per hour, making it ideal for large-scale dredging operations

According to the AISLive data, the dredger has been at Gaven Reefs since 24 May. This corroborates background briefings by Philippine officials, who have told IHS Jane's that three dredgers - including Tian Jing Hao and another called Nina Hai Tuo - are at Gaven Reef along with a large tugboat.

According to Philippine officials who have had access to naval aviation photos of the areas in question, Tian Jing Hao is moving "seabed material to a reclaimed area". Philippine military reports say "reclamation operations at Gaven Reef are expected to be a month or more, barring any environmental setbacks

The CGI plans show a runway, hangars for fast jets, a port, wind turbines, and greenhouses. (China State Shipbuilding Corporation)

AISLive tracking of **Tian Jing Hao's** activities in the South China Sea shows that it has been moving between reefs since 17 December 2013. Satellite imagery provided to IHS Jane's confirms it was operating at Johnson South Reef - part of the Union Reefs - in February and March 2014. Other ships may also have been present in these areas, but were unidentifiable due to clutter or coverage issues."

James Hardy, London and Krispen Atkinson & Richard Hurley, London and Michael Cohen, Manila - IHS Jane's Defence Weekly, 20 June 2014

ooo

Notes:

1) Woody Island has a length of 1.7 km, width of 1.2 km, area of 320 hectares (2.1 km^2). China turned Woody Island into a small city, so they could claim a 200-nautical-mile "exclusive economic zone" and continental shelf for the entire Paracel Archipelago. It is a calculated move to seize the Paracels, making "sovereignty legitimate"!

2) There are 14 projects in this area, scattered over 100 nautical miles wide and 80 miles long on Vietnam's Eastern Sea. Six coral reefs became small islands for military bases: Two reefs in Sin Cowe Group: Johnson Reef and Hughes Reef, and the other four: Gaven Reef, Fiery Cross Reef, Eldad Reef in Namyit Group, and Cuarteron Reef in Spratly Group.

All of these reefs were occupied by China in 1988.

Photos of Johnson Reef from satellite in July (2014) show China building piers, planting coconut trees, building roads and houses. The reef consisting mainly of sand and rocks has become an apple-shaped white island. Photos from Google Earth also reveal construction equipment.

According to analysts, Beijing has moved rapidly with improvements in the South China Sea. The abundant natural resources and the construction capabilities have helped China to thrive in comparison with all other countries. The increase of infrastructures and buildings on the reefs/islands/banks (and other maritime features) has given Beijing an advantage in claiming sovereignty over this Sea.

When Chigua becomes a large-scale maritime base, a 30-hectares artificial island, the Vietnamese base on the Collins Reef (1.9 nautical miles NW of Johnson) has become just a small dot on the Archipelago map.

This newly built massive base is a place for Beijing to show-off her military power, to threaten both the Philippines and Vietnam, in this disputed Archipelago. This base is located about 850 kilometers from the Philippines, 800 kilometers from Vietnam and 1000 kilometers from the Strait of Malacca.

The Philippines national security is greatly threatened. Chinese military bases are so close to it.

According to the current affairs analysts, with the on-going aggressive activities, China is moving from defensive to offensive positions. With Johnson airport is completed and with other existing airfields on Woody Island in the Paracels, Beijing will have a reason to establish a wide "Air Defense Identification Zone" (ADIZ) in the South China Sea. This is a serious concern for many countries, because the year before China already announced an *"air defense identification zone"* over the East Sea.

The Fiery Cross Reef has a similar plan. This reef has a length along the NE-SW axis of 14 nautical miles (nearly 26 km) and a width of 4 nautical miles (7.4 km). Total area is about 110 km². It is a large area. Except for a 1-meter high rock emerging at the southwestern tail, this reef is usually submerged under water at high tide. China turns this reef into an island, so it would be many times larger than Johnson.

According to a statement by Dr Jin Canrong, a professor of international relations, Peking University, quoted by SCMP, the project to change the Fiery Cross Reef to an island has been submitted to China Central Government for approval. When the construction plan is completed it will be twice the size of the U.S. Diego Garcia military base, a 44-km2 base in the Indi*an Ocean. The construction of these artificial islands will start, depending on the progress of construction of the Johnson South artificial Island (đ*ảo Gạc Ma). Last month, China media leaked information that on the South Johnson Island, besides an airfield, a seaport is ready to accommodate ships up to 5,000 tons.

Ly Kiet, a naval expert at the Chinese Naval Research Institute noticed: on the artificial island Fiery Cross, there will be an airport and seaports. At present time, this place is a small base. Over 20 years ago, Beijing already built an observatory for a marine research agency of UNESCO.

In the Spratly Archipelago, since 1988, China has seized several Reefs of Vietnam: Subi Reef in Thị Tứ Group; Fiery Cross Reef (Chữ Thập) and Gaven Reef in Namyit Group; Johnson and Hughes Reefs (Gạc *Ma, Tư Nghĩa) in Sin Cowe Group; Cuarteron Reef (Châu Viên) in Spratly Group, and Mischief Reef (Vành Khăn) in the Flat Group.*

China is changing Vietnam's reefs. Artificial islands are formed for building large military bases of dozens of kilometers in length. The bases connected with Chinese Sanya naval base in Hainan are taking away the *"Survival Space"* from the Vietnamese people, and posing a threat to the coastal states and the whole region.

The silence of Vietnam's leaders is the evidence that *"a lost child"* has obediently returned to his Parent. As a result, they have correctly carried out the 4-NOs policy as instructed by Yang Jiechi. They have endeavored to bring Vietnam into the orbit of China, turning this country into a staging base for China to achieve its hegemonic dream in Asia.

In addition, immediate duties need to be completed . These are tasks necessary to help transfer the entire country in the future to China.   It is Some Other Tasks To Be Done.

2.2.4. FOUR GRAND TASKS PERFORMED TO SERVE RED CHINA STRATEGIC INTERESTS

1. 500 Vietnamese communist cadres to be trained in China:

Deputy Foreign Minister Hồ Xuân Sơn sent a letter dated June 1, 2014 to city and province leaders on the "*16 things to do*", resulted from an agreement on Aptil 2014 between Hu Chunhua, Secretary of Guangdong Party Committee, and Pham Quang Nghi, Secretary of Hanoi Party Committee, and Le Thanh Hai, Secretary of Saigon Party Committee. Hu Chunhua requested Vietnam's Ministry of Foreign Affairs to "develop cooperation programs between the ministries, branches and localities of Vietnam and Guangdong province", attached a list of things to do for references. Hu Chunhua proposed the first task to be performed is preperations for a visit to Guangdong by secretaries of Hanoi, Phạm quang Nghị, and Saigon Le thanh Hai.

The second task is "sending **500 Party cadres to China for training for a period of 5 years**: 100 from the Hanoi Party Committee, 100 from the Saigon Party Committee, and the rest from the provinces from Quang Ninh, Hai Phong, Da Nang, etc.

Besides, Guangdong proposed **to promote economic and trade activities** with Vietnam to boost their trade, and investment into Vietnam so as to create jobs for some localities.

The letter mentioned "trade, tourism, ideologicl studies" between Guangdong province and cities of Vietnam such as Quang Ninh, Da Nang and Ho Chi Minh City (Saigon).

Several important points were emphasized in this letter.

a) Guangdong is the provincial administrative unit of China which writes a letter to the Vietnam Ministry of Foreign Affairs to carry out party and government works. Vietnam is not considered as equal to a provincial administrative unit of China. And Vietnam Ministry of foreign affaris just executes directives from Guangdong Province as stated.

b) To educate 500 members of the Vietnam Communist Party. This training includes many subject matters, but it emphasizes on 'ideological studies' for members of the party committees at the local level. After 5 years of training, Viietnamese trainees would become efficient local agents to run cities or provinces on behalf of China. Thus, China has a whole bunch of local Sino puppets/rulers deployed at the grassroots level. So, native rulers as the local authorities are executors of or the ones who implement the Chinese policies to tightly control Vietnam..

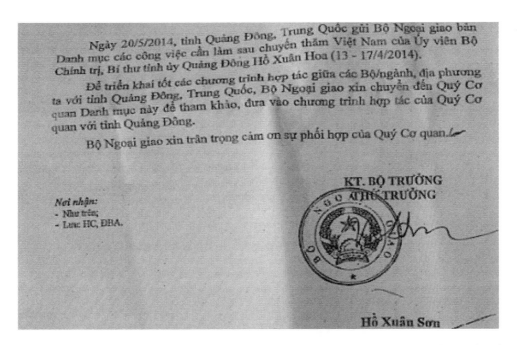

Part of Ho xuan Son' letter to   Secretaries of Hanoi, Saigon…. re. "16 tasks to be done" as suggested by Secrretary of the CPC Guang Dong

Note: Numerous Vietnamese cadres have been trained by communist China. This is the public part of the June 2011 Treaty. No body knows how many high ranking officers in the Communist Party of Vietnam who have secretly been trained, since the re- normalization of diplomacy in 1991.

Those cadres were trained in "ideology" to become loyal to Mao's Socialism, faithful servants of the Chinese Communist Party after returning to Vietnam.

What has been happening every day in Vietnam shows that numerous Vietnamese Party cadres as China agents have held key positions in the government structures, at all levels. They are everywhere in the state agencies, from central to local levels in the police, judicial and defense (military) sectors, especially in the area of information/propaganda (directly controlled by the CPV, culture, education, tourism and sports...)

Tens of thousands of such people are Sino puppets/authorities currently ruling Vietnam, on behalf of the communist China.

The open-border policy has flooded criminals, promoted human trafficking, brought drugs and toxic foods into Vietnam. Even domestic food production has toxic ingredients provided by China. Dangerous Chinese toxins are found everywhere in Vietnam. People have opposed but nothing changed. As a result, local authorities and high-rank leaders are controlling Vietnam on behalf of Re China.

Some reports say that several tour guides told tourists *"Vietnam is a part of China"*. People have criticized this, but it was ignored by CPV leaders in the Tourism industry.

Recently, the Yandi Company (a Chinese Co.) hung banners to welcome Chinese tourists visiting Hue (Vietnam's ancient capital). On the banner, Hue is called "*Đại Nam Hải* 大 南 海 " (Grand South Sea). The Hue authorities ignored it, but Hue citizens were angry. A tourism city official said this was done by Yandi tourism company headquartered in Nha Trang. Hue authorities said that it was not their responsibility. The head of tourism industry in Nha Trang was also quiet.

2.7 million Chinese tourists came to Vietnam in 2016. Millions of Chinese tourists were told by Vietnamese officials that "*Vietnam is part of China*". Particularly, tourists who come to Hue "are visiting Đại Nam Hải".

Chinese naval ships sank Vietnamese fishing boats. About 800 state-owned Vietnamese news agencies used the terms *"strange ships"("unfamiliar ships", "unknown ships", "unidentified vessels) that killed Vietnamese fishermen...* Chinese enterpreneurs went deep into rural areas of South Vietnam to trick farmers: buying leeches, ordering crops, roots, leaves, even water buffalo hooves (to do damage to Vietnam agriculture, because Vietnamese farmers use water buffalos as a principal means for plowing and harrowing rice fields). They have caused disasters, social chaos. They destroy lives and Vietnam agriculture. How could Vietnam's government turn a blind eye on this disaster?

Hundreds of Chinese youth publicly held Chinese flags with banners and actions contrary to Vietnamese sovereignty. They marched in the streets of Saigon on the occasion of the 2008 Olympic Games, and were protected by police in uniform.

In some cases people protesting against China in Hanoi and Saigon identified the police that suppressed them as Chinese secret agents sent in from China.

Vietnam's Defense Minister, General Le Duc Anh ordered Vietnam Navy soldiers not to fire back against China' navy when they were assigned to do construction work on Johnson Reef in March 1988. General Phung Quang Thanh, the Minister of Defense ordered Vietnam's Coast

Guard to withdraw, while China placed the HD 981 rig on the continental shelf of Vietnam. They were not allowed to fire back, even the Chinese navy killed four coast guards and wounded several, on May 2014. To lessen the international outrage, Phung Quang Thanh stated that the Rig incident was a small matter, like *"a family conflict"*!

An example of Vietnamese leaders shamefully bow their heads to China!

How many Vietnamese communists playing a role of China puppets who are ruling Vietnam are there? I am not surprised when watching a video in which Brigadier General of Public Security, Truong Giang Long, Deputy Director General, General Department of Public Security, in October 2016, said that China ***"has installed hundreds of cadres, perhaps plus another hundreds "*** into the Vietnamese Communist Party and Government.

Over the past decade, China has established and controlled an agency in Vietnam to formally command, coordinate, and supervise activities. It is the Bilateral Cooperation Committee. Currently, the State Councilor Yang Jiechi and Deputy Prime Minister Pham Dinh Minh are co-chairs. There are many conferences between the Parties and Government officials of the border provinces and some provinces of Vietnam, on the implementation of Chinese policies, organized and guided by this Committee.

2. Unifying the border armed forces under Chinese leadership.

On October 17, 2013, being invited from the Ministry of Public Security of China, the CPV hurriedly ordered Lt. General Võ Trọng Việt, a pro-Chinese general, member of the CPV Central Commitee, who was then the Border Guards Commander to go to Fangcheng, Guangxi where he worked with a Chinese local Border Security Defense Team of the General Department of the Choang Ethnic Autonomous Region Border Defense Forces. Aa a head of the Vietnam delegation, Lt Gen Viet humbly bowed down to Brigadier General Wu Dongli 武冬立, a commander of the Border Defense forces of the Chinese Security Ministry.

Gen. Viet signed an agreement on "Three-Tier Border Defense Cooperation":

三级边防合作机制

a). China-Vietnam cooperation between the Security Border Guard Commands.

b). China-Vietnam cooperation between Ministries of Defense.

c). China-Vietnam cooperation between Border Management Departments.

Vietnam shall comply with the inspection order of the Chief of the Mong Cai International Border Gate Station

Vietnam shall commit to implement this "Three-Tier" policy, and shall be protected by China's Border Guard Security Division of the port city of Fangcheng.

As such, the VCP accepts the unification of the Security Border Guard Forces, National Defense Forces and Border Management Deprments. Briefly, the Unified Border Forces of both countries now are under the command and supervision of the Chinese comand at the Fencheng Distric level.

3. Vung Ang Autonomous Region, a territorial concession of the 21st Century

An economic report on June 25, 2015 said that General Manager of Hung Nghiep Formosa Company, Yang Hongzhi sent a letter to Deputy Prime Minister Hoang Trung Hai proposing to establish Vung Ang as a special economic zone on an area of 3,300 ha, to serve the Son Duong deep-water port and build enterprises such as iron, steel, and power plants, etc.

This proposal was intended for Vung Ang region to become an "autonomous region" inside Vietnam.

Through Taiwanese Formosa, a "front company for China", China has invested 6.5 US billion to build this project. Since it started until now, the entire area has been a territorial concession where no one is allowed to enter, even the local government officials.

It is an exclusive economic zone (EEZ) in Kỳ Anh, Hà Tĩnh province.

This is the largest industrial park in the North Central Coast of Vietnam. It is rumored to be a gathering place of the Chinese communist secret forces. On May 1, 2015, China put HD 981 oil rig into operation on the continental shelf of Vietnam in the Paracel Archipelago. Angry local residents rose up to protest. They burned down Chinese factories and attacked Chinese communist workers there. Some were killed, others injured. On May 14, 2015, China sent ships to evacuate more than 4,000 workers and engineers, and bring them back to China, but this number is still a small fraction. There are still about 10,000 Chinese workers.

For a long time, Chinese who came here, have built their own roads, private streets, and got married to Vietnamese women ... turning this area into a colony in a strategic region of Vietnam. Most of the workers here are undoccumented under Vetnam laws. People also said that many Chinese people are secretly armed, behave like the military.

If this is an autonomous region, sooner or later Chinese working in the Central Highlands will demand for such privilege. Which means that Vietnam will fall uder the control of Beijing.

Its importance for national security and defense lies also in the Triangle: Sanya Naval Base in Hainan, Cua Viet in Quang Tri and Vung Ang in Ha Tinh.

After Le Hong Anh returned to Vietnam in August, it was confirmed that China demanded to bring in 20,000 men to work here.

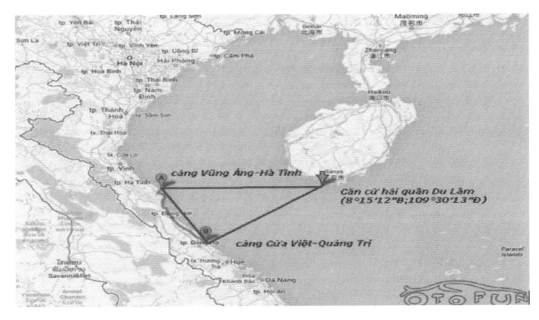

National Security

VUNG ANG INDUSTRIAL PARK

NO TRESPASSING

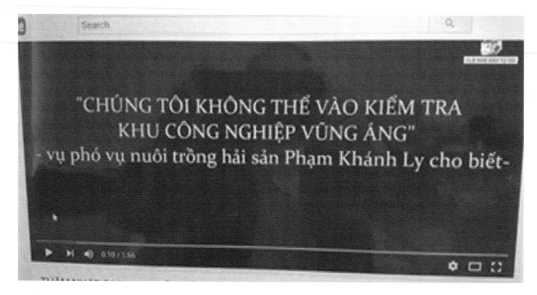

"We can't enter the Vung Ang Industrial Park to investigate.." Pham khanh Ly, Deputy Director, Sea Food Raising Services said.

Local residents are allowed to collect trash left ouside the Park

Người dân khu vực Sihanoukville đã đến bãi rác để nhặt lấy những túi nilon mà Formosa đã thải ra (ảnh: BAN)

Media reporters invited to press conference: "We are throughly checked, including personal belongings"

If the Viet are silent

Additional Information: A former high-ranking official, Trịnh xuân Thanh, former Chairman, General Corporation oF Contruction re. Oil ang Gas, was kidnapped n Germany by CPV agents under the command of Lt.Gen To Lam and flown home in July 2017. He revealed huge corruptions and embezzlements. That Project costed $6 billion dollars. Other Chinese projects costed 10 billions. The $16 billion dollars were transferred to Ban Viet Bank, chaired by Nguyen Thanh Phuong, daughter of Prime Minister Nguyen Tan Dung.

Đông Đô Đại Phố (East Capital Grand Town)

A grand new "China town"was built in 2011 at Bình Dương city, named Đông Đô Đại Phố, east of Saigon. It is a large modern town of 26 hectares, including an administrative center, an Eastern International University, a 1,000-bed hospital, and a large cultural center for sports, conferences and weddings. There are shopping malls, a financial center, hotels, townhouses, houses, and a golf course. There is a large city park. This town is mainly for Chinese elites with Chinese customs and traditions. Vietnamese laws are ignored. Vietnamese law enforcement officers are not allowed to control their activities.

By 2010, about 120,000 Chinese moved to Binh Duong city. Millions of Chinese are moving into Vietnam to settle as new citizens. East Capital Grand Town is a kind of Political Center of 'Han Dynasty', a large administrative complex for governing South Vietnam if and when Vietnam is transferred to China.. This is part of the process of **Sinicization 中國化.**

China has accounted for 90%. of the total economic and development bidding projects. Of 65 projects nationwide, China owns about 60 projects, with Chinese workers everywhere in those "Exclusive Economic Zones" (EEZ). *Đông Đô Đại Phố* has a Chinese Trade Center and several Chinese administrative offices to govern South Vietnam.

Business Center

The Cultural Center has been completed

Industrial Park

Eastern International University construction is completed

The 1,000-bed hospital is nearing completion

One of the many residences

2.3. PROTEST AGAINST RED CHINA' SCHEMEM OF EXPANSIONISM WITH COLLUSION OF VIETNAMESE COMMUNIST LEADERS AS PARTNERS IN CRIME

This dossier was sent to the leaders of 192 members of the United Nations by Nguyen Trung Chau, President of the Federation of Associations of former Vietnamese Political Prisoners when the leaders attended the United Nations General Assembly meeting in August 2011.

COMMITTEE ON PROTECTION OF TERRITORIAL INTEGRITY OF VIETNAM

Dr. Nguyen van Canh, President
June 31, 2011

PROTEST AGAINST CHINA'S HEGEMONY WITH COLLUSION OF THE COMMUNIST PARTY OF VIETNAM (CPV)

2.3.1. PART I: CHINA'S EXPANSIONISM.

Scheme of taking over the South China Sea and Activities threatening Peace and Stability in the region.

1. In Jan. 1974, China sent a fleet south to take the Republic of Vietnam's Paracels. The RVN naval forces strongly and heroically resisted China's aggression. In a fierce battle, the defending forces killed Admiral Phuong Quang Kinh, commander of the operation and 5

colonels, sinking one ship and disabling another. However, the RVN could not defend their territorial waters. Paracels was lost to China.

Since then, China has built many concrete military installations in the Paracels, using the archipelagoes as a stronghold to advance to the South. Woody is the most important island with so many structures built for military purposes: a large and modern runway (2.7 km long) for military jets, large buildings for offices, barracks to house hundreds of troops, ammunition depots, ports for warships, a communication tower, and huge containers to collect 140,000 tons of rainwater a year...

In Spratlys, in March 1988, China sent war ships to take 6 islets or reefs. Chinese war ships suddenly appeared and opened fire on 64 Socialist Republic of Vietnam (SRV) soldiers while in the water, carrying supplies on their heads or backs to their comrades staging on Johnson reef. They were killed instantly. They had no place to hide, no means and no opportunity to defend themselves. The Johnson reef was one of the six taken at that time. As of the late 1990's, 16 reefs/islets had been occupied by China.

A dozen fortified structures emerging from the waters were erected on the reefs. Two areas where more concrete buildings have been built are Mischiefs and Fiery Cross Reef. Four colossal structures on Mischiefs close to the Philippines appear to serve as outposts to control the sea-lanes from Malacca to the North. The lanes lie to the west of the Philippines coast. Five structures are found on the Fiery Cross reef. One of them is supposedly a missile-launching platform.

With a secret new nuclear naval base revealed in 2004 in Sanya in the Southern tip of Hainan, China clearly shows her intent to control the region. In December 2007, she moved Type 094 second-generation nuclear ballistic missile submarines (SSBN) to the base. The Jin Class/ type 094 is equipped with 12 long-range nuclear multi warheads missiles that could reach a target as far away as 7000 or 8000 km. China now has five of them. A source from the US Defense Department estimates that China will have five more in ten years. A Jin class submarine was seen when it entered the cave at the base. The cave can host 20 of them. The base has built two 800m long piers for aircraft carriers, three piers for submarines with a modern de-magnetism facility and a network of underground tunnels with infrastructures ready for use.

China showed that she has produced Dong Fong 23D, a long-range anti ship ballistic missile with a maximum range of 2,700 km and ability to strike moving targets at sea. Super jets J-15's have been added to increase her air capabilities in her expansion scheme.

Thi Lang, an aircraft carrier built from a Ukraine wrecked carrier will be put in operation within weeks and as a result will threaten peace and stability in the entire region.

For the past few months, China's military activities in the region have been more aggressive: opening fire on the Filipino fishermen working in their waters and sending naval ships to patrol provocatively even in Malaysian waters. On July 25, President Aquino told the Filipino congress that the Philippines would use military power to protect their land. The Philippines buys ships, planes and weapons, and conducts military exercises with American and allied troops. Chinese ranking officials have not hesitated to convey open and direct threats to her neighbors, when telling them *"don't play with fires"*, or *"China is a great power"* (as Yang Jiechi, Minister of Foreign Affairs told ASEAN members) even in international forums like the Hanoi ASEAN meeting in July 2010. This testifies to the fact that her ambitions to control the South China Sea are not in question and that her intent is to use force if needed to dominate the region.

Indeed, she has prepared to move forward to put all of Asia under her control.

Late last March, Cui tiankai, Chinese Deputy Foreign Affairs Minister openly told visiting American Deputy Secretary of State, James Steinberg that China has a core interest in the South China Sea. It is as important as the one she has in Taiwan, and Tibet. With this, China informs the US that the South China Sea is her pond and insists that the US, an outsider or an external force, should not meddle with the ASEAN internal problem. To her, the US involvement has caused tension and instability for the region.

2. Back in June 2006, China re-drew a new map with a U shape on the South China Sea. The entire area is 3.5 million square kilometers and the U shape map represents 3 million kilometers. She claims that the area within the map belongs to her.

Since 2007, China has aggressively increased her activities in the newly claimed waters. The activities show that she intents to exercise her sovereignty over the region:

- Conducting military exercises using live ammunitions in an area South of Paracels, on a yearly basis. One large-scale military exercise was done on Fiery Cross with combined airborne and marine troops in September 2009. The drill was announced to practice the defense of China's 'frontier against invasion'.

- Forbidding Vietnamese fishermen to fish in an area north of the 15th parallel (North of Spratlys). The reason is to protect marine resources (from May to August, every year)

- Naval ships, sometimes disguised as marine vessels are used to patrol on Paracels and Spratlys. The purpose is to harass Vietnamese fishermen, discouraging them from coming in.

- In July 2007, Chinese naval ships surrounded Vietnamese fishing wooden boats that were working near the Spratly Island. They killed one Vietnamese fisherman, and sank some boats. This event occurred in front of a Vietnamese naval ship. Reportedly, the ship stayed idle and watched, and then quietly left the scene.

- During the last four years, China has increased her brutal and uncivilized activities against Vietnamese fishermen. Every year, a dozen cases of arrests for 'violations of China's territorial waters' are made, though the fishermen are working on the waters that belong to Vietnam, and where their ancestors fished for several thousand years ago. Victims are taken into custody on any of the following islands: Hainan, Lincoln, Woody or Roberts. They are required to pay a ransom for violations of "Chinese waters."

In most cases, they are beaten seriously. In others, they were killed.

In all cases, they were robbed of all products and belongings. Their fishing equipment is confiscated. In September 2009, 27 Vietnamese fishing boats from Quang Ngai with 230 fishermen on board were denied taking refuge at the Roberts Island from an approaching hurricane.

In Jan. 2005, three Chinese naval vessels suddenly attacked 3 wooden boats owned by fishermen from Thanh Hoa while fishinig in the Tonkin Bay. 9 were killed instantly. Some 34 of them were arrested and taken to Hainan. They were fishing on the west side of the boundary of the newly drawn map by the 2000 Treaty. Such types of activities are designed to deny Vietnamese fishermen access to the areas where they have worked for a hundred years. China prefers to exercise her sovereignty over Paracels and Spratlys at the expenses of the lives of hundreds of Vietnamese fishermen rather than pursue the spirit of human rights that she accepts when joining the United Nations Organization.

When no signs of Vietnamese are present in the areas, the two archipelagoes become China's property.

China knows that she can't take the South China Sea without substantial and positive contributions of the CPV. As a result, she has used all necessary means including possible ruses to conquer the latter to work for her objective.

China herself is the cause of Instability and Danger to Peace in the region and to the world.

2.3.2. PART II. VIETNAMESE COMMUNISTS' COLLUSION IN CHINESE SCHEME OF EXPANSION

On June 28, 2011, Hong Lei, spokesman of the China Ministry for Foreign Affairs announced that there is a mutual agreement between PRC and SRV dated June 25 for both sides to carry out "what they have agreed on" to seek a permanent and stable solution to the South China Sea matter.

In the announcement, PRC stated that negotiation is a must. Both sides agree not to allow "*external forces* "to be involved in the internal affairs of the real players in the region. However, PRC does not forget to threaten SRV by saying that SRV could not do anything to "*undermine the friendship with and trust from China*." This includes making unfavorable public statements, carrying out any such adverse activities, or implying collaboration with or taking sides with the USA. Even a public demonstration by private Vietnamese citizens to say "Paracels and Spratlys belong to Vietnam" is considered as an unacceptable activity.

The announcement mentioned that the mutual agreement was reached between Dai Bingguo, a ranking member of the Communist Party of China (CPC) in charge of foreign affairs and Ho xuan Son, Vietnamese deputy minister for foreign affairs. They do not make public what they have agreed on. The Vietnamese people suspect that this type of "secret dealings" will again lead to more territorial concessions as happened in the past:

-SVR secretly transferred many regions bordering the frontier with China. Chains of mountains in Hà Giang and Lang Son provinces are now lying inside China through the 1999 treaty. Twelve years has past since then and both sides have not made public the map attached to the Treaty.

-In the Tonkin Bay, SRV also through the 2000 treaty has transferred 11, 520 square kilometers to China. Besides, with the treaty of cooperation on mutual fishing in the Bay, Chinese fishermen are working near the coast of Vietnam. On the other hand, Vietnamese fishermen are not allowed to fish in areas designated in the treaty, even though they belong to Vietnam. As a result, 9 of them were massacred by Chinese naval ships and 34 were arrested as mentioned above in the 2005 incident even when they fished on the West side of the boundary.

Moreover, with regards to implementation of national policies, the SVR government has acted just as a PRC agency that executes the latter's decisions in Vietnam.

The SRV Ministry of Information has tightened its grip on news agencies, including 800 newspapers/magazines not to cover any story 'deemed' hostile to PRC. A few years ago, a newspaper in Hanoi published an article covering contaminated foods imported from China. An official from Chinese Foreign Affairs ministry called SRV Ambassador Nguyen trieu Luat to Beijing at midnight giving him a warning about the coverage. Recently a member of SRV National Assembly complained that in the economic field, 90 % of projects to produce energy, to build roads and bridges have been granted to Chinese corporations...

In November 2007, when the PRC announced that the two archipelagoes, Paracels and Spratlys of Vietnam, had been annexed to Hainan province and are under management of the Sansha district, Vietnamese students staged strong protests against the decision in Hanoi as well as in Saigon on Dec.9 and 16. A few days later, on Dec. 18, Qin Gang, spokesman of the PRC Foreign Affairs in a news conference for the foreign press stated in Beijing "*we hope that the government of SRV will have a responsible attitude and at the same time have effective measures to prevent actions that would undermine the bilateral relationships*".

In the following weeks, the entire SRV government including the ministry of education, Hanoi Polytechnic University, police, and tribunals together with CPV apparatus was mobilized to violently suppress the protests against China's invasion. Even today, such activities are still going on. Dieu Cay, an independent reporter and others who in 2008 strongly opposed PRC annexation of the islands to China and Pham thanh Nghiên, a young female student, who resisted China's scheme of aggression by sitting in her home with a slogan "*Paracels and Spratlys belong to Vietnam*" are still in prison.

ooo

2.3.3. PART III PICTURES

2.3.3.1.   I. MAP OF GREATER CHINA (redrawn in 2010)

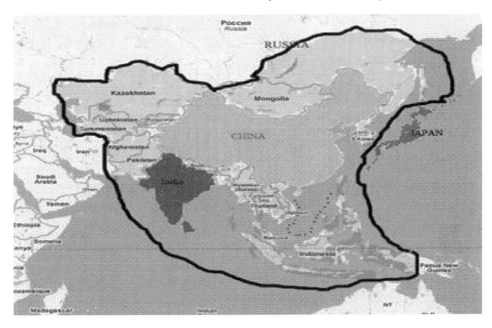

2.3.3.2.   II. CHINESE Military BUILD-UPS IN EASTERN SEA

A. Paracels:

1. Woody Island: General view

2. A portion in North East of Woody: Ammo. Depots

3. One of the two multi- storey buildings: headquarter and office

4. Building on Woody

5. A PRC Navy headquarter on Duncan island where a fierce battle between PRC fleet and RVN naval defending forces on Jan.19, 1974 occurred and where Chinese Admiral Phuong quang Kinh and his 5 colonels lost their lives.

16° 12' 43.33" N 111° 38' 25.15" E
6. A structure on Discovery Island.

7. Tree Island with a communication tower

B. Spratlys:

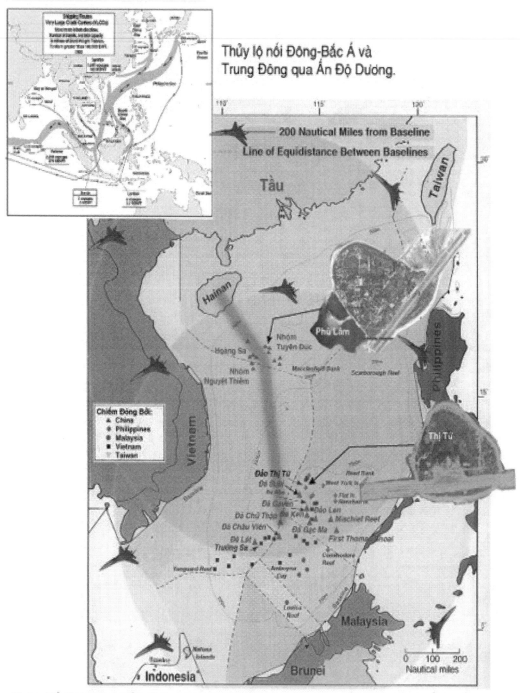

Thủy lộ nối Đông-Bắc Á và
Trung Đông qua Ấn Độ Dương.

Trục chiến lược Nam Hải - Hoàng Sa - Trường Sa. Hai vòng tròn màu xanh nhạt biểu thị tầm hoạt động
an toàn cho loại phản lực SU-27 của Không quân Hán tặc. Ng: middlebury.com, globalsecurity.org, googleearth.com.

1. Strategic Axis (from Hainan via Paracels to Spratlys)

Khám Phá Căn Cứ Tàu Ngầm ... Bí Mật Của Trung Cộng

Một sự đe dọa trầm trọng tại vùng biển Đông (biển Nam Trung Hoa): Dưới một hòn đảo, Trung Cộng đã cho xây một căn cứ tàu ngầm khổng lồ. Một đặc khu giống y như trong phim gián điệp James Bond 007, cùng những Hàng Không Mẫu Hạm có thể ẩn nấp ở đây. Từ đặc khu cảng này có thể gây ra một sự đe dọa nguy hiểm lâu dài cho các quốc gia láng giềng Đông Nam Á khác.

Hình chụp từ vệ tinh chỉ rõ các đường ngầm ra vào khu cảng đầu não của Trung Hoa.

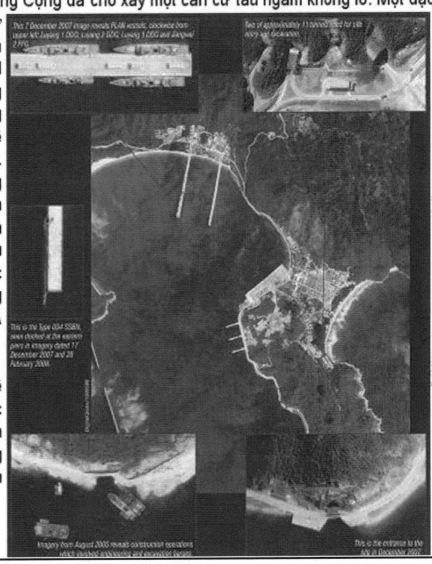

2. Sanya or Yulin Naval Base, Hainan: 2 piers for aircraft carriers and 3 for sub marines. Underwater Entrance of the cave. At upper right corner: system of underground tunnels; and left corner: a pier with four sub. identified.

3. Nuclear Jin class/-094 submarine; six ICBM multi warheads missiles on each side.

9° 53' 15.06" N 115° 31' 19.56" E

4. Headquarter, Mischiefs Reef (2008)

5. Another structure in Mischief Reef.

6. Fiery Cross Reef

7. **Missile launching pad** and platform for Change Z-8 helicopters (116 meters, long and 96 meters, wide), Fiery Cross.

8. **Johnson South** was one of the six reefs taken by PRC in March 1988. This is the place where 64 SRV soldiers were killed while they were in the water, unarmed, carrying supplies to their comrades defending the reef.

9° 42' 50.27" N 114° 17' 9.59" E

2.3.3.3.   III. CHINA NAVY'S VICIOUS TREATMENTS TOWARD VIETNAMESE FISHERMEN

- Chinese Naval forces violently attack Vietnamese fishermen.

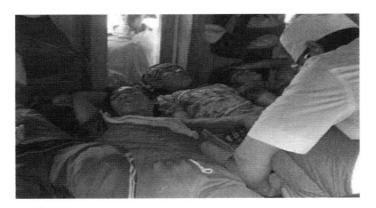

1. Wounded fishermen were in carried in from Paracels

2. Remains of a dead fisherman

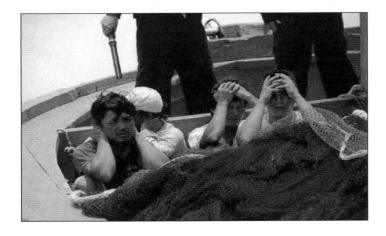

3. Fishermen arrested by Chinese naval forces

4. A fisherman's boat is sinking after being hit by a PRC Naval ship

2.3.3.4.   **IV. HEGEMONY WITH CHINESE CHARACTERISTICS**

-Yang Jiechi, China Foreign Minister told Singapore Foreign Minister George Yeo at the ASEAN Regional Security Meeting in Hanoi, July, 2010: *"China is a great nation, yours is only a small state."*

-Every year China has received economic assistance from the USA. In 2010, she received about US $270 million as a grant-in-aid for development. China still claims that she is an underdeveloped country though economically she is ranked second only after the USA. She is a big US creditor. Her ambitions to dominate the world are unlimited. She builds up her military might to threaten every major country in the world, and uses it to achieve her goals by any means she has available, though civilized countries never consider the way she does it as appropriate.

Chinese Destroyer 556 during the invasion 1988

Destroyer 556 was one the four Chinese battleships involved in carrying out a surprise attack on unarmed SRV soldiers who were instantly murdered in the waters while making routine trips to carry supplies to their comrades-in arms staging on Johnson Reef as they had done for the last ten years. Johnson (09 46 N 114 22E) is one of the six reefs taken by PRG. Others are Len Dao (09 46 N 114 22E), Chigua (09 55 N 114 29 E). Sin Cowe (09 51N 114 22E.)

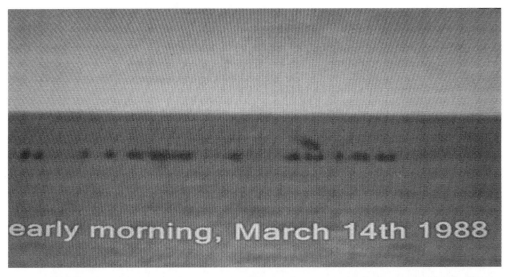

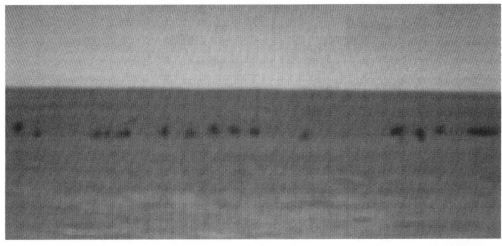

Chigua is one of six reefs taken by Chinese Navy in 1988

2.3.3.5.   **V. COMMUNIST PARTY OF VIETNAM's VICIOUS CRACKDOWN ON PROTESTERS: SUPPRESSING ANTI-CHINA PROTESTS**

A. Terrorism in Hanoi, July 17, 2011

1. The officer in white pinpointing a target to be captured is Lt. Col. Canh, Deputy Director, for Security Affairs, Hoan Kiem District, Hanoi. He is surrounded by a large group of secret

service officers conducting an anti-protest operation in Hanoi where students rose up against Chinese ship violations of the continental shelf of Vietnam and cutting off a Vietnam ship cables while it did seismic work on Vietnam's continental -shelf.

2. The person wearing sunglasses and the one with a hat on are targets to be captured. The one with sunglasses is Nguyen chi Duc.

3. The man in yellow is Capt. Phạm hải Minh, Deputy Chief of the anti-demonstration task force, Hoan Kiem District, Hanoi who is receiving orders from Col. Canh. Minh waits at the door of the bus, then uses his right foot to stomp the face of an unknown student, who has been tightly held by 4 secret service agents. He is one of over 100 demonstrators captured during a protest in Hanoi on July 17, 2011. Later on, the victim is identified as Nguyen chí Đức.

Photo: DanLamBao, Hà nội, 17 July 2011 - Communist officer Minh stomps Duc's face

405

4. Nguyen chí Đức whose face was stamped by Capt. Minh receives a bouquet from an unknown supporter the next day after he is freed from the police station.

5. Nguyen tien Nam, a student is arrested by secret service agents in a protest in Hanoi on 24 April 2008 when the Chinese Olympic torch is carried through Vietnam. This is the same method to suppress protesters. The secret service agent happened to be Capt. Minh who stomped Nguyen chi Duc's face on July 17.

B. Terrorism in Saigon, 12 June 2011

1. Secret service agents arrest a protester

2. Police arrest a protester - Photo:CTV Hà Nội

3. A robust secret service agent uses his judo skills to arrest and torture a young protester in Saigon.

C. Protest in Hanoi, 24 July 2011

1. Vietnamese teenagers demand PRC to respect International laws

2. 200 people join the protest

2. Bui thi Minh Hang, a protester, showing her anger against the Chinese invasion, and two teenagers carrying a slogan by her side

3. Demonstration against Chinese aggressors.

4. Demonstrators against Chinese aggressors who massacre innocent
and unarmed fishermen.

5. Demonstrators against Chinese aggressors

SAIGON, A CHINA TOWN IN VIETNAM.

In 2008, when the Olympic torch was carried through Saigon, Beijing sent hundreds of youth from China to Vietnam. They marched in Saigon streets, guided and protected by SRV police in uniform, as they did in Beijing, while Vietnamese students were not allowed to take to the street.

Display of PRC flags while marching in Saigon.

Notes: The CPV has mostly employed secret service agents who pretend to be protesters and march together with them in order to identify who is a leader or who is active, then make arrests as seen. The agents have been trained to deal with protestors opposing the invaders.

In one report, in some demonstrations like the ones on July 10 or 17 in Hanoi, over a hundred protesters are arrested by secret service agents (not by police) and the ratio of secret service agents and protesters is 5 to 1.

Besides, in the July 24 demonstration, CPC sent teams of Chinese secret agents from Beijing to Hanoi to directly command the anti-demonstration operations.

There have been 8 consecutive demonstrations against Chinese aggressors on every Sunday in both Hanoi and Saigon, since June 5 to July 24. It appears that the CPV leadership continues to resist against the demand of the Vietnamese people to protect the integrity of the Vietnamese territory, to safeguard the lives of Vietnamese fishermen. The reason as to why they act ferociously against the protestors is that the ultimate objective of the CPV is to help China to occupy the South China Sea at the expenses of the Vietnamese people, and in spite of the world aspiration for peace and stability.

The real danger to peace and stability to South East Asia and the world comes from CPV's collusion with Beijing in the latter's scheme of expansion.

000

On August 30, 2011, Nguyen Trung Chau, President of the Federation of Associations of Former Vietnamese Political Prisoners sent a letter to 192 world leaders attending the United Nations's General Assembly. This letter was sent along with an attached Dossier of the Committee on Protection of Territorial Integrity of Vietnam denouncing the Chinese Hegemony and condemning the Communist Party of Vietnam (CPV) as an accomplice for China to seize the Eastern Sea of Vietnam, the South China Sea, and even Asia. The goal was to alert world leaders about the dangers of this expansion, especially with the help of the leaders of the Communist Party of Vietnam.

The Letter and Documents were also sent to the US President Barack Obama.

Attached is a response from President Obama outlining a strategy for dealing with Beijing expansionism?

2.3.4. RELATED DOCUMENTS TO THE DOSSIER

2.3.4.1.   THE LETTERS

1. Letter from Nguyen Trung Chau to President Obama

Federation Of Association Of Former Vietnamese Political Prisoners
62 W. Kingsbridge Rd, Bronx, Newyork 10468. Tel (718) 364-3673
Email: "" <tonghoictnctvn@yahoo.com>

August 15, 2011

The honorable Ban Ki-moon, Secretary General And Members of the United Nations UN Headquarters

New York, NY 10017

Dear Mr. Ban and Ladies and Gentlemen:

Subject: Danger of Instability in the South East Asian Region

The Federation of Association of Former Vietnamese Political Prisoners (herein called the Federation) is an organization established in the USA by a number of former Vietnamese political prisoners who survived brutal atrocities perpetrated by the communist party of Vietnam (CPV) after the Republic of Vietnam was taken militarily in 1975.

The Federation is an international organization composed of 33 chapters in the North America and 4 others in Europe and Australia.

The Federation, endorsed by a number of community-based organizations in North East of the USA, calls your attention to the fact that during the past year the situation in South East Asia Region becomes increasingly tense and this could lead to a danger to peace and stability that people all over the world is longing for. In fact, on June 25, 2011, Ho xuan Son, a deputy minister of the Socialist Republic of Vietnam (SRV) met in Beijing with Dai Bingguo, a senior official member of the communist party of China (CPC) in charge of external affairs about implementation of "what both sides have agreed on" to solve the South China sea problem. The concerned parties have never openly defined what does their mutual agreement mean. However, the content of the agreement reflects provocative mentality of those Chinese expansionists who have caused tension in the region for the past months. And also, it includes details telling the world that the CPV is moving a bolder step in providing the expansionists with another opportunity for their naval forces to position themselves in a part of the region as a new starting point to move south and further.

Being a loving peace people, we strongly condemn the CPC for its scheme of hegemony and the CPV for their services to the former.

Attached is a copy of research on this important matter for your consideration and we wish that appropriate measures be taken to maintain peace and stability for the region in particular and the world in general.

Sincerely yours,

Nguyen trung Chau,

President

2. Replying Letter from President Obama to Nguyen Trung Chau

In his reply to Mr. Nguyen Trung Chau, President Obama outlined the strategy to deal with the dangers of Beijing's expansion scheme. President Obama's strategy was **to strengthen the existing coalition and to develop the new cooperation...**

THE WHITE HOUSE
WASHINGTON

October 4, 2011

Nguyen Trung Chau
President
Federation of Association of
Former Vietnamese Political Prisoners
62 West Kingsbridge Road
Bronx, New York 10468

Dear Nguyen:

Thank you for writing. I have heard from many Americans about our Nation's foreign policy, and I appreciate your perspective.

As President, my highest priority is the safety of the American people. My Administration is using every element of our national power to keep our country secure, prosperous, and free. We have renewed our leadership in the world by strengthening old alliances and forging new partnerships to meet common challenges such as preventing terrorist attacks, reversing the global economic crisis, responding to pandemic disease, and confronting climate change.

are in the midst of a four-year effort to secure all vulnerable materials worldwide to prevent nuclear terrorism at its source. Looking forward, we will continue to partner with other nations to fulfill our shared aspirations: to support our families, to have the freedom to choose leaders and worship as we please, and to live in peace and security.

I will advance these interests in my work with other governments. However, meeting these common challenges will also require active, engaged citizens. Real progress does not just come from governments and international institutions. Lasting change comes from those who are willing to speak up for the future we desire.

Thank you, again, for writing, and I invite you to learn more about our foreign policy at: www.WhiteHouse.gov/issues/foreign-policy.

Sincerely,

[signature]

This is an analysis of the US strategy, to prevent Chinese expansionism.

2.3.4.2.   THE USA AND ASIA SECURITY

Nguyen Van Canh - January 1, 2014

The scope of this article is a discussion on China scheme of expansionism in Asia. The South China Sea and part of the Pacific Ocean are China's targets. What measures the United States is taking, against aggressive China in order to maintain Peace and Stability for this region and the world?

I. THE ARTERIAL SEA LANE OF THE WORLD THROUGH THE SOUTH CHINA SEA

 Some Important data we need to know:

- SHIPS NAVIGATING THROUGH THE SOUTH CHINA SEA:

Every year, about 100,000 trips going through the South China Sea, to the Indian Ocean, transporting over a quarter (1/4) the world's goods. (Source: Malaysian Prime Minister's office) According to Malaysia's Ministry of Fisheries, in 2010 alone, more than 74,000 ships passed through the Malacca Strait, carrying 30% of the world's goods and a quarter (1/4) of the world oil, equivalent to 11 million barrels of oil per day.

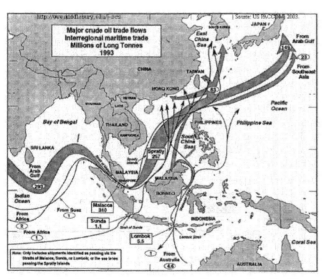

The United Nations Conference on Trade and Development (UNCTAD) estimates that roughly 80 percent of global trade by volume and 70 percent by value is transported by sea. Of that volume, 60 percent of maritime trade passes through Asia, with the South China Sea carrying an estimated one-third of global shipping. Its waters are particularly critical for China, Taiwan, Japan, and South Korea, all of which rely on the Strait of Malacca, which connects the South China Sea and, by extension, the Pacific Ocean with the Indian Ocean. This vital "arterial" maritime route is critically important for the survival of commerce for Japan, South Korea and China. South Korea and Japan also depend on this sea route for oil import.

- VALUE OF TRADE: The total value of goods transferred through the South China Sea is estimated at $5 trillion USD a year.

- The trading value for America and Asia in 2010 through Malacca is US$ 1,300 billion, and through the whole region in 2014 is estimated at 3,140 billion USD. An estimated $3.4 trillion in trade passed through the South China Sea in 2016. US Secretary of State Hilary Clinton said the US-Korea Trade Treaty created 70,000 jobs in 2011.

II. CHINA'S SCHEME TO OCCUPY THE EASTERN SEA & EXPANSION INTO THE PACIFIC OCEAN

A. Core Interests In The Eastern Sea: (South China Sea):

- In March 2010, Cui Tiankai, Deputy Foreign Minister, in the presence of Dai Bingguo, a member of the State Council of China, informed Jeffrey A. Bader and James B. Steinberg of the US Department of State when they visited Beijing, about ***the core interest of China in the South China Sea, and this interest is equivalent to that in Taiwan, Xin jiang and Tibet"***. That means China now considers the South China Sea to be her property.

On May 24-25, 2010 at the Strategic and Economic Dialogue Conference in Beijing, Dai Bingguo reiterated that statement to Clinton that China considered the South China Sea to be **China's core interest**. It is the official message that informs the United States that South China Sea is her territorial waters and the passage through the South China Sea must have China's permission. The exploitation of natural resources such as oil exploration in this area will also be prohibited.

- On August 19, 2013, when visiting the United States, at a press conference at the US Pentagon, Chinese Defense Minister General Chang Wanquan emphasized: *"No one should have the idea that China will exchange that core interest"*. In order to achieve that goal, China has spent decades, possibly more than half a century, in preparing for it!

1). Enactment of Laws. China unilaterally has considered the Eastern Sea as her property, since China was ruled by Mao Zedong and the communists. In 1958, Zhou Enlai published a document stating that Paracel and Spratly Archipelagos of (South) Vietnam have been under the China's sovereignty. Then Premier Pham Van Dong sent an diplomatic note to acknowledge China's claim. Later, China published a map showing the South China Sea, with new boundary covering a large area of the Sea. In February 1992, the National Assembly of China enacted a law declaring that scientific and military ships passing through the South China Sea have to seek permission, otherwise they would be sunk.

By May of that year, Red China signed a contract with the US oil company Crestone, based in Denver, Colorado, to explore and exploit oil and gas in an area, 25,000 square kilometers, south of the Paracels. In June 2006, China published another wider "9-dash-line map" to claim sovereignty. The west boundary on this map lies near the coast of Vietnam. Then in November 2007, the Chinese State Council announced the establishment of the Sansha district of Hainan Province. Sansha/Tam Sa 三沙 district is the administrative unit that governs the three archipelagos: Paracels, Spratlys and Zhongsha. This act is to ***annex*** 附件 Vietnam's Eastern Sea into China territory. In July 2012, China raised Sansha district to the city level, with a government agency including the Military Command to defend this Sea.

2). Activities to assert sovereignty over Eastern Sea:

-With the Socialist Republic of Vietnam (SRV): In 1956, Red China sent troops to occupy the eastern part of Paracel Archipelago, the Amphitrite Group. In 1974, they sent a fleet of battleships to invade the Crescent Group, to the west of this archipelago. At that time, the

Republic of South Vietnam's Navy (RSVN) occupied this area. Fierce cross-fires occurred at the Duncan (đảo Quang Hoà) and Drummond Islands (đảo Duy Mộng), but RVN failed to protect the territorial sea. Since then, the Paracel Archipelago fell under China's control.

Regarding the Spratlys, in 1988, China brought four destroyers into Spratlys waters. They then suddenly shot and killed 64 of 74 soldiers, unarmed while in the water to deliver supplies to the Vietnamese troop stationed at Johnson Reef. At this time, China occupied six reefs or dunes of the Spratlys. In 1994, the Philippines discovered a wooden structure with a Chinese flag at a site east of the Mischief Reef, near the Philippines. Philippines deputy Foreign Minister went to China to oppose this. China replied that it was only a temporary structure for Chinese fishermen to shelter from the sun, rain and storm. After that, the Philippines sent a naval ship to destroy that structure using explosives.

By the mid-2000s, many solid military structures have been built on the reefs of Vietnam such as Mischief Reef, Fiery Cross Reef, Johnson South Reef (Gạc Ma)..... Over a dozen of fortified structures emerged out of the water in this area. About 16 reefs and dunes are occupied by China's navy. Important structures are located south of the Spratly Archipelago. Since 2007, China has increased her activities on this Sea, in the Spratly archipelago, to assert her claimed sovereignty. In July 2007, a Chinese naval ship killed a Vietnamese fisherman and sank several other Vietnamese fishing boats operating in the Spratly Island. This incident was witnessed by a Vietnamese naval vessel. China's military performed drills with live ammunition in the north of the Spratly Archipelago. To increase patrolling on this Sea, their fishing and naval vessels are disguised as civilian vessels. From May to August each year, China prohibits Vietnamese fishermen to operate in the area north the 15th parallel, for "preserving ocean resources". The Chinese Navy has been very aggressive on the Sea. In September 2010, their military exercises took place on a large scale on the Fiery Cross Reef. China arrogantly increased their threat, manipulation, intimidation, suppression, shooting and killing of Vietnamese fishermen all over these two archipelagos of Vietnam. In 2010, there were 200 arrests of Vietnamese fishermen. They were detained on Woody, Robert and Lincoln Islands, robbed of all the catch, fishing gear confiscated, and ransom demanded. China constantly attacked, mistreated, beat and killed Vietnamese fishermen. On June 25, 2011, Chinese surveillance ships entered Vietnam contiental self cutting cables of Vietnam geological survey ship Binh Minh 2 operating in an area 120 nautical miles from Dai Lanh, Tuy Hoa province; two weeks later, on June 9 they cut the cables of Viking 2, of Vietnam, at an area 140 nautical miles frrom Vung Tàu Seaport

In July, a report said a Chinese ship pulled out a Vietnamese ship from where it is doing oil search on Vietnam continental self, while Hanoi tried to hide the news. This incident was published a few months later however with a photo showing "*Vietnamese ship pulling Chinese ship out of Vietnam waters*".

Since 2009, China has threatened the British Oil Company BPH exploiting gas in south of Côn Sơn island, intimidated the US ExxonMobil, demanding this compaany to terminate its oil/gas contract with Vietnam. In July 2011, the Indian amphibious ship Airavat visited Nha Trang, on its way back, about 45 nautical miles away, this ship was warned for "*unauthorized navigating in Chinese waters*". Then in September, China opposed the ONCG oil company of

India operating on the continental shelf of Vietnam, though it has a contract wiith Vietnam since 2004...

All of the above Chinese activities are justified by declaring that the Chinese waters have been violated.

In adittion, the Chinese communists have tried to use the Vietnamese Communists as puppets to surrender Vietnam's Eastern Sea to China. China has insisted to resolve the South China Sea disputes by bilateral negotiations only. With this method, China has bribed, intimidated and manipulated the Socialist Republic of Vietnam in many ways, in order to gain control of Vietnam's Eastern Sea. The bilateral negotiation tactics aim at neutralizing the US stance on the internationalization of the South China Sea, and also to divide ASEAN while the US policy is to solve the dispute by multilateral negotiations: one side is Communist China and the other side is all countries of the ASEAN.

- With the Philippines: China also applies the similar tactics: On February 25, 2011, two Filipino fishing vessels were shot at by a Chinese battleship carrying missiles. They used live ammunitions to fire, threatened and ordered the Filipino fishing vessels to leave the aea immediately. It was about 140 nautical miles from Palawan Island. Shortly thereafter, on March 2, 2012, 12 Chinese marine surveillance ships threatened a Filipino explorer ship and demanded it to leave the area near Reed Bank, offshore of the Palawan Island.

- With Malaysia: Red China naval ships also used live ammunitions to threaten Malaysia fishermen offshore.

B. Hegemonic Expansion in the South China Sea:

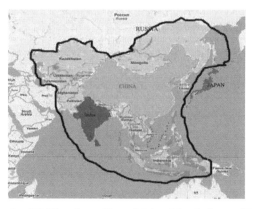

- The "Han" Map published in 2010: On this map, the entire Asia continent is the territory of China, including the entire East Asia except Japan, Southeast Asia, India, Pakistan, Afghanistan. The five former Soviet nations located east of the Caspian coast are also part of China territory.

- The expanded Pacific map with two Defense lines.

a) *String of Islands Defense Line* : This line starts from Japan to the Philippines. The four allied nations of the United States: Japan, South Korea, Taiwan and the Philippines lie within this defense line.

b) *"Distant Defense Line"*: This perimeter of this defense covers a large area from Indonesia via Guam going down to Australia. The Chinese extends the "defense belt" with an intent to occupy the entire Western Pacific, i.e. China asserts her sovereignty over this part of the Pacific Ocean, pushing the United States westtward to Hawaii. In addition, China has a scheme of expansion towards the Indian Ocean with 'String of Pearls': seaports are located in this sequence, starting from Sihanook ville (Cambodia), Kyauk Pyu (Burma), then Chittagong, (Bangladesh), Hambantot (SriLanka,) Cocos Island, Maldives, through Gwadar (Pakistan) to Djibouti (Africa).. The ambition to establish this chain is to help China control the Indian Ocean and expand to Africa and South America. The main contributor to this scheme is Burma.

C. Coordination of military, economic, and political forces to confront the US in order to occupy the South China Sea and expand in the Pacific Ocean. –**Military forces**: China has produced J20, submarines JIN CLASS (094), aircraft carrier Liaoning, Dong Fong 21D; establishing a massive "Sanya" naval base in Hainan with massive military structures on the two Paracel and Spratly Archipelagos, etc. -**Economic & Financial forces:** China has a huge surplus of foreign currency and it is used to bribe leaders, putting pressure on some ASEAN countries, especially targeting the Socialist Republic of Vietnam, Cambodia, Laos, and Burma to serve as puppets to implement the Dai Han plan.

III. THE UNITED STATES REACTIONS

At the above-mentioned Strategic and Economic Dialogue Conference in Beijing, Secretary of States Hillary Clinton politely replied to Dai Bingguo that "we do not agree" (when Dai frankly told her that China has a core interest in South China Sea) and that the United States has a **national interest in the region**. By June 2010, at the Shangri-la Defense Dialogue Conference, in Singapore, U.S. Secretary of Defense, Robert Gates stated that *"The South China Sea is not only important for the coastal states, but also for all the countries that have economic and security interests in Asia, therefore freedom of navigation and economic development must be maintained. We are not on any side in the dispute of sovereignty; but we **oppose the use of force and actions that hinder freedom of navigation.** We object to any attempt to intimidate US oil companies or companies of any country that have engaged in legitimate economic activities. All parties must work together to resolve differences using peaceful, multilateral efforts in accordance with common international laws. The 2002 Declaration of Conduct was an important step in this direction and we hope that the work that needs to be done specifically will continue"*. Gates also emphasized the freedom of movement in the air and on the sea surface of the entire Pacific Ocean. As such, the United States regards these regions as the common property of everyone, though he did not mention the use of power to defend America's stance.

- In July 2010, Secretary of State Hillary Clinton, in a statement at the ASEAN Conference in Hanoi, reiterated that the United States distinguished these two issues: maritime navigation and disputed sovereignty in the South China Sea.

- **Navigation issue in the South China Sea:** America advocates Freedom of Navigation. Every nation has the right to freedom of movement on this sea, no one is allowed to stop that. Clinton said this is the **national interest** of the United States. The United States will defend and have a clear and hard line policy.

- **Sovereignty dispute over the islands.** America does not take side with any one. All countries must negotiate peacefully, **without forces**, to confirm their sovereignty. This was approved since 2002 when the nations in dispute met in Cambodia and signed the Declaration of Conduct (DOC):

ASEAN and China are on opposite sides. The US advocates **multilateral negotiations** to resolve sovereignty disputes. It is the **American policy of internationalization of the South China Se**a. To implement this policy, through Defense Secretary Robert Gates' statement in Shangri-la, and that of Secretary of State Hillary Clinton in Hanoi, in August 2010, the US sent aircraft carrier George Washington to Vietnam, and it was anchored at Da Nang offshore, across Sanya base on Hainan Island, China. Vietnamese naval officers were invited to visit the ship, to play sports, and practice a sea rescue. The USA also sent the aircraft carrier Ronald Reagan to Okinawa to strengthen its 7th Fleet. This is a USA show of power, reflecting the US announcements on the American national interests.

In fact, the United States made such preparations years ago. Attention was made to the statement of the Deputy Commander of the Chinese People's Liberation Army, posted in China News on April 7, 1992. General Zhang Xusan said that the duty of the Chinese navy is to support the exploitation under the waters, including protection of disputed islands in the Spratly archipelago. At this time, Vice Admiral Zhang Lianzhong, Chinese Navy Commander, informed China News Services that the Central Military Commission ordered the navy to be ready to defend its territorial waters and surrounding areas. So with the deep sea economic exploitation projects, the situation will be more complicated, and the fight to protect the waters will become fierce.

Beijing's expansion plan does not stop in the South China Sea, but extends throughout Asia, the Pacific and also around the world, including to the United States. In recent years, this evidence has been found.

As early as the mid-2000s, under President Bush, the United States cooperated with India: the lifting of the embargo on nuclear technology to help this country to be an ally in the future. US President Barack Obama also had a plan with more details. In a letter dated October 4, 2011 replying to Nguyen Trung Chau (President of the Federation of Associstions Former Vietnamese Political Prisoners), he wrote "*My government is using every element of a nation's power to keep our nation safe, prosperous and free. We have re-established our leadership over the world by **_strengthening old alliances and consolidating new partnerships_** to deal with common challenges such **as terrorist attacks and global economic crisis...**"* President Obama re-emphasized this idea at the ASEAN Summit held in New York on September 2010:

"As President of the United States, I explicitly affirm that the United States has a goal to play a leadership role in Asia. We strengthen old alliances. We consolidate new partnerships. We renew our commitment to regional organizations including ASEAN...".

2.3.4.3. OLD ALLIANCES AND NEW PARTNERSHIPS

2.3.4.3.1. POLITICS AND MILITARY

The United States strategy is to form an arc to overpower Beijing. This arc includes the United States, India, Philippines, Japan, and Australia. Washington's allies from Northeast Asia to Southeast Asia, and the South Pacific. All have participated in a new strategy with the goal of blocking China's ambitious expansion.

-**With ASEAN,** on July 22, 2009, US Secretary of State signed the Treaty on Non-aggression with ASEAN.

-**PHILIPPINES:** On November 12, 2009, Washington and Manila signed an agreement allowing 600 US soldiers to be stationed in the Philippines. After New York was attacked on 9/11/2001, the USA provided military assistance to the Philippines to deal with the armed extremist Islamic organizations. Dealing with the current situation, the Philippines requested US military aids for national independence. The US Commander for the Asia Pacific visited the Philippines to pledge support. The United States has provided military training for two years for the Philippines. An advanced jet fighter squadron was transferred to the Philippines Air Forces. President Aquino asked for the second squadron. The Philippines received two Destroyers.

Both the Philippines and the United States agreed to protect the Philippines in accordance with a Defense Treaty signed in 1951. Philippine Foreign Minister Albert del Rosario on January 27, 2012 said Manila would accept a greater US military presence, to help protect the Philippines' interests and ensure peace in the region, amid tensions with China. He wanted more joint military exercises with the United States and more US military troops in the Philippines. The Washington Post reported on Jan 26, 12 that negotiations continue and will take place on Jan. 26 and 27 in Washington before a meeting at a higher level will be held in Marh in Washington. A senior Philippines official said: "*We could follow examples of other countries: Australia, Japan, Singapore... the Philippines is not the only country doing this. We expect the best for regional peace and stability. No one wants to confront China*". In early 2013, the Philippines invited the United States to use the Subic Bay as a military base, and in August 2013, a negotiation for the US navy to be stationed there will begin..

- On June 8, 2012, President Barack Obama met president Benigno Aquino at the White House. During the meeting, the two leaders reviewed their national defense ties, and discussed strengthening bilateral cooperation. President Obama also discussed trade with President Aquino, including the TPP Trans-Pacific Partnership. President Aquino visited the United States amid tensions between the Philippines and China, after the clash between ships in the Scarborough Shoal. Manila affirmed this island is within Philippines' exclusive economic zone of 200 miles, while Beijing claimed this island is hers.

At the same time, General Martin Dempsey, chairman of the Joint Chiefs of Staff, also discussed with President Aquino the cooperation between the two nations, with focus on international terrorism and extremist Islamic armed groups. General Dempsey also discussed the ensuring of freedom of navigation in the South China Sea. The two leaders did not discuss *"territorial sea disputes, but called on all parties concerned to resolve this issue through international laws, without using forces"*.

Washington has assisted to modernize the Philippines' military equipment. Manila agreed to increase the number of US troops stationed in the Philippines. The Obama administration has pledged to increase the United States presence in Asia. US Defense Secretary, Leon Panetta announced a plan to shift most of US battleships to the Asia Pacific towards 2020. In a joint statement released on August 23, 2013, the Commanders of the US and Philippines militaries reaffirmed their determination to maintain freedom of navigation at sea in Southeast Asia. This pledge was emphasized again on the occasion that the delegations of these two military allies began a new round of negotiations in Washington on expanding the US military presence in the Philippines.

The Joint statement of General Emmanuel Bautista, Philippines military leader and General Martin Dempsey, Chairman of the Joint Chiefs of Staff, said : *"We share a common interest in maintaining freedom of navigation, legal trade unencumbered, and transport of people and goods at sea". The joint statement emphasized: "We are determined to strengthen the security environment in Southeast Asia so as to protect the interests of all who respect the value of trade across regions without obstruction, and also to give warnings to those who want to restrict or act in threatening the free trade"*.

Also according to the Philippine Ministry of Foreign Affairs, the Increased Rotational Presence (IRP) agreement would go into details of the campaigns that will be conducted in the future, while the number of US troops allowed to stay in the country will «depend on the size of the campaigns that both sides will accept". So far, the United States has regularly conducted joint exercises with the Philippines, and there is a rotating force of about 500 troops present in the southern Philippines. With the agreement on strengthening a rotating presence in talks, the Pentagon may send more troops and advanced equipment to the Philippines, or join in upgrading bases in the Philippines.

- On July 16, 2013, the USA and the Philippines negotiated more on military cooperation, and the USA provided funding for additional storage facilities for temporary US humanitarian aid military equipment and supplies. However at a news conference in Manila, Philippines ambassador Jose Cuisia said his country rejected the permanent US military presence in the Philippines. Manila was ready to receive US fighters and warships to improve its national defenses. In recent years, US military forces have been rotating to visit the Philippines more, due to a bilateral agreement signed in 1998. However, a new deal will become necessary if Washington wants to build facilities to support the temporary deployment of U.S. military operations in the Philippines.

According to Mr. Cuisia, the two countries had negotiated since 2011 on "common use" of civilian and military facilities in the Philippines, and informal negotiations have reached the ministry level. Both parties hope to reach an agreement before President Benigno Aquino ends his term in June 2016. Mr. Cuisia said a new treaty could allow the United States to store equipment and supplies in the Philippines to prepare for humanitarian aid and disaster relief. This will reduce delays in getting equipment from other places to the region, such as from US bases in Guam or Honolulu.

United States sent super attack submarines to the Philippines

Fast Attack Submarine USS North Carolina of US Navy has arrived and docked at the Philippines' Subic Freeport, near the Scarborough Reef. Here, the Philippines and Chinese ships confronted, according to Philippine Navy spokesman, Lieutenant Colonel Omar Tonsay. According to Tonsay, the modern Virginia-class submarine docked at Subic Freeport has a mission to support U.S. troops in the Philippines. It is not related to the earlier confrontation between the Philippines and China regarding the issue of sovereignty over the horseshoe-shaped Scarborough Shoal (China calls it the island of Huangyan 黃岩).

According to the United States Pacific Command, this submarine has a length of 350 feet and a weight of more than 7,800 tons when diving. The USS North Carolina is one of the "invisible" submarines equipped with the most advanced state-of-the-art technology in the world at that time.

- On September 18, 2013, the United States and the Philippines begin joint military exercises (drills) at a naval base on the coast of Luzon Island in the South China Sea — near the disputed area, between Manila and Beijing. Facing the turbulence from China's maritime sovereignty claims, the US and the Philippines emphasized their military cooperation. About 2,000 US Marines and Philippine troops take part in this annual exercise in the South China Sea, just before President Obama's first official visit to the Philippines on October 11-12, 2013.

- On August 4, 2013, Manila's second US-bought battleship BRP Ramon Alcaraz has arrived and docked at the former US Navy base in Subic Bay. It is to strengthen the Philippines Navy while the sovereignty dispute over the sea and islands between the Philippines and China has become increasingly fierce. Ramon Alcaraz is a refurbished ship of the US Coast Guard, dating back to World War II. The ship complemented the first battleship BRP Gregorio del Pilar. It is also an old US Coast Guard vessel purchased by the Philippines in August 2011.

The Manila government has welcomed the acquisition of this ship as a step to enhance the Philippines Navy's combat capability against the increasing Chinese military presence in the West Philippines Sea (South China Sea). It was announced by Foreign Minister Albert del Rosario at a conference on maritime security in Bruxelles, last month.. At the conference, he condemned China for having caused tension in the region, probably implying Chinese vessels invading the islands within the exclusive economic zone of the Philippines. Since May last year, Chinese fishing vessels, with escort of Chinese battleships, often have entered and exited Philippine waters as they do in their waters. Manila has the weakest naval force in Asia, and is unable to prevent these Chinese encroachments. So the Philippines are rushing to modernize the naval forces.

Some purchased US warships are not enough to deal with the giant Chinese navy. So Manila also is looking at purchasing more warships from other nations, such as France

-In March 08, the Philippines orders a French battleship La Tapageuse, 26-year-old, cost 6 million euros, will be delivered in April 2009. This is the first battleship purchased from France. The Philippines Coast Guard also bought 10 multi-purpose patrol vessels from Japan.To increase capabilities for national defense, the Philippines's Department of National Defense moved the airbases and naval bases into the Subic Bay, a deep-water seaport having available runway and airport facilities.

The Philippines plans to purchase 10 multi- missioned patrol ships within an aid program from Japan.

Besides the strenghtening denfense capabilties, the Philippines is having a project to move its air and navy baese to the Subic Bay, because there is a deep wat seaport, a runway and facilities available for its air forces.

In addition to the already purchased battleships, the Philippines navy still needs support from its American ally. The Philippines Minister of Foreign Affairs Albert del Rosario stated on July 31, 2013 that US reconnaissance planes have provided valuable information about the Chinese military activities around the area over which China asserts sovereignty.

 On June 17, 2012, the Gulf News on line quoted a source from the Philipppines military as saying that Manila and Washington have set up a surveillance center in the South China Sea, where for the past two months the Philippines and China have tense relations in the Scarborough Shoal (Bãi Cạn). According to Colonel Arnulfo Marcelo Burgo, spokesman for the Philippines military, the Manila government has planned to buy a Landing Craft Utility (LCU), two coastal surveillance systems, over one hundred communication devices, three battle systems for night use, aerial cameras, radar etc. Those devices will be used by the Philippines Navy and the marine surveillance center. Also according to Philippines military representatives, the surveillance systems will help detect foreign ships penetrating into the territorial seas of the Philippines, especially the exclusive economic zone (within 200 nautical miles), persuant to The United Nations Convention on The Law of The Sea (UNCLOS). The surveillance systems are also used to prevent the transnational crimes, human trafficking, pirates, drug smuggling, illegal fishing, and to protect of Philippines' marine resources. Before that, Major Catherine Wilkinson of the US Armed Forces said: **«We are at the initial period of the plans to assist the Philippines to set-up the National *Center for Coastal Monitoring»*.** This center will also assist the Philippines Navy to generally monitor the entire territorial sea under this nation's sovereignty.

Also in 2013, the US Hamilton-class coast guard vessel acquired by the Philippines Navy patrols in the South China Sea.

- JAPAN: Japan is protected by the United States in accordance to the 1951 treaty. Japan also has established a cooperation structure with the United States, Australia and India. The United States, India and Japan have decided to form a three-way security structure for communication. This information was revealed by an Indian newspaper on 9/1/2011. Senior diplomatic officials from the three nations, the United States, India and Japan met in Washington on 12/19/2011, for the first meeting within a newly formed trilateral dialogue mechanism. Japan has also taken several steps to defend itself in case of an invasion. Japan has produced more submarines, missiles and has discussed the issue of rearmament. Japan really needs the United States support for defense. On 4/22/2011, Japan Minister of Defense Toshimi Kitazawa said that Japan needs to strengthen its military relations with the United States and South Korea, to restrain communist China's expansion.

Japan's Minister of Defense declared that Tokyo's priority is to make the US-Japanese relations "solid as a rock". Japan's Ministry of Defense has publicly announced a new strategy on national security. It mainly will focus on military potential on the territorial waters and airspace, in the South and the West, to deal with China's military modernization. In particular, according to Minister Kitazawa, Japan has discussed with the United States, South Korea and Australia, a plan to strengthen cooperation in the field of Information Technology counter-attack. It is through a cooperation program called «Tomodachi» (Friendship), that the US Navy has sent over 13,000 soldiers and 16 battleships, including the aircraft carrier Ronald Reagan to Japan. Kitazawa also visited Washington to discuss bilateral issues, including the strengthening the US-Japanese military alliance for regional security. Starting March 2010, Japan has negotiated to purchase 40 advanced fighter aircrafts. Boeing company could sell more F-15 or F-18 Super Hornet aircraft to Japan. Japan has 16 submarines available and could increase to 22 or more. Early 2013, Japan announced the launch of a state-of-the-art modern aircraft carrier. At the ASEAN Conference held in Brunei, on August 28, 2013, Japan Minister of Defense Onodera announced Japan would play a key role in the South China Sea, if the war breaks out. Under the USA umbrella, Japan cooperated with the Philippines tightly.

Towards this direction, under the umbrella of the United States, Japan has also cooperated closely with the Philippines. On a visit to Japan, on September 27, 2011, Philippine President Benigno Aquino met with Prime Minister Yoshihiko Noda to discuss regional issues, in the context of Manila seeking support from Tokyo, regarding the South China Sea's sovereignty dispute among China and some Southeast Asian nations.

According to the Japanese media Tokyo and Manila signed military cooperation agreements to strengthen relations for the maritime security. In an interview on 9/26/2011, a senior official from Japanese Prime Minister Noda's office said, leaders from the Philippines and Japan would review the capability of having frequent joint exercises of the Coast Guards from both nations and to have frequent consultations between naval officials from both nations. Japan provided state-of-the-art coast guard ships to the Philippines. The Naval Forces from the United States, Australia and Japan have conducted joint military exercises in the South China Sea for the first time in 2012.

At year end 2013, Japan said it will provide some coastal patrol vessels to Vietnam.

- **INDIA** On 6/6/2012 in a conference with the Indian prime minister Manmohan Singh, the U.S. Secretary of Defense Leon Panetta emphasized the role of India as a "hyphen between the West and East Asia". In a conference with his Indian counterpart A.K Antony, the U.S. Secretary of Defense discussed the NATO plan to withdraw all combat forces from Afghanistan by year end 2014. They also talked about the U.S. selling more weapons to India and cooperating in military training between the two countries. Panetta's trip to India was set in a broader context, because the purpose of the US Secretary of Defense's trip to New Delhi was also to strengthen the national defense ties between the United States and India, in dealing with China's growing military and economic power.

President Barack Obama publicly announced the new strategy in Asia, and India was mentioned as a key partner of the United States. US officials still view India and the United States as having similar tradition on democracy, also sharing common concerns on China and the Islamic organizations. The United States has encouraged India to implement its "Look East" policy. The United States is also working hard to establish a trilateral security alliance with India and Japan. Since 2005, U.S. Congress approved the Nuclear Cooperation Agreement with India: to abolish the embargo on nuclear weapons for India, a first step. In 2008, US Congress passed a law authorizing the US administration to provide fuel and nuclear technology to India. In November 2011, Australia provided uranium to India. The United States and Australia have openly encouraged India to implement its "Look East" policy.

Therefore, for a long time, the United States has made preparations for India to take an important role in Asia. On a larger scale, the United States is also working hard to establish a trilateral security dialogue with India and Japan. Japan currently has no hesitation to show her intention to strengthen ties with India. The USA - Australia -India -Japan strategic alliance has been formed. The Australian warships travel more frequently in the Indian Ocean. Battleships of Australia and India had military exercises (drills) in the Indian Ocean. Australia and India have played larger roles agaisnt China's plot towards Africa and South America, not to mention India's important role in the South China Sea. To strengthen its power, India has ordered six Scorpène-class submarines from France. This type of submarines are also used by Malaysia. The Indian Navy is already equipped with at least 18 modern submarines , and incease 10 new more in 2013, along with a second new aircraft carrier to be launched. On November 16, 2013, finally, Russia handed over to India an old renovated Soviet Union aircraft carrier. At times, the delay in delivery of this aircraft carrier caused tension in the bilateral relationship between Russia and India.

When being asked about India's position on recent disputes over the South China Sea, Indian Foreign Minister S.M. Krishna said: "*India considers Biển Đông (Eastern Sea/South China Sea) as the world's property. I think those trade routes must be liberated from any intervention from any nation*". Regardless of warnings from China, Krishna said Biển Đông area must be used to enhance the trade-related activities between the nations within their coastlines. Foreign Minister Krishna emphasized: "*This has been accepted by China and the ASEAN countries, in their dialogues together. Therefore, I think India supports the theory of freedom of navigation on prosperous trade routes*".

India will not give up its interests on the South China Sea.

To prove its words, India has sent battleships many times to this area, to exchange and perform military exercises (drills) with a few Southeast Asian countries. In the past battleships from India once visited the seaports of the Philippines, Brunei, Malaysia, Vietnam....Recently India announced it is going to send four Navy vessels, the INS Rana, Shakti, Shivalik and Kurmak to make a friendly visit to Shanghai seaport in China for a few weeks. However, one interesting thing to recognize is that the Navy vessels of INS Rana and Shakti visited Subic Bay in the

Philippines, the other two vessels made a brief visit to Hai Phong port, Vietnam, while Manila and Beijing are having sovereignty disputes over the Scarborough shoal.

The sending of Navy vessels from India to Biển Đông (South China Sea) caught the attention of the Chinese media.

The "Look East" policy of India.

According to several sources, the South China Sea is the main focus in the "**Look East**" policy of India. Therefore, New Delhi is very concerned about matters related to the South China Sea.

In July 2012, Indian and U.S. officials held talks on several important projects, mainly to build the "**East-West Economic Corridor in the Greater Mekong Sub-Region**" in Southeast Asia. The project included three nations: the USA, India and Japan. This project will create a tremendous corridor for transportation and trade, from India through Myanmar, Thailand, Cambodia, Laos and finally Vietnam. Japan pledged to provide capital support for this project.

The "Look East" policy was initiated by India since the early 1990s. It is to expand trade cooperation between India and Southeast Asian countries. It is beneficial for India's economic development. The "Look East" policy is considered the key strategy for India's foreign policy. It is considered to be a way to build and strengthen ties between India and Southeast Asian countries.

To implement the Look East policy is a strategy for India to break up China's siege.

The "Look East" policy also has increased contacts with China. Therefore in recent years, India has stepped up its "Look East" policy. People have speculated that the United States and India have tried to contain China's moves. China seems to deliberately "suppress" India on land from the North, East and West, to restrain this South Asian tiger from becoming a new power. Therefore, obviously for survival, India wants to overcome this disadvantage by strengthening its cooperation with ASEAN. On the other hand, India could not sit still watching the South China Sea fall easily into China's hands, as suggested by the USA. The United States wants Asia to have several powerful nations to constrain China. India is a goal for Washington to reach. To gain special support from powerful nations worldwide would make New Delhi confident amid China's warnings that a non-regional nation should not interfere with Beijing's internal affairs...

India - Japan strengthen cooperation on national defense

With China in view, on 01/25/2014, Japan and India's Prime Ministers affirmed some plans to "*further strengthen*" the cooperation on national defense between the two countries. The deal was reached during a summit meeting in New Delhi, between Indian Prime Minister Manmohan Singh and his Japanese counterpart Shinzo Abe visiting India for three days. Speaking after the annual summit conference with Manmohan Singh, Shinzo Abe declared: "*When a strong India and a mighty Japan come together, miraculous things could happen.*

According to the Japanese prime minister: *"Japan and India's relation has greater potential than any other bilateral relationship in the world"*.

In a joint communiqué released after the meeting, the two leaders of Japan and India *affirm the determination to strengthen even more cooperation bilateral on national defense"*. Singh and Abe also reiterated their determination to co-conduct Naval exercises on a *"regular basis with a higher frequency"*. Specifically, the Indian Prime Minister said that New Delhi and Tokyo have decided to conduct joint exercises at sea at least once a year. India and Japan have also participated in multi-national naval exercises (drills), called "Malabar", including the United States and Australia. As for Japan, on this trip to India, Prime Minister Abe promoted the sale of ShinMaywa US-2 seaplanes to the Indian Armed Forces. This is a specialized unarmed aircraft to use for the search and rescue operations, in line with the ban on arms exports that Tokyo has imposed on itself.

Speaking while in Tokyo on 5/28/2013, Prime Minister Manmohan Singh said that India and Japan have shared strong strategic interests in expanding cooperation on national security and in promoting regional stability. Singh also added: Ensuring the open free sea routes for maritime navigation is vital to the prosperity of the region, due to the dependence on imported oil resources from the Middle East.

"The relationship of India and Japan is important, not only because of the economic cooperation, but also because we view Japan as an essential natural partner in search of peace and stability in this vast area", emphasized Prime Minister Singh. "We share our concerns on the maritime security in dealing with the mutual challenges of energy security. Our strong economic ties need an open international trading system based on laws for development"

– **AUSTRALIA** The cooperation between the United States and Australia is very close. On 09/15/2011, in San Francisco, the United States and Australia held their annual dialogues at the high level of Secretaries of State and Defense. On this occasion the two countries updated the Joint Defense Agreement signed in 1951. This is a new field of cooperation: a war against information technology. According to analysts, this routine annual dialogue was to reconfirm the roles of Australia and the United States in the Asia-Pacific and the South Pacific regions, while China has expanded influences there. In a joint statement, Washington and Canberra officially urged India to advance its Look East policy. Australia and the United States also emphasized a need to establish an economic corridor, within the framework of the Trans-Pacific Partnership (TPP), without China. President Barack Obama made that announcement during his two-day visit to Australia, starting November 16, 2011. At a joint news conference with Obama, Australian Prime Minister Julia Gillard said that, at first, the United States would send 250 Marines to Northern Australia starting in mid-2012.

According to Australian Prime Minister Julia Gillard, sending US Marines to Northern Australia was to strengthen the military alliance between the two nations. The number of American soldiers gradually is increased from 250 to 2,500. At a press conference, President Obama emphasized the development of the US-Australia military cooperation. His visit to Asia-Pacific nations was to send out a clear signal to the allies in this region. He declared: *"This region has great strategic importance to us. Even though we have to approve many decisions on budgets in the U.S. However the US presence in Asia - Pacific is still my top priority".*

To protect the natural resources in the North, to monitor the unrest situation in the South China Sea, to increase the military presence on the Indian Ocean are the missions of the Australian Navy in the realignment strategy for national defense. The rising power of China is regarded as a threat. Reuters reported on Jan.30, 12 that the Australian strategists for national defense have urged the strengthening of military forces in northern Australia where, there are many natural resources, from metal to oil and gas. The Australian Navy needs to have more assault ships and amphibious ships. Australia should be ready to deal with the instability and challenges in Asia, at the same time to increase its "presence" in the Indian Ocean. To prepare a new defense strategy for the next two decades, Australia needs to acquire 12 submarines, three more destroyers with air strike capability, 100 stealth F35 fighters from the United States.

- **MALAYSIA:** It took a long time for Malaysia to officially participate in joint military exercises with the United States. On 06/23/2013, the US and Malaysian Navies had 10 days of the annual CARAT 2013 military exercises offshore of Malaysia. The highlight this year was to participate in the military exercises with the USS Freedom, an advanced Littoral Combat Ship. It is the first of four US coastal ships to be stationed at Singapore in few years to come. The CARAT Malaysia 2013 drills included military training activities on land and a four-day training exercise offshore mobilizing over 1,000 naval and US Marines. Besides the USS Freedom, there was the destroyer USS Curtis Wilbur, the landing craft USS Tortuga, the rescue ship USNS. Malaysia had the escort flagship KD Jebat, equipped with guided missiles, along with the maritime patrol ship KD Kelantan.

Malaysia is strengthening its military and receives the first nuclear submarine from the French port of Toulon. This submarine is named Tunku Abdul Rahman after Malaysia's first prime minister. Another Malaysian submarine, named after the second Prime Minister Tun Abdul Razak, is delivered at the Spanish port of Cartagena. Both are from the Scorpène class capable of attacking the opponents' ships and submarines, using rockets, torpedos and mines from a depth of 200m. Those two submarines significantly empower Malaysia in her capability to defend her territorial waters. In 2009, Malaysia purchased two Scorpène submarines. The two attack submarines were ordered from 2002 in a comprehensive modernization policy led by Deputy Prime Minister Najib Razak (who had been a defense minister and finance minister). He initiated military upgrades with a contract to buy 18 Russian Su-30 MKM fighters, eight Italian MB-339CD training aircrafts, four Airbus heavy transport aircrafts made by Group A400M in Europe, along with 48 PT-91M tanks from Poland, and various weapons for the air force, navy and infantry.

Malaysia announced the establishment of a new naval base in the coastal city of Bintulu, Sarawak state, less than 100 km from James Shoal, a submerged reef in dispute with China. The stationed troops at this base have the objective to protect the area and the national oil/gas reserves. There is a threat from China on James Shoal. Malaysia Defense minister Hishammudin Tun Hussein reveals the first marine battalion established by the military. This new unit basically has paratroopers, recruited from the army, air forces, and navy. According to Jane's Defence Weekly, Malaysia government has asked the United States to assist in forming Marines, mainly in training and equipment. Kuala Lumpur wants to buy some unused equipment of the U.S. military, after withdrawing from Afghanistan.

Malaysia also plans to buy US attack helicopters used at sea, such as the Apache, Super Cobra, or the Tiger type from Eurocopter Group. Kuala Lumpur also is in serach for buying a new amphibious ship to replace the burned one. According to Jane's Defense Weekly, Malaysia negotiates with France to buy a Mistral ship, and with South Korea to buy the landing crafts. The United States also wants to sell its Denver ship to Malaysia. Observers link Malaysia's decision to establish a new naval base in Bintulu and a Marine unit with a series of Chinese naval ships and coastal patrol ships entering Malaysian offshore waters on the east and part of Spratly Islands claimed by Malaysia.

- INDONESIA: The US-Indonesia bilateral relation was interrupted 12 years, due to the serious human rights violations by Indonesian special forces Kopassus under president Suharto regime. When the Suharto regime collapsed, their military relations had gradually improved since 1998. The breakthrough was in July 2010, when Panetta's predecessor, US Secretary of Defense Robert Gates, announced the resumption of cooperation with the Kopassus forces "*in a limited and gradual step-by-step manner*". U.S. Secretaty of Defense Leon Panetta's visit to Bali this time is to further strengthen the process of military cooperation with Indonesia, a nation considered essential for the US's policies in Asia.

Previously, the US-Indonesia military cooperation was primarily carried out at a high-rank level. Both sides have increased the exchange of personnel and experts, as well as organizing additional joint drills. In 08/26/2013, US Department of Defense provided eight Apache attack helicopters AH-64E to Indonesia. At a press conference in Jakarka, the US Secretary of Defense Chuck Hagel announced that action was taken to strengthen Indonesia's military capabilities.

The cooperation on national defense between South Korea and Indonesia was also established. South Korean Defense Minister Kim Kwan-jin will travel in September to Indonesia to discuss the sale of submarines worth 1.1 billion dollars. The submarines sold to Indonesia could accommodate 40 sailors and are equipped with eight weapons launchers capable of firing the torpedoes and guided missiles. Those submarines are powered by electricity and diesel and weigh 1400 tons. Paul Burton from the security intelligence group IHS Janes told Radio Australia that, in the situation of tense territorial disputes among regional nations, the acquisition of submarines has helped Indonesia to defend her territorial sovereignty and to protect its abundant natural resources in the South China Sea, especially the oil and gas. According to Burton, in 2013, China already has 60 submarines while Indonesia only has two old models. Therefore, Jakarta quickly strengthens its combat capabilities for its Navy. In fact, South Korea and Indonesia have cooperated closely in national defense. In May 2011, Indonesia purchased 16 jet training aircraft T50 Golden Eagle from Korea Aerospace Industry company. Indonesia was the first nation in Southeast Asia to acquire some submarines from the Soviet Union, as early as 1967. In 1978, Jakarta bought two diesel submarines from West German to replace the Soviet ships. In 2012, Indonesia's Defense Ministry announced that by 2020, Indonesia will have a submarine fleet of 12. It will take at least 12 submarines for

Indonesia to be able to control many strategic points and access routes in this island nation of a thousand islands.

The Indonesia Navy has orderd three South Korean U-209 submarines which will be delivered to Jakarta around 2015 - 2016. Besides, Indonesia is considering to acquire old submarines, Kilo-class, then refurhish them or buy new ones from South Korea. The current break in Australia-Indonesia relations could potentially lead to the end of the two countries' current defense agreement, commonly known as the Lombok Treaty. Signed in already purchased 2006, the treaty provides the basis for Australia-Indonesia defense cooperation. In addition to calling for regular consultations on defense and security issues, the treaty lists several specific areas of cooperation, including law enforcement cooperation against the smuggling of people, drugs, and arms, intelligence sharing, and counter-terrorism. After Yudhoyono's announcement that Indonesia is cutting off cooperation in many of these fields, it's unclear what the fate of the treaty will be.

-**THAILAND:** U.S. Secretaty of Defense Leon Panetta visited Thailand on 11/15/2012, to strengthen the military relations between the United States and regional countries. An unspoken goal is to increase military might, while China is on the rise. For Thailand military, the United States wants to restore a higher strategic dialogue, to enhance the contacts between the military units. In a joint statement after a meeting in Bangkok, the two allies pledged to upgrade the bilateral military alliance, to a level suitable for 21st century. This time, the United States pledged "*a long-term presence in the Asia-Pacific region*" and recognized Thailand as a "regional leader".

The US has organized dozens of drills with Bangkok, including the on-large-scale Cobra Gold military exercises. In 2011, the military exercises mobilized nearly 13,000 soldiers from 24 countries. In 2013, the United States gave to Thailand two battleships of Oliver Hazard Perry-class, produced in USA from 1975-2004. This battleship is 124 m long and weighs 4,100 tons. The maximum speed is 54 km/h and the ship has a range of 8,300 km and a crew of 176 people. These battleships are equipped with three types of anti-aircraft missiles, to destroy battleships and hunt submarines. This battleship is also equipped with 76mm cannon, 40mm machine gun, and a runway wide enough for two multi-purpose helicopters. In 2013, the United States gave an old warship to Thailand. The Royal Thailand Navy, in October 2013, announced the purchase of three submarines over 10 years. In the past, due to internal conflicts, the plan to purchase some old 206-A submarines from Germany failed.

- **SINGAPORE:** The US has established a support base here. There were 4 modern destroyers, as the Landing Craft Support ship (LCS), a type of coastal battleships frequently stationed here. In a statement released March 12, 2013, Singapore's Defense Minister Ng Eng Hen informed that he has reviewed and evaluated a project to replace the F-15 and F-16 fighter jets with a modern model F-35, manufactured by US American Lockheed Martin. The F-35 is viewed as a suitable aircraft for the needs of modernizing Singapore's fighter fleet. In an effort to modernize its best-equipped military in Southeast Asia, Singapore replaced the fleet of Challenger submarines from Sweden in the 1990s. Singapore has 5 attack submarines. Singapore buys one of the two submarines, Västergötland-class, (A17). In late November

2013, Singapore ordered two German 218 submarines, to replace the Challenger-class submarines.

- **BURMA:** Since Burma switched to a democracy, cooperation with the United States has been tightened since late 2011. Burma (Myanmar) has been supported by the US, in many ways, to escape China's influence. Burma turned cold to China. In the past, with a Burmese dictator, China see this nation as the back door to the Indian Ocean and Africa for natural resources. Now this door has been sealed. In June 2013, Burma discussed with Russia to buy two Kilo submarines. That same month, at a Pakistani naval base, 20 Burmese naval officers were trained to familiarize them with submarines. Burma wants to develop a submarine fleet before 2015.

Burma has been closer to India than China.

India rolled out the red carpet to welcome Burmese President Thein Sein officially visiting India on October 14, 2011 for four days. He held talks with Indian Prime Minister Manmohan Singh and the two countries issued a joint statement. 13 Burmese ministers accompanied President Thein Sein. This is an opportunity for New Delhi to have closer ties with its neighbor Burma having been heavily influenced by China, the main rival of India in the region. President Thein Sein spent two days visiting Buddhist sites, before arriving in New Delhi. When Burma president Thein Sein arrived in New Delhi, an Indian official Harsh Shringla said at a news conference: *"New Delhi is ready to help Naypidaw build a democracy that is still in its infancy"*. He also said a delegation of Burmese parliamentarians is invited to visit India. Thein Sein's visit is an opportunity for the two countries to cooperate for regional security. Burma has assured India that it does not allow anyone to use its territory for hostile anti-Indian activities.

Explanation of the two Maps:

1) The American map for strategic defense is to *"Reinforce Old Alliance and Strengthen New Cooperation"*, mentioned in the Obama letter. The main point of this strategy is that each nation must defend itself, in dealing with an aggression by expansionists. The United States will lead an effort to support but will not send troops to battles. Allied nations will rpovide support if war breakes out.

2) A map of the US Army stations and logistics locations of the US Military.

These two maps show the US circle formed to contain China.

Looking at these two maps, we could see Vietnam is not in the US Alliance for defense, thus it could be the target for American attack. The United States views Communist Vietnam as China's ally, who has contributed to China's expansionism. As a result, Nguyễn minh Triết asked for a battleship in an aid program, when he met US President George Bush at the White House. His request was denied. Reason? Because US laws **prohibit to aid lethal weapons to any Communist country**. US President Obama also rejected a request for military aids by Vietnamese president Trương Tấn Sang at a visit to the United States, although he implicitly appeared to be sided with US. A reason cited: **Vietnam has violated human rights**. If Vietnam plays an important role in the US policy to contain China, then US could immediately seize this rare opportunity for cooperation. The U.S. Administration could seek Congress' approval for an exemption from the provision of lethal weapon aids. It could be approved easily (case of president Nguyễn minh Triết). Or, US government does not cite the human rights issue to deny Sang' request. Also the way to receive a head of state by a US president is in line with this policy. The case of communist president Trương tấn Sang is a clear signal.

2.3.4.3.2. ECONOMIC & TRADE: THE TRANS-PACIFIC PARTNERSHIP (TPP) COOPERATION

This is a comprehensive agreement, including all major areas of free trade such as: the exchange of goods, origin of goods, compensation in trade, measures for food hygiene and safety, plants and animals, technical barriers of trade, service exchanges, intellectual properties, and procurement for the governments on the basis of competition. By 2015, all barriers of tariffs will be removed.. Throughout the negotiations before the signing of TPP, all trade partners agree on its goals. It is a coalition of economies -the developed and developing member countries- to become a unique free-trade community with no more tariff barriers. This trade community will consist of 800 million people holding 40% of the world's economy, including two key countries: the United States and Japan as the first and third economic superpowers in the world.

The United States also set conditions for the TPP partners:

- Compliance with regulations on trade, origin of goods, technical barriers and service exchanges. - TPP partners must respect the laws protecting the intellectual property rights, inventions and transparency in the competition policy.

Also within the TPP framework, the contracts signed with the governments must have the following provisions:

- To protect workers and protect the environment; jobs must conform to human dignity.

- Must encourage the free flow of information (newspaper, media). Although TPP is considered a successor of P4, it is actually initiated from the USA. TPP also aims at preventing China's military and economic expansion in the west of the Asia Pacific.

In short, the US set conditions that TPP partners must comply with the rules of trade, on the origin of goods, the technical barriers, and the exchange of services. TTP member nations must respect the laws protecting the intellectual property rights, protecting the invetionss, and must be transparent in the competition policy. There are tight rules and regulations for TPP partners. So China is pushed to a dilemma. If joining TPP, China's state-owned entreprise monopoly system based on free market economy can't exist and the regime will collapse. And if it stayed outside, it will be frustrated and craving the benefits, because the demand for goods and services to 800 million people in the region is irresistible. The Trans-Pacific Partnership Treaty governs and strictly prohibits what deceitful China is currently doing: commercial fraud, toxic foods, piracy of intellectual property rights, exploiting laborers, merchandises exported from forced labor camps, media censorship, information suppressed, human rights violation, people's properties confiscated, monopoly of state-owned enterprises, no competition, no privatization ... Through deceitful tactics by traditions, China has a trade surplus with the United States. In 2011, this surplus was reduced to 160 billion dollars (from 270 billion dollars in 2010). If TPP could fully function, merchandises and services in this bloc will freely circulate. That time, Chinese goods and services will not be exported massively anymore. It is especially hard for China to possibly penetrate this Trans-Pacific bloc and it will loose a market of 800 million people. This situation could put China in jeopardy: hundreds of millions of Chinese workers will be unemployed, while 300 millions Chinese farmers have migrated to cities to seek jobs. This trend has sparked social turmoils in China, possibly leading to the collapse of this communist regime.

RESPONSE FROM CHINA

Being aware of the US's large scale, decisive, and comprehensive plan in Asia, therefore, at the East Asia Summit in Bali, China's head of government Wen Jiabao 温家宝 admitted that he did not raise the issue of *"multilateral negotiations on the South China Sea"*. The day before, Wen arrogantly declared that "outside powers" should not interfere in the internal disputes between China and ASEAN countries. Wen added that it would be "impolite if not responding to the concerns of [his] neighbors regarding this request". That "request" was from 17 Heads of State attending the Conference, along with president Obama. They demanded a solution for South China Sea, by organizing the multilateral conferences, instead of unilateral talks as wanted by China then and now. Wen also asked to have a private meeting with US President Obama to talk on this matter. Why did Wen Jiabao have such a sudden toned-down change? At this Conference, there were 17 of 19 heads of State interested in an alliance with the United States, especially after Obama announced two moves: The United States has established a military base at Darwin to protect Southeast Asia, and Secretary of State Hillary Clinton was assigned to visit Burma. This is a gesture to extend friendship and alliance with this country.

2.3.4.3.3.   HOW WILL THE SITUATION DEVELOP?

Over the past few years, China has demonstrated aggressive behavior in its scheme of hegemony over the South China Sea. This is just the beginning. China has even prepared

another step in order to take over all of Asia. At the same time, China has asserted sovereignty over the entire western region of the Asia Pacific. China is trying to ward off the US influence by drawing a new map showing defense belts on the Pacific Ocean. China even dreams to reign over the entire world, and the United States is the key target to be eliminated . Becoming a great power at sea is an important step. Two important paths to help China carry out her conspiracy on supremacy in this period:

-     Burma with a military dictatorship is a gateway to the Indian Ocean, connecting the "String of Pearls" outlined in a network of Chinese military and commercial facilities along the sea lines.
-    The Socialist Republic of Vietnam with a Vietnamese Communist Party controlled by China, with puppets assisting Chinese masters to control South China Sea, a staging base from which Red China reigns over the etine region.
-

Now Burma is determined to advance to democracy. This nation has wisely realized that its military dictatorship causes political problems and wants to cooperate with the US. Burma is transforming strongly to advance toward democracy. Thus, a link in this pearl chain has broken. In addition, the United States is building a naval base on Cocos island, offshore in Indian Ocean. Thus, clearly, this path is out of reach for China for now.   -

-The second path: Vietnam society and Vietnam communist leaders are controlled by Red China, through numerous different tactics. It is hard for Vietnam to escape Beijing's strong grips. Vietnam is in a "half and half" position, struggled between China and the United States. However, because of personal interests, Vietnam leaders are still complying with China, the enemy of Vietnamese people throughout history. Vietnam leaders are local Sino hpuppets being charged by the foreigner China with helping her expansion policy. Vietnamese leaders continue to surrender land, sea, and islands to China — while many Southeast Asian countries have allied themselves with the United States to protect their sovereignty and independence, against the hegemony expansion.

Beijing is a cruel, sly and brutal enemy of peoples in the world. Will the Communist Party of Vietnam (CPV) have enough **courage and ability** to escape China's supreme domination at every levels of government — especially within the CPV structure? Beginning with its master Ho Chi Minh, communist cadres have worked hard through decades to establish the systematic communist structures all over Vietnam, at all levels, in many fields of national activities!

- The USA encirclement is growing stronger to control the expansionism of China. Another military base is established in Darwin, Northern Australia. Another point to emphasize in the area of logistics: The United States has the ability to set up large maritime logistics bases to support a distant war. The US Navy continues to improve with high technology incorporated in warships to replace the "giant" Navy crew, to make room for supplies in every aircraft carrier. In the early 1980's an aircraft carrier could utilize 16,000 sailors. In the middle of the next decade the number of sailors is reduced to 6,000, thanks to the advances in science and technology. Today, only 4,600 sailors are needed on the aircraft carrier with enhanced combat ability and more advanced weapons. An aircraft carrier is a huge city being active and floating on the sea for several months. The United States is moving forward to reuse the military base at Subic Bay. In August 2013, the Phillippines announced this news. The older US military bases in Asia were strengthened in South Korea, Japan, Taiwan, and Singapore. And the United States developes a new military base in Guam (1). The United States has transformed this Guam military base into a massive logistics base for the Naval Air Forces. Currently, the US has brought at least two of the most advanced striking aircraft squadrons to the garrison, not to mention the B-52 squadron available there.

This massive logistics base is an important source of supplies for military necessities and different types of weapons. Here I do not mention weapons of the United States SDI defense plan. This plan caused the collapse of the Soviet Union in the late 1980s. Dealing with the tremendous destructive power of the American military power in the coming years, which way will China go? Perhaps Chinese communist leaders will not give up their ambition on expansionism. They are choosing the "soft" path by showing off and continuing to strengthen their military power, including the "*digital information*" wars. They are waiting for opportunities even if it takes 50 years or more to defeat their top enemy: the United States! Will that burning ambition help them succeed? Or will it burn China down to destruction?

UPDATED: Feb. 16, 2020

President President Trump's policies to replace those of Pres. Obama:

1) **Withdrawl from TTP**

President Trump solves the economic and trade problems with China by means of **bilateral negotiations**. China for years has taken advantage of the multi- cooperation beween countries, especialy within WTO, having a surplus of $US 500 billion/ year in trade against the USA, on unequal basis, including theft of intellectual properties… This situation must be stopped. Tariffs is a means to deal with this problem, in order to require China to reduce the surplus. Both sides agreed on it a Phase I few monhs ago. Intellectual properties theft, environment, workers protection, restructure of Red China economy…..are also problems to be solved to satisfy Pres. Trump's dmandes.

2) " Free and Open Indo-Pacific Policiy" to replace President Obama 's " Pivot to Asia."

The new policy includes a) Promotion and establishment of rule of law, freedom of navigation and free trade; b) Pursuit of Economic prosperity and c) Commiitment for peace.

Militarily, the USA has esablished a Indo-Pacific command to deal with China expansion. Under President Trump policy, US activities performed in the South China Sea have increased to execise freedom of navigation. Ships of 7th fleet have navigated within 12 miles of Chinese artificial islands more often. A four Diamond Alliance composed of Japan, Australia, India and the USA is created, strongly supported by Great Britain, France and others to contain a dangerous China whose expansionist activity threatens to overturn a basic tennet of the international order: the freedom of navigation on the sea. Japan and India play an important role in this strategy. A soutce from the US congress said that a budget for the operation would be $20.B in the next five years.

(1) The map contains stars of US encirclement locations to eliminate two Chinese defense lines in the Pacific: a) "String of islands" defense line; and 'distant defense" line, b.) A ' string of pearls;' strategy (along the coast South East Asian countries and Indian Ocean to Djibouti (Africa).

2.4. CHINA NEW MILITARY BASE SYSTEM IN THE SPRATLY ARCHIPELAGO

DECLARATION

OF

COMMITTEE ON PROTECTION OF TERRITORIAL INTEGRITY OF VIETNAM

ON

A NEW CHINESE NAVAL BASE SYTEM IN THE SPRATLY ARCHIPELAGO & THE COMMUNIST PARTY OF VIETNAM (CPV)

Nguyen van Canh*.
January 22, 2015

For the past decades, China has gradually asserted her sovereignty over the East Sea or Bien Dong of Vietnam (South China Sea). In 1988, she sent her naval forces to take six reefs in Spratlys. Then she built fortified structures on them to assert her sovereignty. In June 2007, she re-drew a U-shape map covering 80% of the Bien Dong area, claiming that it is hers. In Nov 2007, she established the 三沙 Sansha District in Woody island of the Paracel Archipelago (Paracels) to administer Spratlys and Paracels of Vietnam.

This is an act to officially annex them to China's territory.

In front of the flagrant infringement on the Vietnamese waters by China, the CPV leaders showed little interest in protection of their national territory.

Photo courtesy of Dũng Đô Thị's blog. (Trà Mi, RFA, June 16, 2008) -- About 50,000 students in Hanoi protested the Invasion

No positive action was taken to defend it. On the contrary, they mobilized the entire governmtal machinery (including police, court, prison house, military personnel, with support of local communist party chapters) to suppress protests of students who took to the street in Hanoi and Saigon against Red China's invasion.

The more concessions they made to the Communist Party of China (CPC) leaders, the more the latter increased their activities to assert their claims of sovereignty over Bien Dong Last May (2014) the Chinese Naval Base System (NBS) was established as a another step for China to achieve her goal: real and only owner of the entire waters.

2.4.1. CHINA'S SCHEME OF EXPANSION.

early morning, March 14th 1988

Early in May 2014, international media spread news warning that Red China was constructing a huge man-made island on the Johnson South Reef (JSR) to transform the whole reef into a naval base, with the purpose to control the Asian waters.

The JSR belongs to Vietnam. In March 1988, China sent four destroyers of her naval forces from Hainan to take it, killing some 64 unarmed Vietnamese Communist soldiers while swimming and carrying supplies to their comrades stationing there to defend the reef. It is worth saying that after having used heavy weapons to attack the swimmers; Chinese came in on PT boats, looking for those who were still alive to kill them with small guns.

37mm anti-aircraft gun fired at unarmed Vietnamese sailors and sappers

The JSR is composed of coral, sitting on top of the Sin Cowe chain to the South West, and is one of the six islands that China plundered from Vietnam on March 14. This area is located on the south side of Spratlys.

On May 5, 2014, China Global Times "semi-secretly" disclosed that "China has created a man-made island that 'could be JSR' in the Spratlys on which there are a naval airport and a seaport to accommodate China's ships that will be used for 'swift response' in case of war." Later, another medium in China said that the JSR Island is a station that provides supplies to fishermen only. Offices, vacation houses and farms and a harbor large enough to serve ships of up to 5000 tons will also be built.

On June 7, 2014 South China Morning Post (SCMP) reported that China has turned the JSR into a giant man-made island. On it, the naval airport, separate seaports for military and civilian ships are built. Houses for civilians, installations for tourism are also projected. Dredgers are sucking sand from the bottom of the sea for that purpose.

On May 13, 2015, the Filipino Ministry for Foreign Affairs denounced, "China is building a man-made island named JSR, which includes a military airport"

In response to the Filipino denunciation, on May 15, 2014, Chinese Foreign Ministry Spokesperson Hua Chunying in Peking replied that "*China has an undisputed sovereignty over the region that includes JSR; therefore, China has a right to build whatever she wants.*"

000

China has constructed another man-made island in the Fiery Cross Reef (FCR) area. FCR is on the West of JSR. On January 2015, Gen Gregorio Catapang Jr, Chief of General Staff of the Filipino Armed Forces stated: *"About 50% of the man made island has been completed…It is built on the reef [FRC] that China took from Vietnam in 1988…This is a*

serious concern, because it could be used for another purpose than peace…."

Picture: Chinese Military Base in Woody; Military Headquarter on Woody

A Filipino website entitled Rappler on Jan. 6, 2015 quoted a source from the Filipino armed forces as saying that the runway being built on the Fiery Cross is 2000 meters long and will be completed by the year end.

In November 2014, IHS Jane Review published a satellite photo showing a runway and a seaport on the reclaimed island of which the length is 3 km and the width is 300 m.

To a Filipino military expert, it is no doubt that the runway will be used for Chinese military jets that help to put the entire region under her control, while the seaport is to accommodate

supplies ships and other vessels for China to implement her plans of expansion.

The man made JSR and FCR islands in NBS come into existence to address Chinese demands for territorial expansion to the South.

The Chinese naval base established on Woody island in Paracels being served as a command headquarter for the entire region has **limitations** and can't do the job as China intends. She needs to build naval bases further south.

As a consequence, the six reefs that China took from Viet Nain 1988 are her choice.

Limitations 1: The distance from Woody to JSR is 800 km. And the distance between Woody and Barque Canada Shoal sitting in the South most point of Spratlys at the 3rd parallel is 1,780 km. Therefore, China cannot control the ASEAN waters and further South.

Limitation 2: The size of Woody Island is too small to be used as a naval base. The Woody area is 1.3 to 2 square kilometers, while the giant JSR base upon completion will be as large as the U.S. Diego Marcia naval base in the Indian Ocean.

Limitation 3: China's ambitions are very high. Her scheme is to annex the entire Asia into her territory. Conquering Asia is just one step before moving forward to Africa and other continents. Therefore a larger base is needed.

After JSR base is hooked up with Fiery Cross, which is being built, and with others, the base system will become a chain of fortified outposts that spread over 44 kilometers.

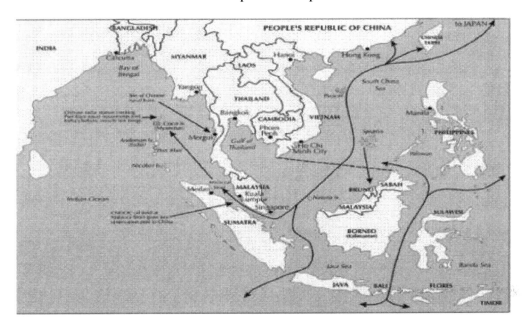

At the present times, 3 or 4 fortified structures have been built on the Mischiefs reef, which is on the East of JSR. Among them, some are seen as big as a colossal hotels erected out of the water. The chain of fortified outposts will support those on Mischiefs to control the water lanes, especially to monitor the US 7th fleet military ships that travel from the Indian Ocean through Malacca to East Asia along the West coast of the Philippines.

MAP SHOWING CHINA's NEW NAVAL BASE SYSTEM (NBS)

The NBS is composed of four man-made islands sitting on the following reefs: 1) Subi Reef (*Đá Xu Bi*); 2) Mischiefs (*Vành Khăn*); 3) Fiery Cross Reef (*Bãi Đá Chữ Thập*); 4) Cuarteron Reef (*Bãi Đá Châu Viên*).

China is reclaiming the islands and build naval bases on them, with airstrips for military jets with hangars, seaports for naval ships, barracks for soldiers, supply facilities…

This is a huge complex stretching over 80 nautical miles from North to South and about 150 miles, East-West. In the middle of the area is the Union Banks where a system of 4 other reefs lies and China has constructed naval fortresses on them.

EAST SEA

(SOUTH CHINA SEA)

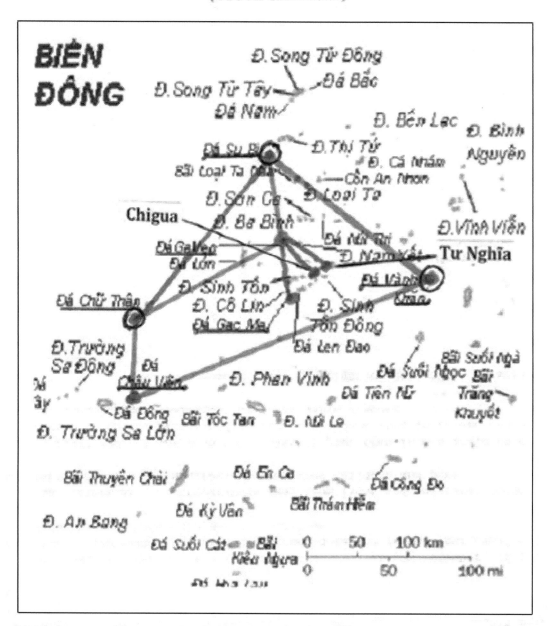

HỆ THỐNG CĂN CỨ HẢI QUÂN TC.
1) Đá Gaven (Gaven Reef): 10° 12' N 114° 14' E; 2) Ến Đất (Eldad Reef) : 10° 21' N 114° 42' E;
3) Đá Vành Khăn (Mischief Reef): 09°58'N 115° 42' E; 4) Đá Châu Viên (Cuarteron Reef): 08°50'N
112°47' E; 5) Đá Chữ Thập (Fiery Cross Reef): 09°38' N 112°57'. 6) Chuỗi đảo Quần Tụ (Union
Banks)

442

UNION BANKS

SERIES OF ISLANDS GROUP

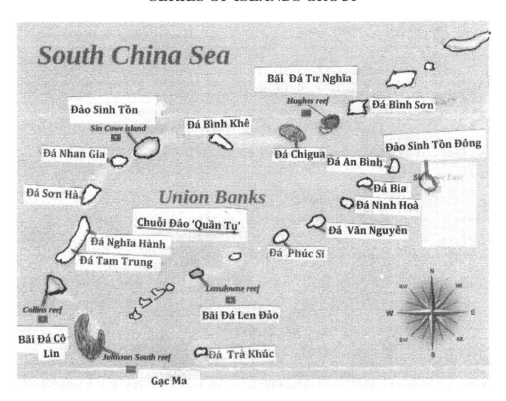

SERIES OF ISLANDS GROUP

Đá Gạc Ma (Johnson South Reef): 09'43' N 114' 17' E; Đá Cô lin (Johnson North or Collins Reef): 09'45' N 114' 14 E; Đảo Sinh Tồn (Sin Cowe Island): 09'51' N 114' 22' E; Đá Chigua (Kennan Reef): 09'55'N 114'29'E; Đá Tư Nghĩa (Hughes Reef): 09'55'N 114' 30' E; Đảo Sinh Tồn Đông (Sin Cowe East Island): 09'55'N 114'33'E. Đá Len Đảo (Lansdowne Reef): 09'46'N 114'22'E.

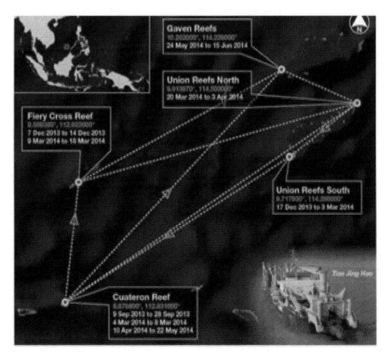

CHINESE RECLAIMING THE FIVE REEFS TAKEN FROM VIETNAM

At least Tian Jiang Hao, Nina Hai Tao and a third dredger operated from September, 2013 to June 14 between 5 above reefs, escorted by an war ship of Mien Duong type, armed with missiles and others including a landing craft for protection.

Cuarteron Reef   9-28 September 2013, 4-8 March 2014, 10 April to 22 May 2014

Union Reefs South   17 December 2013 to 3 March 2014

Union Reefs North   20 March to 3 April 2014

Fiery Cross Reef   7-14 December 2013 and 9-17 March 2014

Gaven Reefs   24 May to 15 June 2014

Tian Jian Hao, giant dredging vessel of China, 127 meters long. It has the capacity to perform soil suction from the deep sea. It can suck 4,500 tons of sand per hour. Tian Jian Hao is the largest of the three dredgers operating in the area.

One of the vessels, Giang vệ type, armed with missiles for protection of construction with landing crafts for supplies present at the sites of construction.

THREATS POSED TO ASEAN COUNTRIES AND THE WORLD.

Rolio Golez, Filipino former National Security Advisor warned that the military base that China is building on JSR island will be a great threat to all Asian and Pacific countries. On October 6, 2014, Channel ANC of the Filipino TV remarked "the whole South East Asia will be in danger after the Chinese Communist Government completes the illegal construction of the military base on JSR island in Spratlys with an airstrip. JSR belongs to Vietnam. Mr. Golez confirmed that the Chinese Communist Government wants to change the balance of power in South East Asia through the construction of the new naval base.

"The Chinese Communist Government wants consolidate its power on the South China Sea and turn it into its own lake. They assert that they own the U-shape water territory that she drew in 2007. They want to change the power, since the U.S. is playing a dominant role there. It begins to challenge the U.S. The JSR military base will be used to resupply and support their destroyers. In addition, one can see the runway with the length of 1.6 kilometers. This is very dangerous because this is a base for military aircrafts, like the Chinese aircraft J-11 that could operate as far as 3,200 kilometers. JSR island is the central point and the diameter of the area is more than 1,600 kilometers. Thus the neighboring countries in Asia are within their range of operation. Therefore, all of our military bases will be threatened".

Former ambassador of Philippines, Paranaque, noted that if the military base is completed, Chinese's jet planes will easily access to the Philippines, Vietnam, and part of Malaysia within 1,000 miles. Chinese airstrip will help Chinese jets to control the entire region.

2.4.2. CHINESE EXPANSIONISM AND THE COMMUNIST PARTY OF VIETNAM (CPV)

For over the past decades, China'claim in the disputed area has been more and more assertive: denial to Vietnamese fishermen to work in their traditional seas by means of 'killing, arrest and imprisonment for violations of Chinese waters'; Chinese naval ships sinking their boats; Chinese sea surveillance ships cutting off cables of Vietnamese seismic research ships on Vietnam' self continents; putting pressure on Vietnamese authorities to arrest and imprison those students who call for defending Paracels and Spratlys or who protest against China's activities in assert sovereignty over the islands, threatening and demanding foreign oil corporations that are exploiting oil in the Vietnamese waters to leave.

On May 1, 2014, China moved to take a bolder action: placing by surprise a huge mobile Oil Rig HD-981, in the shelf-continent of Vietnam for exploration. The Oil Rig was escorted by a fleet at first of some 90 ships of all types including four warships armed with missiles, a number of sea surveillance ships, sea police ships ...., and later on the number of vessels increased to 135. When the rig moved in, the Chinese gave a warning to Vietnamese sea police to leave the area and the limit was 3 miles away from the rig. General Phung quang Thanh, Defense Minister responding to their demands immediately gave order to sea police units to withdraw from the site. Vietnamese police ships then operated far outside from the oil rig and watched. However some of their ships were sunk by Chinese vessels though they were about 10 miles away. Others were damaged when hit by Chinese vessels. Total loss was 24 ships. Some members of the police forces were killed, and others got injuries.

China claimed that the oil rig operated in her waters.

This was a provocation and real invasion by forces.

On the part of the Vietnamese government, no positive concrete measures were taken to defend the territory. Indignant before the government's inaction against the foreign aggressors, and also afraid of more territorial concessions made to China as it happened in the past, about fifty thousand Vietnamese gathered in Bình Dương in a protest against the aggression. Some factories owned by Chinese were burned down or destroyed. In Hà Tĩnh, protestors became violent. Two Chinese workers were killed, and four got injuries.

The fact that China moved the oil rig to the Vietnamese waters put the CPV leaders in an awkward position: on one hand, they could not resist the Vietnamese people's demand to protect the national territory against the invaders; on the other, they were under strong pressure from China to make more concessions by accepting the fact that HD 981 operated in the waters that China claimed theirs. Under the circumstances, the most important thing for the CPV leaders is to find a way to help ease the boiling situation inside Vietnam:

On May 11, at an ASEAN meeting in Myanmar SRV Prime Minister Nguyen tan Dung claimed that China's action constitutes a gross danger to the safety and freedom of maritime movement through the South China Sea. On 5/21/2014, he came to Manila, talked about a legal measure with Filipino President Aquino who filed a lawsuit against China for violations of the Filipino waters. The discussion which was widely published by Vietnamese media made people think that Dung was considering a legal action to stop China's invasion. But actually it is not true. It is only a kind of old tactics that he has used to temporarily ease the tension inside the country.

Why have the CPV leaders adopted a policy of accommodation to China's demand on territory, instead of looking for ways to defend it? Why did they keep quiet and pretend not to know any thing about the fact that since 2013, China openly built a man made island on JSR with giant dredgers moving back and forth for a long period of times in Spratlys, while the Filipino government voiced against China's expansionism on their behalf?

The answer would be as follows:

Back in April 2011, when Gen. Guo Boxiong, vice chairman of the Communist Party of China (CPC) Military Central Commission, came to Hanoi and met with CPV leaders: Secretary General Nguyen phu Trong, Premier Nguyen tan Dung, Chief of State Nguyen minh Triet, …. Leaders of both parties agreed on a number of principles based on which both sides use to 'solve the conflict problems' related to South China Sea:

1) **Bilateral and friendly consultation** to find a solution to the conflict;

2) **Not allowing any third country** to intervene in solving the Spratlys problems;

3) **Guiding public opinions** and being alert about not making statements or taking any actions that could lead to damage of friendship or loss of trust of the people of the two countries.

In June of the same year, these points was officially ratified into *"a Mutual Agreement On The Solution To The Disputes In South China Sea"* signed in Beijing by Ho xuan Son, Deputy Minister of the Socialist Republic of Vietnam Ministry of Foreign Affairs and his Chinese counterpart, Cui Tankai under the 'supervision" of Dai Bingguo, Chinese Vice Premier in charge of foreign affairs.

The spirit of Agreement shows that the CPV and CPC are not on an equal footing. It looks like a relationship between a 'master' and a 'servant', or that between a Kingdom and a client state in the feudal times:

In the Agreement, there is a one way order from China, and Vietnam is to carry it out, even with no rights to complaints.

China placed its HD 981 in the Vietnamese waters off the Quang Ngai coast, but claimed that it sits in her waters. Of course, Vietnam had not been consulted about it. Also, after the oil rig had been in place and under the pressure from Vietnamese people, Nguyen phu Trong asked to see Xi Jinping, his request was turned down. The construction of 14 projects on the five reefs in Spratlys taken from Vietnam has been going on for more than two years, probably without the CPV's consent.

In the agreement, the Chinese side has all privileges and rights, but no duties while Vietnam is not allowed, or forbidden even to complain: 'she can't make statements that could cause a loss of trust in China.'

China thought that the Communist Party of Vietnam leaders have been tightly bound by the agreement, and that in the previous years they had endeavored to carry out what they have committed themselves to do and that they were able to successfully control the situation inside and also outside Vietnam. **A policeman in civilian clothes tortured a student who protested against China in Saigon for her aggression.**

In fact inside the country, public opinion has been strictly controlled by the CPV to satisfy Beijing's demands. Leninist techniques have been fully used to make opposition to China

shattered. Those who actively and strongly protest against China about her move to assert sovereignty are either isolated or imprisoned. Most of them are brutally or ferociously treated. Voices that call for protection of Paracels and Spratlys are suffocated. Even, those who hold a sign with a slogan *"Paracels & Spratlys belong to Vietnam"* are in jail. Viet Khang, a young artist, who just composed a short anti- Chinese song some 3 years ago, was arrested and until now his whereabouts is unknown.

The CPV leaders have successfully mobilized the entire machinery of government with the local party cells 's support (police, court, prison house, local party cell, military personnel) in maintaining 'public order' as stipulated in the Agreement.

Internationally, the CPV leaders did not make any statement or take any action that could "harm the good relationship with China": no comments/ opinion/ action that could damage it. Their fishermen have continuously been brutally harassed. Some of them were killed. Many others were arrested and jailed for violations of the Chinese waters though they worked in the waters of Vietnam. In many instances, their wooden boats were hit and sunk by Chinese Naval vessels. The CPV official mass media only stated that it was 'tầu lạ', a 'strange ship' that did it. They dared not point the fingers at Chinese naval ships, though victims knew their identities. All the 'tầu lạ' left the scenes without rescuing victims while in the water. Therefore, no countries could blame Chinese for their illegal and <u>immoral</u> acts. Also, adhering to the Agreement, SRV did not take a legal action against the oilrig HD-981 though it operated illegally in the Vietnamese water. Or, the CPV keeps silence while the CPC Navy builds man made islands in Spratlys.

China fell satisfied with what the CPV had done.

Believing in the satisfactory results that the CPV leaders have got in terms of carrying out duties prescribed in the Mutual Agreement, China moved a bolder step forward to assert her sovereignty over Bien Dong: placing the HD 981 in the Vietnamese waters in May. If this is successful, the entire South China Sea becomes Chinese territory quickly.

The fact that Nguyen tan Dung's declarations in Myanmar and Manila were contrary to the June. 2011 agreement, made China think that the CPV leaders tried to escape her control.

As a consequence, China sent Yang Jiechi Vice Premier in charge of foreign affairs to Vietnam on June 30, 2014.

What did Yang tell Nguyen phu Trong, Nguyen tan Dung, Truong tan Sang was not disclosed? However, two days later when he was back in Beijing, it was reported that he bluntly criticized the CPV leaders for not abiding the principles in the agreement that both Ministries of foreign affairs signed in June 2011.

It was also reported that Yang told Chinese media that he went to Hanoi to bring "a prodigal/lost child back to his motherland", and that the CPV leaders now must fully carry out **four DON'Ts** :

1). Don't ever underestimate China's strong and unswerving determination and her capabilities of protection of sovereignty over Spratlys (of course by force).

2). Don't ever use records or data that Vietnam claims they are historical documents to assert 'historic' sovereignty over Spratlys. If so, it would create a misunderstanding to the world communities and also to the Vietnamese people about this matter.

3). Don't bring in any third country that would intervene in this matter.

4). Don't go off track from an ever-good relationship with China.

It is humiliating!

Surprisingly the four DON'Ts that Yang told the Vietnamese communist leaders to do have highly been respected since then.

The Chinese goals? Vietnam leaders could drag this matter as long as possible, so China could have times to finish building Naval Base System quietly and successfully.

000

In summary, it is no surprise that the CPV leaders have tried to comply with the above commitments they have made under the June. 2011 Agreement. This is an act of connivance on part of the CPV leaders in the Chinese scheme of expansion in South China Sea. As an owner, they keep silence or do not take any action, such as call for help while the powerful aggressors accelerate the construction of the base system, no country could intervene. When the base becomes a "*fait accomplit*", no one can revert the situation. It is no doubt that the JSR, FCR and other man-made islands in the Chinese NBS will be complete in few years. It is then a home for China's war ships, jets, arsenals…Once Chinese troops and their equipment are deployed there, the CPV leaders will be told to withdraw their troops from islands and reefs

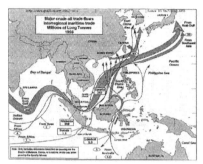 that they have occupied and hand them to China. The CPV leaders would not dare do so because they would be blamed of 'selling Bien Dong to foreign aggressors'. And they would do nothing, but allow Chinese Navy to send in warships to kill those soldiers who were told to station there to defend "the country". It will be the same way that the CPV leaders did to their 64 Vietnamese soldiers in 1988 in Johnson South Reef area. The very issue is now raised by People's Army Brigadier General Le ma Lương, Director of the Military History Museum in Hanoi by disclosing that "the soldiers were not allowed to open fires when Chinese moved in", when he talked in a public meeting in Hanoi last year. Then no battle occurred at all. However, the CPV media until now has publicized that they lost a "battle" while defending the Johnson South Reef and others. The Communist Party of Vietnam leaders will again sacrifice their men in order to protect interests granted them by Chinese.

The outposts built on reefs that sit within or near the NBS perimeter are Nam Yết (Namyit Island), Đảo Sinh Tồn (Sin Cowe Island), Đảo Trường Sa (Spratly Island), Đá Tây (West Reef), Collins, Lansdowne… are targets for the scheme.

This is the way the CPV transfers the ownership of Spratlys to China. After it has belonged to China, the NBS would then poses a serious danger to the security of all countries in Southeast Asia and then all other countries in the world.

First, the Chinese scheme would directly neutralize the call for freedom of maritime and aerial movements voiced by US Defense Secretary Robert Gates 4 years ago in Shangri-La. Secretary Gates also stated that the US would defend it and also protect American oil companies doing exploitation oil in South China Sea. Ships or airplanes then could not enter or go through Bien Dong or South China Sea to the North East of Asia from Malacca without China's permission because it is 'Chinese waters'. And the US national interest in Bien Dong declared by Secretary of State Hilary Clinton at the same time in Hanoi is in jeopardy.

Second, the security of all South East Asia countries will be seriously threatened.

With the USA, the value of merchandises that went through Malacca to Bien Dong in 2010 was US $1,300 billions. Her economic interests will be in trouble, while total values of all countries combined were 5,000 billions.

2.4.3. PICTURES AND NOTES

1). GAVEN REEF *(dá Ga Ven)*

According to the AISLive data, the dredger has been at Gaven Reefs since 24 May 2014. This corroborates background briefings by Philippine officials, who have told IHS Jane's that three dredgers - including Tian Jing Hao and another called Nina Hai Tuo - are at Gaven Reef along with a large tugboat.

The CHINESE GOVERNMENT INSTITUTE (CGI) plans show a runway, hangars for fast jets, a port, wind turbines, and greenhouses. (China State Shipbuilding Corporation. James Hardy, London and Krispen Atkinson & Richard Hurley, London and Michael Cohen, Manila-IHS Jane's Defense Weekly, 20 June 2014.)

2). JOHNSON SOUTH REEF (đá Gạc Ma)

A seaport that can serve ships of up to 5,000 tons, will provide supplies and support to destroyers, and a runway 1.6 km long for J-11 with a range of operation of 3000 km. Satellite photos show that infrastructure has been built: a pier, roads, houses, rows of coconut trees. Its area is 30 hectares. The distance from JSR to Vietnam is 800km, to Philippines is 850 km and to Malacca Strait is 1000km.

EXISTING FORTIFIED STRUCTURES

9°42' 50.27" N 114° 17' 9.59" E 9 43 N 114° 17 E

3). CHIGUA/KENNAN REEF (đá Ken Nan/ Chigua)

The military fortified structures have existed since 1990's. On the roof of the white building, there are two satellite antennas, diameter of 2.5 meters, and 2.4 meters high 09 55 N 114 29 E.

4). FIERY CROSS REEF (*Bãi Đá Chữ Thập*)

The Reef is 14 miles long (almost 26 km), 4 miles wide (7.4 km), lying along the Northeast-Southwest axis. Upon completion, the man made island will be twice as large as the US Diego Garcia in Indian Ocean. The area of the island is 44 km^2

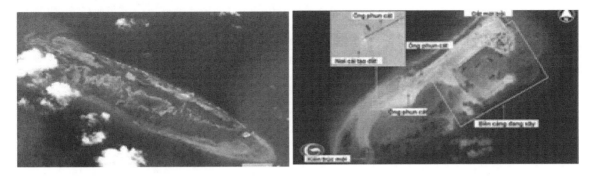

In Nov. 2014, HIS Jane Defense Magazine released a satellite photo showing an airstrip and a seaport. It is 3 km long and 300 wide.

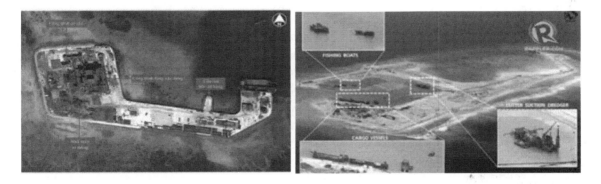

Airbus Defense & Space's satellite photo taken on November 14, 2014 shows that this man made island in the Fiery Cross area is much larger that Itu Aba presently occupied by Taiwan.

EXISTING FORTIFIED STRUCTURES on FERRY CROSS REEF

Headquarters

Supplies Facility: Antenna with 70-73 MHZ frequency system can operate within 180km radius. Two poles for antennas seen on top of building with equipment equivalent to RW2-1 of American destroyers.

<u>Missile launching Platform</u>, 116 meters x 96 meters, to be used as base for the missile launchers to shoot down the U.S.satellites. Antenna for communication on top of building

Office

Under Construction

5). CUARTERON REEF (*Đá Châu Viên*)

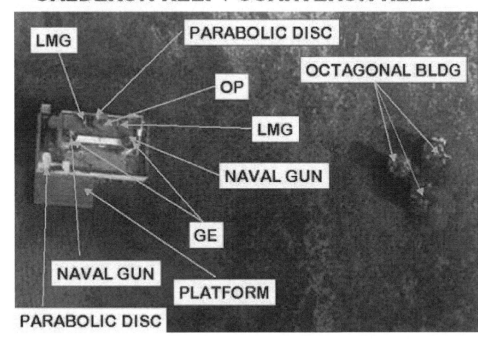

CALDERON REEF / CUARTERON REEF

LMG: Light Machine Gun

GE: Gun Emplacement

OP: Observation Post

6). MISCHIEF REEF (Đá Vành Khăn)

7. SUBI REEF (Đá Xu Bi)

DECLARATION

On behalf of peace, WE, the Committee

a) Condemn the Communist Party of Vietnam leaders for serving the CPC leaders as lackeys that contribute to the Chinese scheme of expansion and conniving with them in conquering SEA countries including Vietnam.

b) Demand the Communist Party of Vietnam leaders to withdraw from a role of a puppet which provides service that benefits the enemy of the Vietnamese people and of the peace loving people throughout the world.

c) Condemn the Communist Party of China leaders for their scheme of expansion. They aim at conquering other countries by force, annexing them to the territory of China. Their ambitions are a cause of inability to the region and to the world.

d) Call for an international involvement in stopping China's illegal activities. In order to protect the countries in Southeast Asia from being dominated by the expansionist 's ambitions, a strong, positive and urgent support from the whole world for this cause is needed.

e) Call on the US government and its peace loving people to have a clear-cut and aggressive determination to deal with the fact that China has moved steadily forward to swallow Asia and then later on the whole world. The only country in the entire world that is capable of dealing with this situation is the United States of America.

photo Vo Thieu

Together with other former Vietnamese Police Officers in uniform on the platform, Major Thai van Hoa reads the Proclamation of the Committee on Protection on Territorial

Integrity of Vietnam, calling President Barack Obama to reconsider his conduct of war to deal with the enemy who is waging a multifaceted warfare against the USA. America needs a comprehensive plan action

President Obama policy *of* "**strengthening old alliances and forging new partnership to meet common challenges**" and **redeployment of military forces** throughout Asia and Australia, also including TPP is absolutely necessary but not adequate. The reason is that he is thinking of building up military strength to meet challenges in a **conventional warfare**. Because of this, SOUTH CHINA SEA IS ALMOST BEING IN THE COMMUNIST PARTY OF CHINA'S HAND.

If this happens, the legitimate US interests as stated by Secretary of Defense Robert Gates and Secretary of State Hilary Clinton will be neutralized. And the trouble for America and the world would begin from this point. Remember that the potential enemy of America has a mind of a fox that is playing a multifaceted war game, using all possible means, including immoral ones. A honest Gentleman 'America' can't deal with it efficiently.

The strategy we need is an effective comprehensive plan of action to radically eradicate the roots of the problem.

Made in California January 22, 2015

Nguyen van Canh

REFERENCES:

Nguyen van Canh "*Paracels & Spratlys and National Sovereignty*", Center for Vietnam Studies, 5th edition, 2014; and "*Territorial Sovereignty and Chinese Expansionism*", Center for Vietnam Studies.

Photo Vo Thieu

460

ADDITIONAL MATERIALS RE. THE COMMITTEE 's DECLARATION

Professor Canh 'criticizes' President Obama for conduct of the war against Red China that poses a threat to the world and America. He deploys political and military forces in a conventional way to face the enemy, while the latter wages a multifaceted warfare. Any thing available could be used to attack and defeat this country, including immoral ones. This enemy has a mind of a " fox" that lies still, waits for an opportunity to suddenly stab his adversary at the back. A "Gentleman America" can't win this war.

In a solemn ceremony of very large Vietanmese Community gathering organized in Westminster, CA on January 27, 2015, former Major Thai van Hoa read the Committee's Call upon Preident Obama to re-consider his concept in conduct of .the war aginst Red China.

The following is President Obama answers:

THE WHITE HOUSE

WASHINGTON

May 20, 2015

Nguyen van Canh
Redwood City, California

Dear Nguyen van Canh:

Thank you for writing. I have heard from many Americans about United States-China relations, and I appreciate your perspective.

I believe there is much to be gained from a closer working relationship with China. Indeed there are very few global challenges, if any, we can address effectively without China's active cooperation. They are a global economic power, and engagement with China's government is an important step in recovering from the financial crisis that devastated economies around the world. Both of our nations seek to lay a foundation for sustainable growth and lasting prosperity.

My Administration is also working with China on a number of security issues, including stopping North Korea's nuclear program, rolling back the advance of extremists in Pakistan, and ending the humanitarian crisis in Darfur. The United States and China share common interests on a host of issues—including energy security and climate change, food safety and public health, and nuclear non-proliferation and counter-terrorism. We want to work with them to address these issues in the years ahead.

Improved relations with China will require candor and open discussion about those issues on which we may disagree. We must address human rights, democracy, and free speech. We must also work to ensure that our nations play by the rules in open and transparent economic competition. These important matters will be essential elements of our ongoing dialogue with China.

Thank you, again, for writing. For more information on my foreign policy agenda, I encourage you to visit www.WhiteHouse.gov/Issues/Foreign-Policy.

Sincerely,

461

EAST SEA
(SOUTH CHINA SEA)

HỆ THỐNG CĂN CỨ HẢI QUÂN TC.
1) Đá Gaven (Gaven Reef): 10° 12' N 114° 14' E; 2) Én Đất (Eldad Reef) : 10° 21' N 114° 42' E;
3) Đá Vành Khăn (Mischief Reef): 09°58'N 115° 42' E; 4) Đá Châu Viên (Cuarteron Reef): 08°50'N
112'47' E; 5) Đá Chữ Thập (Fiery Cross Reef): 09°38' N 112°57'. 6) Chuỗi đảo Quần Tụ (Union
Banks)

China naval bases on the Spratly Archipelago include eight man-made islands. There are many fortified structures built for military purposes, such as airports, hangars, warehouses for military supplies, facilities to install air defense weapons, rockets, barracks for the stationed troops, hospitals and military seaports...

The following are eight reefs with updated photos and information.

Those are 1) Subi; 2) Gaven; 3) Hughes Reef (*Tư Nghĩa*); 4) Chigua or Kennan; 5) Mischief (*Vành Khăn*); 6) South Johnson Reef (Gạc Ma); 7) Fiery Cross Reef (*Đá Chữ* Thập); and 8) Cuarteron Reef (*Đá Châu viên*).

The three largest Chinese military bases are Subi, Mischief and Fiery Cross, forming a triangular belt to control the entire South China Sea. Subi is at top. Each military base has a runway of 3,000 m long for large aircraft to take-off and land, and a wide seaport with a long dock for large Chinese Navy ships. These three military bases cover the entire Spratly (*Trường* Sa) region of Vietnam. In the middle are Johnson South Reef, Chigua and Hughes Reef. Gaven is on North West. On the South is the Cuarteron Reef (Châu Viên). This system of eight military bases is capable of controlling the entire Spratly Archipelago and posing threats to the entire region. By year-end 2017, communist China had already established the communication facilities, radar, and rocket storage for military purposes, and built other essential infrastructures.

Later at appropriate times, China would only need to demand the Vietnamese Navy to withdraw from some currently occupied islands. Then China completes her occupation of South China Sea.

Note: On new maps recently distributed by China, Vietnamese names are already erased.

1. SUBI REEF (ĐÁ XU BI) Coordinates: 10.9133°N 114.062°E

Subi is an underwater coral reef. It is 57 km in length and 35 km in width. Before the renovation in 2014, Subi was a naval base with a fortified structure and a dock capable of accommodating 160 soldiers. It had an on-site helipad, equipped with 37mm anti-aircraft guns, three small piers, and a radar station to monitor weather.

Now, China has transformed this rocky bank (reef) into a 3.95-km2 naval base (1.53 sq miles^2). It consists of barracks, warehouses, hangars, a 4-story structure, an airstrip 3,250 m long and 250 m wide, including a road next to the runway for aircraft, and a large seaport for the naval ships; a 55m high lighthouse has been in operation since April 2016.

Construction of 24 hangars for fighter jets, four for larger aircraft, transparent domes for radar placed on three towers, and a radar tower next to runway has been completed. Also, there is a row of high-frequency antennas, circled at the island's end on the south. Along with the radar facilities on other islands, this high-frequency radar is nearby a structure built for island defense, for protection against air or rocket attacks. A squadron of 24 jet fighters has been deployed.

This base is 238 nautical miles from Palawan, Philippines, and 503 nautical miles from China.

Subi Reef
(north rim)
18 July, 2015

Subi Reef
(northwest rim)
18 July, 2015

Subi Reef
(southwest rim)
18 July, 2015

SUBI REEF updated May 24, 18

Tara Francis Chan
May 24, 2018, 1:24 AM
A satellite photo of Subi Reef on March 20. Planet Labs/Handout via REUTERS

• Satellite imagery shows that China has put nearly **400 buildings** on Subi Reef in the South China Sea.

• Data shows that the number of buildings on Subi Reef is about double that on China's other large outposts in the hotly contested region, known as the Spratly Islands.

• Experts are concerned about China's increasing militarization of the South China Sea, and they say it may plan to station a large number of troops on Subi Reef.

• Buried storage facilities (ammos & other materials) have been constructed along the north side of Subi.

• In May 18,, China released footage of H-6K nuclear-capable bombers landing on another island in the South China Sea. **Runways and hangars built on Subi could accommodate such** bombers.

2. GAVEN: 10.1230°N 114.1330°E

The Gaven Reef has two sections: The north is 86 hectares wide. Part of the south island is 67 hectares. By 2015, China had added 15.3 hectares, creating an island of 0.135 km². On it, the Chinese communists have built a 6-story structure, barracks, warehouse, gun arsenal, firearm emplacement, communication facilities, radar, and large seaport with a ship dock...

April 12, 2015

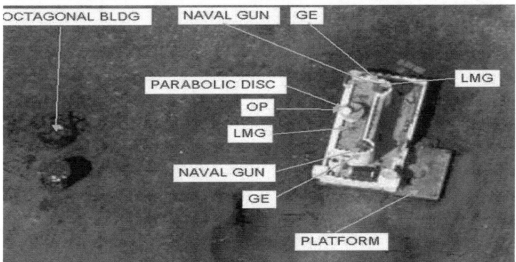

OCTAGONAL BLDG

NAVAL GUN

GE

PARABOLIC DISC

OP

LMG

LMG

NAVAL GUN

GE

PLATFORM

华 阳 岛 （2014年7月19日）

STRUCTURE

GAVEN updated 2017

Gaven Reef May 9, 2015

As of November 2015, China has created an artificial island of 13.6 hectares in Gaven Reef.

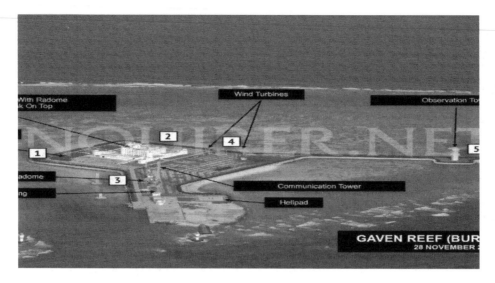

1. A solar panel array, constructed in tandem with the administrative building in 2015.

2. The headquarters/administrative center on Gaven Reefs, built in 2015. The octagonal structures jutting out from each corner sport gun emplacements, which are covered up in the aerial Inquirer photos.

3. A communications tower, with accompanying blue radomes. The tower went up in 2015, followed by the radomes in the first half of 2016.

4. Three of six wind turbines on Gaven Reefs (the other three can be seen between the communication tower and administrative building). All six turbines appear to have been erected in 2015.

5. A tall tower housing a sensor/communications facility topped by a radome, completed in 2016.

3. HUGHES REEF Coordinates: 9°55′N114°30′E

Jane's experts have analyzed the Hughes Reef (Tư Nghĩa). On the reef of only 380 m², China dredged the seabed, filled the island with sediments to reclaim it as a wide artificial island of over 75,000 m².

Jane's Defense Weekly compared photos of the Hughes Reef at three different times. On the photo taken on 3/30/2014, the Hughes Reef was still a tiny underwater reef. Photos in August 7, 2014 showing this reef already became an artificial island. Photo on 1/30/2015 showed the ongoing constructing of facilities on the island: the helipad, runway, airway, piers, and the buildings.

In short, by the end of 2016, China has filled 7.6 hectares sediments, installing the anti-aircraft guns, CIWS Rockets, and the military structures…

This is 9-story building structure with radar on top

China has filled 6.8 hectares of sediments. The main structure has 6 stories of 4,128 m² wide. This seaport consists of a small pier and another one for a ship 103m long.

This island is 187 nautical miles from Palawan, and 784 nautical miles from China.

4. CHIGUA/KENNAN REEF Coordinates: 9.715 N 114.287 E

ON-GOING CONSTRUCTION OF THREE (3) RECTANGULAR AND ONE (1)
OCTAGONAL CONCRETE STRUCTURES AT CHIGUA(KENNAN) REEF (PROC)
ALTITUDE: 5,000 FEET
LAT/LONG: N 09° 54' 10.95" E 114° 29' 52.39"
28 JANUARY 2015

KEENAN REEF
(PHOTO TAKEN: 12 APRIL 2015)

CHIGUA/KENNAN updated 2017

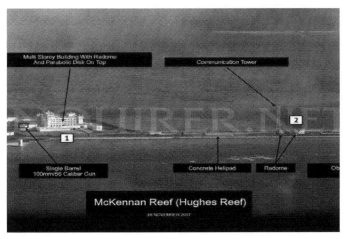

1. The administrative/headquarters building, constructed in 2015.

2. A communications tower with accompanying blue radomes. The tower went up in 2015 and the radomes were installed by the middle of 2016.

3. A tall tower with a sensor/communications facility topped by a radome, completed in early 2016.

5. MISCHIEF REEF (Đá Vành Khăn) Coordinates: 9°55′N115°32′E

This is a reef of 9 km in length and 6 km in width. It has been filled with 27 hectares sediments. Mischief reef is a marine lagoon in a 36-km² reef, with a depth of 20 to 30 meters. The lagoon has 1m high waves, and 20m waves offshore at 1000m depth or more, very suitable for submarines.

China has built a 3-story structure, along with 5 facilities with 8-sided shape rebars (steel reinforcing rod in concrete) for military purposes, and a 3,250-meter runway 55 meters wide. There are four large hangars, 24 to house fighter jets, four artillery systems, two radar systems, one cement factory, and the ship docks.

A radar tower was built in the middle of the island and three large towers in the southwest corner. Situated next to the 3 towers, a radome shows that China also followed the same model of construction pattern as on Subi and the Fiery Cross. Retractable roof could be open or closed for rocket storage. A squadron of 24 jet fighters and have been deployed there.

AMTI/CSIC 9/8/15

Runway

a stealth

AMTI/CSIS July 22, 2016

MISCHIEF REEF updated Dec. 2017

1. A large sensor/communications facility topped by a radome, completed in 2017.

2. One of the four point defense facilities built around the base in 2016.

3. Three towers housing sensor/communications facilities with radomes, completed in 2017.

4. Underground storage tunnels, likely for ammunition and other material were built during 2017. In the Inquirer's photo, the tunnels are already buried, but AMTI's satellite image shows the tunnels in an earlier, exposed state. Identical buried storage facilities have been constructed at Fiery Cross and Subi Reef. There is also more underground storage built along the north side of Mischief (and at Fiery Cross and Subi).

5. The base's 3,000-meter runway has been complete since 2016.

6. Hangar space for 8 combat aircraft, completed by late 2016.

7. One of Mischief's five hangars for larger aircraft, completed by late 2016.

8. A sensor/communications facility topped by a radome paired with what is believed to be an administrative building for the airfield.

9. Hangar space for 16 combat aircraft, completed by late 2016. An omnidirectional radio beacon for guiding inbound aircraft toward the airfield.

10. An omnidirectional radio beacon for guiding inbound aircraft toward the airfield.

6. JOHNSON SOUTH REEF (ĐÁ GẠC MA) - Coordinates: 9.715°N 114.287°E

This reef has an area of 7.2 km²; it was filled with 10.9 hectares sediments for land reclamation. By 2014, there was a 3-story building structure in the center, between two radar towers, a reinforced concrete platform, a ship dock, communication facilities, barracks, and helipads. Now this has become a 100,000 m² artificial island.

This base is 194 nautical miles from Palawan Island. China reclaimed 10.9 hectares of artificial island, with 3-story structure in the center, 2 radar towers on sides, a small peer, a large ship dock, two helipads, and three satellite antennas.

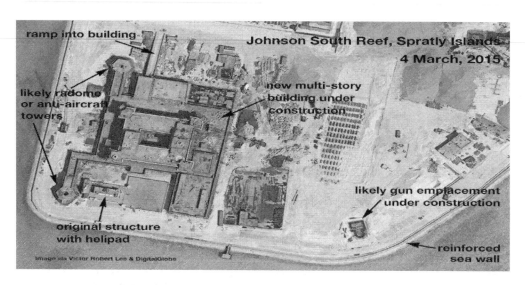

ramp into building

Johnson South Reef, Spratly Islands
4 March, 2015

likely radome or anti-aircraft towers

new multi-story building under construction

likely gun emplacement under construction

original structure with helipad

reinforced sea wall

Image via Victor Robert Lee & DigitalGlobe

MABINI (JOHNSON) REEF

OLD STRUCTURE

SOUTH JOHNSON REEF (Đá Gạc Ma) updated 2017

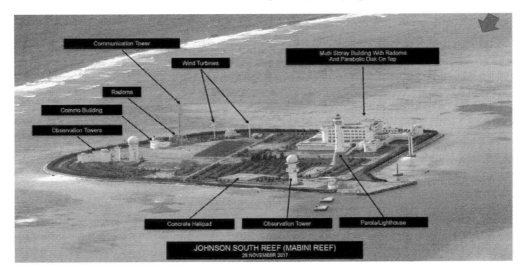

Some photographs show cargo ships and supply vessels, which the newspaper said appeared to be delivering construction materials to the China-controlled islands. Others show runways, hangars, control towers, helipads and radomes as well as a series of multistorey buildings that China has built on reefs such as Fiery Cross, Subi, Mischief, McKennan, Johnson South, Gaven and Cuarteron.

1. The Inquirer described the reefs as "island fortresses". Bonnie Glaser, an expert in Asia-Pacific security issues from the Center for Strategic and International Studies, called the images *"the most complete, detailed batch of aerial pics available"* of China's military outposts in the South China Sea. A point defense emplacement, completed in 2016. The guns on the structure are covered up in the images.

2. A communications tower with accompanying blue radomes. As on Cuarteron, Gaven, and Hughes Reefs, the tower was built in 2015 and the radomes completed in 2016.

3. A solar panel array built in late 2015 or early 2016.

4. Two wind turbines installed in late 2015.

5. A tall tower housing a sensor/communications facility topped by a radome, completed in late 2015.

6. A large lighthouse.

7. The administrative/headquarters building, including point defenses, was completed in early 2016.

7. FIERY CROSS REEF (ĐÁ CHỮ THẬP) Coordinates: 9°32′57″N112°53′21″E

China spent $5 billions to build this base within 10 years. The Fiery Cross Reef has an area of 5km², three meters higher than sea level.

It was filled with 10 hectares sediments for land reclamation, and has a 3,000 meter runway. The runway is 130m wide, including a road next to the runway for aircraft . It has hangars for large aircrafts, reconnaissance aircraft (spy planes), jet fighters, bombers, barracks, hospitals and seaports. There is a command post with radar, control tower for air and sea, and a barracks for 200 soldiers. There are two helipads for helicopters, 10 satellite antennas and a radar tower. By September 9, 2014, an area of 3000 m long and 200-300 m² wide was filled with sediments for land reclamation. J-11 aircrafts were brought into the island.

Construction was finished for all 24 fighter jet hangars and 4 other hangars for transport aircrafts, aerial refueling planes, or bombers. By January 2017, transparent radomes were installed on three large towers on the northwest island and on a tower north, toward the end of the airstrip. Several transparent radomes are on the airstrip at north, with a significant system of radar and sensors.

The Fiery Cross Reef is 14 nautical miles in length (nearly 26 km) along the NE-SW axis, and four nautical miles (7.4 km) in width, with a total area of 110 km². This reef is submerged at high tide, except for a 1-m high rock emerged on the southwest reef. If China renders this submerged reef into an island above water, this Johnson Reef would be many times larger.

Fiery Cross Island (đảo Chữ Thập) is now three times larger than Itu Aba *(đảo Ba Bình)* which was previously the largest island.

Image via Victor Robert Lee &
DigitalGlobe

Fiery Cross Reef
(northeast portion)
13 July, 2015

Image via Victor Robert Lee &
DigitalGlobe

Fiery Cross Reef
(midsection)
13 July, 2015

Image via Victor Robert Lee &
DigitalGlobe

Fiery Cross Reef
(southwest portion)
13 July, 2015

Hospitals

Lighthouse

FIERY CROSS, updated Dec. 2017

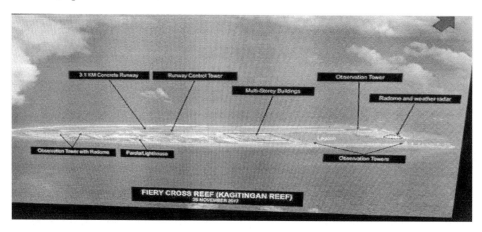

Buried storage facilities were constructed along the north side at Fiery Cross and Subi Reefs.

8). CUARTERON REEF (ĐÁ CHÂU VIÊN) Coordinates :8°51′50″N112°49′40″E

China built an area of 24.6 hectares, a 6-story structure, a small pier, and a large dock for 130m long ships.

CALDERON REEF / CUARTERON REEF

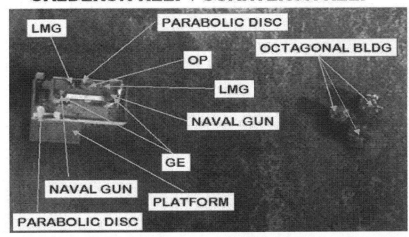

LMG
PARABOLIC DISC
OP
OCTAGONAL BLDG
LMG
NAVAL GUN
GE
NAVAL GUN
PLATFORM
PARABOLIC DISC

LMG:
Light
Machine
Gun

GE:
Gun
Emplacement

OP:
Observation
Post

CALDERON (CUARTERON) REEF

"HAIYANG SHAN"
YUTING-II CLASS TYPE 072II-CLASS
LANDING SHIP BOW #936

ORIGINAL STRUCTURE

Cuarteron Reef (Updated 2017)

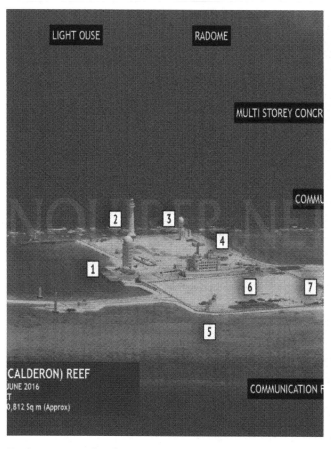

1. A tall tower housing a sensor/communications facility topped by a radome, completed in early 2016.

2. A lighthouse built in 2015, one of the first buildings constructed on the reef.

3. One of two point defense emplacements completed in 2016.

4. A large administrative building, similar to ones built on Gaven, Hughes, and Johnson Reefs.

5. A second point defense emplacement, also completed in 2016.

6. A large radar array, likely for high frequency over-the-horizon radar. Because the array consists of a grid of vertical poles, satellite images taken from directly overhead do a poor job of depicting the array. The Inquirer photos thus offer a much more enlightening perspective.

7. A communications tower completed in 2015. The two blue radomes on the ground beside the tower in the satellite images do not appear in the aerial photos and were constructed in 2016

2.5. TRANSFERRING OF VANGUARD BANK-RIFLEMAN BANK (TƯ CHÍNH-VŨNG MÂY):

CHINA BROUGHT IN TWO OIL RIGS TO THE VANGUARD-RIFFLEMAN BANK

Nguyễn Văn Canh
July 31, 2017

Information from the international media: The Vietnamese Communist Party (CPV) suddenly ordered Repsol company to suspend its oil/gas exploration on lot 136-03 at Vanguard Bank (*khu Tư Chính*), and leave. This oil/gas lot is located on Vietnam's continental shelf, adjacent to South Côn Sơn basin on the East. Then, China moved into this area the two drilling oilrigs Hai Duong 708 and Hai Duong 760.

Repsol, an oil company from Spain, has operated there for many years. Repsol acquired the right to exploit oil from Talisman, a Canadian Oil Company, for a price of $300 million. Previously, Hanoi permitted Talisman to exploit oil in this area.

Recently, Repsol announced the discovery of oil in this area.

Therefore, it was an act of official transferring to China our Vietnam's sovereign rights over that territory. Particularly in this case, at this place, the Communist Party of Vietnam already has signed a prior contract with Repsol to explore and exploit oil. Repsol has spent a lot of money to explore and now they found oil.

How could this territory transfer seem unusually easy and fast? Doing this, Vietnamese communist leaders have to accept two facts:

 a) To be exposed to Vietnamese people and the world, as despicable leaders of a people who condone an aggressor's unruly behavior and his motivation to dominate Vietnam.

b) To loose significantly large portions of profits from this oil resources for Party leaders. Indeed, through accusations from Trịnh xuân Thanh, former President of PetroVietnam Construction Corporation, so much money was stolen and fell into Party leaders' pockets, from the illegal oil sale over the past 30 years, especially since the era of the late Prime Minister Vo Van Kiet. It was estimated over $90 billions were stolen. Particularly during 10 years ruling by Nguyễn Tấn Dũng, this amount was $36 billions.

To understand as why did the CPV leaders accept this position, we need to repeat again the foundation of China-Vietnam relationship laid out since April 2011 by general Guo Boxiong 郭伯雄 (Quách bá Hùng), Vice Chairman of the Chinese Central Military Commission.

Here, Guo set the directions and principles, dictating what Vietnam leaders have to perform in order to eliminate oppositions to China's scheme; for the purpose of safeguarding her sovereign rights already acquired previously over the South China Sea (see. App. 9 above)

May 1, 2014 China suddenly moved the oilrig HĐ-981 into the maritime waters nearby Triton Island (*đảo Tri Tôn*) within the Paracel archipelago belonging to Vietnam. It operated under protection of China's powerful navy. China said that the rig "*operates within her territorial waters and her sovereign rights*". When the oilrig advanced into position, Vietnam's coast guard ship was immediately ordered to move away three nautical miles from the oilrig, and then four nautical miles as ordered by Chinese Navy. Phùng Quang Thanh, National Defense Minister of Vietnam, was more cautious and ordered the Vietnamese coast guard ships to move ten nautical miles away from the Chinese oilrig. However, a Vietnamese Coast Guard ship was still hit and sunk there by a Chinese naval ship. Some others were badly damaged. Four Vietnamese coastguardsmen killed, and others were injured. The total loss was 24 Vietnamese ships.

Bringing an oilrig into the Paracels this way, blatantly violating Vietnamese waters, clearly is an act of war, an aggressive invasion.

Vietnamese leaders were motionless. Ten days later, the people of Vietnam expressed their anger. There were many violent anti-China protests. At Hà Tĩnh province, people broke into Chinese special zones. This violent confrontation caused death to two Chinese workers and injury to others. 4,000 Chinese workers hurriedly returned to China by ship. At Bình Dương province, Vietnamese people set fire to several Chinese factories, including those not from China. Some Chinese had to flee to Cambodia.

Vietnam's leaders were frustrated at reactions from angry Vietnamese people.

Communist Party of Vietnam General Secretary Nguyễn phú Trọng asked to see Xi Jinxing to resolve this problem, but he was not welcomed.

At Tây Hồ district in Hanoi, to calm down the popular enraged opposition, Trong mentioned Vietnam's sovereignty over Hoang Sa archipelago. In Saigon, President Trương tấn Sang also talked with voters about sovereignty. When attending the Asian Conference in Burma on May 11, Prime minister Nguyễn Tấn Dũng was more clever, saying: "*That act [of China]} threatened the maritime security.... No exchange of sovereignty for the unrealistic vague friendship*". At the same time, he visited Philippines on May 21 and talked about the Philippines claiming case at the International Court of Arbitration (talking about the claim, but not discussing or learning about it).

All of the above were made known to the public. However practically it aimed to cover up the fact that the CPV leaders have been bound by "*Guo Boxiong Agreement*" and the Treaty, therefore no further action was taken. **Photo by Chinese media in Beijing.**

Now, the CPV leaders' behaviors caused China to "misunderstand". China thought that Vietnam's leaders plotted against China, because Trọng and Sang 'mobilized' people to demand for sovereignty over Biển Đông (Vietnam's East Sea). Dung engaged in the 'international campaign', implicitly calling for US intervention, because China is a reason for unsafe navigation on this sea. The US has claimed that it is necessary to protect free ships passing through the area freely and safely.

To China, those CPV acts were serious violations of the previously committed agreement and also Red China suspects Hanoi leaders of seeking way to escape her control, China State Councilor Yang Jiechi 杨洁篪 (Dương Khiết Trì), director of Foreign Affairs Office of Communist Party of China, on June 30 was sent to Hanoi where he **childed** Vietnam's leaders, telling them that "the lost/prodigal children must return to the mother country, to be forgiven."

At the same time, he reminded Hanoi leaders about two points in the Guo Agreement, and asked them to abide by strictly.

1) DO NOT EVER CITE ANY RECORD FROM VIETNAM TO CLAIM THAT VIETNAM HAS THE HISTORIC SOVEREIGNTY OVER THE TWO ARCHIPALAGOS (criticizing CPV General Secretary Nguyễn phú Trọng and President Trương tấn Sang when they talked to voters about sovereignty, while Prime minister Nguyễn Tấn Dũng talked about safety of movement in South China Sea…

2) DO NOT BRING OTHER NATIONS INTO THE SOUTH CHINA SEA DISPUTE (criticizing Prime minister Nguyễn Tấn Dũng about his statement at the Asian Conference about China acts, a reason for unsafe navigation on the sea, thus engaging the United States and other nations into the dispute against China. China also worried about Vietnam following Philippines to submit territorial claims to the International Court.

In addition, Yang also prohibited Vietnam leaders on two other matters:

1) DO NOT UNDERESTIMATE CHINA'S CAPABILITY TO PROTECT HER SOVEREIGNTY OVER THE ISLANDS OF BIỂN ĐÔNG, implying a threat directly to Vietnam leaders.

2) DO NOT JEOPARDIZE THE GOOD RELATIONSHIP CURRENTLY HAVING WITH CHINA. (2)

General Fan Changlong 范长龙 the Vice Chairman of China's Central Military Commission canceled his previously planned visit on June 18, 2017 because Vietnam's leaders could not satisfy China's demand. China demanded Vietnam to unilaterally cancel the prior contract with Repsol, allowing China to take over the project of exploiting oil/gas on lot 136-03. If not, the consequence will be serious. In early July 2017, China dispatched a fleet of 134 ships into the South China Sea. Vietnam's leaders were informed that if China's demands were not fulfilled, then China would seize those islands in the Spratly Archipelago being occupied by Vietnam.

In addition to the fleet of 134 ships above, China has eight military bases on eight islands in the Spratlys. Among them, there are three important bases: Subi, Mischief and Fiery Cross.

There is a large airport, with a squadron of jet fighters already deployed on each of them. Each squadron has 24 aircrafts. There are vast seaports, arsenals for weapons and missiles, radar systems, telecommunications facilities...

Those are critical reasons urging Vietnam's leaders to painfully/unilaterally cancel the contract with Repsol. Under humiliation and shame, they allowed China to move in the Vanguard Bank of Vietnamese territory. The two oilrigs of HD-708 and HD-760 were at the Vanguard Bank.

*****

On this occasion, the Vietnamese people warned the communist authorities of their cowardice, and seriously condemned their acts of selling the nation.

Let's proudly look up to the Republic of South Vietnam's Navy (RSVN). On January 19, 1974, the small South Vietnamese naval forces bravely confronted a large aggressive Chinese fleet of over 40 battleships. Operation Commander Chinese Admiral Phuong Quang Kinh died in this fierce maritime battle against South Vietnam's Navy defending the Paracels. This Deputy Commander of China's South Sea Fleet died along with five other Chinese colonels and others.

We commemorate the brave spirit of the Republic of South Vietnam's Navy fighting against foreign aggression. At year-end 2009, the Committee on Protection of Territorial Integrity of Vietnam mobilized Vietnamese people worldwide to organize the "Global Paracel Day" on Jan 19, 2010. Vietnamese communities worldwide responded to the call to have solemn ceremonies. Particularly those refugees who escaped from communist Vietnam and settled in Europe, Australia, Canada and the United States joined the event. The Vietnamese people paid tribute to and honored those brave soldiers of the Republic of (South) Vietnam Navy. It is not only to honor the 74 heroic Navy fallen soldiers who sacrificed for our nation's border protection, in the battle of Paracel Islands in January 19, 1974 but also to show to the whole world that the sovereignty of Vietnam over the two archipelagos is undisputable.

Two outstanding ceremonies were solemnly held for the purposes:

1) In Southern California, organized by the Mekong Naval Association. It was conducted at the Vietnam-American Veteran Memorial Monument in Westminster city where 2,000 people attended. Very touching.

2) In North California, the Bạch Đằng Navy Association and local groups, at San José American GI Forum on Story Road, performed another ceremony. About 1,000 people attended.

Photos of the ceremonies are posted at the end of the book.

Vietnamese Communist Party leaders should follow the heroic ARVN soldiers in the 1974 sea battle. **Don't be cowards anymore!**

Vietnamese people do not forgive those cowardly and shameful communist leaders surrendering and selling-off the nation to the enemy.

EAST SEA
(SOUTH CHINA SEA)

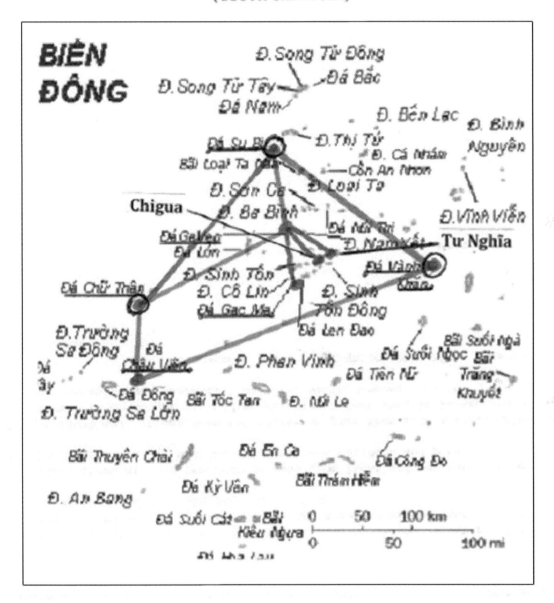

HỆ THỐNG CĂN CỨ HẢI QUÂN TC.
1) Đá Gaven (Gaven Reef): 10' 12" N 114' 14' E; 2) Én Đất (Eldad Reef) : 10' 21' N 114' 42' E;
3) Đá Vành Khăn (Mischief Reef): 09'58'N 115' 42' E; 4) Đá Châu Viên (Cuarteron Reef): 08'50'N
112'47' E; 5) Đá Chữ Thập (Fiery Cross Reef): 09'38' N 112'57'. 6) Chuỗi đảo Quần Tụ (Union
Banks)

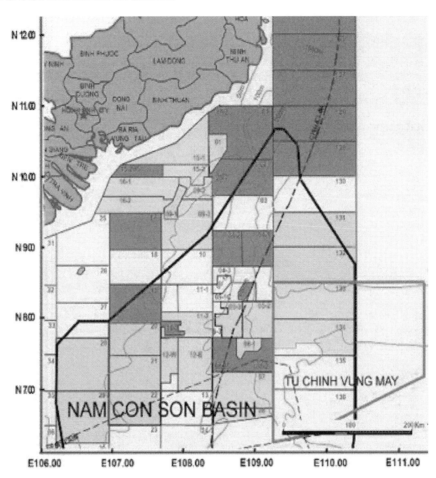

Repsol were exploiting oil/gas on LOT 136-03 at the Vanguard Bank (*khu Tư Chính*) and Rifleman Bank (*bãi Vũng Mây*).

THE OIL RIGS HD-708 and HD-760 AT VANGUARD BANK -- RIFLEMAN BANK

Photo by QUANG NGUYEN China moved the oil rigs into this area, to replace REPSOL, to extract oil for benefits with no cost of searching.

SOME MILITARY STRUCTURES:
 Photos by Center for Strategic and International Studies (CSIS), Washington

HUGHES REEF: 9-story Structure with radar on the High Tower (CSIS)

 A Stealth and hangar on the MISCHIEF Reef.

Hospital on the FIERY CROSS Reef (Bãi đá Chữ Thập) (CSIS)

FIERY CROSS (updated December 2017)

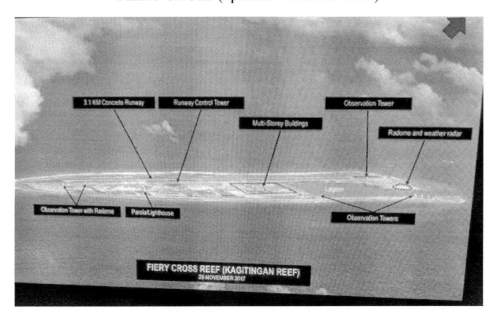

Buried storage facilities have been constructed along the north side

2.6. CHINA EXPANSIONISM

Nguyen van Canh
June 17, 2019

Extracted from "Hồ Sơ Hoàng SA & Trường Sa và Chủ Quyen Dân Tic" (Dossiers on Paracels & Spratlys and National Sovereignty) by Nguyễn văn Canh *, UBBVSVTLT, 6th edition, 2017.

Summary: After defeating Chiang Kai-shek in 1949, Communist China took power. She released a 9 -dash line map of the South China Sea that included Vietnam's Paracels and Spratlys, claiming the 3.5 million-km2 seas is hers.

In January 1974, China sent a fleet of 41 ships of her naval forces to take Paracels from the Republic of Vietnam. In March 1988, four destroyers with heavy weapons attacked unarmed members of Vietnamese engineer corps who were in the waters, carrying construction materials to South Johnson Reef and occupied it. 64 out of the 74 men were killed. At those times, 5 other reefs in the neighborhood were taken. In 1992, she occupied others.

Presently, in Paracels, a large military complex has existed. On Woody Island, there is a large airfield with a 3000m x 250 m runway, and jet fighters have been deployed. Ammo. And missiles depots are in the North side. Larger seaports have been built. A tall communication tower and radars and other facilities have been in operation. A large multi-story building is served as a military headquarter for the region. Several hundred solders have been stationed there. On other islands in the archipelago, military fortified fortresses have been erected.

In Spratlys, a system of naval bases built on eight artificial islands is found in the middle of the sea. The three largest and most important are Subi, Mischief and Fiery Cross, on each of which an airfield with a 3000m x 250m runway has been completed to accommodate large aircrafts when landing and taking off. And also on each, a squadron of 24 long-range bombers is being deployed; not including some most advanced aircraft j-20's or long range stealth fighters. They are combat-ready. Seaports, weapons with missiles and ammunition depots, advanced infrared sense radar network and communication facilities, gun emplacements are also detected. Along north sides of Subi and Fiery Cross, there are underground depots of supplies and materials. Anti- aircraft and also anti-ship missiles are camouflaged.

China now can project its military power anywhere in Southeast Asia and as far away as northern Australia. She is capable of securing the area, including blocking the Malacca Straits anytime she wants.

With support of Sanya Naval base in Hainan, China uses Paracels and Spratlys as a staging base from which she plans to move forward: **Claiming sovereignty over the Western region of the Pacific and also conquering Southeast Asia countries then annexing them to China.**

* Dr Nguyen van Canh: Before 1975, professor of Law & Politics, Saigon Law School; in the USA, Visiting Scholar, Hoover Institution on Peace, War and Revolution, Stanford University

SANYA NAVAL BASE IN HAINAN

Entrance of a case that could house 20 submarines, type 094

Submarine, type 094 equipped with 12 long-range missiles,
(6 on each side). It could carry nuclear warheads

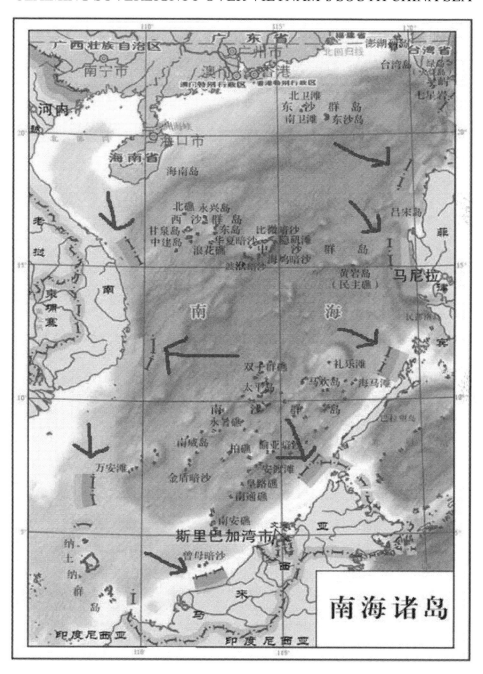

A. PARACELS

Woody Island

J 7s on Woody

CNN June 21,19: 4 J 10s seen on Woody; (range 500 mi
(CSIS- AMTI/Digital Globe)

CHINA's NAVAL FORCES HEADQUARTER ON WOODY ISLAND

B. SPRATLYS

A system of bases

Some photographs show cargo ships and supply vessels, which the Inquirer said appeared to be delivering construction materials to the China-controlled islands. Others show runways, hangars, control towers, helipads and radomes as well as a series of multi-storey buildings that China has built on reefs such as Fiery Cross, Subi, Mischief, McKennan, Chigua, Johnson South, Gaven and Cuarteron. The Inquirer described the reefs as "island fortresses". Bonnie Glaser, an expert in Asia-Pacific security issues from the Center for Strategic and International Studies, called the images "the most complete, detailed batch of aerial pics available" of China's military outposts in the South China Sea. A point defense emplacement was completed in 2016. The guns on the structure are covered up in the images. A communications tower with accompanying blue radomes is erected. As on Cuarteron, Gaven, and Hughes Reefs, the tower was built in 2015 and the radomes completed in 2016. A solar panel array: built in late 2015 or early 2016. Two wind turbines installed in late 2015. A tall tower housing a sensor/communications facility topped by a radome, completed in late 2015. There is a large lighthouse

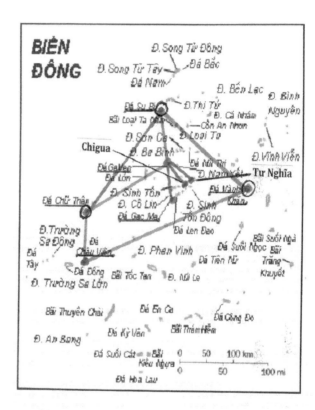

EASTERN SEA
(SOUTH CHINA SEA)

HỆ THỐNG CĂN CỨ HẢI QUÂN TC.
1) Đá Gaven (Gaven Reef): 10° 12' N 114° 14' E; 2) Én Đất (Eldad Reef) : 10° 21' N 114° 42' E; 3) Đá Vành Khăn (Mischief Reef): 09°58'N 115° 42' E; 4) Đá Châu Viên (Cuarteron Reef): 08°50'N 112°47' E; 5) Đá Chữ Thập (Fiery Cross Reef): 09°38' N 112°57'. 6) Chuỗi đảo Quần Tụ (Union Banks)

FORTIFIED MILITARY INSTALLATIONS IN SPRATLYS:

1. SUBI

Reuters, March 20, 2018: 400 buildings have been constructed; buried storage facilities constructed along the North side of Subi; Runways and hangars could accommodate H-6K nuclear capable bombers.

2. GAVEN

A solar panel array, constructed in tandem with the administrative building in 2015. The headquarters/administrative center on Gaven Reefs, built in 2015. The octagonal structures jutting out from each corner sport gun emplacements, which are covered up in the aerial *Inquirer* photos. A communication tower, with accompanying blue radomes. The tower went up in 2015, followed by the radomes in the first half of 2016. Three of six wind turbines on Gaven Reefs (the other three can be seen between the communication tower and administrative building). All six turbines appear to have been erected in 2015. A tall tower housing a sensor/communications facility topped by a radome, completed in 2016. Headquarters built in 2015 with gun emplacements, radomes and 6 turbines; Solar Panel on building; a sensor/communications facility topped by a radome, completed in 2016.

As of November 2015, China has created an artificial island of 13.6 hectares in Gaven Reef.

3. MISCHIEF

A sensor/commo facility with radomes, completed in 2017; one of 4-point facilities in 2016; 3 sensor/como facility with radomes on top, 2017, underground tunnels (for ammunitions & materials), a 3000m runway with **hangar space for 8 combat aircrafts completed 2016; one of five hangars for larger aircraft;** an administrative building a sensor/communications facility topped by a radome Hangar space for 16 combat aircrafts (2016)

Hangar

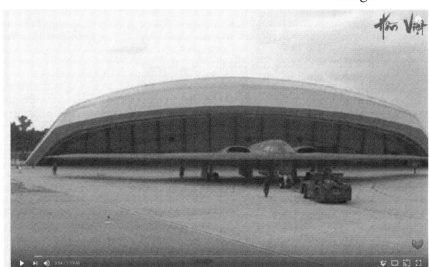

Stealth & hangar

4. JOHNSON SOUTH

A commo tower with blue radomes completed in 2016; a solar panel array built in late 2015; two wind turbines; a tall tower housing a sensor/communications facility topped by a radome, completed in late 2015; a large lighthouse; administrative building also completed.

5. FIERY CROSS

It costs China 5 billion US dollars to build this fortress

514

Hospital

Missiles launching platform,

- 96 m x 116 m (to shoot down

American satellites.) No satellites available, American aircraft carriers no longer receive guidance, and disorient…

6. CUARTERON REEF

A tall housing sensor/communications facility with a radome (2016); a lighthouse (2015); one of two point defense emplacements (2016); a large administrative building; a second point defense emplacement (2016); a large radar array, likely for high frequency over-the-horizon radar. The array consists of a grid of vertical poles; satellite images taken from directly overhead do a poor job of depicting the array. A communications tower completed in 2015. The two blue radomes on the ground beside the tower in the satellite images do not appear in the aerial photos and were constructed in 2016

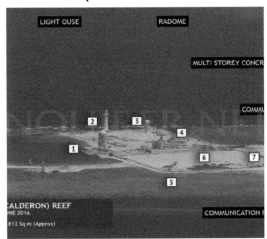
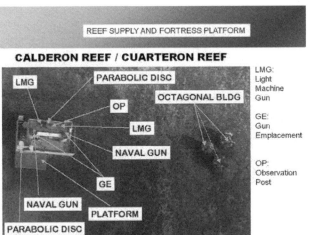

CHINA's SCHEME OF EXPANSION IN THE REGION

1. Greater China

2. West Region of the Pacific belongs to China

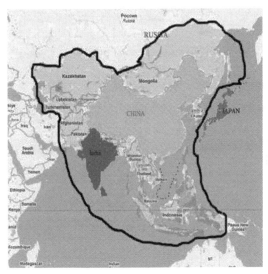

d Second Island Chains. *PRC military theorists conceive of two island "chains"*

Map 6.
Source: US Department of Defence, Annual Report to Congress: Military Power of the People's Repub;lic of China 2007.

In order to claim sovereignty over the Western Region of the Pacific, China Naval forces set up two lines of defense: **a) Chains of islands defense line: from**

Japan down to the Philippines; b) far-distant line of defense: from Indonesia through Guam down to Australia.

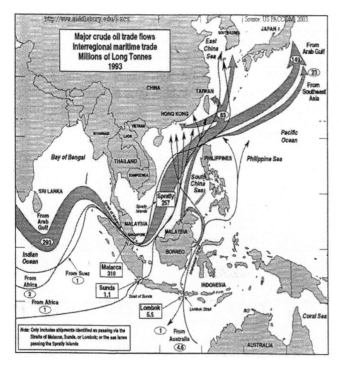

SEA LANE FROM INDIAN OCEAN TO NORTH EAST OF ASIA

Sea-lane goes from Indian Ocean through Malacca Strait to South China Sea, then North East of Asia. Annual World trade values are estimated at 53,000 billion US dollars. The USA share is $13,000 billion.

Militarily, China is capable of blocking the Malacca Strait at any time. But she dare not because she is not strong enough. She could lie in wait, even for 3 or 4 decades to come until she feels she is ready. If this happens, it will have an unthinkable impact on the US economy, not to mention about political and other situations in the US.

WHAT ARE CHINA's AMBITIONS IN THE "CENTURY OF CHINA" by 2049?

Young men and women sent from China held this banner before the former Republic of Vietnam National Assembly in 2008, in Saigon, before the Beijing Olympic began.

ONE WORLD ONE DREAM AND ONE CHINA

ONE BELT ONE ROAD INITIATIVES

To achieve this goal, China announced the OneBeltOneRoad Initiative (BRI) Strategy with 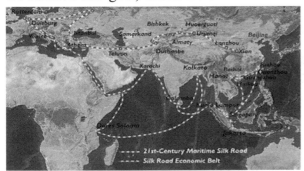 US$ 1,000 billion dollars earmarked for this Expansionism purpose. Li Keqiang, Chinese Premier in a conference on BRI held in Beijing few months ago stated that 126 countries and 29 world organizations have joined the program. The latest country is Italy who recently has adhered to this program since April 2019.

How does this program work? China State Bank and "private" Banks loan money to countries that need to develop their infrastructure such as roads, bridges, railways, seaports, airports etc.... even with easy conditions, even without conditions required. The loan amount  in many cases is more than $ US 20 billion. When times come to pay back the loaned money, debtors who are not able to have resources available to pay back have to make concessions by allowing China to use strategic areas for a period of 40, 60 or 99 years., where she builds military installations, or where she has exclusive rights to exploit mineral resources. This is called **debts traps**.

What areas does China want? Seaports, airports, areas that sit on the BRI road

-In Asia, seaports are places where China looks at. The following countries that allowed China uses their seaports under the conditions are Sri Lankra, Myanmar, Bangladesh, Pakistan, Maldives, Teheran…

-In Africa, areas where there are mineral resources such as gold, copper, zinc, iron, silver aluminum etc.. Zimbabwe, Congo, Kenya, Marco, Nigeria, Djibouti, Anglo, Namibia etc. are examples.

Esimerkkejä kiinalaisten ostoista ja sijoituksista infrastruktuurikohteissa

-In Europe, many countries have received financial aids from China. Italy is an example. Italy has allowed China to use Trieste in Northern part of Italy. It is a seaport that lies on the border of Adriatic Sea, leading to the Balkan area, connected with a railroad leading to Northern and Central Europe. Italy has also agreed to have China exploit the Geona port that faces Mediterranean Sea. These are two of 14 European ports, which are operated with money from China. Another Italy's Vado port on the Mediterranean Sea has been conceded to China. Xi Jinxing came to Italy on March 21, 19 and agreed to provide Italy 20 US $ billion. Previously, in 2000, Italy had received from China 14 billion Euros.

Besides, China has another secret plan. Those countries that received aids from China are places where China sends Chinese in under the name of economic cooperation and economic aids. This is the way Chinese slowly build colonies. In Africa, millions of Chinese from mainland came and have settled down. In Europe, she bought small farms and Chinese peasants are seen in many places. It is said that some 30 millions have been relocated from China. In Beijing, there is a University that trains young female students militarily with skills to be good wives and then China export them to Western hemisphere under the **Maosan Plan**: **to get married with white men, and foster Chinese families for future use.**

The first batch of the program is 1,000, 000 girls.

In order to achieve what is called CHINA **DREAM,** the USA is the main target for attack. China wages a war with many fronts: economic, monetary, intelligence including planting agents in R & D of Corporations, research institutions, universities, propaganda, cyberwar, exporting young girls to the USA etc. These are just secondary. **The main means to defeat America is bio/chem warfar**e, waged at DC, where several million people die, not necessarily using nuclear warfare.

When the USA collapses, all western countries will surrender.

Here comes the **"CENTURY OF CHINA"**.

2.7. THE PERMANENT COURT OF ARBITRATION AT THE HAGUE

DECLARATION

OF

THE COMMITTEE ON PROTECTION OF TERRITORIAL INTEGRITY OF VIET NAM

Subject: The Permanent Court of Arbitration Decision on South China Sea

Two years has passed since the Court promulgated its decision on China's illegal occupation of the Eastern Sea, the Socialist Republic of Vietnam continues to keep quiet. Therefore, the Committee on Protection of Territorial Integrity of Vietnam on behalf of Vietnamese at home as well as overseas here by publicly recognizes and honors the Court decision.

A solemn ceremony is held in San Jose, CA on July 19, 2018 to warmly welcome the decision of the Court on the Eastern Sea made on July 12, 2016. The decision has nullified the illegal occupation of the Eastern Sea of Vietnam by Chinese hegemonistic expansionists and has restored justice in favor of the weak. The Court decision has also offered an opportunity for the Vietnamese people to re-assert Vietnam's undisputable sovereignty over the Eastern Sea, in spite of Ho and the CPV's secret and illegal exchange of the two archipelagos for aids to invade South Vietnam.

In the face of flagrant invasion of Vietnam's Eastern Sea (Southeast Asia Sea) by China, the Committee On Protection Of Territorial Integrity Of Vietnam publicly and repeatedly demanded through its proclamations on September 15, 2009, on September 1, 2012, and on June 11, 2014, that the Communist Party of Vietnam order its government- the Socialist Republic of Vietnam, to file a claim against China in the International Permanent Court of Arbitration at The Hague. The Communist Party kept silent.

After the Philippines filed a claim with the International Court of Justice, Den Hague, against China alleging the latter's intrusion into its sovereignty over a portion of Spratly Islands, the Court on July 12, 2016 ruled that China conduct was in contravention of International Laws of the Seas and protocols, including its nine-dash line announced map. It is illegal. China protested vehemently that ruling.

The Communist Party of Vietnam continued its silence, despite the fact that the said decision and ruling are applicable to the entire Eastern Sea, the major part of which lies under Vietnam's sovereignty. Among 10 islands examined by the court, eight belong to Vietnam

This silence leads only a conclusion that the Communist Party of Vietnam was complicit with China, indirectly rejecting said rulings and decisions.

The derelict in its duty / abdication of its responsibility to prosecute the nation's claim in connection with sovereignty and the silence after the announcement of the Court rulings and decisions are clear evidence of the Communist Party of Vietnam acknowledging China's illegitimate control of the Nation's territories over the Eastern Sea.

Therefore, the Committee on Protection of Territorial Integrity of Vietnam, on behalf of the Vietnamese people, the world over, proclaims on July 29, 2018 before the people of Vietnam and before International communities the sovereignty of Vietnam over the Eastern Sea (Southeast Asian Sea).

PICTIURES

Former Major Thai Van Hoa and Ms. Pham My Linh as MCs of the ceremony

Former Republic of Vietnam Police Officers salutes Vietnam Flag at the ceremony.

Organizing Committee

Proclaiming the Court Decision

400 members of local communities attending the ceremony

2.7.1. THE COURT DECISION

. . . .

12 July 2016

RULING

The Hague's Permanent Court of Arbitration ruled that "**China has no historical rights**" based on the "nine- dash line" map.

AWARD

On 12 July 2016, the Permanent Court of Arbitration published an arbitration award by the tribunal which it states is final and binding as set out in the Convention.[30][42] Conclusions expressed in the award included the following:

Regarding the "Nine-Dash Line" and China's claim in the maritime areas of the South China Sea[43]_____ • The [UNCLOS] Convention defines the scope of maritime entitlements in the South China Sea, which may not extend beyond the limits imposed therein.[44]

• China's claims to historic rights, or other sovereign rights or jurisdiction, with respect to the maritime areas of the South China Sea encompassed by the relevant part of the 'nine-dash line' are contrary to the Convention and without lawful effect to the extent that they exceed the geographic and substantive limits of China's maritime entitlements under the Convention. The Convention superseded any historic rights or other sovereign rights or jurisdiction in excess of the limits imposed therein.[45]

Regarding the status of features as above/below water at high tide (Submissions no. 4 and 6)

•High-tide features: (a) Scarborough Shoal, (b) Cuarteron Reef, (c) Fiery Cross Reef, (d) Johnson Reef, (e) McKennan Reef, and (f) Gaven Reef (North).[46]

•Low-tide elevations: (a) Hughes Reef, (b) Gaven Reef (South), (c) Subi Reef, (d) Mischief Reef, (e) Second Thomas Shoal.[47]

•Hughes Reef lies within 12 nautical miles of the high-tide features on McKennan Reef and Sin Cowe Island, Gaven Reef (South) lies within 12 nautical miles of the high-tide features at Gaven Reef (North) and Namyit Island, and that Subi Reef lies within 12 nautical miles of the high-tide feature of Sandy Cay on the reefs to the west of Thitu.[48]

Regarding the status of features as rocks/islands (Submissions no. 3, 5, and 7)

•**Scarborough Shoal** contains, within the meaning of Article 121(1) of the Convention, naturally formed areas of land, surrounded by water, which are above water at high tide. However, under Article 121(3) of the Convention, the high-tide features at Scarborough Shoal **are rocks that cannot sustain human habitation or economic life** of their own and accordingly shall have no exclusive economic zone or continental shelf.[49]

•**Johnson Reef, Cuarteron Reef, and Fiery Cross Reef** contain, within the meaning of Article 121(1) of the Convention, naturally formed areas of land, surrounded by water, which are above water at high tide. However, for purposes of Article 121(3) of the Convention, the high-tide features at Johnson Reef, Cuarteron Reef, and Fiery Cross Reef **are rocks that cannot sustain human habitation or economic life of their own** and accordingly shall have no exclusive economic zone or continental shelf.[50]

•The high-tide features **at Gaven Reef (North) and McKennan Reef are rocks that cannot sustain human habitation or economic life** of their own and accordingly shall have no exclusive economic zone or continental shelf.[51]

•Mischief Reef and Second Thomas Shoal are both low-tide elevations that generate no maritime zones of their own [and] that none of the high-tide features in the Spratly Islands are capable of sustaining human habitation or an economic life of their own within the meaning of those terms in Article 121(3) of the Convention. All of the high-tide features in the Spratly Islands are therefore legally rocks for purposes of Article 121(3) and do not generate entitlements to an exclusive economic zone or continental shelf. There is, accordingly, no possible entitlement by China to any maritime zone in the area of either Mischief Reef or Second Thomas Shoal and no jurisdictional obstacle to the tribunal's consideration of the Philippines' Submission No. 5.[52]

•Both Mischief Reef and Second Thomas Shoal are located within 200 nautical miles of the Philippines' coast on the island of Palawan and are located in an area that is not overlapped by the entitlements generated by any maritime feature claimed by China. It follows, therefore, that, as between the Philippines and China, Mischief Reef and Second Thomas Shoal form part of the exclusive economic zone and continental shelf of the Philippines.[53]

Regarding alleged interference with the Philippines' sovereign rights in its EEZ and continental shelf (Sub. no. 8)

•China has, through the operation of its marine surveillance vessels with respect to M/Veritas Voyager on 1 to 2 March 2011 **breached Article 77** of the Convention with respect to the Philippines' sovereign rights over the non-living resources of its continental shelf in the area of Reed Bank [and] that China has, by promulgating its 2012 moratorium on fishing in the South China Sea, without exception for areas of the South China Sea falling within the exclusive economic zone of the Philippines and without limiting the moratorium to Chinese flagged vessels, breached Article 56 of the Convention with respect to the Philippines' sovereign rights over the living resources of its exclusive economic zone.[54]

Regarding alleged failure to prevent Chinese nationals from exploiting the Philippines' living resources (Submission no. 9)

•China has, through the operation of its marine surveillance vessels in tolerating and failing to exercise due diligence to prevent fishing by Chinese flagged vessels at Mischief Reef and Second Thomas Shoal in May 2013, **failed to exhibit due regard for the Philippines' sovereign rights with respect to fisheries in its exclusive economic zone.** Accordingly, China has breached its obligations under **Article 58(3)** of the Convention.[55]

Regarding China's actions in respect of traditional fishing at Scarborough Shoal (Submission no. 10)

•China has, through the operation of its official vessels at Scarborough Shoal from May 2012 onwards, **unlawfully prevented Filipino fshermen** from engaging in traditional fishing at Scarborough Shoal.[56]

Regarding alleged failure to protect and preserve the marine environment (Submissions no. 11 and 12(B))

•China has, through its toleration and protection of, and failure to prevent Chinese fishing vessels engaging in harmful harvesting activities of endangered species at Scarborough Shoal, Second Thomas Shoal and other features in the Spratly Islands, **breached Articles 192 and 194**(5) of the Convention. [57]

•China has, through its island-building activities at Cuarteron Reef, Fiery Cross Reef, Reef and Mischief Reef, breached Articles 192, 194(1), 194(5), 197, 123, and 206 of the Convention.[58]

Regarding occupation and construction activities on Mischief Reef (Submission no. 12)

•China has, through its construction of installations and artificial islands at Mischief Reef without the authorization Gaven Reef (North), Johnson Reef, Hughes Reef, Subi of the Philippines, breached Articles 60 and 80 of the Convention with respect to the Philippines' sovereign rights in its exclusive economic zone and continental shelf [and], as a low-tide elevation, Mischief Reef is not capable of appropriation.[59]

Regarding operation of law enforcement vessels in a dangerous manner (Submission no. 13)

•China has, by virtue of the conduct of Chinese law enforcement vessels in the vicinity of Scarborough Shoal, created serious risk of collision and danger to Philippine vessels and personnel. The Tribunal finds China to have violated Rules 2, 6, 7, 8, 15, and 16 of the COLREGS and, as a consequence, to be in breach of Article 94 of the Convention.[60]

Regarding aggravation or extension of the dispute between the parties (Submission No. 14)

•China has in the course of these proceedings aggravated and extended the disputes between the Parties through its dredging, artificial island building, and construction activities [in several particulars itemized in the award].[61]

Regarding the future conduct of the parties (Submission no. 15)

•Both Parties are obliged to comply with the Convention, including its provisions regarding the resolution of disputes, and to respect the rights and freedoms of other States under the Convention. Neither Party contests this.[62} …..

EPILOGUE

You have finished reading this documentary book. A question is raised as to whether Ho Chi Minh and Vietnam Party leaders know what they have done to people of Vietnam? **They do!**

In fact, in ta book entitled "**Beijing: against the movement for people's liberation**". Khoa Học Xã Hội Publisher, Hanoi, 1982, the Communist Party of Vietnam gave some details on China's expansionism.

-Part I of this book, *en*titled "**Maoism- A Threat to Humanity**", includes: A section with this title "**Southeast Asia - the foremost target to be conquered for expansionism**": *"The birth of an independent, unified socialist Vietnam has been an obstacle to the implementation of China's hegemony policy in this region"* (page 58). And, *"China is concerned that a strong independent Vietnam will hinder the implementation of China's strategic moves in Southeast Asia"* (page 65).

About China's territorial ambitions: *"People's Republic of China not only has ambition for the territory of Socialist Republic of Vietnam, but also Burma, Laos, and even the islands along the border of the Philippines and Malaysia"* (page 64).

Mao tse Tung*:" Vietnam is a stepping stone from which we advance to the South. We must take it"*, Nguyen van Canh. *"Ho so HS & TS và Chủ Quyền Dân Tộc"* Center for Vietnam Studies., 7th edition, 2017 p.28.

Le Duan, Secretary Genenral of the Communist Party of Vietnam;

"We fight the Americans. That means a fight for the Soviet Union and China".

Entrance of Le Duan's mausoleum.

In short, they are aware of it and determined to execute Red Chinas' orders.

527

PHOTOS ON THE PARACEL GLOBAL DAYS

In response to the Committee On Protection Of Territorial Integrity Of Vietnam, some 20 Vietnamese communities overseas worldwide organize the Paracel Global Day on January 19, 2010 to **commemorate 74 Vietnamese Navy men** who sacrificed in fighting Chinese aggressors in the Paracels and, also to **assert Vietnam's sovereignty** over the two archipelagos.

The following are photos of two ceremonies: one in Westminster, South California, and the other in San Jose, Norh California.

IN SOUTH CALIFORNIA:

Over 1000 Vietnamese participate in the ceremony held in January 17, 2010

IN NORTH CALIFORNIA

Some 1,200 Vietnamese attend the ceremony held on January 24, 2010 at GI Forum, San Jose.

Nguyễn thanh Hà, Secetary General of the Committee on Paracels makes a recapitulation of the events on September, 26, 2010.

NGUYỄN VĂN CANH

The author was a professor at Saigon Faculty Law, Saigon, lecturer at the Command and General Staff College, and the National Defense College of the Republic of (South) Vietnam Armed Forces.

In the United States: Visiting Scholar at Hoover Institution on War, Revolution, and Peace, Stanford University; Co-Director, Oral Life History Project, East Asia Institute, UC Berkeley, California.

-Author of books and research articles published in magazines and newspapers (in English and Vietnamese). Attended several international conferences on Vietnam and Southeast Asia

The Author wishes to thank the following individuals:

For Financial Support:
Phan Hong Long, President of Van Hanh University Alumni Association
Tran Huy Bich, Ph.D
Hoang Cam, M.D
Le Van Thanh, former President of Van Hanh University Alumni Association
Paul Bick Esq..

For Translation & Editing:
Mary & Michael Nguyen
Stephen J. Dunham, John Birch Society
Raymond Fadeley, (ret) English Professor

Graphic Design
Nguyen Thanh Ha